Under and Applying Cryptography and Data Security

Understanding
and Applying
Cryptography
and Data Security

Adam J. Elbirt

CRC Press
Taylor & Francis Group
Boca Raton London New York

CRC Press is an imprint of the
Taylor & Francis Group, an **informa** business
AN AUERBACH BOOK

CRC Press
Taylor & Francis Group
6000 Broken Sound Parkway NW, Suite 300
Boca Raton, FL 33487-2742

First issued in paperback 2019

© 2009 by Taylor & Francis Group, LLC
Auerbach is an imprint of Taylor & Francis Group, an Informa business

No claim to original U.S. Government works

ISBN-13: 978-1-4200-6160-4 (hbk)
ISBN-13: 978-0-367-38579-8 (pbk)

Library of Congress Cataloging-in-Publication Data

Elbirt, Adam J.
  Understanding and applying cryptography and data security / Adam J. Elbirt.
    p. cm.
  Includes bibliographical references and index.
  ISBN 978-1-4200-6160-4 (alk. paper)
  1. Computer security. 2. Cryptography. I. Title.

QA76.9.A25E43 2008
005.8--dc22   2008028154

Visit the Taylor & Francis Web site at
http://www.taylorandfrancis.com

and the Auerbach Web site at
http://www.auerbach-publications.com

Dedication

To Danielle, Jacob, and Rachel — the impossible became real because of you. You are the shining lights of my life and bring joy to my heart.

Contents

5 Symmetric-Key Cryptography: Block Ciphers   83

List of Figures

List of Tables

About the Author

Adam J. Elbirt is a Senior Member of Technical Staff at the Charles Stark Draper Laboratory, Inc. He is also a member of the Eta Kappa Nu and Sigma Chi honorary societies.

Elbirt has given seminars for such prestigious universities as Worcester Polytechnic Institute, the New Jersey Institute of Technology, and the University of Massachusetts Lowell. He was a founding member of the Center for Network and Information Security and recently completed a six-year term as a professor of computer science at the University of Massachusetts Lowell.

Prior to joining the Charles Stark Draper Laboratory, Elbirt held senior engineering positions at Viewlogic Systems and NTRU Cryptosystems. He holds a doctor of philosophy degree from Worcester Polytechnic Institute where he performed his research in the area of reconfigurable hardware architectures designed to accelerate cryptographic algorithms. Elbirt has published numerous articles in journals and conference proceedings and many of his implementations broke previous encryption throughput performance records for symmetric-key algorithms.

Acknowledgments

I would like to deeply thank Christof Paar, chair for Communication Security of the Horst Goßrtz Institut for IT Security at the Ruhr-Universitaßt Bochum. Christof was my advisor and mentor at Worcester Polytechnic Institute from 1998 through 2002, and much of my lecture notes and thus the topics examined in this textbook are based on his rigorous and comprehensive lectures, examples, and practical implementation knowledge. It is through Christof's guidance and love for cryptography and information security that I first became interested in these areas and I would like to express my heartfelt appreciation to him.

I would also like to extend my thanks to Ralph Spencer Poore, Managing Partner of PiR Squared Consulting LLP, for his time and effort spent reviewing the text.

Chapter 1

Introduction

1.1 A Brief History of Cryptography and Data Security

For over 4,500 years, cryptography has existed as a means of secretly communicating information. Egyptian hieroglyphics are the first example of the use of cryptography to hide information from those not "in the know". The use of cryptographic ciphers is central to events surrounding historical figures such as Julius Caesar, Queen Elizabeth I, Mata Hari, and Alfred Dreyfus, while playing a significant role in the Allies' victory over the Axis powers during World War II, directly affecting the outcome of the Battle of Midway and other engagements [88]. For those interested in cryptographic history, books such as *Brute Force: Cracking the Data*

1

Encryption Standard [52], by Matt Curtin, and *The Codebreakers. The Story of Secret Writing* [148], by David Kahn, provide interesting reading on how cryptography has affected world events.

Cryptography in its more contemporary form was fathered by Claude Shannon in 1949 [283]. Widely known for his work in electronic communications and digital computing, Shannon established the basic mathematical theory for cryptography and its counterpart, cryptanalysis. Shannon's methods relied on a unique shared secret, referred to as the *key*, that allowed two parties to communicate securely as long as this key was not compromised. This class of algorithms, known as private-key, secret-key, or symmetric-key, was the sole method of secure communication until 1976, when Whitfield Diffie and Martin Hellman proposed a revolutionary key distribution methodology [70]. This methodology led to the development of a new class of algorithms, termed public-key or asymmetric-key, where a pair of mathematically related keys are used and one of these keys is made *public*, obviating the need for a secret shared specifically between two parties. Today, information systems typically use a hybrid approach, combining the benefits of symmetric-key and public-key algorithms to form a system that is both fast and secure.

1.2   Cryptography and Data Security in the Modern World

Cryptography currently plays a major role in many information technology applications. With more than 188 million Americans connected to the Internet [110], the use of cryptography to provide information security has become a top priority. Many applications — electronic mail, electronic banking, medical databases, and electronic commerce — require the exchange of private information. For example, when engaging in electronic commerce, customers provide credit card numbers when purchasing products. If the connection is not secure, an attacker can easily obtain this sensitive data. In order to implement a comprehensive security plan for a given network to guarantee the security of a connection, the following services must be provided [202, 275, 296]:

- *Confidentiality*: Information cannot be observed by an unauthorized party. This is accomplished via public-key and symmetric-key encryption.

- *Data Integrity*: Transmitted data within a given communication session cannot be altered in transit due to error or an unauthorized party. This is accomplished via the use of *Hash Functions* and *Message Authentication Codes* (MACs).

- *Message Authentication*: Parties within a given communication session must provide certifiable proof validating the authenticity of a message. This is accomplished via the use of *Digital Signatures*. The only communicating party that can generate a *Digital Signature* that will successfully verify as belonging to the originator of the message is the originator of the message. This process validates the authenticity of the message, i.e. that the claimed originator of the message is the actual originator of the message.

- *Non-repudiation*: Neither the sender nor the receiver of a message may deny transmission. This is accomplished via *Digital Signatures* and third-party notary services.

- *Entity Authentication*: Establishing the identity of an entity, such as a person or device.

- *Access Control*: Controlling access to data and resources. Access is determined based on the privilege assigned to the data and resources as well as the privilege of the entity attempting to access the data and resources.

1.3   Existing Texts

There are numerous books available that present cryptography and data security concepts from a variety of perspectives [202, 296, 298, 301]. While useful as reference texts when examining specifics of cryptographic algorithm and protocol implementation, these texts tend to be written from a mathematics perspective versus engineering and computer science viewpoints. Even books such as *Applied Cryptography* [275], by Bruce Schneier, are not truly suited to classroom environments, though they are written to be accessible to those with a less formal mathematics background. Moreover, mathematics-based books fail to provide real-world examples that span the implementation domains of hardware, software, and embedded systems. This book describes cryptography and data security from the "how do I implement the algorithms and protocols" point of view, with relevant examples and homework problems that will be coded in software languages, such as assembly and C, as well as hardware description languages, such as VHDL and Verilog, to evaluate implementation results. The goal of these implementation comparisons is to provide students with a feel for what they may encounter in actual job situations, examining tradeoffs between code size, hardware logic resource requirements, memory usage, speed and throughput, power consumption, etc.

1.4 Book Organization

This book is organized with emphasis on cryptographic algorithm and protocol implementation in hardware, software, and embedded systems. To that end, it is useful to hierarchically classify the different subject areas that will be examined. Figure 1.1 details the breakdown of relevant topics. We use the term *cryptology* to refer to the generic study of secret messages, but it is often used interchangeably with the term *cryptography* [89].

Different types of symmetric-key cryptographic algorithms are presented in Chapters 2-5. Basic substitution ciphers will be examined and the concept of cryptanalysis, or code breaking, will be introduced. Cryptography and cryptanalysis cannot exist without the other — cryptanalysis provides the necessary scrutiny to validate the security (or lack thereof) of a cryptographic algorithm.

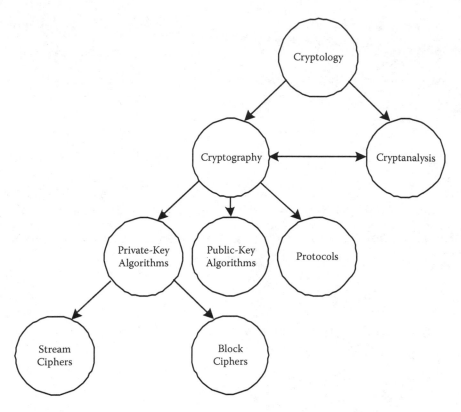

Figure 1.1: Overview of the Field of Cryptology

These ideas will lead to a study of both stream ciphers, in which data is *encrypted* and *decrypted* a single bit at a time, and block ciphers, in which data is broken into blocks for encryption and decryption. Both the Data Encryption Standard (DES), which expired in 1998 [275], and the Advanced Encryption Standard (AES) algorithm *Rijndael*, chosen by the National Institute of Standards and Technology (NIST) in October 2000, will be explored in detail with particular emphasis placed on the tradeoffs between hardware and software implementations in addition to attacks that have been proposed in recent publications.

Chapters 6-9 will focus on public-key cryptographic algorithms. Initial discussions will center around the underlying mathematics behind the computation of inverses, knowledge that will be critical in understanding cryptosystems such as *RSA* and those based on the *Discrete Logarithm* problem. An extended discussion will be presented on efficient implementations of public-key algorithms through the use of fast exponentiation techniques, the *Chinese Remainder Theorem*, and *Montgomery Arithmetic*. Tradeoffs between public-key and symmetric-key algorithms will be examined, leading to the development of hybrid architectures that address the *Key Distribution* problem while also maintaining a reasonable level of performance. Finally, attacks against public-key algorithms will be investigated, the results of which will be used to determine the minimum key lengths necessary to maintain acceptable levels of security.

The understanding of cryptographic algorithms gained in Chapters 2-9 will be used as the foundation for the construction of cryptographic protocols. Chapter 10 will examine the different components necessary for the creation of cryptographic protocols, such as *Digital Signatures*, *Message Authentication Codes* (MACs), and *Hash Functions*. These components will be analyzed in terms of the services they provide in combination with each other when attempting to create cryptographic protocols that are fast, efficient, and secure. Finally, Chapter 11 will investigate different security services and their impact on the construction of cryptographic protocols. The issues related to *key establishment* and *key*

distribution will be examined with respect to the constructed protocols, with particular focus on the use of certificates to establish
identity during the communication process.

The material for this book is derived from the author's teach-
ing notes and research publications, with other books and research
articles in recent literature used as supplementary material to provide information on state-of-the art implementations when evaluating different methods. The book is designed to be used in
electrical engineering and computer science courses focused on applied cryptography, where students are taught not only the underlying mathematics theory behind cryptographic algorithms, but
also how to efficiently implement these algorithms for a variety of
target technologies.

1.5   Supplements

The files required for various homework problems, as well as supplementary reading, can be found at www.understandingcryptography.
com <http://www.understandingcryptography.com/>.

Chapter 2

Symmetric-Key Cryptography

When examining Figure 1.1, it is interesting to note that until 1973, when James Ellis, Clifford Cocks, and Malcolm Williamson first developed the concept of public-key encryption [121], and 1976, when Whitfield Diffie and Martin Hellman proposed their revolutionary key distribution methodology [70], all cryptosystems were symmetric-key based. Based on Figure 1.1, it is clear that cryptographic algorithms used to ensure confidentiality fall within one of two categories: symmetric-key (also known as secret-key and private-key) and public-key. Symmetric-key algorithms use the same key for both encryption and decryption. Conversely, public-key algorithms use a public key for encryption and the verification of *Digital Signatures* while using a private key for

9

decryption and the generation of *Digital Signatures*. Modern cryptosystems tend to be hybrid systems that include both symmetric-key and public-key algorithms. In a typical session, a public-key algorithm will be used for the exchange of a session key and to provide authenticity through *Digital Signatures*. The session key is then used in conjunction with a symmetric-key algorithm. Symmetric-key algorithms tend to be significantly faster than public-key algorithms and as a result are typically used in bulk data encryption [275]. The two types of symmetric-key algorithms are block ciphers and stream ciphers. Block ciphers operate on a block of data whereas stream ciphers encrypt individual bits. Block ciphers are typically used when performing bulk data encryption, and the data transfer rate of the connection directly follows the throughput of the implemented algorithm [82].

2.1   Cryptosystem Overview

Figure 2.1 shows the setup of a typical symmetric-key cryptosystem in which two parties, denoted as *Alice* and *Bob*, desire to communicate in secret over an open channel such as the Internet. However, a third party, denoted as *Oscar*, wishes to determine the contents of the communication and potentially modify said contents without the knowledge of either *Alice* or *Bob*.

To achieve these goals, two options are available to *Alice* and *Bob*. The first option is to protect the open channel. However, this option is not practical when considering the vast size, com-

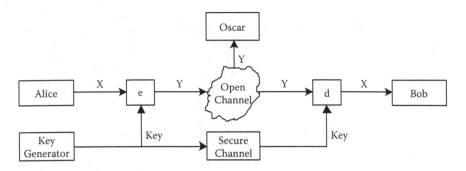

Figure 2.1: Typical Symmetric-Key Cryptosystem

plexity, and distributed nature of channels such as the Internet. The second and more viable option is the use of cryptography. *Alice* must encrypt the message X before sending it across the open channel so that *Oscar* can only access Y, the encrypted message. *Oscar* will be unable to translate Y to X without knowledge of the *Key*.

To facilitate the use of cryptography, it is useful to develop a notation defining a number of terms and variables for use in cryptosystem specification:

- X is the *plaintext* and is of finite length.

- $P = \{x_1, x_2, \ldots x_p\}$ is the *plaintext space*, representing all possible inputs.

- Y is the *ciphertext* and is of finite length.

- $C = \{y_1, y_2, \ldots y_p\}$ is the *ciphertext space*, also representing all possible inputs.

- k is the *key* and is of finite length.

- $K = \{k_1, k_2, \ldots k_l\}$ is the *key space* and is finite.

- e_{k_i} is the encryption function such that $e_{k_i}(X) = Y$.

- d_{k_i} is the decryption function such that $d_{k_i}(Y) = X$.

- e_{k_i} and d_{k_i} are inverse functions for identical keys such that $d_{k_i}(Y) = d_{k_i}(e_{k_i}(X)) = X$.

Example 2.1: Consider a substitution cipher that operates on the English alphabet. In this case, both the plaintext space P and the ciphertext space C are the letters A through Z. The key space K is the set of all unique mappings of the letters A through Z to the letters A through Z. For the first letter to be mapped there are twenty-six possible mappings, for the second letter to be mapped there are twenty-five possible mappings, and so on. Therefore, the size of the key space is $26 \times 25 \times 24 \times \ldots \times 2 \times 1 = 26!$.

Example 2.2: Consider a substitution cipher that operates on the Greek alphabet. In this case, both the plaintext space P and the ciphertext space C are the letters α (alpha) through ζ (zeta). The key space K is the set of all unique mappings of the letters α through ζ to the letters α through ζ. For the first letter to be mapped there are twenty-four possible mappings (because there are twenty-four letters in the Greek alphabet). For the second letter to be mapped there are twenty-three possible mappings, and so on. Therefore, the size of the key space is $24 \times 23 \times 22 \times \ldots \times 2 \times 1 = 24!$.

Example 2.3: Consider the Data Encryption Standard (DES), a 64-bit block cipher. *DES* accepts a 64-bit plaintext block and a 56-bit key as inputs and produces a 64-bit ciphertext block as its output. Therefore, both the plaintext and ciphertext spaces are the set of all possible 64-bit values, resulting in both spaces having a size of 2^{64}. Similarly, the key space K is the set of all possible 56-bit values, resulting in the key space having a size of 2^{56}.

2.2 The Modulo Operator

To facilitate the understanding of cryptographic algorithms and attacks against these algorithms, it is useful to examine relevant discrete mathematics number theory. The *Modulo* operator, denoted as *mod* in equations, is defined as the remainder r of the division of a value a by the modulus m. More formally, if a, r, and m are integers, $m > 0$, and $0 \leq r < m$, computing a modulo m is denoted as $a \equiv r \bmod m$.

Example 2.4: Let $a = 15$ and $m = 4$. Therefore a modulo m is computed as:

$$a \equiv r \ mod \ m$$
$$15 \equiv 3 \ mod \ 4$$

because the remainder of a divided by m is 3.

It is important to note that r is chosen such that $0 \leq r < m$. The computation of the *Modulo* operation may be expressed as $a = (q \cdot m) + r$ or $a - r = (q \cdot m)$, where q is the quotient of a divided by m. But why is the requirement that $0 \leq r < m$ imposed? This requirement is necessary because the remainder r is not unique, as will be shown in **Example 2.5**.

Example 2.5: Let $a = 15$ and $m = 4$. Therefore, a modulo m is computed as $15 \equiv 3 \ mod \ 4 \equiv 7 \ mod \ 4 \equiv 11 \ mod \ 4$ because the remainder of a divided by m is 3 in all cases.

Example 2.6: Let $a = -15$ and $m = 4$. Therefore, a modulo m is computed as:

$$a \equiv r \bmod m$$
$$-15 \equiv 1 \bmod 4$$

The remainder of a divided by m is -3. However, -3 is outside of the bounds of $0 \leq r < m$. Continually adding the modulus m to the remainder r when r is negative will guarantee that r is within the bounds of $0 \leq r < m$. In this case, adding the modulus to the remainder once yields $r = -3 + 4 = 1$ which is within the desired range $0 \leq r < m$. Adding multiples of the modulus increases the quotient. However, when performing the *Modulo* operation the only concern is the remainder. Modifying the quotient has no impact upon the remainder and is thus a viable method of converting a negative calculated value for the remainder to a value that meets the requirement $0 \leq r < m$.

Most high level software languages have a built in operator for the *Modulo* operation. In the case of C, the % is used as the modulus operator.

Example 2.7: The C statement to compute 67 modulo 13 is:

  r = 67 % 13; /* r = 67 mod 13 = 2 */

Example 2.8: The C statements to compute -38 modulo 11 is:

  r = -38 % 11; /* r = -38 mod 11 = -5 */

  r = r + 11; /* r = -5 + 11 = 6 */

C exhibits unusual behavior when implementing the *Modulo* operation on negative numbers. In such cases, the result calculated using the % operator is in the range $-m \leq r < 0$ instead of being in the range $0 \leq r < m$. To adjust for this condition so as to meet the requirement that $0 \leq r < m$, the modulus m must be added to the remainder r to yield a new value for r that is in the required range $0 \leq r < m$.

The computational aspects of performing the *Modulo* operation in a base-10 system must be considered when implementing hardware and software systems that employ such arithmetic operations. Division must be performed regardless of whether the desired result is the quotient or the remainder. Base-10 division in both software and hardware tends to be slow and resource intensive. As a result, computer architects and software developers will go to great lengths to avoid performing division. One method of avoiding division is to apply a transformation to a basis which results in division and multiplication becoming shifting operations. An example of such a transformation is *Montgomery Arithmetic* (see Section 7.2.4.4).

An important property of the *Modulo* operation is that it may be applied to intermediate results within an equation. When applied to intermediate results, this associative property simplifies future calculations by reducing the size of the data to be operated upon.

Example 2.9: Compute $5^{17} \bmod 11$ without applying modulo reduction to intermediate values.

$$
\begin{aligned}
5^{17} &= 762,939,453,125 \bmod 11 \\
762,939,453,125/11 &= 69,358,132,102 + r \\
762,939,453,125 &= 69,358,132,102 \cdot 11 + r \\
r &= 762,939,453,125 - (69,358,132,102 \cdot 11) \\
r &= 3
\end{aligned}
$$

From this it is evident that $r \equiv 3 \bmod 11$. In this case, the exponentiation results in a large number — 762,939,453,125 — which must then be reduced via division. Both of these operations become exceedingly complex due to the multi-precision arithmetic that must be performed. A more computationally friendly alternative is demonstrated in **Example 2.10**.

Example 2.10: Compute $5^{17} \bmod 11$ by applying modulo reduction to intermediate values.

$$5^{17} = 5^5 \cdot 5^5 \cdot 5^5 \cdot 5^2 \bmod 11$$
$$5^{17} = 3,125 \cdot 3,125 \cdot 3,125 \cdot 25 \bmod 11$$
$$5^{17} = (3,125 \bmod 11 \cdot 3,125 \bmod 11 \cdot 3,125 \bmod 11 \cdot 25$$
$$\bmod 11) \bmod 11$$

$$3,125/11 = 284 + r_1$$
$$3,125 = 284 \cdot 11 + r_1$$
$$r_1 = 3,125 - 284 \cdot 11$$
$$r_1 = 1$$

$$25/11 = 2 + r_2$$
$$25 = 2 \cdot 11 + r_2$$
$$r_2 = 25 - 22$$
$$r_2 = 3$$

$$5^{17} = (1 \cdot 1 \cdot 1 \cdot 3) \bmod 11$$
$$5^{17} = 3$$

Examples 2.9 and **2.10** illustrate that computing smaller intermediate exponentiation values and modulo reducing these values often results in an implementation (in either hardware or software) that is faster and less resource intensive versus computing the entire exponentiation and applying the modulo reduction at the end of the exponentiation process.

2.3   Greatest Common Divisor

The *Greatest Common Divisor* or *gcd* of two numbers, a and b, is defined as the largest integer that evenly divides both a and b. Computation of the *gcd* of two elements requires that the elements be decomposed into their integer prime factors. If the *gcd* of two elements is one, then the elements are said to be *relatively prime* to each other.

Example 2.11: Compute the *gcd* of 440 and 128.

Factoring 440 and 128 yields:

$$
\begin{aligned}
440 &= 2^3 \times 5 \times 11 \\
128 &= 2^7 \\
gcd(440,\ 128) &= 2^3
\end{aligned}
$$

2.4   The Ring Z_m

Having established an understanding of the *Modulo* operator, the *Ring Z_m* is now defined as consisting of:

1. The set $Z_m = \{0, 1, 2, \ldots m-1\}$.

2. Two operations:

   (a) Addition (denoted as +) such that $a + b \equiv c \bmod m$ for all elements $a, b, c \in Z_m$.

   (b) Multiplication (denoted as ×) such that $a \times b \equiv c \bmod m$ for all elements $a, b, c \in Z_m$.

Example 2.12: Compute the addition and multiplication of 3 and 5 in the *Ring Z_7*.

$$m = 7$$
$$3 + 5 = 8 \equiv 1 \bmod 7$$
$$3 \times 5 = 15 \equiv 1 \bmod 7$$

The *Ring Z_m* has a number of properties of note [301]:

- 0 is the additive identity element such that $a + 0 = a \bmod m$ for all elements a in the set Z_m.

- $-a$ is the additive inverse of any element a such that $a + (-a) \equiv 0 \bmod m$ for all elements a in the set Z_m. Note that $-a$ must be adjusted to $-a + m$ to comply with the requirement that $0 \le a < m$.

- The addition operation is closed, such that $a + b \equiv c \bmod m$ for all elements a, b, $c \in Z_m$.

- The addition operation is commutative, such that $a + b = b + a$ for all elements a, $b \in Z_m$.

- The addition operation is associative, such that $(a + b) + c = a + (b + c)$ for all elements a, b, $c \in Z_m$.

- 1 is the multiplicative identity element such that $a \times 1 = a \bmod m$ for all elements a in the set Z_m.

- a^{-1} is the multiplicative inverse of any element a such that $a \times a^{-1} \equiv 1 \bmod m$. An element a in the set Z_m has a multiplicative inverse if the $gcd(a, m) = 1$ (a and m are relatively prime to each other).

- The multiplication operation is closed, such that $a \times b \equiv c \bmod m$ for all elements a, b, $c \in Z_m$.

- The multiplication operation is commutative, such that $a \times b = b \times a$ for all elements a, $b \in Z_m$.

- The multiplication operation is associative, such that $(a \times b) \times c = a \times (b \times c)$ for all elements a, b, $c \in Z_m$.

2.5   Homework Problems

Homework Problem 2.5.1: Find the additive inverse for all elements contained in the *Ring* Z_m for $m = 6$ and $m = 13$.

Homework Problem 2.5.2: Find the multiplicative inverse for all elements contained in the *Ring* Z_m for $m = 4$, $m = 9$, and $m = 13$. Why is Z_{13} different from Z_4 and Z_9?

Homework Problem 2.5.3: Find the multiplicative inverse for 5 in Z_9, Z_{11}, and Z_{12}.

Homework Problem 2.5.4: Find all the elements contained in the *Ring* Z_m that are relatively prime to m for $m = 5$, $m = 10$, $m = 12$, and $m = 26$.

Homework Problem 2.5.5: Write a C program to find all elements contained in the *Ring* Z_m that are relatively prime to m. Write a user interface that queries the user for m and then prints the values for the elements in the *Ring* Z_m that are relatively prime to m to the screen.

Homework Problem 2.5.6: Write a C program to find the multiplicative inverse for all elements contained in the *Ring* Z_m. Use the program from **Homework Problem 2.5.5** to query the user for m and then determine if an element in the *Ring* Z_m has an inverse, i.e. the element is relatively prime to m. If an inverse exists for an element under test, use trial-and-error to determine the element's inverse. Create an output file that has two columns; the first column will be the elements in the *Ring* Z_m and the second column will be the multiplicative inverse of each element. If an element does not have a multiplicative inverse, enter a dash in the multiplicative inverse column.

Homework Problem 2.5.7: Using the C program from **Homework Problem 2.5.6**, add code that will measure and output to the screen the time required to find the multiplicative inverse for all elements contained in the *Ring* Z_m. Test the program for $m = 2^{10}$, $m = 2^{15}$, $m = 2^{20}$, $m = 2^{25}$, and $m = 2^{30}$. Draw a graph that plots m versus program execution time.

Chapter 3

Symmetric-Key Cryptography: Substitution Ciphers

Substitution ciphers encrypt text by substituting one character for another. In this case, the key is the user-defined substitution mapping for the characters contained in the plaintext space.

3.1 Basic Cryptanalysis

Cryptanalysis, or code breaking, occurs when *Oscar* attempts to recover plaintext sent over an open channel without knowledge of the key used to encrypt the plaintext. Recall that in **Example 2.1** it was determined that a substitution cipher whose plaintext and ciphertext spaces are the English alphabet has a key space of size $26! \approx 4 \times 10^{26}$. One method of performing cryptanalysis on a substitution cipher (or any cryptosystem) is to try all possible mappings (or keys) to see if the decrypted text is intelligible. This method is referred to as the *Brute Force* or *Exhaustive Key Search* method. Although this method is inefficient, *Exhaustive Key Search* does provide an upper bound for the complexity, time, and resources required to attack a system. Unfortunately (or fortunately, for *Oscar*), other attacks may exist that reduce these parameters, making *Oscar's* job significantly easier. Moreover, these attacks may not always be based in mathematical analysis. Social engineering attacks are often cheaper and easier solutions versus more traditional cryptanalysis, achieving the same results through bribery, trickery, etc. [74, 276].

In the case of a substitution cipher, each plaintext character always maps to the same ciphertext character for a given mapping. As a result of this characteristic, *Statistical Analysis* may be used to extract information from the ciphertext; the nature of the mapping transfers any statistical properties contained in the plaintext to the ciphertext. Therefore, in the case of **Example 2.1**, where the plaintext and ciphertext spaces are the English alphabet, *Oscar* can take advantage of the known properties of the English language to obtain the plaintext from a given ciphertext. From Table 3.1, *Oscar* knows the frequency of occurrence of each letter in the English alphabet [301]:

Letter	Probability	Letter	Probability
A	.082	N	.067
B	.015	O	.075
C	.028	P	.019
D	.043	Q	.001
E	.127	R	.060
F	.022	S	.063
G	.020	T	.091
H	.061	U	.028
I	.070	V	.010
J	.002	W	.023
K	.008	X	.001
L	.040	Y	.020
M	.024	Z	.001

Table 3.1: Probability of Occurrence of 26 Letters in the English Language

Other references may be used to determine the most frequently occurring two- and three-letter sequences in the English language, beginning and ending letter frequencies for words, and high probability letter combinations (such as "q" being followed by "u") [99]. Determining a word in this manner reveals the mapping for all letters contained in the word, a significant improvement versus the *Exhaustive Key Search* attack method. Similar analyses have been performed for other languages, including French, German, Italian, Portuguese, and Spanish [101, 118]. Clearly, for any cipher to be secure, the resultant ciphertext must appear to have no correlation to and thus reveal no statistical data about the plaintext.

When performing cryptanalysis, it is important to define the assumed basic operating conditions under which the attacker must function. These rules, known as *Kerckhoffs' Principle* [156], state that:

1. *Oscar* knows the cryptosystem in use, including the algorithms used to perform encryption and decryption.

2. *Oscar* does not know the key.

Clearly *Oscar* must have some basic knowledge of the cryptosystem in use if he is to have any hope of performing an attack. It is also clear that if *Oscar* knows the key for the cryptosystem in use, he can immediately decrypt the ciphertext without performing any attack, because the decryption function is known to him. Moreover, *Oscar* may masquerade as either *Alice* or *Bob*, encrypting messages and sending them to either party, both of whom will successfully decrypt the ciphertext and assume that the message came from their counterpart. Because *Alice* and *Bob* share the same key, the underlying assumption is that if *Alice* receives a message, the message must have come from *Bob* (and vice versa). A system that relies solely upon symmetric-key encryption fails to provide the security services of message authentication and non-repudiation of the message, as described in Section 11.1.

At first glance, *Kerckhoffs' Principle* would seem to violate common sense in that by keeping the details of a cryptosystem hidden, the system should be more secure, much like the secret formula to *CocaCola*®. However, history has demonstrated that the strength of cryptographic algorithms and cryptosystems is validated only through public scrutiny over extended periods of time.

Such systems eventually have their underlying algorithms revealed and are usually demonstrated to be poorly designed once the design details are made public.

Based on *Kerckhoffs' Principle*, four classifications of attacks on a cryptographic algorithm may now be defined:

1. **Ciphertext-Only**:

   - *Oscar* knows the ciphertext $y_1 = e_k(x_1)$, $y_2 = e_k(x_2)$, ...
   - *Oscar* wants to know either the plaintext x_1, x_2, ... or the key k.

2. **Known-Plaintext**:

   - *Oscar* knows some plaintext-ciphertext pairs $(x_1, y_1 = e_k(x_1))$, $(x_2, y_2 = e_k(x_2))$, ...
   - *Oscar* wants to know the key k.

3. **Chosen-Plaintext**:

   - *Oscar* knows some plaintext-ciphertext pairs $(x_1, y_1 = e_k(x_1))$, $(x_2, y_2 = e_k(x_2))$, ... and is able to choose x_1, x_2, ...
   - *Oscar* wants to know the key k.

4. **Chosen-Ciphertext**:

   - *Oscar* knows some plaintext-ciphertext pairs $(x_1, y_1 = e_k(x_1))$, $(x_2, y_2 = e_k(x_2))$, ... and is able to choose y_1, y_2, ...
   - *Oscar* wants to know the key k.

These classifications will be used when discussing attacks on cryptosystems examined in later Sections.

3.2 Shift Ciphers

A shift cipher is a type of substitution cipher in which each letter of an alphabet is assigned a number. Each letter is then encrypted by shifting its numerical value by a fixed amount and translating the new number back to its corresponding letter in the alphabet. Note that for an alphabet with l letters, a shift cipher with a shift value of 0 passes the plaintext through as the ciphertext. Shift values greater than $l - 1$ are not unique because they are equivalent to shift values of $(l - 1) \bmod l$. Therefore, the plaintext, ciphertext, and shift value (the key) must all be contained in Z_l. For an alphabet with l letters using a shift value of k, the shift cipher is defined as:

$$P = Z_l$$
$$C = Z_l$$
$$K = Z_l$$

$$x \in P$$
$$y \in C$$
$$k \in K$$

$$Encryption: e_k(x) = (x + k) \; mod \; l = y$$

$$Decryption: d_k(y) = (y - k) \; mod \; l = x$$

Using this definition, shift ciphers for specific languages and alphabets may now be examined.

Example 3.1: Consider the English language and associated alphabet with the mapping of $A \Leftrightarrow 0$, $B \Leftrightarrow 1$, ... , $Z \Leftrightarrow 25$. Encrypt the plaintext

$$X = CRYPTOGRAPHY$$

$$X = 2, \; 17, \; 24, \; 15, \; 19, \; 14, \; 6, \; 17, \; 0, \; 15, \; 7, \; 24$$

using a shift cipher with a value of $k = 3$.

Encryption

$x_0 = 2$	$\rightarrow e_3(2) = 2 + 3 \bmod 26$	$= 5 \bmod 26$		$= F$
$x_1 = 17$	$\rightarrow e_3(17) = 17 + 3 \bmod 26$	$= 20 \bmod 26$		$= U$
$x_2 = 24$	$\rightarrow e_3(24) = 24 + 3 \bmod 26$	$= 27 \bmod 26$	$\equiv 1 \bmod 26$	$= B$
$x_3 = 15$	$\rightarrow e_3(15) = 15 + 3 \bmod 26$	$= 18 \bmod 26$		$= S$
$x_4 = 19$	$\rightarrow e_3(19) = 19 + 3 \bmod 26$	$= 22 \bmod 26$		$= W$
$x_5 = 14$	$\rightarrow e_3(14) = 14 + 3 \bmod 26$	$= 17 \bmod 26$		$= R$
$x_6 = 6$	$\rightarrow e_3(6) = 6 + 3 \bmod 26$	$= 9 \bmod 26$		$= J$
$x_7 = 17$	$\rightarrow e_3(17) = 17 + 3 \bmod 26$	$= 20 \bmod 26$		$= U$
$x_8 = 0$	$\rightarrow e_3(0) = 0 + 3 \bmod 26$	$= 3 \bmod 26$		$= D$
$x_9 = 15$	$\rightarrow e_3(15) = 15 + 3 \bmod 26$	$= 18 \bmod 26$		$= S$
$x_{10} = 7$	$\rightarrow e_3(7) = 7 + 3 \bmod 26$	$= 10 \bmod 26$		$= K$
$x_{11} = 24$	$\rightarrow e_3(24) = 24 + 3 \bmod 26$	$= 27 \bmod 26$	$\equiv 1 \bmod 26$	$= B$

Therefore it is evident that the ciphertext

$$Y \; = \; 5, \; 20, \; 1, \; 18, \; 22, \; 17, \; 9, \; 20, \; 3, \; 18, \; 10, \; 1$$

$$Y \; = \; FUBSWRJUDSKB$$

for the plaintext $X = CRYPTOGRAPHY$ using $k = 3$. Note that a shift cipher with $k = 3$ is known as a *Caesar Cipher* because this form of shift cipher was used by Julius Caesar to protect messages passed to and from his military commanders [305].

When considering attacks against shift ciphers, two obvious options present themselves, both of which are *Ciphertext-Only* attacks. The first option is an *Exhaustive Key Search* attack. In the case of a shift cipher, the key space size is equal to the number of letters in the alphabet and thus is easily searched. Clearly, the key space of a shift cipher is not sufficiently large for the cipher to be considered secure.

The second option for attacking a shift cipher is to take advantage of the fact that each plaintext letter will always map to the same ciphertext letter for a given key, i.e. the shift value. Therefore, *Statistical Analysis* in the form of letter frequency analysis may be performed to determine the plaintext from the ciphertext, as described in Section 3.1. It is clear that a shift cipher reveals a correlation between the ciphertext and the plaintext and is thus not secure.

3.3   Affine Ciphers

An affine cipher is a special case of the shift cipher, using a mapping that is more complex than just a simple shifting of the plaintext values. For an alphabet with l letters, the affine cipher is defined as:

$$P = Z_l$$
$$C = Z_l$$

$$x \in P$$
$$y \in C$$
$$k = (a, b) \in Z_l$$

$$Encryption: \; e_k(x) = (a \cdot x + b) \; mod \; l = y$$
$$Decryption: \; d_k(y) = (a^{-1} \cdot (y - b)) \; mod \; l = x$$

The decryption function is derived by manipulating the encryption function to solve for x, noting that $(a^{-1} \cdot a) \; mod \; l \equiv 1 \; mod \; l$:

$$Encryption: \; e_k(x) = (a \cdot x + b) \; mod \; l = y$$
$$(a \cdot x) \; mod \; l = (y - b) \; mod \; l$$
$$(a^{-1} \cdot (a \cdot x)) \; mod \; l = (a^{-1} \cdot (y - b)) \; mod \; l$$
$$((a^{-1} \cdot a) \cdot x) \; mod \; l = (a^{-1} \cdot (y - b)) \; mod \; l$$
$$Decryption: \; d_k(y) = (a^{-1} \cdot (y - b)) \; mod \; l = x$$

Note that because the affine cipher requires the use of a^{-1}, the $gcd(a, l) = 1$ must be true for a^{-1} to exist. Therefore the size of the key space varies based on l, the number of letters in the language's alphabet. In particular, the size of the key space will depend on the number of elements $1 \leq a \leq l - 1$ that are relatively prime to l, which is defined as $\phi(l)$ (also known as *Euler's Phi Function*) and will be discussed further in Section 6.6. Using $\phi(l)$ the size of the affine cipher's key space may now be defined as $K = \phi(l) \cdot l$ because there are $\phi(l)$ possible choices for a and l possible choices for b, the two parameters that form the key k. Using these definitions, affine ciphers for specific languages and alphabets may now be examined.

Example 3.2: What are the valid choices for a and thus the size of the key space for an affine cipher that is based on the English language and associated alphabet?

To answer this question, the elements within Z_{26} that are relatively prime to 26, i.e. that have a $gcd(a, 26) = 1$, must be determined because there are 26 letters in the English alphabet. Therefore, all elements $1 \leq a \leq 25$ must be factored into their integer prime factors and compared with the integer prime factors of 26.

$$1 = 1$$
$$2 = 2$$
$$3 = 3$$
$$4 = 2^2$$
$$5 = 5$$
$$6 = 2 \cdot 3$$
$$7 = 7$$
$$8 = 2^3$$
$$9 = 3^2$$
$$10 = 2 \cdot 5$$
$$11 = 11$$
$$12 = 2^2 \cdot 3$$
$$13 = 13$$

$$14 = 2 \cdot 7$$
$$15 = 3 \cdot 5$$
$$16 = 2^4$$
$$17 = 17$$
$$18 = 2 \cdot 3^2$$
$$19 = 19$$
$$20 = 2^2 \cdot 5$$
$$21 = 3 \cdot 7$$
$$22 = 2 \cdot 11$$
$$23 = 23$$
$$24 = 2^3 \cdot 3$$
$$25 = 5^2$$

$$26 = 2 \cdot 13$$

Based on these results it is evident that $\phi(26) = 12$ because all of the even numbers $1 \leq a \leq 25$ share a factor of 2 with 26 while 13 shares a factor of 13 with 26. Therefore, the size of the key space of this affine cipher is computed as $K = \phi(l) \cdot l = 12 \cdot 26 = 312$.

Example 3.3: Consider the English language and associated alphabet with a key $k = (a = 5, b = 9)$. Encrypt the plaintext:

$$X = CRYPTOGRAPHY$$
$$X = 2,\ 17,\ 24,\ 15,\ 19,\ 14,\ 6,\ 17,\ 0,\ 15,\ 7,\ 24$$

Encryption

$x_0 = 2$	$\rightarrow e_{(5,9)}(2) = 5 \cdot 2 + 9 \bmod 26$	$= 19 \bmod 26$		$= T$
$x_1 = 17$	$\rightarrow e_{(5,9)}(17) = 5 \cdot 17 + 9 \bmod 26$	$= 94 \bmod 26$	$\equiv 16 \bmod 26$	$= Q$
$x_2 = 24$	$\rightarrow e_{(5,9)}(24) = 5 \cdot 24 + 9 \bmod 26$	$= 129 \bmod 26$	$\equiv 25 \bmod 26$	$= Z$
$x_3 = 15$	$\rightarrow e_{(5,9)}(15) = 5 \cdot 15 + 9 \bmod 26$	$= 84 \bmod 26$	$\equiv 6 \bmod 26$	$= G$
$x_4 = 19$	$\rightarrow e_{(5,9)}(19) = 5 \cdot 19 + 9 \bmod 26$	$= 104 \bmod 26$	$\equiv 0 \bmod 26$	$= A$
$x_5 = 14$	$\rightarrow e_{(5,9)}(14) = 5 \cdot 14 + 9 \bmod 26$	$= 79 \bmod 26$	$\equiv 1 \bmod 26$	$= B$
$x_6 = 6$	$\rightarrow e_{(5,9)}(6) = 5 \cdot 6 + 9 \bmod 26$	$= 39 \bmod 26$	$\equiv 13 \bmod 26$	$= N$
$x_7 = 17$	$\rightarrow e_{(5,9)}(17) = 5 \cdot 17 + 9 \bmod 26$	$= 94 \bmod 26$	$\equiv 16 \bmod 26$	$= Q$
$x_8 = 0$	$\rightarrow e_{(5,9)}(0) = 5 \cdot 0 + 9 \bmod 26$	$= 9 \bmod 26$		$= J$
$x_9 = 15$	$\rightarrow e_{(5,9)}(15) = 5 \cdot 15 + 9 \bmod 26$	$= 84 \bmod 26$	$\equiv 6 \bmod 26$	$= G$
$x_{10} = 7$	$\rightarrow e_{(5,9)}(7) = 5 \cdot 7 + 9 \bmod 26$	$= 44 \bmod 26$	$\equiv 1 \bmod 18$	$= B$
$x_{11} = 24$	$\rightarrow e_{(5,9)}(24) = 5 \cdot 24 + 9 \bmod 26$	$= 129 \bmod 26$	$\equiv 25 \bmod 26$	$= Z$

Therefore it is evident that the ciphertext

$$Y \;=\; 19,\; 16,\; 25,\; 6,\; 0,\; 1,\; 13,\; 16,\; 9,\; 6\; 1,\; 25$$

$$Y \;=\; TQZGABNQJGBZ$$

for the plaintext $X \;=\; CRYPTOGRAPHY$ using $k \;=\; (a \;=\; 5,\; b \;=\; 9)$.

The same *Ciphertext-Only* attacks against shift ciphers may be applied to affine ciphers. Even with 312 valid combinations of a and b, the key space of an affine cipher is not sufficiently large for the cipher to be considered secure should it be subjected to an *Exhaustive Key Search* attack. Moreover, even with the expanded key space versus the key space of a shift cipher, an affine cipher exhibits the same property that each plaintext letter will always map to the same ciphertext letter for a given key. Therefore,

Statistical Analysis in the form of letter frequency analysis may be performed to determine the plaintext from the ciphertext, as described in Section 3.1. Therefore, although a large key space is necessary for a cipher to be strong, this feature alone is not a sufficient condition to guarantee the strength of a cipher. In general, symmetric-key algorithms with key spaces ranging in size between 2^{56} and 2^{64} provide only short-term security versus *Exhaustive Key Search* attacks (see Section 5.1 for a discussion of *DES*, a block cipher that employs a 56-bit key, as detailed in **Example 2.3**). Symmetric-key algorithms with key spaces of size 2^{128} are required for long-term security versus *Exhaustive Key Search* attacks given current computing capabilities.

Known-Plaintext, *Chosen-Plaintext*, and *Chosen-Ciphertext* attacks may also be applied to affine ciphers. In the case of a *Known-Plaintext* attack, knowledge of two plaintext letters and their corresponding ciphertext letters is sufficient to determine the key $k = (a, b)$, as demonstrated in **Example 3.4**.

Example 3.4: Compute the affine cipher key $k = (a, b)$ if the letter C, represented as 2, maps to the letter T, represented as 19, and the letter R, represented as 17, maps to the letter Q, represented as 16.

The problem statement yields the equations:

$$19 = a \cdot 2 + b \bmod 26$$
$$16 = a \cdot 17 + b \bmod 26$$

Subtracting the first equation from the second equation allows us to solve for a, noting that $15^{-1} \bmod 26 \equiv 7 \bmod 26$:

$$-3 \bmod 26 \;=\; a \cdot 15 \bmod 26$$

$$23 \bmod 26 \;=\; a \cdot 15 \bmod 26$$

$$15^{-1} \bmod 26 \cdot 23 \bmod 26 \;=\; 15^{-1} \bmod 26 \cdot a \cdot 15 \bmod 26$$

$$7 \cdot 23 \bmod 26 \;=\; a \bmod 26$$

$$161 \bmod 26 \;=\; a \bmod 26$$

$$5 \bmod 26 \;=\; a \bmod 26$$

Solving for a allows us to solve for b:

$$19 \;=\; a \cdot 2 + b \bmod 26$$

$$19 \bmod 26 \;=\; 5 \cdot 2 \bmod 26 + b \bmod 26$$

$$19 \bmod 26 \;=\; 10 \bmod 26 + b \bmod 26$$

$$19 \bmod 26 \;-\; 10 \bmod 26 \;=\; b \bmod 26$$

$$9 \bmod 26 \;=\; b \bmod 26$$

$$16 \;=\; a \cdot 17 + b \bmod 26$$

$$16 \bmod 26 \;=\; 5 \cdot 17 \bmod 26 + b \bmod 26$$

$$16 \bmod 26 \;=\; 85 \bmod 26 + b \bmod 26$$

$$16 \bmod 26 \;=\; 7 \bmod 26 + b \bmod 26$$

$$16 \bmod 26 \;-\; 7 \bmod 26 \;=\; b \bmod 26$$

$$9 \bmod 26 \;=\; b \bmod 26$$

Therefore, it is evident that the key $k \;=\; (5,\ 9)$, matching the results of **Example 3.3**.

In the case of a *Chosen-Plaintext* attack, careful plaintext selection immediately yields the values of the key $k = (a, b)$, as demonstrated in **Example 3.5**.

Example 3.5: Compute the affine cipher key $k = (a, b)$ if the letter A, represented as 0, maps to the letter J, represented as 9, and the letter B, represented as 1, maps to the letter O, represented as 14.

The problem statement yields the equations:

$$9 = a \cdot 0 + b \bmod 26$$
$$14 = a \cdot 1 + b \bmod 26$$

The first equation immediately yields $b = 9$. Substituting this value for b into the second equation allows us to solve for a:

$$14 = a \cdot 1 + 9 \bmod 26$$
$$14 \bmod 26 - 9 \bmod 26 = a \bmod 26$$
$$5 \bmod 26 = a \bmod 26$$

Therefore, it is evident that the key $k = (5, 9)$, matching the results of **Examples 3.3** and **3.4**.

In the case of a *Chosen-Ciphertext* attack, careful ciphertext selection is sufficient to determine the key $k = (a, b)$, as demonstrated in **Example 3.6**.

Example 3.6: Compute the affine cipher key $k = (a, b)$ if the ciphertext letter A, represented as 0, maps to the plaintext letter T, represented as 19, and the ciphertext letter B, represented as 1, maps to the plaintext letter O, represented as 14.

The problem statement yields the equations:

$$0 = a \cdot 19 + b \bmod 26$$

$$1 = a \cdot 14 + b \bmod 26$$

Subtracting the second equation from the first equation allows us to solve for a, noting that $5^{-1} \bmod 26 \equiv 21 \bmod 26$:

$$-1 \bmod 26 = a \cdot 5 \bmod 26$$

$$25 \bmod 26 = a \cdot 5 \bmod 26$$

$$5^{-1} \cdot 25 \bmod 26 = 5^{-1} \cdot a \cdot 5 \bmod 26$$

$$21 \cdot 25 \bmod 26 = a \bmod 26$$

$$525 \bmod 26 = a \bmod 26$$

$$5 \bmod 26 = a \bmod 26$$

Solving for a allows us to solve for b:

$$19 = a \cdot 2 + b \bmod 26$$

$$19 \bmod 26 = 5 \cdot 2 \bmod 26 + b \bmod 26$$

$$19 \bmod 26 = 10 \bmod 26 + b \bmod 26$$

$$19 \bmod 26 - 10 \bmod 26 = b \bmod 26$$

$$9 \bmod 26 = b \bmod 26$$

$$16 = a \cdot 17 + b \bmod 26$$

$$16 \bmod 26 = 5 \cdot 17 \bmod 26 + b \bmod 26$$

$$16 \bmod 26 = 85 \bmod 26 + b \bmod 26$$

$$16 \bmod 26 = 7 \bmod 26 + b \bmod 26$$

$$16 \bmod 26 - 7 \bmod 26 = b \bmod 26$$

$$9 \bmod 26 = b \bmod 26$$

Therefore, it is evident that the key $k = (5,\ 9)$, matching the results of **Examples 3.3**, **3.4**, and **3.5**.

It is clear based on **Examples 3.2**, **3.4**, **3.5**, and **3.6** that an affine cipher is not secure because numerous attacks may be applied to easily obtain the key $k = (a,\ b)$.

3.4   Homework Problems

Homework Problem 3.4.1: You receive the ciphertext

PKVUADHUAAOLTAVMVYNLAYBAOPQBZADHUAAOLTAVYLTLTILYTL

encrypted using a shift cipher. Assume the mapping of $A \Leftrightarrow 0$, $B \Leftrightarrow 1$, ... , $Z \Leftrightarrow 25$. Perform a letter frequency analysis attack to extract the plaintext from the ciphertext using the statistics provided in Table 3.1. How many letters must be identified before the key is successfully recovered? Which of the four types of attacks described in Section 3.1 did you perform? Who said the decrypted text?

Homework Problem 3.4.2: Write a C program to decrypt the ciphertext

NYSYXDSYAXDKYALMWVKYADWDPROPYSNYSYXDKYACZM

encrypted using an affine cipher with the parameters $a = 9$ and $b = 2$. Assume the mapping of $A \Leftrightarrow 0$, $B \Leftrightarrow 1$, ... , $Z \Leftrightarrow 25$. Who said the decrypted text?

Homework Problem 3.4.3: Write a C program to encrypt your first, middle, and last names using a shift cipher with the parameter $k = 7$. To create the plaintext, concatenate the three names with no punctuation marks or spaces. Your program must function properly for both upper-case and lower-case letters.

Homework Problem 3.4.4: Write a C program to encrypt the plaintext "The only thing we have to fear is fear itself" using an affine cipher with parameters a and b that will be specified as command line switches. Your program must print the resultant ciphertext to the screen, ignore punctuation marks and spaces, and check that the value entered for a is valid, returning an error if this is not the case. Show the resultant ciphertext for $a = 11$ and $b = 15$.

Homework Problem 3.4.5: What is the size of the key space of an affine cipher that uses the letters of the Greek alphabet?

Homework Problem 3.4.6: What is the size of the key space of an affine cipher that uses the letters of the Russian alphabet?

Homework Problem 3.4.7: Assume an affine cipher with parameters $a = a_1$ and $b = b_1$ is used to encrypt letters from the English alphabet. **Example 3.2** demonstrated that the size of the key space in this case is 312. If the ciphertext is encrypted a second time using an affine cipher with parameters $a = a_2$ and $b = b_2$, explain why the effective key space will be the same even though the plaintext has been encrypted twice.

Homework Problem 3.4.8: An affine cipher is applied to the English alphabet. The mapping of letters to integers is $A \Leftrightarrow 0$, $B \Leftrightarrow 1$, ..., $Z \Leftrightarrow 25$. Let $b = 2$.

a) Which of the integers — 9, 10, 11, 12, 13 — are valid values for a?

b) Use the largest possible value from part (a) for a and encrypt the message *BLACK ELK* using 8 for b.

c) The decryption process may be expressed as $d_k(y) = x = c \cdot (y + d) \bmod 26$. What are the values for c and d based on your answer for part (b)?

Homework Problem 3.4.9: A message is double encrypted with $y = e_{k_1}(e_{k_2}(x))$ where $e_{k_1}()$ and $e_{k_2}()$ are two affine ciphers with parameters $a_1 = 25$, $b_1 = 20$, $a_2 = 17$, and $b_2 = 21$.

a) Find the parameters c and d such that $x = c \cdot (y + d) \bmod 26$ decrypts a message encrypted via the double encryption method.

b) Decrypt the message $ZHUTKRBT$ using the mapping of letters to integers $A \Leftrightarrow 0$, $B \Leftrightarrow 1$, ... , $Z \Leftrightarrow 25$.

Homework Problem 3.4.10: Consider an affine cipher used for encryption and decryption that distinguishes between upper- and lower-case letters, resulting in a plaintext and ciphertext space of size 52.

a) What is the size of the key space for this affine cipher?

b) Given the parameters $a = 3$ and $b = 11$, and that the upper-case letters are assigned the values 0 through 25 for A through Z, and the lower-case letters are assigned the values 26 through 51 for a through z, decrypt the ciphertext $vlnnlrGtnxqqn$.

Homework Problem 3.4.11: Consider an affine cipher that encrypts and decrypts messages written using an alphabet containing twenty-five symbols.

a) How large is the key space of the affine cipher for this alphabet?

b) The ciphertext $y = $ 23, 9, 11, 7, 23, 9, 8, 21, 2 was encrypted using the key ($a = 13$, $b = 5$). What is the plaintext?

Homework Problem 3.4.12: Consider an affine cipher that encrypts and decrypts messages written using an alphabet containing twenty-one symbols.

a) How large is the key space of the affine cipher for this alphabet?

b) The ciphertext y = 18, 4, 20, 20, 15, 6, 15, 16, 5, 0, 19, 16 was encrypted using the key (a = 13, b = 5). What is the plaintext?

Homework Problem 3.4.13: Consider an affine cipher that encrypts and decrypts messages written using an alphabet containing thirty symbols.

a) How large is the key space of the affine cipher for this alphabet?

b) The ciphertext y = 26, 20, 29, 22, 29 was encrypted using the key (a = 17, b = 1). What is the plaintext?

Homework Problem 3.4.14: Write a VHDL architecture to implement the affine cipher encryption specified in **Homework Problem 3.4.8**. Assume that the input and output characters are represented by their binary 5-bit values and that the parameters a and b are fixed per **Homework Problem 3.4.8**. Your implementation must update the output ciphertext on every rising edge of the clock. Use the following entity declaration for your implementation:

```
LIBRARY ieee;
USE ieee.std_logic_1164.ALL;
USE ieee.std_logic_arith.ALL;
USE ieee.std_logic_unsigned.ALL;
ENTITY affine IS
   PORT ( plaintext  : IN  std_logic_vector (4 DOWNTO 0);
          clk, rst   : IN  std_logic;
          ciphertext : OUT std_logic_vector (4 DOWNTO 0));
END affine;
ARCHITECTURE behav OF affine IS
BEGIN
-- Your code goes here
END behav;
```

Specify the target technology used to implement the design and the maximum operating frequency as specified by your place-and-route tools. How much time is required to encrypt an input of 2^{20} random 5-bit characters based on your maximum operating frequency assuming a new 5-bit character is input every clock cycle?

Homework Problem 3.4.15: Write a VHDL architecture to implement any affine cipher encryption based on any language with up to 256 symbols. Assume that the input and output characters are represented by their binary 8-bit values and that the parameters a and b are 8-bit inputs. Also assume that a will be chosen by the user to be relatively prime to 256. Your implementation must update the output ciphertext on every rising edge of the clock. Use the following entity declaration for your implementation:

```
LIBRARY ieee;
USE ieee.std_logic_1164.ALL;
USE ieee.std_logic_arith.ALL;
USE ieee.std_logic_unsigned.ALL;
ENTITY gen_affine IS
   PORT ( plaintext  : IN  std_logic_vector (7 DOWNTO 0);
          a,b         : IN  std_logic_vector (7 DOWNTO 0);
          clk, rst    : IN  std_logic;
          ciphertext : OUT std_logic_vector (7 DOWNTO 0));
END gen_affine;
ARCHITECTURE behav OF gen_affine IS
BEGIN
-- Your code goes here
END behav;
```

Specify the target technology used to implement the design and the maximum operating frequency as specified by your place-and-route tools. How much time is required to encrypt an input of

2^{20} random 8-bit characters based on your maximum operating frequency assuming a new 8-bit character is input every clock cycle?

Homework Problem 3.4.16: Write a C program to implement any affine cipher encryption based on any language with up to 256 symbols. Assume that the input and output characters are represented by their 8-bit ASCII values and that the parameters a and b are inputs specified by the user. Write a user interface that queries the user for a, b, and an input file containing ASCII characters. Your program must check that the input value for a is valid and you must include code that will measure and output to the screen the time required to encrypt the input file.

Homework Problem 3.4.17: Write a C program that will create a text file with 2^{20} ASCII characters. Your program should repeatedly cycle through all of the valid ASCII codes until 2^{20} characters have been written to the output file. Once the output file has been generated, use the file as the input to the C program of **Homework Problem 3.4.16**. Compare your results with the time calculated to perform the same task in hardware in **Homework Problem 3.4.15**.

Chapter 4

Symmetric-Key Cryptography: Stream Ciphers

Recall that the two types of symmetric-key algorithms are block ciphers and stream ciphers, and that block ciphers operate on a block of data whereas stream ciphers encrypt individual bits. Therefore, in the case of a stream cipher we have the plaintext message $X = x_1, x_2, \ldots$, the key $Z = z_1, z_2, \ldots$, and the ciphertext $Y = y_1, y_2, \ldots$. Because stream ciphers encrypt a single bit at a time, $x_i, y_i, z_i \in \{0, 1\}$. The ciphertext Y is defined as $y_1 = e_{z_1}(x_1)$, $y_2 = e_{z_2}(x_2)$, $\ldots$ where the most common form of stream cipher encryption is modulo 2 addition, i.e. $y_i = e_{z_i}(x_i) = x_i + z_i \; mod \; 2$. Decryption is of the form of modulo 2 subtraction, which is equivalent to modulo 2 addition, i.e. $x_i = d_{z_i}(y_i) = y_i - z_i \; mod \; 2 = y_i + z_i \; mod \; 2$. Moreover, both operations are equivalent to the bit-wise exclusive-OR (denoted as XOR) operation, as detailed in Table 4.1.

a	b	a + b mod 2	a - b mod 2	a $\oplus$ b
0	0	0	0	0
0	1	1	-1 mod 2 $\equiv$ 1 mod 2	1
1	0	1	1	1
1	1	2 mod 2 $\equiv$ 0 mod 2	0	0

Table 4.1: Modulo 2 Addition, Subtraction, and Bit-Wise XOR

Figure 4.1 shows the setup of a typical stream cipher implementation in which two parties, *Alice* and *Bob*, desire to communicate in secret over an open channel. A third party, *Oscar*, wishes to determine the contents of the communication and potentially modify said contents without the knowledge of either *Alice* or *Bob*. However, with the use of the stream cipher, *Oscar* can only access the ciphertext y_i as it is sent over the channel. Note that encryption and decryption are the same because $x_i \oplus z_i \oplus z_i = x_i$. This equation holds true because of the XOR properties $z_i \oplus z_i = 0$ and $x_i \oplus 0 = x_i$. Using the XOR operation for encryption and decryption was originally proposed by Gilbert Vernam in 1917 and was patented in U.S. Patent 1310719 in 1919 for use in the Baudot teletype. Stream ciphers that utilize the XOR operation to combine the plaintext X with the key Z to generate the ciphertext Y are known as Vernam ciphers [90].

Therefore, it is evident that stream cipher encryption and decryption are easy to implement; in hardware, using 2-input XOR gates, and in software, using bitwise XOR instructions. For hardware implementations, the unit-gate model approximation is used such that a 2-input XOR gate is counted as two gate equivalents [314]. For software implementations, encrypting or decrypting a

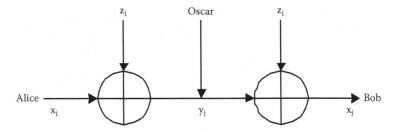

Figure 4.1: Typical Stream Cipher Implementation

single bit at a time is inefficient when instructions that perform bit-wise functions typically operate on single or multiple bytes of data. When operating on ASCII character data, software-based stream cipher encryption and decryption work well given that ASCII characters are seven bits in length and extended ASCII characters are eight bits in length. When encrypting or decrypting binary data streams in software, the data must be organized in groupings that match the processor word size (which dictates the number of bytes operated on by an individual instruction). This allows for efficient software-based stream cipher encryption and decryption for all but the leftover bits when the size of the data stream is not evenly divisible by the processor word size.

Having established hardware and software implementations of stream cipher encryption and decryption, what remains is how to generate the key $Z = z_1, z_2, \ldots$ such that *Oscar* is unable to decrypt the ciphertext Y and potentially alter the resultant plaintext X. If *Oscar* can recreate the key Z, he can decrypt the ciphertext y by combining the key and the ciphertext through an XOR operation. Therefore, it is critical that the key Z appear to be random such that *Oscar* cannot perform an attack using *Statistical Analysis* (or any other method) to extract the key.

4.1 Random Numbers

Generating random numbers may seem trivially easy but is in fact quite difficult. Recall that when examining substitution ciphers in Section 3.1, *Statistical Analysis* attacks were applied to determine the plaintext from the ciphertext. Similarly, if correlations exist between results of a supposedly random number generator, *Oscar* can exploit these correlations when attacking the cryptosystem. As detailed in [166, 275], because computers are deterministic, the best a computer can do is to act as a pseudo-random number generator to produce numbers and sequences that appear to be random but are computed from some initial value, usually termed a *seed*. Two examples of pseudo-random number generators are linear congruential generators and *Linear Feedback Shift Registers*.

It is important to note that although pseudo-random number generators may pass statistical randomness tests such as those found in [166], this does not guarantee that such generators are useful in cryptographic applications. This is because such applications require cryptographically secure pseudo-random number generators that have the additional property of being unpredictable [275]. Keeping *Kerckhoffs' Principle* in mind, we must assume that *Oscar* knows the method used to generate the pseudo-random stream of numbers or bits. Therefore, for a pseudo-random number generator to be cryptographically secure, it must generate number streams (or bit streams) in a manner such that it is not computationally feasible for *Oscar* to reproduce the stream and thus generate the next number or bit in the stream.

4.2 The One-Time Pad

The concept of security is unusual in that it is nearly impossible to state that something is proven to be secure. The opinion of an algorithm's or cryptosystem's strength of security is based on the scrutiny applied by cryptanalysts over time. The more time that passes without attacks being proposed that significantly reduce the complexity of obtaining the key (or keys) below the threshold of *Exhaustive Key Search*, the more secure the algorithm or cryptosystem. If it can be demonstrated that an algorithm or cryptosystem cannot be compromised, even if *Oscar* has access to unlimited computing resources, then such an algorithm or cryptosystem is termed *Unconditionally Secure*.

The only cryptosystem that is proven to be unconditionally secure is known as the *One-Time Pad*. The *One-Time Pad* was developed as a result of Joseph Mauborgne's suggestion that the key used in the Baudot teletype be random, and this idea was patented in the 1920s. However, it was not until the late 1940s that Claude Shannon successfully proved the *One-Time Pad* to be unconditionally secure [90]. The *One-Time Pad* is defined as:

$$X = \{x_0,\ x_1, \ldots\} \in P$$
$$Y = \{y_0,\ y_1, \ldots\} \in C$$
$$K = \{k_0,\ k_1, \ldots\} \in K$$

$$x_i,\ y_i,\ k_i \quad \in \quad \{0,\ 1\}$$

$$Encryption: \ e_{k_i}(x_i) \ = \ (x_i + k_i) \ mod \ 2 \ = \ y_i$$
$$Decryption: \ d_{k_i}(y_i) \ = \ (y_i + k_i) \ mod \ 2 \ = \ x_i$$

The *One-Time Pad* is unconditionally secure if keys are used only once and the keys are random, i.e. no correlations exist between keys. This is demonstrable by examining the system of linear equations that results from implementing the *One-Time Pad*:

$$y_0 = (x_0 + k_0) \ mod \ 2$$
$$y_1 = (x_1 + k_1) \ mod \ 2$$
$$y_2 = (x_2 + k_2) \ mod \ 2$$
$$\vdots$$
$$y_i = (x_i + k_i) \ mod \ 2$$

As long as each k_i is independent, the system of linear equations cannot be solved because each equation has one known element, y_i, and two unknown elements, x_i and k_i.

Unfortunately, implementing a *One-Time Pad* is not practical. As previously discussed, generating random key bits, i.e. bits that are independent, is extremely difficult, especially for long keys. The *One-Time Pad* is vulnerable to attack if a key is reused. Moreover, the nature of the *One-Time Pad* is such that key lengths must match the message length, resulting in a system that scales poorly. Finally, and arguably most significantly, the *One-Time Pad* does not address key distribution once the key has been generated. Given the lack of feasibility of a true *One-Time Pad*, more practical systems that attempt to replace the random key stream used in the *One-Time Pad* with a pseudo-random key stream generated from a small number of random key bits must be considered. Such an implementation yields a cryptosystem that is more easily realized in practice, as shown in Figure 4.2.

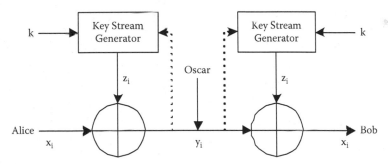

Figure 4.2: Practical Stream Cipher Implementation

Clearly, such an implementation is not unconditionally secure as in the case of the *One-Time Pad*. Therefore, more realistic levels of security when defining a cryptosystem must be considered. A cryptosystem is considered to be *Computationally Secure* if the best possible algorithm available to *Oscar* for successfully compromising the system requires a very large number of computations. In such a situation, it is not feasible for *Oscar* to have sufficient computing power to break the cryptosystem. Of course the computing power available to *Oscar* varies widely depending on whether *Oscar* is an individual, a company, a government, or somewhere in between. Moreover, computational security is based on the best known algorithm, and the required number of computations necessary to ensure computational security may change dramatically if a more powerful algorithm for attacking the cryptosystem be developed. The same is true should a significant advance in computing technology occur. As such, cryptosystems whose security is based on a very hard problem that has been studied by cryptanalysts are of greater interest. Such cryptosystems are termed *Relatively Secure*, although these systems may also fall victim to technology advancements and the development of a more powerful attack as scrutiny and cryptanalysis of the underlying algorithm(s) continues over time.

4.3   Key Stream Generators

When considering key stream generators for implementing the more practical stream cipher shown in Figure 4.2, two possibilities exist. *Asynchronous* key stream generators use the ciphertext y_i as a feedback term. This is indicated by the dotted lines in Figure 4.2. *Synchronous* key stream generators do not use the ciphertext y_i as a feedback term and instead rely only on the key k and previously generated key stream bits $(z_{i-1}, z_{i-2}, \ldots, z_1)$ to generate the next key stream bit z_i. The term *Synchronous Stream Cipher* is used to describe stream ciphers that use key stream generators that generate the key stream independent of the plaintext and the ciphertext, i.e. that use synchronous key stream generators. The term *Asynchronous Stream Cipher* is used to describe stream ciphers that synchronize automatically. In all cases, *Alice* and *Bob* must reach a state where their key stream generators are synchronized so that each z_i arrives at the same time as its corresponding y_i because loss of synchronization will result in corruption of the plaintext x_i upon decryption of the ciphertext y_i.

4.3.1 Linear Feedback Shift Registers

Linear Feedback Shift Registers (LFSRs) are often used to generate key streams for practical stream ciphers. An *LFSR* is made up of storage elements and a feedback network, as detailed in Figure 4.3.

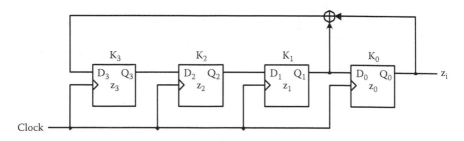

Figure 4.3: Example LFSR Implementation

The number of flip-flops in the *LFSR* is denoted as m. In the case of Figure 4.3, $m = 4$. The m *LFSR* storage elements are represented as D flip-flops, denoted as K_i, that are initialized to a chosen value, represented in Figure 4.3 as (z_3, z_2, z_1, z_0). The right-most flip-flop produces the output key stream z_i. The left-most flip-flop's input is the XOR of the outputs of certain flip-flops within the feedback network, and the input to all other flip-flops is the output of the previous flip-flop, i.e. $D_i = Q_{i+1}$. It will become evident that choosing which flip-flop outputs to XOR to create the input to the left-most flip-flop is the critical factor to guarantee a key stream z_i that is of maximum length before repeating its output sequence. Based on the configuration of Figure 4.3, the values (z_3, z_2, z_1, z_0) propagate through the D flip-flops from left to right and are shifted out to form the key stream z_i via output Q_0 of flip-flop K_0.

Example 4.1: What is the pattern generated for z_i given the *LFSR* of Figure 4.3 and the initial vector of $(z_3 = 1, z_2 = 0, z_1 = 0, z_0 = 1)$?

The *LFSR* of Figure 4.3 yields the following equations for the flip-flop inputs:

$$D_0 = Q_1$$
$$D_1 = Q_2$$
$$D_2 = Q_3$$
$$D_3 = Q_1 \oplus Q_0$$

Based on these equations and knowing the initial vector $(z_3, \; z_2, \; z_1, \; z_0)$ yields equations for each z_i beginning with z_4, remembering that $z_i \; = \; Q_0$:

$$z_4 \; = \; z_0 \oplus z_1$$

$$z_5 \; = \; z_1 \oplus z_2$$

$$z_6 \; = \; z_2 \oplus z_3$$

$$z_7 \; = \; z_3 \oplus z_4$$

$$\vdots$$

$$z_{i+4} \; = \; z_i \oplus z_{i+1}$$

Therefore, the pattern generated by the *LFSR* for z_i is:

$$z_4 \; = \; z_0 \oplus z_1 \; mod \; 2 \; = \; 1 \oplus 0 \; = \; 1$$

$$z_5 \; = \; z_1 \oplus z_2 \; mod \; 2 \; = \; 0 \oplus 0 \; = \; 0$$

$$z_6 \; = \; z_2 \oplus z_3 \; mod \; 2 \; = \; 0 \oplus 1 \; = \; 1$$

$$z_7 \; = \; z_3 \oplus z_4 \; mod \; 2 \; = \; 1 \oplus 1 \; = \; 0$$

$$z_8 \; = \; z_4 \oplus z_5 \; mod \; 2 \; = \; 1 \oplus 0 \; = \; 1$$

$$z_9 \; = \; z_5 \oplus z_6 \; mod \; 2 \; = \; 0 \oplus 1 \; = \; 1$$

$$z_{10} \; = \; z_6 \oplus z_7 \; mod \; 2 \; = \; 1 \oplus 0 \; = \; 1$$

$$z_{11} \; = \; z_7 \oplus z_8 \; mod \; 2 \; = \; 0 \oplus 1 \; = \; 1$$

$$z_{12} \; = \; z_8 \oplus z_9 \; mod \; 2 \; = \; 1 \oplus 1 \; = \; 0$$

$$z_{13} \; = \; z_9 \oplus z_{10} \; mod \; 2 \; = \; 1 \oplus 1 \; = \; 0$$

$$z_{14} \; = \; z_{10} \oplus z_{11} \; mod \; 2 \; = \; 1 \oplus 1 \; = \; 0$$

$$z_{15} \; = \; z_{11} \oplus z_{12} \; mod \; 2 \; = \; 1 \oplus 0 \; = \; 1$$

$$z_{16} \; = \; z_{12} \oplus z_{13} \; mod \; 2 \; = \; 0 \oplus 0 \; = \; 0$$

$$z_{17} = z_{13} \oplus z_{14} \bmod 2 = 0 \oplus 0 = 0$$

$$z_{18} = z_{14} \oplus z_{15} \bmod 2 = 0 \oplus 1 = 1$$

$$z_{19} = z_{15} \oplus z_{16} \bmod 2 = 1 \oplus 0 = 1$$

$$z_{20} = z_{16} \oplus z_{17} \bmod 2 = 0 \oplus 0 = 0$$

$$z_{21} = z_{17} \oplus z_{18} \bmod 2 = 0 \oplus 1 = 1$$

$$z_{22} = z_{18} \oplus z_{19} \bmod 2 = 1 \oplus 1 = 0$$

$$z_{23} = z_{19} \oplus z_{20} \bmod 2 = 1 \oplus 0 = 1$$

$$z_{24} = z_{20} \oplus z_{21} \bmod 2 = 0 \oplus 1 = 1$$

$$z_{25} = z_{21} \oplus z_{22} \bmod 2 = 1 \oplus 0 = 1$$

$$z_{26} = z_{22} \oplus z_{23} \bmod 2 = 0 \oplus 1 = 1$$

$$z_{27} = z_{23} \oplus z_{24} \bmod 2 = 1 \oplus 1 = 0$$

Therefore it is evident that for the key stream

$$z_i = 100110101111000100110101110 \ldots$$

the key stream begins repeating at z_{15}, and the length of the key stream before repeating is 15.

Figure 4.3 may be generalized to represent any *LFSR*, as shown in Figure 4.4. Note that each c_i represents a feedback coefficient controlling an on-off switch, where a zero represents an open switch (and thus no connection) and a one represents a closed switch (and thus a completed circuit). The switch itself is represented as a multiplier using the $\otimes$ symbol.

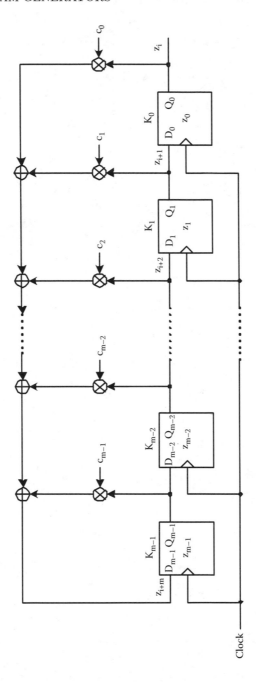

Figure 4.4: Generalized LFSR Implementation

Example 4.2: What are the values for m and the feedback coefficients c_i for the *LFSR* in Figure 4.3?

The *LFSR* of Figure 4.3 yields four flip-flops; therefore, $m = 4$. For this number of flip-flops, there must be four feedback coefficients, (c_3, c_2, c_1, c_0). The input to flip-flop K_3 is the XOR of the outputs of flip-flops K_1 and K_0. The outputs of flip-flops K_3 and K_2 are not used as feedback terms. As a result, the four feedback coefficients are $(c_3 = 0, c_2 = 0, c_1 = 1, c_0 = 1)$.

Based on the generalized *LFSR* representation detailed in Figure 4.4, the key stream z_i generated by such an *LFSR* is characterized by the following equations:

$$z_{i+m} = z_{i+m-1}c_{m-1} + \ldots + z_{i+1}c_1 + z_i c_0 \bmod 2$$

$$z_{i+m} = \sum_{j=0}^{m-1} z_{i+j}c_j \bmod 2; \; c_j \in \{0, 1\}; \; i = 0, 1, 2, 3, \ldots$$

The generalized *LFSR* key k may now be defined as:

$$k = (m, (z_{m-1}, z_{m-2}, \ldots z_2, z_1, z_0),$$

$$(c_{m-1}, c_{m-2}, \ldots c_2, c_1, c_0))$$

Example 4.3: What is the key k for the *LFSR* in Figure 4.3 using the initial vector of $(z_3 = 1, z_2 = 0, z_1 = 0, z_0 = 1)$?

The *LFSR* of Figure 4.3 has parameters $m = 4$ and ($c_3 = 0$, $c_2 = 0$, $c_1 = 1$, $c_0 = 1$). Therefore, the key $k = ((m = 4, (z_3 = 1, z_2 = 0, z_1 = 0, z_0 = 1), (c_3 = 0, c_2 = 0, c_1 = 1, c_0 = 1))$.

When examining *LFSR* sequences, it is important to note that for an *LFSR* of size m, there are a total of 2^m possible patterns and thus the *LFSR* sequence must repeat after 2^m clock cycles. Although 2^m is the theoretical maximum sequence length that may be generated by the *LFSR*, a pattern where the m flip-flops are all initialized to zero will always repeat itself and therefore cannot be included as part of a larger sequence. Therefore, the largest possible sequence that may be generated by an *LFSR* is of length $2^m - 1$. In general, only maximum length *LFSRs* are of interest in order to achieve the longest possible pseudo-random key stream for a given implementation. However, there is no guarantee that an *LFSR* will generate a maximum length sequence as in the case of **Example 4.1**. Moreover, an *LFSR* may generate different sequences depending on the initial vector, as demonstrated in **Examples 4.4** and **4.5**.

Example 4.4: What is the sequence generated by the *LFSR* defined by the key $k = ((m = 4, (z_3 = 1, z_2 = 0, z_1 = 0, z_0 = 1), (c_3 = 1, c_2 = 1, c_1 = 1, c_0 = 1))$?

The *LFSR* yields the following equations for the flip-flop inputs:

$$D_0 = Q_1$$
$$D_1 = Q_2$$
$$D_2 = Q_3$$
$$D_3 = Q_3 \oplus Q_2 \oplus Q_1 \oplus Q_0$$

Therefore, the pattern generated by the *LFSR* for z_i is:

$$z_4 = z_0 \oplus z_1 \oplus z_2 \oplus z_3 \bmod 2 = 1 \oplus 0 \oplus 0 \oplus 1 = 0$$
$$z_5 = z_1 \oplus z_2 \oplus z_3 \oplus z_4 \bmod 2 = 0 \oplus 0 \oplus 1 \oplus 0 = 1$$
$$z_6 = z_0 \oplus z_3 \oplus z_4 \oplus z_5 \bmod 2 = 0 \oplus 1 \oplus 0 \oplus 1 = 0$$
$$z_7 = z_0 \oplus z_4 \oplus z_5 \oplus z_6 \bmod 2 = 1 \oplus 0 \oplus 1 \oplus 0 = 0$$
$$z_8 = z_0 \oplus z_5 \oplus z_6 \oplus z_7 \bmod 2 = 0 \oplus 1 \oplus 0 \oplus 0 = 1$$
$$z_9 = z_0 \oplus z_6 \oplus z_7 \oplus z_8 \bmod 2 = 1 \oplus 0 \oplus 0 \oplus 1 = 0$$

Therefore, it is evident that the key stream $z_i = 1001010010 \ldots$, the key stream begins repeating at z_5, and the length of the key stream before repeating is 5.

Example 4.5: What is the sequence generated by the *LFSR* defined by the key $k = ((m = 4, (z_3 = 1, z_2 = 0, z_1 = 0, z_0 = 0), (c_3 = 1, c_2 = 1, c_1 = 1, c_0 = 1))$?

The *LFSR* yields the following equations for the flip-flop inputs:

$$D_0 = Q_1$$
$$D_1 = Q_2$$
$$D_2 = Q_3$$
$$D_3 = Q_3 \oplus Q_2 \oplus Q_1 \oplus Q_0$$

Therefore, the pattern generated by the *LFSR* for z_i is:

$$z_4 = z_0 \oplus z_1 \oplus z_2 \oplus z_3 \, mod \, 2 = 0 \oplus 0 \oplus 0 \oplus 1 = 1$$
$$z_5 = z_1 \oplus z_2 \oplus z_3 \oplus z_4 \, mod \, 2 = 0 \oplus 0 \oplus 1 \oplus 1 = 0$$
$$z_6 = z_0 \oplus z_3 \oplus z_4 \oplus z_5 \, mod \, 2 = 0 \oplus 1 \oplus 1 \oplus 0 = 0$$
$$z_7 = z_0 \oplus z_4 \oplus z_5 \oplus z_6 \, mod \, 2 = 1 \oplus 1 \oplus 0 \oplus 0 = 0$$
$$z_8 = z_0 \oplus z_5 \oplus z_6 \oplus z_7 \, mod \, 2 = 1 \oplus 0 \oplus 0 \oplus 0 = 1$$
$$z_9 = z_0 \oplus z_6 \oplus z_7 \oplus z_8 \, mod \, 2 = 0 \oplus 0 \oplus 0 \oplus 1 = 1$$

Therefore, it is evident that the key stream $z_i = 0001100011 \ldots$, the key stream begins repeating at z_5, and the length of the key stream before repeating is 5.

LFSRs are often specified as polynomials of the form:

$$P(x) = x^m + c_{m-1} \cdot x^{m-1} + \ldots + c_1 \cdot x + c_0$$

Example 4.6: What is the polynomial representation of the *LFSR* defined by the key $k = ((m = 4, (z_3 = 1, z_2 = 0, z_1 = 0, z_0 = 1), (c_3 = 1, c_2 = 1, c_1 = 1, c_0 = 1))$?

The *LFSR* yields the following polynomial:

$$P(x) = x^m + c_{m-1} \cdot x^{m-1} + \ldots + c_1 \cdot x + c_0$$

$$P(x) = x^4 + c_3 \cdot x^3 + c_2 \cdot x^2 + c_1 \cdot x + c_0$$
$$P(x) = x^4 + x^3 + x^2 + x + 1$$

Example 4.7: What is the polynomial representation of the *LFSR* defined by the key $k = ((m = 4, (z_3 = 1, z_2 = 0, z_1 = 0, z_0 = 0), (c_3 = 0, c_2 = 0, c_1 = 1, c_0 = 1))$?

The *LFSR* yields the following polynomial:

$$P(x) = x^m + c_{m-1} \cdot x^{m-1} + \ldots + c_1 \cdot x + c_0$$

$$P(x) = x^4 + c_3 \cdot x^3 + c_2 \cdot x^2 + c_1 \cdot x + c_0$$
$$P(x) = x^4 + x + 1$$

LFSRs may be classified as one of three types:

1. LFSRs with sequences of maximum length. These LFSRs are described by Primitive Polynomials.

2. LFSRs that do not generate sequences of maximum length but whose sequence lengths are independent of the initial values z_i. These LFSRs are described by Irreducible Polynomials that are not Primitive (all Primitive Polynomials are also Irreducible).

3. LFSRs that do not generate sequences of maximum length and whose sequence lengths depend on the initial values z_i. These LFSRs are described by Reducible Polynomials.

From a hardware implementation perspective, area-efficient LFSRs are easily realized. For an LFSR of degree m, a total of m D flip-flops and at most $m - 1$ XOR gates are required for an implementation. Once again using the unit-gate model approximation such that a 2-input XOR gate is counted as two gate equivalents [314], and assuming that the D flip-flops are implemented as SRAM using an estimate of four gates per SRAM bit [242], the total number of gates is calculated as at most $(m \cdot 4) + [(m - 1) \cdot 2] = 6m - 2$ gate equivalents. When examining the timing of a hardware implementation of an LFSR, performance will be heavily dependent on the number of non-zero feedback coefficients used in calculating the input to the left-most D flip-flop denoted as $K_{m - 1}$. Assuming the use of 2-input XOR gates and a binary tree implementation to sum the feedback terms, such an implementation would require $log_2(m)$ levels of logic to calculate the input to D flip-flop K_{m-1}.

Software implementations of *LFSRs* need to operate on the feedback coefficients at the bit level. Bit-level operations require that the data be unpacked and then repacked, all to compute the 1-bit result z_i. This sequential computation of z_i results in a significant performance degradation versus hardware implementations which effectively perform the computation of z_i in parallel. Moreover, storage of the data in registers, a practice normally used to improve performance versus storage of data in memory, negatively impacts performance for an *LFSR* implementation. This decrease in performance is caused by the difficulty in chaining registers in most processor instruction sets, a requirement for *LFSRs* with degree m that exceeds the width of the processor's registers. All of these factors lead to software implementations of *LFSRs* tending to exhibit considerably reduced performance versus hardware implementations.

4.3.2 Clock Controlled Shift Register Key Stream Generators

The goal of a clock controlled shift register key stream generator is to combine multiple smaller *LFSRs* to generate a significantly longer pseudo-random key stream z_i. Types of clock controlled shift register key stream generators include stop-and-go, alternating step, and shrinking [50]. Figure 4.5 shows the schematic for a stop-and-go generator. The output of *LFSR* 1 is gated with the system clock to control *LFSR* 2 and *LFSR* 3. If the output of *LFSR* 1 is a zero, then *LFSR* 3 is clocked; when the output of *LFSR* 1 is a one, then *LFSR* 2 is clocked. The outputs of *LFSR* 2 and *LFSR* 3 are combined via an XOR operation to form the final key stream z_i.

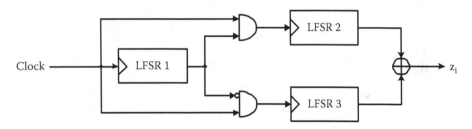

Figure 4.5: Clock Controlled Shift Register Implementation

The following design rules must be followed in order to guarantee the security of the stop-and-go generator:

1. Each of the three *LFSRs* must generate sequences of maximum length.

2. Each of the three *LFSRs* must have approximately the same sequence length of 2^{128}, i.e. $m \approx 128$ for each *LFSR*.

3. Each of the three *LFSRs* must have sequence lengths that are relatively prime to each other. In such cases, the sequence length of the stop-and-go generator is the product of the sequence lengths of the individual *LFSRs*.

4.3.3   Attacks Against LFSRs

The most straightforward attack against an *LFSR* is a *Known-Plaintext* attack in which the degree m of the *LFSR* is known and $2 \cdot m$ plaintext bits are known. *Oscar's* goal is to determine the feedback coefficients of the *LFSR*, c_i, so as to reconstruct the key stream. Once the key stream is known, *Oscar* can decrypt all ciphertext that passes over the open channel and, if he so chooses, modify and then re-encrypt the plaintext before sending out the new ciphertext over the open channel. The recipient of the modified ciphertext will believe that the resultant plaintext is valid even though it has been sent by *Oscar*. This demonstrates the catastrophic nature of a system's failure to provide message authentication when based solely on a stream cipher.

Oscar initiates the attack by reconstructing the first $2 \cdot m$ bits of the key stream by taking advantage of the nature of the XOR operation:

$$y_i = z_i \oplus x_i \bmod 2$$
$$z_i = y_i \oplus x_i \bmod 2$$

Once the first $2 \cdot m$ bits of the key stream are known, *Oscar* employs the generalized *LFSR* characterization equation $z_{i+m} = \sum_{j=0}^{m-1} z_{i+j} \cdot c_j \bmod 2$; $c_j \in \{0, 1\}$; $i = 0, 1, 2, 3, \ldots$, used to generate the key stream, to solve for each feedback coefficient c_i:

$$
\begin{aligned}
i = 0 &\quad \to z_m = z_{m-1}c_{m-1} + z_{m-2}c_{m-2} + \dots + z_1 c_1 + z_0 c_0 \bmod 2 \\
i = 1 &\quad \to z_{m+1} = z_m c_{m-1} + z_{m-1}c_{m-2} + \dots + z_2 c_1 + z_1 c_0 \bmod 2 \\
i = 2 &\quad \to z_{m+2} = z_{m+1}c_{m-1} + z_m c_{m-2} + \dots + z_3 c_1 + z_2 c_0 \bmod 2 \\
&\quad \vdots \\
i = m-1 &\quad \to z_{2m-1} = z_{2m-2}c_{m-1} + z_{2m-3}c_{m-2} + \dots + z_m c_1 + z_{m-1}c_0 \bmod 2
\end{aligned}
$$

This yields a total of m equations with m unknowns, the individual feedback coefficients c_i. Arranging the system of equations in matrix form yields:

$$
\begin{pmatrix}
z_0 & z_1 & \cdots & z_{m-1} \\
z_1 & z_2 & \cdots & z_m \\
\vdots & & & \vdots \\
z_{m-1} & z_m & \cdots & z_{2m-2}
\end{pmatrix}
\begin{pmatrix}
c_0 \\
c_1 \\
\vdots \\
c_{m-1}
\end{pmatrix}
=
\begin{pmatrix}
z_m \\
z_{m+1} \\
\vdots \\
z_{2m-1}
\end{pmatrix}
\bmod 2 \quad (4.1)
$$

Reorganizing the system of equations allows *Oscar* to directly solve for the individual feedback coefficients c_i:

$$
\begin{pmatrix}
c_0 \\
c_1 \\
\vdots \\
c_{m-1}
\end{pmatrix}
=
\begin{pmatrix}
z_0 & z_1 & \cdots & z_{m-1} \\
z_1 & z_2 & \cdots & z_m \\
\vdots & & & \vdots \\
z_{m-1} & z_m & \cdots & z_{2m-2}
\end{pmatrix}^{-1}
\begin{pmatrix}
z_m \\
z_{m+1} \\
\vdots \\
z_{2m-1}
\end{pmatrix}
\bmod 2
$$

$$(4.2)$$

As a result, once *Oscar* has observed $2 \cdot m$ output bits of the degree m *LFSR*, he can solve for the feedback coefficients c_i if he has the matching known plaintext. This attack is quite feasible — consider electronic mail messages and their associated headers. Such a header is easily observed by *Oscar* from a legitimate encrypted communication between himself and *Alice*. At this point, *Oscar* now has the known plaintext necessary to perform the attack on an *LFSR* of degree m, assuming that the electronic mail header has at least $2 \cdot m$ bits.

Stream ciphers are also extremely vulnerable to key reuse attacks, once again due to the nature of the XOR operation. Recall that the ciphertext is computed as $y_i = x_i \oplus z_i$. Therefore, if *Oscar* knows that the same key stream is used to encrypt two messages, M_1 and M_2, then *Oscar* can recover the combined messages by performing the XOR operation on the two ciphertexts y_{M_1} and y_{M_2}:

$$y_{M_1} = z_i \oplus x_{M_1} \bmod 2$$

$$y_{M_2} = z_i \oplus x_{M_2} \bmod 2$$

$$y_{M_1} \oplus y_{M_2} = z_i \oplus z_i \oplus x_{M_1} \oplus x_{M_2} \bmod 2$$

$$y_{M_1} \oplus y_{M_2} = x_{M_1} \oplus x_{M_2} \bmod 2$$

If either x_{M_1} or x_{M_2} is known, then the other message is easily recovered. As an example, assume x_{M_1} is known. x_{M_2} is recovered by performing the XOR operation of $x_{M_1} \oplus x_{M_2} \oplus x_{M_1} = x_{M_2}$. Even if neither message is known, $x_{M_1} \oplus x_{M_2}$ acts much like a substitution cipher because both x_{M_1} and x_{M_2} are language constructs. This fact may be exploited to extract the complete plaintexts by guessing likely plaintexts and performing the XOR operation on the guessed plaintext and $x_{M_1} \oplus x_{M_2}$. This method was used by Brigadier John Tiltman, a British cryptographer, to break the German Lorenz cipher during World War II after a German operator made the mistake of resending an encrypted message with the same key but with slight modifications to the text [91].

4.4 Real-World Applications

Stream ciphers tend to be smaller and faster than block ciphers and have been used in a number of practical applications. Two examples of commonly used stream ciphers are *RC4* and *A5*. The *RC4* cipher, developed by Ron Rivest of RSA Security, is arguably the most widely deployed stream cipher. *RC4* is used by the *Secure Sockets Layer* (SSL) and *Wireless Equivalent Privacy* (WEP) protocols to secure Internet traffic and wireless networks, respectively. *RC4* is fast and efficient in both hardware and software because it does not make use of *LFSRs*, relying instead on byte-wise manipulations. Much like *RC4*, the *A5* cipher, which is based on irregularly clocked *LFSRs*, is also used in mobile applications. *A5* provides speech encryption as part of the Global System for Mobile Communications (GSM) cellular telephone standard. It is interesting to note that both *RC4* and *A5* have been broken, yet both stream ciphers remain heavily deployed in existing applications. This is a testament to the concept of *Relative Security*, discussed in Section 4.2, where cryptosystems may appear to be secure but eventually fall victim to technology advancement and the development of more powerful attacks. *RC4* and *A5* are deployed in systems when the security provided by these ciphers has been deemed sufficient based on the importance of the data being transmitted and the likelihood of someone wanting to attack the system. Clearly such a determination must be made on a case-by-case basis, leading to the generalized conclusion that not all cryptosystems are suitable for every application.

4.5   Homework Problems

Homework Problem 4.5.1: What is the sequence generated by the $LFSR$ characterized by ($c_2 = 1$, $c_1 = 0$, $c_0 = 1$) starting with the initial vector ($z_2 = 1$, $z_1 = 0$, $z_0 = 0$)?

Homework Problem 4.5.2: What is the sequence generated by the $LFSR$ characterized by ($c_2 = 1$, $c_1 = 0$, $c_0 = 1$) starting with the initial vector ($z_2 = 0$, $z_1 = 1$, $z_0 = 1$)? How is the sequence related to the sequence generated in **Homework Problem 4.5.1**?

Homework Problem 4.5.3: Determine all sequences generated by the $LFSR$ characterized by the polynomial $P(x) = x^4 + x + 1$. Draw a schematic of the $LFSR$. Is the $LFSR$ described by a *Primitive*, *Irreducible*, or *Reducible Polynomial*?

Homework Problem 4.5.4: Determine all sequences generated by the $LFSR$ characterized by the polynomial $P(x) = x^4 + x^2 + 1$. Draw a schematic of the $LFSR$. Is the $LFSR$ described by a *Primitive*, *Irreducible*, or *Reducible Polynomial*?

Homework Problem 4.5.5: Determine all sequences generated by the $LFSR$ characterized by the polynomial $P(x) = x^4 + x^3 + x^2 + x + 1$. Draw a schematic of the $LFSR$. Is the $LFSR$ described by a *Primitive*, *Irreducible*, or *Reducible Polynomial*?

Homework Problem 4.5.6: A *Known-Plaintext* attack is to be conducted upon an $LFSR$-based stream cipher. The plaintext that was encrypted was:

$$P = 1001\ 0010\ 0110\ 1101\ 1001\ 0010\ 0110$$

By tapping the open channel, the observed ciphertext is:

$$C = 1011\ 1100\ 0011\ 0001\ 0010\ 1011\ 0001$$

What is the degree m of the *LFSR* used to generate the key stream? What is the initial vector of the *LFSR*? Determine the feedback coefficients of the *LFSR*. Draw a schematic for the *LFSR* and verify the output sequence z_i.

Homework Problem 4.5.7: In order to process English letters, each of the twenty-six upper-case letters and the numbers 0, 1, 2, 3, 4, and 5 are represented by a 5-bit vector of the form:

$$A \Leftrightarrow 0 = 00000_2$$
$$B \Leftrightarrow 1 = 00001_2$$
$$\vdots$$
$$Z \Leftrightarrow 25 = 11001_2$$
$$0 \Leftrightarrow 26 = 11010_2$$
$$1 \Leftrightarrow 27 = 11011_2$$
$$\vdots$$
$$5 \Leftrightarrow 31 = 11111_2$$

The degree of the *LFSR* is $m = 6$ and every message is known to start with the header *UML*. The ciphertext *L2DLKZCOJ* is then observed on the open channel. What is the initial vector of the

LFSR? What are the feedback coefficients of the *LFSR?* Write a program in C which generates the entire sequence of the *LFSR* and determines the entire plaintext. Note that the inverse of:

$$
\begin{pmatrix}
1 & 1 & 1 & 1 & 1 & 1 \\
1 & 1 & 1 & 1 & 1 & 0 \\
1 & 1 & 1 & 1 & 0 & 0 \\
1 & 1 & 1 & 0 & 0 & 0 \\
1 & 1 & 0 & 0 & 0 & 0 \\
1 & 0 & 0 & 0 & 0 & 0
\end{pmatrix}
\tag{4.3}
$$

is:

$$
\begin{pmatrix}
0 & 0 & 0 & 0 & 0 & 1 \\
0 & 0 & 0 & 0 & 1 & 1 \\
0 & 0 & 0 & 1 & 1 & 0 \\
0 & 0 & 1 & 1 & 0 & 0 \\
0 & 1 & 1 & 0 & 0 & 0 \\
1 & 1 & 0 & 0 & 0 & 0
\end{pmatrix}
\tag{4.4}
$$

Homework Problem 4.5.8: The goal is to encrypt a network link which is part of an Asynchronous Transfer Mode (ATM) network. Data on the link is transmitted at full ATM speed, i.e. 155 Mbps. Note that 1 *Mbit* $= 2^{20}$ *bits*. An *LFSR*-based stream cipher is chosen as the encryption methodology. What is the minimum degree of the stream cipher in order to ensure that there is no repetition in the key stream within a full day, i.e. twenty-four hours?

Homework Problem 4.5.9: *One-Time Pads* can easily be generalized to work in alphabets other than binary. For manual encryption, an especially useful *One-Time Pad* is one that operates on letters. Develop a *One-Time Pad* system that operates with the letters A, B, ... Z represented by the numbers 0, 1, ... 25. What does the key stream look like? What are the encryption and decryption functions?

Homework Problem 4.5.10: Using the encryption and decryption functions developed in **Homework Problem 4.5.9**, decrypt the ciphertext *UANIXC KOLHAAC*, which was encrypted using the *One-Time Pad RSIDPY DKAWOAP*.

Homework Problem 4.5.11: Assume a *One-Time Pad* in which a short key of 1,000 bits in length is used repeatedly. With what attacks can the cipher be immediately broken?

Homework Problem 4.5.12: Assume a *One-Time Pad* key is stored on a CD with 1 Gbyte storage capacity. Discuss the real-world implications of such a system. Address life cycle of the key, storage of the key both during and after the life cycle, key distribution, generation of the key, etc.

Homework Problem 4.5.13: Describe why an *Exhaustive Key Search* attack against a *One-Time Pad* is not feasible.

Homework Problem 4.5.14: Consider the alternating stop-and-go generator detailed in Figure 4.5. The three *LFSRs* are specified by the polynomials and initial vectors:

LFSR	*Polynomial*	*Initial Vector*
1	$x^2 + x + 1$	$z_0 = 1,\ z_1 = 0$
2	$x^3 + x + 1$	$z_0 = 1,\ z_1 = 0,\ z_2 = 0$
3	$x^5 + x^2 + 1$	$z_0 = 1,\ z_1 = 0,\ z_2 = 0,\ z_3 = 0,\ z_4 = 0$

Draw the schematic for the stream cipher. Compute the first eight output bits.

Homework Problem 4.5.15: It generally holds true for stream ciphers built from *LFSRs* that the sequence length is the product of the sequenced lengths of the individual *LFSRs* if the individual lengths are all relatively prime. Is this condition fulfilled for the stream cipher generated in **Homework Problem 4.5.14**? What is the length of the generated sequence?

Homework Problem 4.5.16: An *LFSR* is characterized by the polynomial $x^4 + x^3 + 1$ and the initial vector $(z_0 = 1, 0, 0, 0)$.

a) What are the feedback coefficients c_0, c_1, c_2, and c_3?

b) Draw the block diagram of the *LFSR*.

c) Is this a maximum-length *LFSR*?

d) Encrypt the binary message $1001\ 1100\ 1100_2$.

e) What is the maximum message length that should be encrypted using this stream cipher?

Homework Problem 4.5.17: An *LFSR* of degree m is described as $z_{i+m} = \sum_{j=0}^{m-1} c_j z_{i+j} \bmod 2$; $i = 0, 1, 2, \ldots$ where z_k are the outputs and c_j are the m binary feedback coefficients. Breaking an *LFSR* requires determining the m unknown coefficients c_j, $j =$ 0, 1, ... , $m - 1$, by observing the output bits z_k. Assume that m is known. Derive the matrix equation for breaking the *LFSR* of degree m with $2m$ known outputs z_k.

Homework Problem 4.5.18: Consider the *LFSR* stop-and-go generator. The first *LFSR* is of degree $m_1 = 2$ and the feedback coefficients are given by $x^2 + x + 1$. The second *LFSR* is of degree $m_2 = 3$ and the feedback coefficients are given by $x^3 + x + 1$.

   a) Choose the third *LFSR* from:

   1. $m_3 = 4$, $x^4 + x + 1$

   2. $m_3 = 7$, $x^7 + x + 1$

   3. $m_3 = 9$, $x^9 + x + 1$

where each of the *LFSRs* has maximum period. Which *LFSR* results in the longest sequence length for the stop-and-go generator?

   b) Assume the initial vector for the first *LFSR* is $(z_0 = 1, 0)$ and the initial vector for the second *LFSR* is $(z_0 = 1, 0, 0)$. Use your answer from part (a) with an initial vector of $(z_0 = 1, 0, \ldots, 0)$ for the third *LFSR*. Draw the circuit diagram and compute the first five bits of the key stream.

Homework Problem 4.5.19: Consider the *LFSR* characterized by the polynomial $x^3 + x + 1$ and the initial vector $(z_0 = 1, z_1 = 1, z_2 = 0)$. What are the feedback coefficients for the *LFSR*? Is this a maximum length *LFSR*?

Homework Problem 4.5.20: Consider the *LFSR* characterized by the polynomial $x^4 + x^2 + x + 1$ and the initial vector $(z_0 = 1, 0, 1, 0)$. What are the feedback coefficients for the *LFSR*? Is this a maximum length *LFSR*?

Homework Problem 4.5.21: Consider the *LFSR* characterized by the polynomial $x^{128} + x + 1$ and an initial vector of all ones. Write a VHDL architecture to implement the *LFSR* assuming that the user will provide a *start* signal to indicate when the *LFSR* should begin generating the output key stream. Use the following entity declaration for your implementation:

```
LIBRARY ieee;
USE ieee.std_logic_1164.ALL;
USE ieee.std_logic_arith.ALL;
USE ieee.std_logic_unsigned.ALL;
ENTITY lfsr IS
   PORT ( clk, rst, start : IN  std_logic;
             z_i                : OUT std_logic);
END lfsr;
BEGIN
ARCHITECTURE behav OF lfsr IS
-- Your code goes here
END behav;
```

Specify the target technology used to implement the design and the maximum operating frequency as specified by your place-and-route tools. What is the bit length of the output key stream before the cycle repeats? How much time is required to encrypt an input of 2^{20} bits based on your maximum operating frequency, assuming a new bit is combined with the output key stream via the XOR operation every clock cycle?

Homework Problem 4.5.22: Assume a software implementation of the *LFSR* specified in **Homework Problem 4.5.21**. If the software implementation is able to generate the next sixteen bits of the output key stream z_i every ten clock cycles and the system operates at 4 GHz with a 16-bit processor word size, how much time is required to encrypt an input of 2^{20} bits assuming that the combination of the output key stream via the XOR operation requires one additional clock cycle? Compare your results with the time calculated to perform the same task in hardware in **Homework Problem 4.5.21**.

Chapter 5

Symmetric-Key Cryptography: Block Ciphers

In 1949, Claude Shannon defined two properties necessary for secure cryptosystem design [283]:

1. *Confusion* of the relationship between the plaintext, the ciphertext, and the key.

2. *Diffusion* of the influence of one plaintext or key symbol over as many ciphertext symbols as possible.

Confusion may be achieved via substitution or look-up tables, such as in a shift or affine cipher. *Diffusion* may be achieved via permutation or expansion of the plaintext or key bits [275]. As a rule, a change in one plaintext bit should result in half of the output bits changing on average, and this behavior is known as the *avalanche effect*. The goal is to reduce the correlation between bits and thus make *Oscar's* attempts to break the system more difficult. Combining *Confusion* and *Diffusion* in an iterative manner is standard practice for realizing a secure cryptosystem.

5.1   The Data Encryption Standard

The Data Encryption Standard (DES) was first published in 1975 and was accepted as a Federal Information Processing Standard (FIPS) by the National Bureau of Standards (NBS), now known as the National Institute of Standards and Technology (NIST), in 1977 [229]. *DES* was developed by an IBM research team in response to an NBS solicitation for proposals for an encryption standard to be used to target government information that was not classified but still considered sensitive. The standard was renewed multiple times (in 1983, 1988, and 1993) but finally was allowed to expire in 1998 because the algorithm was no longer considered to be secure based on the computing power available at the time.

5.1.1   Feistel Networks

Many block ciphers may be characterized as Feistel networks. Feistel networks were invented by Horst Feistel [94] and are a general method of transforming a function into a permutation. The basic Feistel network divides the data block into two halves with one half operating on the other half [277]. The function, termed the f-function, uses one of the halves of the data block and a key to create a pseudo-random bit stream that is used to encrypt or decrypt the other half of the data block. Therefore, to encrypt or decrypt both halves requires two iterations of the Feistel network [82].

A generalization of the basic Feistel network allows for the support of larger data blocks. Generalization occurs by considering the swap of the halves of the data block as a circular right shift. This allows for the use of the same f-function but requires multiple rounds to input all of the sub-blocks to the f-function [3]. Figure 5.1 details the block diagram for block ciphers employing both the basic Feistel network and generalized Feistel networks of both three and four blocks. The f-function is represented by the shaded box and the $\oplus$ symbol represents a bit-wise XOR operation.

The basic operations that may be found within an f-function include [82]:

- Bitwise XOR, AND, or OR.

- Modular addition or subtraction.

- Shift or rotation by a constant number of bits.

- Data-dependent rotation by a variable number of bits.

- Modular multiplication.

- Multiplication in a *Galois Field*.

- Modular inversion.

- Look-up-table substitution.

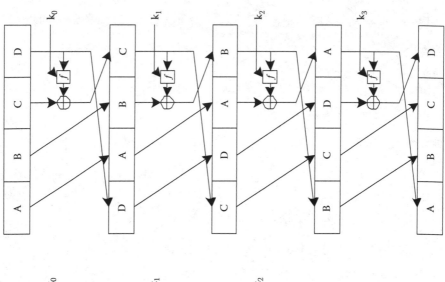

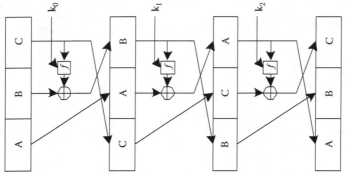

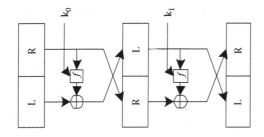

Figure 5.1: Block Diagram for Standard Block Ciphers

5.1.2 Cryptosystem

DES is by far the most popular symmetric-key algorithm in terms of fielded implementations. *DES* operates on a 64-bit block with a 56-bit key using a Feistel network structure with a total of sixteen iterations, also known as *rounds*. Figure 5.2 provides an overview of the *DES* algorithm for encryption and Figure 5.3 details the *DES* round function [229, 275]. As detailed in Section 5.1.1, two iterations are required to encrypt or decrypt the entire 64-bit block. Because *DES* iterates sixteen times, the 64-bit block is encrypted a total of eight times.

As detailed in Figures 5.2 and 5.3, the 64-bit block is divided into *Left* and *Right* halves, denoted as L_i and R_i, where i indicates the round number. The right half of the 64-bit block is operated on by the round key (generated from the 56-bit master key) and then passed through the *f-function* to generate a pseudo-random bit stream. This pseudo-random bit stream is then combined with the left half of the 64-bit block via an XOR operation to generate the next round's right half block. The previous round's right half block will be encrypted in the next round and is therefore mapped directly to the next round's left half block.

The *Initial Permutation* (IP) and *Final Permutation* (FP) are used to rearrange the input and output bits. Note that $FP(IP(x))$ $= x$ such that $FP(x) = IP^{-1}(x)$. Table 5.1 details the mapping of the *Initial Permutation*. Note that the table is read row-wise from left to right. As a result, *IP* input bit 58 is mapped to

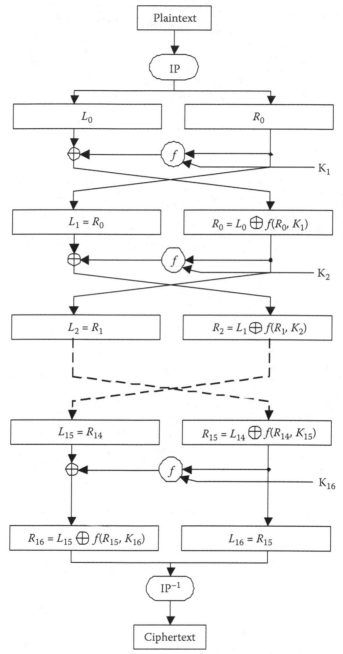

Figure 5.2: DES Encryption Block Diagram

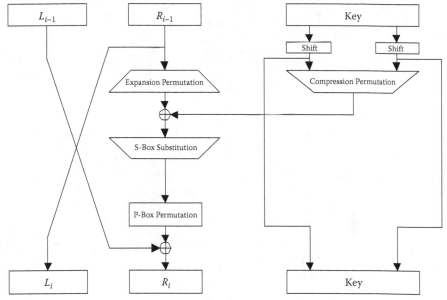

Figure 5.3: DES Round Function

IP output bit 1, IP input bit 50 is mapped to IP output bit 2, etc. The *Final Permutation* is a reverse mapping of the *Initial Permutation* and is detailed in Table 5.2.

IP

58	50	42	34	26	18	10	2
60	52	44	36	28	20	12	4
62	54	46	38	30	22	14	6
64	56	48	40	32	24	16	8
57	49	41	33	25	17	9	1
59	51	43	35	27	19	11	3
61	53	45	37	29	21	13	5
63	55	47	39	31	23	15	7

Table 5.1: DES Initial Permutation (IP)

The *Initial Permutation* and *Final Permutation* have little impact on the security of *DES*. The purpose of the permutations was to ease the I/O transfer of blocks of data between preexisting hardware and newly created *DES* implementations, effectively

FP

40	8	48	16	56	24	64	32
39	7	47	15	55	23	63	31
38	6	46	14	54	22	62	30
37	5	45	13	53	21	61	29
36	4	44	12	52	20	60	28
35	3	43	11	51	19	59	27
34	2	42	10	50	18	58	26
33	1	41	9	49	17	57	25

Table 5.2: DES Final Permutation (FP)

rewiring the incoming bits to meet the needs of the *DES* algorithm while rewiring the outgoing bits to match the bus format of the preexisting hardware interfaces.

The *DES f-function* is shown in Figure 5.4.

The *f-function* begins by expanding the 32-bit datapath to a 48-bit datapath via the *E* expansion in which sixteen bits are cross-wired twice. Table 5.3 details the expansion mapping. Note that the table is read row-wise from left to right. As a result, *E* input bit 32 is mapped to *E* output bits 1 and 47, *E* input bit 1 is mapped to *E* output bits 2 and 48, etc. The expansion process is an example of Shannon's *Diffusion* property.

The expanded datapath is combined with the round key K_i via the XOR operation before being broken up into 6-bit groupings. These groupings are then used as inputs to the *DES S-Boxes*, denoted as S_1 through S_8. The mappings for the *S-Boxes* are shown in Tables 5.4–5.11. The *S-Boxes* are a non-linear mapping such that $S_i(X) \oplus S_i(Y) \neq S_i(X \oplus Y)$ and they are also an

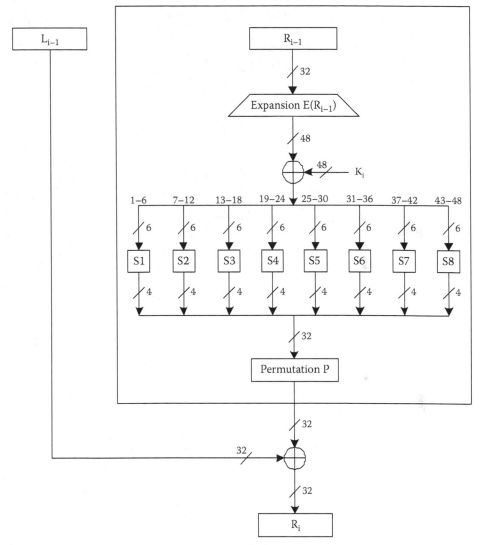

Figure 5.4: DES f-Function

example of Shannon's *Confusion* property. Each *S-Box* outputs a 4-bit vector and is addressed in a row-column manner based on the 6-bit input vector. The input vector is represented as $b_6b_5b_4b_3b_2b_1$; the row address is b_6b_1 whereas the column address is $b_5b_4b_3b_2$. Note that the row addresses range from zero to three and the

E

32	1	2	3	4	5
4	5	6	7	8	9
8	9	10	11	12	13
12	13	14	15	16	17
16	17	18	19	20	21
20	21	22	23	24	25
24	25	26	27	28	29
28	29	30	31	32	1

Table 5.3: DES Expansion (E)

column addresses range from zero to fifteen. Also note that row addresses increment from the top to the bottom of the grid whereas column addresses increment from the left to the right of the grid.

S_1

14	4	13	1	2	15	11	8	3	10	6	12	5	9	0	7
0	15	7	4	14	2	13	1	10	6	12	11	9	5	3	8
4	1	14	8	13	6	2	11	15	12	9	7	3	10	5	0
15	12	8	2	4	9	1	7	5	11	3	14	10	0	6	13

Table 5.4: DES S-Box S_1

S_2

15	1	8	14	6	11	3	4	9	7	2	13	12	0	5	10
3	13	4	7	15	2	8	14	12	0	1	10	6	9	11	5
0	14	7	11	10	4	13	1	5	8	12	6	9	3	2	15
13	8	10	1	3	15	4	2	11	6	7	12	0	5	14	9

Table 5.5: DES S-Box S_2

S_3

10	0	9	14	6	3	15	5	1	13	12	7	11	4	2	8
13	7	0	9	3	4	6	10	2	8	5	14	12	11	15	1
13	6	4	9	8	15	3	0	11	1	2	12	5	10	14	7
1	10	13	0	6	9	8	7	4	15	14	3	11	5	2	12

Table 5.6: DES S-Box S_3

S_4

7	13	14	3	0	6	9	10	1	2	8	5	11	12	4	15
13	8	11	5	6	15	0	3	4	7	2	12	1	10	14	9
10	6	9	0	12	11	7	13	15	1	3	14	5	2	8	4
3	15	0	6	10	1	13	8	9	4	5	11	12	7	2	14

Table 5.7: DES S-Box S_4

S_5

2	12	4	1	7	10	11	6	8	5	3	15	13	0	14	9
14	11	2	12	4	7	13	1	5	0	15	10	3	9	8	6
4	2	1	11	10	13	7	8	15	9	12	5	6	3	0	14
11	8	12	7	1	14	2	13	6	15	0	9	10	4	5	3

Table 5.8: DES S-Box S_5

S_6

12	1	10	15	9	2	6	8	0	13	3	4	14	7	5	11
10	15	4	2	7	12	9	5	6	1	13	14	0	11	3	8
9	14	15	5	2	8	12	3	7	0	4	10	1	13	11	6
4	3	2	12	9	5	15	10	11	14	1	7	6	0	8	13

Table 5.9: DES S-Box S_6

S_7

4	11	2	14	15	0	8	13	3	12	9	7	5	10	6	1
13	0	11	7	4	9	1	10	14	3	5	12	2	15	8	6
1	4	11	13	12	3	7	14	10	15	6	8	0	5	9	2
6	11	13	8	1	4	10	7	9	5	0	15	14	2	3	12

Table 5.10: DES S-Box S_7

S_8

13	2	8	4	6	15	11	1	10	9	3	14	5	0	12	7
1	15	13	8	10	3	7	4	12	5	6	11	0	14	9	2
7	11	4	1	9	12	14	2	0	6	10	13	15	3	5	8
2	1	14	7	4	10	8	13	15	12	9	0	3	5	6	11

Table 5.11: DES S-Box S_8

Example 5.1: *S-Box* S_2 receives the 6-bit input 101011_2. What is the output of the *S-Box*?

The 6-bit input $b_6b_5b_4b_3b_2b_1 = 101011_2$ results in a row address of $b_6b_1 = 11_2 = 3$ and a column address of $b_5b_4b_3b_2 = 0101_2 = 5$. Examining Table 5.5 at the position denoted by row three and column five yields 4 as the output value for S_2.

The 4-bit output vectors from the *S-Boxes* are recombined to form a 32-bit vector which is then passed through the P permutation. The P permutation mapping is shown in Table 5.12. Note that the table is read row-wise from left to right. As a result, P input bit 16 is mapped to P output bit 1, P input bit 7 is mapped to P output bit 2, etc. The output of the P permutation is also the output of the *f-function* and this output is then combined with L_{i-1} via the XOR operation to form R_i.

P

16	7	20	21
29	12	28	17
1	15	23	26
5	18	31	10
2	8	24	14
32	27	3	9
19	13	30	6
22	11	4	25

Table 5.12: DES Permutation (P)

The *DES* encryption *Key Schedule* is shown in Figure 5.5.

The 56-bit key is broken into eight 7-bit groupings and a parity bit is generated for each grouping, resulting in a 64-bit master key.

The master key is first passed through a *Permuted Choice*, denoted as *PC-1*, to strip off the parity bits, leaving only the 56-bit key. The *PC-1* mapping is shown in Table 5.13. Note that the table is read row-wise from left to right. As a result, *PC-1* input bit 57 is mapped to *PC-1* output bit 1, *PC-1* input bit 49 is mapped to *PC-1* output bit 2, etc.

PC-1

57	49	41	33	25	17	9
1	58	50	42	34	26	18
10	2	59	51	43	35	27
19	11	3	60	52	44	36
63	55	47	39	31	23	15
7	62	54	46	38	30	22
14	6	61	53	45	37	29
21	13	5	28	20	12	4

Table 5.13: DES Permuted Choice (PC-1)

The 56-bit key is divided in half, denoted as C_0 and D_0. To generate the round keys K_i, each C_i and D_i are passed through *Cyclic Left Shift* units denoted as *LSi*. The *Cyclic Left Shift* units will shift by one position for $i = 1, 2, 9, 16$. For all other values of i, the *Cyclic Left Shift* units will shift by two positions. The outputs C_i and D_i are then passed through a *Permuted Choice*, denoted as *PC-2*, to generate the round key K_i. The *PC-2* mapping is shown in Table 5.14. Note that the table is read row-wise from left to right. As a result, *PC-2* input bit 14 is mapped to *PC-2* output bit 1, *PC-2* input bit 17 is mapped to *PC-2* output bit 2, etc.

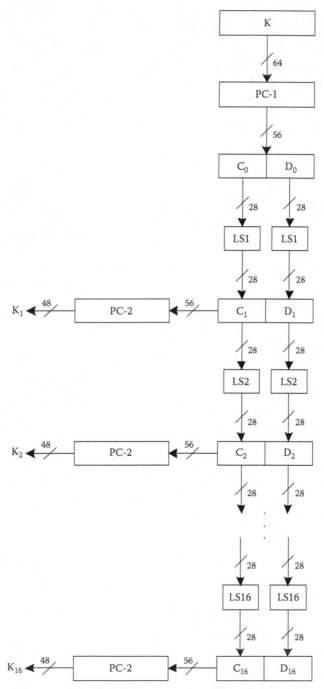

Figure 5.5: DES Encryption Key Schedule

PC-2

14	17	11	24	1	5
3	28	15	6	21	10
23	19	12	4	26	8
16	7	27	20	13	2
41	52	31	37	47	55
30	40	51	45	33	48
44	49	39	56	34	53
46	42	50	36	29	32

Table 5.14: DES Permuted Choice (PC-2)

Note that the total number of shifted positions is calculated as $(4 \cdot 1) + (8 \cdot 2) = 28$, resulting in $C_0 = C_{16}$ and $D_0 = D_{16}$, and thus K_{16} is the same as the 56-bit key derived from the 64-bit master key. This characteristic will be exploited when performing *Key Scheduling* for the decryption process.

DES decryption is essentially the same operation as encryption with a reversed *Key Schedule*. The input to *DES* decryption is the 64-bit ciphertext L_0^d, R_0^d. However, $L_0^d = R_{16}^e$ and $R_0^d = L_{16}^e = R_{15}^e = L_1^d$, where the d superscript is used to denote decryption and the e superscript is used to denote encryption. These equations hold true because the *Final Permutation* at the end of the encryption process is canceled by the *Initial Permutation* at the beginning of the decryption process.

Each round of the decryption process unravels a round of the encryption process. Having solved directly for $L_1^d = L_{16}^e = R_{15}^e$, the value of R_1^d must be determined. If encryption and decryption are implemented in the same manner with the only difference being a reversed *Key Schedule*, then R_1^d may be solved for using the knowledge that:

$$R_1^d = L_0^d \oplus f(R_0^d, \ K_{16})$$

Substituting decryption values for values from the encryption process yields:

$$R_1^d = R_{16}^e \oplus f(L_{16}^e, \ K_{16})$$

This is significant because it is known that:

$$R_{16}^e = L_{15}^e \oplus f(R_{15}^e, \ K_{16})$$

Substituting for R_{16}^e results in:

$$R_1^d = L_{15}^e \oplus f(R_{15}^e, \ K_{16}) \oplus f(L_{16}^e, \ K_{16})$$

However, it is also known that $L_{16}^e = R_{15}^e$. Therefore, this equation may be rewritten as:

$$R_1^d = L_{15}^e \oplus f(R_{15}^e, \ K_{16}) \oplus f(R_{15}^e, \ K_{16})$$

Since $f(R_{15}^e, \ K_{16}) \oplus f(R_{15}^e, \ K_{16}) = 0$ and $L_{15}^e \oplus 0 = L_{15}^e$ due to the nature of the XOR operation, it follows that $R_1^d = L_{15}^e$. This process continues for sixteen rounds such that decryption unravels encryption and the *Final Permutation* at the end of the decryption process cancels the *Initial Permutation* at the beginning of the encryption process. As a result, the completion of the decryption process yields the original plaintext.

Generating a reversed *Key Schedule* for decryption is easily achieved by taking advantage of $C_0 = C_{16}$ and $D_0 = D_{16}$, thus K_{16} is the same as the 56-bit key derived from the 64-bit master key. We therefore implement the decryption *Key Schedule* such that it unravels the shifting of the encryption *Key Schedule*, replacing the *Cyclic Left Shift* units denoted as *LSi* with *Cyclic*

Right Shift units denoted as *RSi*. A *Cyclic Right Shift* unit *RSi* will shift by the same amount as *LSi* but in the opposite direction. The *DES* decryption *Key Schedule* is shown in Figure 5.6.

5.1.3 Modes of Operation

5.1.3.1 Electronic Code Book Mode

In *Electronic Code Book* (ECB) mode, a block cipher is treated as a *code book* or look-up table. In the case of *DES*, which has 56-bit keys, there are a total of 2^{56} possible code books. As long as the key k does not change, the same code book is used to map the plaintext block x to the ciphertext block y. Figure 5.7 shows an *ECB* mode implementation of *DES*.

Because there are no interdependencies between blocks, a block cipher operating in *ECB* mode maps nicely to a pipelined hardware implementation, as will be discussed in Section 5.1.5. However, this feature also leaves block ciphers operating in *ECB* mode susceptible to a *Substitution* attack. Consider a bank transaction where the incoming data stream is composed of the blocks shown in Figure 5.8.

Oscar is capable of viewing the encrypted data stream being sent over the open channel from the sending bank to the receiving bank. *Oscar* can perform a *Substitution* attack as follows:

1. Open an account at the sending bank and deposit a small amount of money.

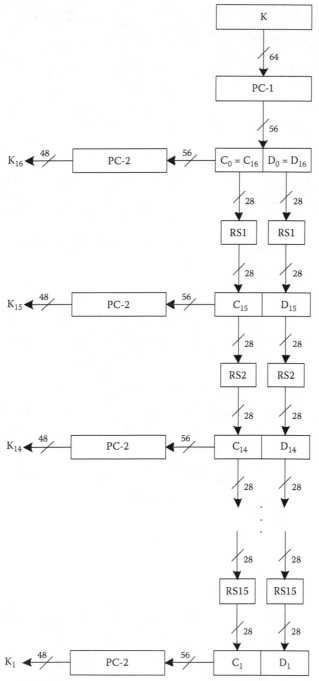

Figure 5.6: DES Decryption Key Schedule

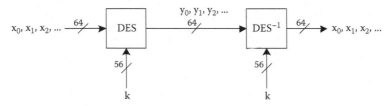

Figure 5.7: Block Cipher Operation in Electronic Code Book Mode

2. Open an account at the receiving bank and then repeatedly transfer $1 from the sending bank to the receiving bank.

3. Knowing the block format of the data stream for the bank transaction (from Figure 5.7) and assuming that the key k does not change, identify and extract the block that contains the encrypted value for the account number to receive the $1 transfer, i.e. *Oscar's* Block 4.

4. Intercept all future transfers from the sending bank to the receiving bank and remove the legitimate Block 4 and replace it with *Oscar's* Block 4.

This attack succeeds regardless of the strength of the encryption algorithm because *Oscar* has defeated the system that uses the algorithm as opposed to the algorithm itself.

5.1.3.2 Cipher Block Chaining Mode

In *Cipher Block Chaining* (CBC) mode, each block is chained to the next block by combining the last encrypted ciphertext block y_{i-1} with the current plaintext block x_i using the XOR operation. The combined result is then encrypted to generate the next

Figure 5.8: Bank Transaction Data Stream

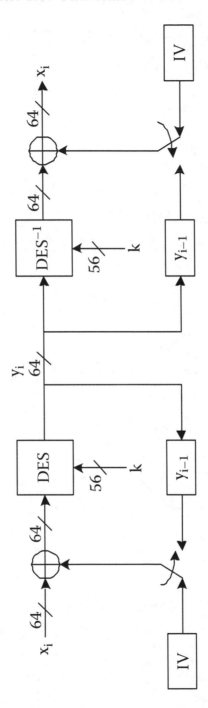

Figure 5.9: Block Cipher Operation in Cipher Block Chaining Mode

ciphertext block y_i, as shown in Figure 5.9 using DES as the block cipher.

A complication arises in the case of the first plaintext block to be encrypted, i.e. x_0, because there is no previous ciphertext block for use in the XOR combining operation. As a result, an *Initialization Vector*, IV, is combined with x_0 to generate the input to the block cipher used to produce the first ciphertext block y_0. All future encryptions use the combination of x_i and y_{i-1}. Therefore, encryption may be defined as:

$$y_0 = DES_k(x_0 \oplus IV)$$
$$y_i = DES_k(x_i \oplus y_{i-1})$$

Similarly, decryption may be defined as:

$$x_0 = IV \oplus DES_k^{-1}(y_0)$$
$$x_i = y_{i-1} \oplus DES_k^{-1}(y_i)$$

Decryption is validated by solving for x_i:

$$x_i = y_{i-1} \oplus DES_k^{-1}(y_i)$$
$$x_i = y_{i-1} \oplus DES_k^{-1}(DES_k(x_i \oplus y_{i-1}))$$
$$x_i = y_{i-1} \oplus x_i \oplus y_{i-1}$$

By making use of the XOR properties $y_{i-1} \oplus y_{i-1} = 0$ and $x_i \oplus 0 = x_i$ it is clear that decryption operates correctly.

Note that IV may be sent over the open channel as plaintext prior to transmission of encrypted data. Knowledge of the IV has no impact on *Oscar's* ability to attack the block cipher, as will be shown in **Homework Problem 5.1.8.12**.

From a performance perspective, block ciphers operating in *CBC* mode do not map nicely to pipelined hardware implementations. Because of the chaining of blocks, processing of plaintext block x_i cannot begin until ciphertext block y_{i-1} has been generated. Using a pipelined hardware implementation would require stalling the pipeline until generation of the ciphertext block y_{i-1} was complete, eliminating the performance gain associated with simultaneously processing multiple data objects. Solutions to this problem will be discussed in Section 5.1.5.

5.1.3.3   Propagating Cipher Block Chaining Mode

The *Propagating Cipher Block Chaining* (PCBC) mode has not been formally standardized and is not a commonly used operating mode though it has been used in protocols such as *Kerberos 4*. *PCBC* mode is a modified version of *CBC* mode designed to propagate errors in multiple output blocks of the ciphertext, as will be illustrated in **Homework Problem 5.1.8.13**. *PCBC* mode is shown in Figure 5.10 using *DES* as the block cipher.

PCBC mode encryption may be defined as:

$$y_0 = DES_k(x_0 \oplus IV)$$
$$y_i = DES_k(x_i \oplus x_{i-1} \oplus y_{i-1})$$

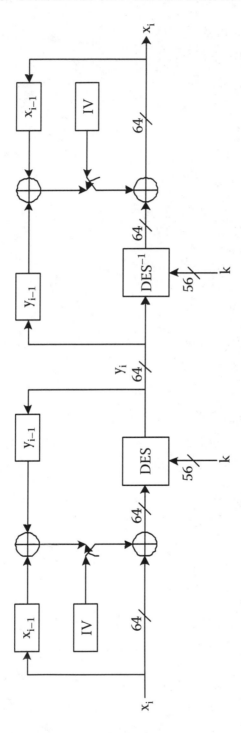

Figure 5.10: Block Cipher Operation in Propagating Cipher Block Chaining Mode

Similarly, decryption may be defined as:

$$x_0 \;=\; IV \;\oplus\; DES_k^{-1}(y_0)$$

$$x_i \;=\; x_{i-1} \;\oplus\; y_{i-1} \;\oplus\; DES_k^{-1}(y_i)$$

5.1.3.4 Cipher Feedback Mode

Cipher Feedback (CFB) mode differs from *ECB* and *CBC* mode in that the block cipher is used as a pseudo-random number generator as opposed to performing encryption and decryption. In such a configuration, the block cipher generates a key stream z_i used to encrypt the plaintext x_i via the XOR operation, resulting in a stream cipher as shown in Figure 5.11.

CFB mode begins by loading the shift register with an *Initialization Vector*, IV. The IV is B bits in length, where B is the block size of the block cipher and a multiple of L, the plaintext block size. The IV is then encrypted by the block cipher, resulting in a B-bit output. The block cipher output is then passed through a selector which selects the L left-most bits of the block cipher output and uses those bits to encrypt the plaintext x_0 via the XOR operation, generating the ciphertext y_0. The shift register is then shifted L positions to the left and the right-most L bits of the shift register are loaded with y_0. The process is repeated such that the block cipher generates a new output based on the new shift register value, updating the pseudo-random bit stream of length L used

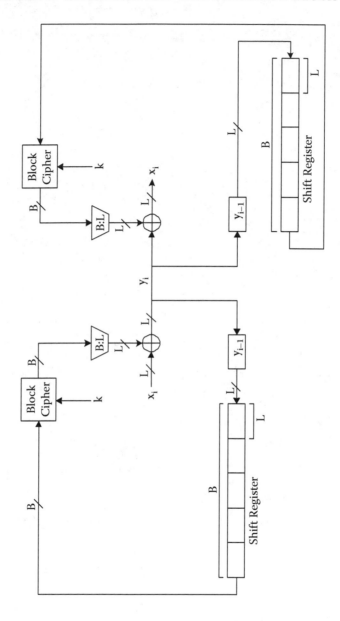

Figure 5.11: Block Cipher Operation in Cipher Feedback Mode

to encrypt the plaintext x_i. If $B = L$ then the selector block is eliminated; otherwise $1 \leq L \leq B$. In the case where DES is used as the block cipher, $1 \leq L \leq 64$.

CFB mode is interesting in that a resultant ciphertext block y_{i-1} is chained to multiple plaintext blocks based on the size of the shift register. The shift register has $\frac{B}{L}$ elements, each of size L bits. As a result, each ciphertext y_{i-1} will impact the output of the block cipher $\frac{B}{L}$ times before it is shifted out of the shift register, a key factor in detecting attempts by $Oscar$ to modify the encrypted data stream, as will be shown in **Homework Problem 5.1.8.13**.

5.1.3.5   Output Feedback Mode

$Output\ Feedback$ (OFB) mode is similar to CFB mode with a minor modification. In CFB mode, the shift register is loaded with the value of $y_{i-1} = x_i \oplus block\ cipher\ output$ whereas in OFB mode the shift register is loaded with the $block\ cipher\ output$. The block cipher in OFB mode is now used as a true synchronous stream cipher because the key stream no longer depends on the plaintext x_i (as is the case in CFB mode), resulting in the system shown in Figure 5.12. It is important to note that OFB mode suffers from the primary stream cipher weakness, i.e. the key stream output sequence will eventually repeat, and thus is vulnerable to attacks discussed in Chapter 4.

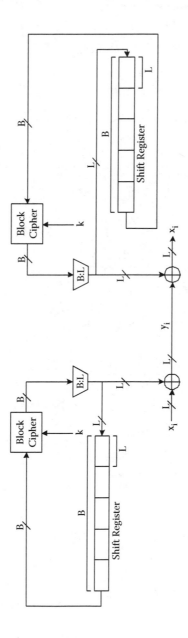

Figure 5.12: Block Cipher Operation in Output Feedback Mode

5.1.3.6   Counter Mode

Counter (CTR) mode is similar to *CFB* mode in that it uses a block cipher as a pseudo-random number generator. However, unlike *CFB* mode, the block cipher in *CTR* mode does not require past ciphertext values to encrypt the current input to the block cipher. This fact is significant because the performance issues associated with block chaining are no longer present. As a result, the use of a pipelined block cipher implementation that allows for the simultaneous processing of multiple input blocks and thus increased throughput is once again worthwhile. *CTR* mode is typically used for high-throughput ATM applications that achieve speeds of 155 Mbps [278]. In the *CTR* mode configuration, a maximum length *LFSR* of the same size as the block cipher is used to generate the block cipher input. The *LFSR* is loaded with an *Initialization Vector* IV. Although the IV does not have to be kept secret, doing so makes the system non-deterministic and thus more difficult to attack. All of the *LFSR* D flip-flops form the *LFSR* state which is encrypted via the block cipher to generate the pseudo-random key stream. Note that the key stream is periodic due to the nature of the *LFSR*, and is of length $n \cdot 2^n$. This key stream is used to encrypt the plaintext block x_i via the XOR operation to yield the ciphertext block y_i. The *LFSR* is then clocked once and the process is repeated for the next plaintext block, resulting in a stream cipher as shown in Figure 5.13.

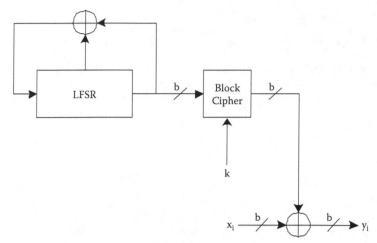

Figure 5.13: Block Cipher Operation in Counter Mode

5.1.4   Key Whitening

Key Whitening is used to increase a block cipher's security versus *Exhaustive Key Search* attacks by increasing the key size of the system without modifying the block cipher itself. *Key Whitening* operates on the plaintext block both prior to encryption by the block cipher and following the end of the block cipher encryption process. *Key Whitening* used in conjunction with *DES* is shown in Figure 5.14. When used in this format, the block cipher is termed DES-X and uses two additional 64-bit keys, k_2 and k_3. In the case of DES-X, encryption is expressed as $y_i = DES_{k_1}(x_i \oplus k_2) \oplus k_3$ and decryption is expressed as $x_i = DES_{k_1}^{-1}(y_i \oplus k_3) \oplus k_2$.

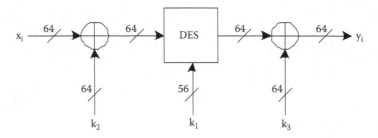

Figure 5.14: DES-X and Key Whitening

5.1.5 Efficient Implementation

DES was designed for fast hardware implementation, and an analysis of the basic building blocks that form the algorithm confirm that efficient, high-throughput implementations are readily achieved. Permutation, expansion, permuted choice, and *Cyclic Left/Right Shift* units do not require logic resources and instead are implemented as wires. The bit-wise XOR operation is used to combine the round key with the expanded R_{i-1}, requiring a total of 32 2-input XOR gates. The *S-Boxes* may be implemented as either $2^6 \times 4$ memory elements or in the form of logic equations based on the mappings in Tables 5.4–5.11. Both methods lead to fast and efficient *S-Box* implementations. With the addition of seventeen 64-bit registers to hold each round's L_i and R_i, a fully pipelined *DES* datapath is easily realized, assuming that the atomic unit of the pipeline is one *DES* round.

It is clear that both encryption and decryption *Key Schedules* are also easily pipelined and synchronized with the pipelined *DES* datapath. One 64-bit register is required to store the master key, and seventeen 56-bit registers are required to hold each round's

C_i and D_i. As a result, a fully pipelined *DES* implementation requires $(17 \cdot 64) + (17 \cdot 56) = 2,040$ storage bits for the pipeline registers. If implementation of the *S-Boxes* as memory elements is assumed, each *S-Box* requires $2^6 \cdot 4 = 256$ storage bits and thus one *DES* round requires $256 \cdot 8 = 2,048$ storage bits. Therefore, the sixteen *DES* rounds require a total of $2,048 \cdot 16 = 32,768$ storage bits for the *S-Boxes*, resulting in a final total of $2,040 + 32,768 = 34,808$ storage bits. The implementation also requires a total of $32 \cdot 16 = 512$ 2-input XOR gates to combine the round key with the expanded R_{i-1} of each round. Once again using the unit-gate model approximation such that a 2-input XOR gate is counted as two gate equivalents [314] and assuming that the storage bits are implemented as SRAM using an estimate of four gates per SRAM bit [242], the total number of gates is calculated as $(34,808 \cdot 4) + (512 \cdot 2) = 140,256$. Such an implementation is easily realized in a single chip, such as a Field Programmable Gate Array (FPGA) or an Application Specific Integrated Circuit (ASIC). To support encryption or decryption of a new block of data every clock cycle in an implementation operating in a non-feedback mode, such as *ECB* or *CTR* mode, also requires that the chip have at least 128 input pins (for the input data and key) and 64 output pins (for the output data). Once again, FPGA and ASIC technology provide more than enough I/O pins to meet these requirements. As a result, numerous fast and efficient *DES* implementations have been reported, reaching throughputs in the Gbps when targeting either FPGAs or ASICs. Examples of such implementations may be found in [202, 312, 327].

As discussed in Section 5.1.3.2, block ciphers operating in feedback modes (such as *CBC* mode) do not map nicely to pipelined hardware implementations because of the chaining of blocks. The chaining requires ciphertext block y_{i-1} to process plaintext block x_i and thus simultaneous processing of the two blocks is impossible, requiring that the pipeline be stalled until generation of the ciphertext block y_{i-1} is completed. However, the stalling of the pipeline may be avoided in an environment with multiple data streams, such as in a network processor. In such a situation, the pipeline may be fully utilized by interleaving the data streams. For a fully pipelined *DES* implementation in which the atomic unit of the pipeline is the *DES* round function, the pipeline will have sixteen stages, thus requiring sixteen interleaved data streams. Let $x_{0_{S_0}}$ denote plaintext block 0 from data stream 0, $x_{0_{S_1}}$ denote plaintext block 0 from data stream 1, etc. Using this notation, the pipeline is filled with blocks $x_{0_{S_0}}$, $x_{0_{S_1}}$, $x_{0_{S_2}}$, ..., $x_{0_{S_{15}}}$. When $x_{0_{S_0}}$ has passed the final stage of the pipeline to yield $y_{0_{S_0}}$, $x_{1_{S_0}}$ is ready to enter the first stage of the pipeline and is combined with $y_{0_{S_0}}$ via the XOR operation to perform *CBC* mode chaining. Thus each data stream is encrypted and decrypted in *CBC* mode while also maintaining full pipeline utilization, maximizing the performance of the implementation. Note that such an implementation must also maintain sixteen *Initialization Vectors*, one for each data stream, to be combined with the first plaintext block x_0 of the associated data stream via the XOR operation.

The analysis proving that the decryption datapath matches the encryption datapath is significant because it implies that the same implementation used for encryption may also be used for decryption as long as the *Key Schedule* is reversed. This feature is crucial when considering hardware implementations with logic resource limitations because separate encryption and decryption *DES* engines are not necessary. However, sharing the same engine does impose a performance limitation because full duplex data communication is not possible when using such a configuration. Therefore, the decision of whether or not to use such a system requires an analysis of the tradeoff between performance and logic resource requirements in the form of chip utilization.

Software implementations of *DES* tend to be significantly slower than hardware implementations. Bit-level manipulations such as those contained in the permutation, expansion, permuted choice, and *Cyclic Left/Right Shift* units do not map well to general purpose processors. General purpose processor instruction sets operate on multiple bits at a time based on the processor word size. Moreover, the *DES S-Boxes* do not use memory in an efficient manner. Software look-up tables would appear to be the obvious implementation choice for the *DES S-Boxes*. However, the *DES S-Boxes* have 6-bit addresses and 4-bit output data, whereas most memories associated with general purpose processors use byte addressing with either 8-bit or 32-bit output data. As a result, many software implementations of *DES* exhibit throughputs that are at least a full order of magnitude slower than hardware implementations.

Even the best software implementations are only capable of throughputs in the range of 100–200 Mbps. Most of these implementations recommend storing the L_i and R_i data as a 48-bit padded word within a 64-bit processor word and implementing the permutations and *S-Boxes* as precomputed look-up tables. Additionally, there is general agreement that the look-up table implementation for the *S-Boxes* is most effective when the size of the look-up tables is minimized, guaranteeing that the data will fit entirely in on-chip cache. Size minimization of the *S-Box* look-up tables is achieved by implementing each *S-Box* in its own look-up table. Finally, one key software optimization is the unrolling of software loops to increase performance. Even when software loops are too cumbersome to unroll, using loop counters that decrement to zero in place of loop counters that increment to a terminal count are shown to greatly increase the performance of software implementations of the *DES* algorithm. However, the unrolling of software loops must be done with great care such that the total data storage space does not exceed the size of the on-chip cache because this would cause extreme performance degradation [31, 129, 244].

5.1.6 Attacks Against DES

Upon its introduction as a standard in 1977, *DES* faced two major criticisms:

1. The 56-bit key was too small, allowing for an *Exhaustive Key Search* attack.

2. IBM refused to divulge the *S-Box* design criteria; as such, the prevailing opinion was that the *S-Boxes* contained a *trap door* that would allow the United States government, in particular the National Security Agency (NSA), to easily decrypt any data encrypted using *DES*.

5.1.6.1   Weak and Semi-Weak Keys

In 1981, the NBS published a FIPS standard outlining the guidelines for implementing *DES* [230]. In the FIPS standard, four weak *DES* keys are identified, each of which causes the bits of C_0 and D_0 to be either all zeros or all ones after *PC-1* has stripped off the parity bits. When this condition occurs, the *Key Schedule* generated from the master key is identical for encryption and decryption, i.e. $K_1 = K_{16}$, $K_2 = K_{15}$, $K_3 = K_{14}$, $K_4 = K_{13}$, $K_5 = K_{12}$, $K_6 = K_{11}$, $K_7 = K_{10}$, $K_8 = K_9$. In this case, encryption and decryption become identical operations such that $DES_{K_w}(DES_{K_w}(x)) = x$. Four 64-bit keys exhibit this property, as detailed in Table 5.15. For these four keys, the parity bit for each byte is set for odd parity.

Key
0101010101010101_{16}
$FEFEFEFEFEFEFEFE_{16}$
$1F1F1F1F0E0E0E0E_{16}$
$E0E0E0E0F1F1F1F1_{16}$

Table 5.15: DES Weak Keys

The FIPS standard also identifies semi-weak key pairs where encryption with one key is identical to decryption with the other key, such that $DES_{K_{sw_1}}(DES_{K_{sw_2}}(x)) = x$. Semi-weak keys yield all zeros, all ones, or patterns of alternating zeros and ones in C_0 and D_0 after PC-1 has stripped off the parity bits. These 64-bit keys include the four previously identified weak keys and twelve other keys. These keys are detailed in Table 5.16 as six pairs, where each pair is denoted as a key and its dual [230]. Note that for the four weak keys, each key is its own dual.

Key	Dual
$E001E001F101F101_{16}$	$01E001E001F101F1_{16}$
$FE1FFE1FFE0EFE0E_{16}$	$1FFE1FFE0EFE0EFE_{16}$
$E01FE01FF10EF10E_{16}$	$1FE01FE00EF10EF1_{16}$
$01FE01FE01FE01FE_{16}$	$FE01FE01FE01FE01_{16}$
$011F011F010E010E_{16}$	$1F011F010E010E01_{16}$
$E0FE0FEF1FEF1FE_{16}$	$FEE0FEE0FEF1FEF1_{16}$

Table 5.16: DES Semi-Weak Keys

The use of weak and semi-weak keys is problematic in systems that employ *DES* to encrypt data multiple times, e.g. double or triple encryption. In these cases, the use of weak and semi-weak keys should be avoided. The likelihood of selecting a weak key or semi-weak key pair at random is quite small given the number of such keys versus the number of possible keys. Many software implementations of *DES* include a weak key check routine to ensure that such a key or key pair is not accidentally selected.

5.1.6.2   Exhaustive Key Search

An *Exhaustive Key Search* attack against *DES* in the form of a *Known-Plaintext* attack was initially proposed by Whitfield Diffie and Martin Hellman in 1977 using a key search machine with a theoretical cost of $20 million. A more detailed design for a hardware-based key search engine was proposed in 1993 by Mike Wiener at a cost of $100,000 with an average search time of thirty-six hours. However, it was not until 1997 that an *Exhaustive Key Search* attack was successful. In June of 1997, *DES* Challenge I was successfully completed via a distributed computing effort in approximately four and a half months. An in-depth history of the computing effort can be found in [52], detailing how resources provided by academia, industry, and the private sector were all coordinated to successfully perform the *Exhaustive Key Search* attack. *DES* Challenge II-1 was successfully completed in thirty-nine days via a distributed computing effort in February of 1998. But it was not until *DES* Challenge II-2 was successfully completed that *DES* was considered to be no longer secure. The *Exhaustive Key Search* attack was carried out via a key search engine built by Electronic Frontier Foundation at a cost of $250,000 with an average search time of fifteen days. This same key search engine was used in combination with a distributed computing effort to successfully complete *DES* Challenge II in January of 1999 in less than twenty-four hours. Based on the established cost and computation time, clearly the construction of such a key search engine is no longer limited to government entities. Therefore *DES* is no longer recommended as a method for ensuring secure data communications.

When examining block ciphers such as *DES*, the straightforward approach to an *Exhaustive Key Search* attack is a *Known-Plaintext* attack. In such an attack, *Oscar* knows (x_0, y_0) for an n-bit block cipher. *Oscar* tests different values for the key k to determine if $e_{k_i}(x_0) = y_0$. This problem becomes more difficult if the key space is larger than the plaintext space (and thus the ciphertext space as well). In such a case, a single $(x_0, y_0$ pair is not sufficient to find the true key because multiple keys will map x_0 to y_0. If the encryption function randomly maps the plaintext space to the ciphertext space, then there are on average $\frac{2^k}{2^n} = 2^{k-n}$ keys that will map x_0 to y_0. However, only one of these candidate keys is the true key. The only way to determine which candidate key is the true key is to have more (x, y) pairs to evaluate versus candidate keys. To eliminate one of the 2^{k-n} candidate keys, each is tested to determine if $e_{k_i}(x_1) = y_1$ for the pair (x_1, y_1). Because there are 2^n possible mappings for x_1, the probability that $e_{k_i}(x_1) = y_1$ is $\frac{1}{2^n}$. Examining a third pair (x_2, y_2), the probability that $e_{k_i}(x_1) = y_1$ and that $e_{k_i}(x_2) = y_2$ is $\left(\frac{1}{2^n}\right) \cdot \left(\frac{1}{2^n}\right) = \frac{1}{2^{2n}}$. Continuing to check additional pairs (x_3, y_3), (x_4, y_4), $\ldots$, (x_t, y_t), the probability that all pairs successfully map x to y for a given key is $\frac{1}{2^{(t-1)n}}$. Since there are 2^{k-n} keys for which $e_{k_i}(x_0) = y_0$, the probability that at least one of those keys successfully maps all of the pairs $(x_1, y_1), (x_2, y_2), \ldots, (x_t, y_t)$ is $\frac{2^{k-n}}{2^{(t-1)n}} = 2^{k-n-tn+n} = 2^{k-tn}$.

Example 5.2: Consider the *IDEA* block cipher. *IDEA* has a 64-bit block size and a 128-bit key size. How many (x, y) pairs are needed to ensure that the key being tested is the correct key with a 99 % probability?

Based on the *IDEA* parameters, $k = 128$ and $n = 64$. Therefore, to ensure that the candidate key is the true key, the likelihood that the wrong key has been chosen must be minimized. If one (x, y) pair is used, the average number of false keys is $2^{k - tn} = 2^{128 - (1 \cdot 64)} = 2^{64}$. If two (x, y) pairs are used, the average number of false keys is $2^{k - tn} = 2^{128 - (2 \cdot 64)} = 2^0 = 1$. If three (x, y) pairs are used, the average number of false keys is $2^{k - tn} = 2^{128 - (3 \cdot 64)} = 2^{-64} = 5.4 \times 10^{-20}$. Therefore, three (x, y) pairs are needed to ensure that the key being tested is the correct key with a 99 % probability.

5.1.6.3 Meet-In-The-Middle

Using a block cipher multiple times to encrypt plaintext would seem to be a reasonable method for increasing the effective key space of a cryptosystem. However, such is not always the case. Consider double encryption using *DES* as shown in Figure 5.15.

The effective key space of this cryptosystem should be $2^{56} \cdot 2^{56} = 2^{112}$, or 2^{2k} for a block cipher with a key size of k bits.

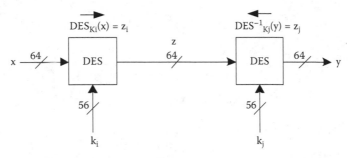

Figure 5.15: Double Encryption Using DES

Whereas a straightforward *Exhaustive Key Search* attack has a computational complexity of 2^{2k}, a key search with significantly reduced computational complexity is possible. This *Known-Plaintext* attack, known as the *Meet-In-The-Middle* attack, requires (x, y) pairs and tries to meet in the middle when computing z, as shown in Figure 5.15. The *Meet-In-The-Middle* attack proceeds as follows:

1. Compute $DES_{k_i}(x_0) = z_i$ for all possible k_i.

2. Store each z_i and its associated k_i in a table in memory.

3. Compute $DES_{k_j}^{-1}(y_0) = z_j$.

4. If z_j is in the table in memory, (k_i, k_j) are candidate key pairs. If z_j is not in the table in memory, discard k_j and test a new key.

This procedure requires that the table in memory have 2^k entries. Each entry has n bits for z_i and k bits for k_i, resulting in a table of size $(n + k) \cdot 2^k$ bits. 2^k encryptions are required to build the table in memory and 2^k decryptions are required in the worst case to compute a z_j that is found in the table, resulting in a total of 2^{k+1} computations. This complexity is significantly less than the complexity of 2^{2k} computed above from an *Exhaustive Key Search* attack. Moreover, the *Meet-In-The-Middle* attack results in double encryption with *DES* increasing the effective key space by only a single bit. Instead of double encryption, consider triple encryption using *DES*, also known as *Triple-DES* or *3-DES*, as shown in Figure 5.16.

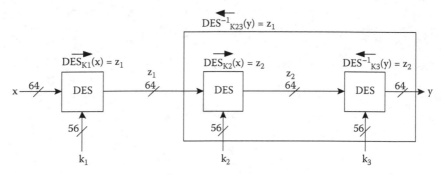

Figure 5.16: Triple Encryption Using DES

In the case of *Triple-DES*, $y = DES_{k_3}(DES_{k_2}(DES_{k_1}(x)))$. The effective key space of this cryptosystem should be $2^{56} \cdot 2^{56} \cdot 2^{56} = 2^{168}$, or 2^{3k} for a block cipher with a key size of k bits. While the *Meet-In-The-Middle* attack may still be applied to *Triple-DES*, the computational complexity is significantly worse versus the *Meet-In-The-Middle* attack applied to double encryption using *DES*. In the case of *Triple-DES*, the *Meet-In-The-Middle* attack is first applied to solve for z_1. In this case, the first *DES* block is used to generate z_1 in the encryption direction while the second and third *DES* blocks are treated as one block that is used to generate z_1 in the decryption direction. The result of this analysis is a solution for k_1. Then the standard *Meet-In-The-Middle* attack is applied to the second and third *DES* blocks to solve for k_2 and k_3. This attack has a computational complexity $\approx 2^{2k}$. Thus the *Meet-In-The-Middle* attack results in *Triple-DES* doubling the effective key space. Whereas single encryption using *DES* is no longer considered secure, *Triple-DES* is considered secure with an effective key space of 2^{112}. Moreover, all of the *DES* implementation issues discussed in Section 5.1.5 also apply to *Triple-DES*.

The number of pairs needed to ensure that a candidate key is the correct key when encrypting multiple times is obtained from the prior analysis performed for single encryption and used in **Example 5.2**. It was determined that the average number of false keys for a block cipher with a key size of k and a block size of n using t (x, y) pairs is $2^{k - tn}$. Encrypting using the same block cipher l times increases the key space from k to $l \cdot k$. Therefore, for l encryptions, the average number of false keys for a block cipher with a key size of k and a block size of n using t (x, y) pairs is $2^{lk - tn}$.

Example 5.3: Consider double encryption using *DES*. How many (x, y) pairs are needed to ensure that the key pair being tested is the correct key pair with a 99 % probability?

Based on the *DES* parameters, $k = 56$ and $n = 64$. Double encryption establishes that $l = 2$. Therefore, to ensure that the candidate key pair is the true key pair, the likelihood that the wrong key pair has been chosen must be minimized. If one (x, y) pair is used, the average number of false key pairs is $2^{lk\ -\ tn} = 2^{(2\ \cdot\ 56)\ -\ (1\ \cdot\ 64)} = 2^{48}$. If two (x, y) pairs are used, the average number of false keys is $2^{lk\ -\ tn} = 2^{(2\ \cdot\ 56)\ -\ (2\ \cdot\ 64)} = 2^{-16} = 1.5 \times 10^{-5}$. Therefore, two (x, y) pairs are needed to ensure that the key pair being tested is the correct key pair with a 99 % probability.

5.1.6.4   S-Box Design Criteria

Addressing the mystery behind the *S-Box* design criteria led to the discovery of two key analytical attacks against *DES*. In 1990, Eli Biham and Adi Shamir proposed the *Differential Cryptanalysis* attack, [32]. *Differential Cryptanalysis* is typically implemented as a *Chosen-Plaintext* attack, although it may also be implemented as either a *Known-Plaintext* or a *Ciphertext-Only* attack. In the *Chosen-Plaintext* attack form, for an unknown key k, *Oscar* chooses the plaintext x_1 and x_2 and observes the resultant ciphertext y_1 and y_2. *Oscar* then computes $\triangle x = x_1 \oplus x_2$ and $\triangle y = y_1 \oplus y_2$ which together are termed a *Differential*. The *Differential* yields information via *Statistical Analysis* as to which keys are more probable values for k. This attack requires approximately 2^{47} (x, y) pairs. Unfortunately, this attack is not feasible in practice — to inject 2^{47} (x, y) pairs would take seven days at a throughput of 5 Mbps and would also require that the key k not change over that time. Even at ATM throughput rates of 155 Mbps, such an attack would still require over five hours to inject the 2^{47} $(x,\ y)$ pairs using the same key k.

Interestingly, the *DES S-Box* mappings are optimally configured to combat *Differential Cryptanalysis* and the prevailing opinion was that both IBM and the NSA knew about *Differential Cryptanalysis* when designing *DES*. This theory was confirmed in 1994 by Don Coppersmith, a member of the IBM research team that developed *DES* [49]. Coppersmith admitted that IBM knew about *Differential Cryptanalysis* as early as 1974 and had intentionally designed *DES* to be strengthened against the attack. Coppersmith also stated that the knowledge of *Differential Cryptanalysis* was kept secret so that the United States could maintain its technical advantage in cryptography over other countries, thus eliminating the *trap door* theory.

In 1993, Mitsuru Matsui proposed the *Linear Cryptanalysis* attack against *DES* [192]. *Linear Cryptanalysis* attempts to find linear approximations to the behavior of *DES* (or any block cipher). *Linear Cryptanalysis* is implemented as a *Known-Plaintext* attack requires approximately 2^{43} known plaintext $(x,\ y)$ pairs. The *DES S-Boxes* are not optimized to combat *Linear Cryptanalysis*. Many theories exist as to why this is the case. It is possible that IBM and the NSA were not aware of *Linear Cryptanalysis*. Alternatively, it has been proposed that IBM and the NSA are aware of a third analytical attack that has not yet been discovered by researchers and that making *DES* resilient against both *Linear Cryptanalysis* and the unknown attack causes conflicting requirements, and as such a design trade-off was made [275].

5.1.7   Homework Problems

Homework Problem 5.1.7.1: Demonstrate the non-linear property of the *DES S-Boxes* by computing the output of $S1$ for the following pairs of inputs. Show that $S1(x_1) \oplus S1(x_2) \neq S1(x_1 \oplus x_2)$ for:

a) $x_1 = 000000_2$, $x_2 = 000001_2$

b) $x_1 = 111111_2$, $x_2 = 100000_2$

c) $x_1 = 101010_2$, $x_2 = 010101_2$

Homework Problem 5.1.7.2: Consider the vector

$$x = (x_1, x_2, \ldots, x_{64})$$

a 64-bit vector. Show that $IP^{-1}(IP(x)) = x$ for the first five bits of x, i.e. for x_i, $i = 1, 2, 3, 4, 5$.

Homework Problem 5.1.7.3: What are the values of (L_1, R_1) for *DES* if the 64-bit input $x = 0000\ 0000\ 0000\ 0000_{16}$ and the 56-bit key $k = 00\ 00\ 00\ 00\ 00\ 00\ 00_{16}$?

Homework Problem 5.1.7.4: If an input word is applied (prior to the *Initial Permutation*) to *DES* that has a 1 at bit position 57 and all other input bits and key bits are 0. Note that the numbering starts from the left (position 1) and moves sequentially to the right (position 64).

a) How many *S-Boxes* get different inputs compared to the case considered in **Homework Problem 5.1.7.3**?

b) What is the minimum number of output bits of the *S-Boxes* that will change according to the *S-Box* design criteria?

c) What is the output after the first round?

d) How many output bits have changed as compared to the case when the plaintext was all zero?

Homework Problem 5.1.7.5: Denote the bit-wise complement of a number A as A'. Show that if $y = DES_k(x)$, then $y' = DES_{k'}(x')$. This states that if the plaintext and the key are complemented, the ciphertext output will also be the complement of the original ciphertext. To prove this property:

a) Show that for any bit strings A, B of equal length, $A' \oplus B' = A \oplus B$ and $A' \oplus B = (A \oplus B)'$.

b) Show that PC-1(k') = (PC-1(k))'.

c) Show that $LS_i(C'_{i-1}) = (LS_i(C_{i-1}))'$.

d) Using the results from parts (a) and (b), show that if k_i are the keys generated from k, then k_i' are the keys generated from k' where $i = 1, 2, \ldots, 16$.

e) Show that $IP(x') = (IP(x))'$.

f) Show that $E(R_i') = (E(R_i))'$.

g) Using all previous results, show that if R_{i-1}, L_{i-1}, k_i generate R_i, then R_{i-1}', L_{i-1}', k_i' generate R_i'.

h) Show that $y' = DES_{k'}(x')$ is true.

Homework Problem 5.1.7.6: Assume that *Oscar* performs a *Known-Plaintext* attack against *DES* with one pair of plaintext and ciphertext. How many keys must be tested in a worst-case scenario if an *Exhaustive Key Search* attack is applied in a straightforward manner? How many keys must be tested on average if an *Exhaustive Key Search* attack is applied in a straightforward manner?

Homework Problem 5.1.7.7: The speed of a hardware implementation of *DES* is mainly determined by the time required to perform a single iteration. This hardware kernel is then used sixteen consecutive times to generate the encrypted output.

a) Assume that a single iteration of *DES* can be performed in one clock cycle. Develop an expression for the minimum clock frequency required to encrypt a stream of data with a data rate of

r bits per second. Ignore the time needed for the *Initial Permutation* and the *Final Permutation*.

b) What is the minimum clock frequency required to encrypt a network link running at an ATM speed of 155 Mbps? What is the minimum clock frequency required to encrypt a network link running at an ATM speed of 622 Mbps? Are these clock rates realistic given current computing capabilities?

c) How many *DES* chips must be used in parallel to encrypt a 1 Gbps data stream and the chips can operate at a maximum clock frequency of 22 MHz?

Homework Problem 5.1.7.8: Assume a *DES* chip with pipelined hardware can perform one encryption (or key test) per clock cycle. If the system is clocked at 50 MHz, how many chips must be run in parallel for an average search time of twenty-four hours? Assume that a worst case run searches through 2^{56} keys. What is the cost for such a machine if one chip costs $10 and there is a 100 % overhead on this price for connecting the chips and building the machine? Why does any design of a key search machine constitute only an *upper security threshold*? The phrase *upper security threshold* means a complexity measure that describes the maximum security that is provided by a given cryptographic algorithm.

Homework Problem 5.1.7.9: Assume a block cipher is used with a key length of 128 bits. Assume a special-purpose chip which searches $5 \cdot 10^7$ keys per second. Also assume that 100,000 of these chips are used in parallel. How long does an average key search take? Relate this time to the age of the universe, which is approximately 10^{10} years.

Homework Problem 5.1.7.10: *Moore's Law* states that computing power doubles every eighteen months. How many years will pass before the key search machine described in **Homework Problem 5.1.7.9** can be built such that the average search time is twenty-four hours?

Homework Problem 5.1.7.11: Consider the storage of data in encrypted form in a large database using *DES*. One record has a size of 64 bits. Assume that the records are not related to each other. Which encryption mode would be most suitable for this system and why?

Homework Problem 5.1.7.12: Consider *Known-Plaintext* attacks on block ciphers by means of an *Exhaustive Key Search* where the key is k bits long. Any *ECB* mode cipher can be broken in a straightforward manner in 2^k steps using one pair of plaintext and ciphertext (x, y).

a) Assume the *Initialization Vector*, IV, in *CBC* mode is not known. This seems to impose another difficulty. Describe the minimum number of pieces of plaintext and ciphertext that are required in order to break a *CBC* mode cipher by an *Exhaustive Key Search* attack. How many search steps are required in a worst-case scenario?

b) Is breaking a block cipher in *CBC* mode by means of an *Exhaustive Key Search* attack considerably more difficult as compared to breaking an *ECB* mode block cipher?

Homework Problem 5.1.7.13: An important issue in choosing a mode of operation in practice is error propagation.

a) Assume an error occurs during transmission in one block of ciphertext, y_i. Which plaintext blocks are affected on *Bob's* side when using *ECB* mode?

b) Assume an error occurs in the plaintext x_i on *Alice's* side. Which plaintext blocks are affected on *Bob's* side when using *CBC* mode?

c) Assume an error occurs during transmission in one block of ciphertext, y_i. Which plaintext blocks are affected on *Bob's* side when using *PCBC* mode?

d) Assume a single bit error occurs in the transmission of a ciphertext character in 8-bit *CFB* mode. How far does the error propagate? Describe exactly how each block is affected.

e) Assume an error occurs in the plaintext x_i on *Alice's* side. Which plaintext blocks are affected on *Bob's* side when using *OFB* mode?

f) Assume an error occurs in the plaintext x_i on *Alice's* side. Which plaintext blocks are affected on *Bob's* side when using *CTR* mode?

Homework Problem 5.1.7.14: *Oscar* wants to attack data that has been double encrypted using the *CAST-64* block cipher. *CAST-64* has a key length of 64 bits and an I/O block size of 64 bits. Using the *Meet-In-The-Middle* attack, how many *(x, y)* pairs should be available so that the probability to determine an incorrect key pair (k_1, k_2) is sufficiently low for a practical attack?

Homework Problem 5.1.7.15: *Triple-DES* with three different keys can be broken with approximately 2^{2k} encryptions and 2^k memory cells, $k = 56$. Design the corresponding attack. How many *(x, y)* pairs should be available so that the probability of determining an incorrect key triple (k_1, k_2, k_3) is sufficiently low?

Homework Problem 5.1.7.16: What are the values of (L_1, R_1) for *DES* if the 64-bit input $x = FFFF\ FFFF\ FFFF\ FFFF_{16}$ and the 56-bit key $k = 00\ 00\ 00\ 00\ 00\ 00\ 00_{16}$?

Homework Problem 5.1.7.17: Assume a 64-bit *DES* key

$$k = 1100\ 0001\ 0000\ 0001\ 0000\ 0001\ \ldots\ 0000\ 0001_2$$

where the leftmost bit is bit 1 and bits 8, 16, 24, ... , 64 are parity bits that are not passed through to PC-1. Compute the sub-key k_{16}.

Homework Problem 5.1.7.18: Write a VHDL architecture to implement the entire *DES Key Scheduling* and encryption operating in *CBC* mode using a non-pipelined architecture. Your implementation must update the output ciphertext on every rising edge of the clock. Assume that the user will provide a *loadkey* signal to indicate that the master key is ready to be loaded from the *plaintext* bus on the next rising edge of the clock. Also assume that the user will provide a *loadiv* signal to indicate that the *Initialization Vector*, IV, is ready to be loaded on the next rising edge of the clock via the *plaintext* bus. Your system must output a *valid* signal to indicate when the output ciphertext is valid, i.e. an encryption has completed. Use the following entity declaration for your implementation:

```
LIBRARY ieee;
USE ieee.std_logic_1164.ALL;
USE ieee.std_logic_arith.ALL;
USE ieee.std_logic_unsigned.ALL;
ENTITY des_cbc IS
   PORT ( plaintext   : IN   std_logic_vector (63 DOWNTO 0);
          clk         : IN   std_logic;
          rst         : IN   std_logic;
          loadkey     : IN   std_logic;
          loadiv      : IN   std_logic;
          valid       : OUT  std_logic;
          ciphertext  : OUT  std_logic_vector (63 DOWNTO 0));
END des_cbc;
ARCHITECTURE behav OF des_cbc IS
BEGIN
-- Your code goes here
END behav;
```

Use the results from **Homework Problems 5.1.7.3**, **5.1.7.4**, and **5.1.7.16** to validate your design. Specify the target technology used to implement the design and the maximum operating frequency as specified by your place-and-route tools. What is the throughput of your implementation?

Homework Problem 5.1.7.19: Write a VHDL architecture to implement the entire *DES Key Scheduling* and encryption in *ECB* mode using a pipelined architecture. Your implementation must update the output ciphertext on every rising edge of the clock. Assume that the user will provide a *loadkey* signal to indicate that the master key is ready to be loaded from the *plaintext* bus on the next rising edge of the clock and that a new key may be loaded while previous encryptions are still in progress. Your system must output a *valid* signal to indicate when the output ciphertext is valid, i.e. an encryption has completed. Use the following entity declaration for your implementation:

```
LIBRARY ieee;
USE ieee.std_logic_1164.ALL;
USE ieee.std_logic_arith.ALL;
USE ieee.std_logic_unsigned.ALL;
ENTITY des_ecb IS
   PORT ( plaintext  : IN  std_logic_vector (63 DOWNTO 0);
          clk        : IN  std_logic;
          rst        : IN  std_logic;
          loadkey    : IN  std_logic;
          valid      : OUT std_logic;
          ciphertext : OUT std_logic_vector (63 DOWNTO 0));
END des_ecb;
ARCHITECTURE behav OF des_ecb IS
BEGIN
-- Your code goes here
END behav;
```

Use the results from **Homework Problems 5.1.7.3**, **5.1.7.4**, and **5.1.7.16** to validate your design. Specify the target technology used to implement the design and the maximum operating frequency as specified by your place-and-route tools. What is the throughput of your implementation?

Homework Problem 5.1.7.20: Compare the throughputs and logic resource requirements of **Homework Problems 5.1.7.18** and **5.1.7.19**. What is the ratio of throughput improvement versus the increased logic resources of **Homework Problem 5.1.7.19** versus **Homework Problem 5.1.7.18**?

Homework Problem 5.1.7.21: Write a C program to implement the entire *DES Key Scheduling* and encryption operating in *CBC* mode. Write a user interface that queries the user for an input file that contains the key K, the *Initialization Vector*, IV, and five plaintexts $P_0 — P_4$, in hexadecimal notation. The program must output the five ciphertexts to the screen in hexadecimal notation and include code that measures the time required to encrypt each of the five ciphertexts, outputting this information to the screen. Specify the computer model used and the amount of available RAM.

Homework Problem 5.1.7.22: Compare the throughputs of **Homework Problems 5.1.7.18** and **5.1.7.21**. What is the ratio of throughput improvement for **Homework Problem 5.1.7.18** versus **Homework Problem 5.1.7.21**?

Homework Problem 5.1.7.23: Write a C program to implement the entire *DES Key Scheduling* and encryption operating in *ECB* mode. Write a user interface that queries the user for an input file that contains the key, K, and five plaintexts $P_0 — P_4$ in hexadecimal notation. The program must output the five ciphertexts to the screen in hexadecimal notation and include code that measures the time required to encrypt each of the five ciphertexts, outputting this information to the screen. Specify the computer model used and the amount of available RAM.

Homework Problem 5.1.7.24: Compare the throughputs of **Homework Problems 5.1.7.19** and **5.1.7.23**. What is the ratio of throughput improvement for **Homework Problem 5.1.7.19** versus **Homework Problem 5.1.7.23**?

Homework Problem 5.1.7.25: Write a VHDL architecture to implement *DES Key Scheduling* and one round of encryption operating in *ECB* mode using a non-pipelined architecture that iterates sixteen times to perform a complete encryption. Assume that the user will provide a *loadkey* signal to indicate that the master key is ready to be loaded on the next rising edge of the clock. Your system must output a *valid* signal to indicate when the output ciphertext is valid, i.e. an encryption has completed. Use the following entity declaration for your implementation:

```
LIBRARY ieee;
USE ieee.std_logic_1164.ALL;
USE ieee.std_logic_arith.ALL;
USE ieee.std_logic_unsigned.ALL;
ENTITY des_ecb_single IS
   PORT ( plaintext  : IN  std_logic_vector (63 DOWNTO 0);
          key        : IN  std_logic_vector (63 DOWNTO 0);
          clk        : IN  std_logic;
          rst        : IN  std_logic;
          loadkey    : IN  std_logic;
          valid      : OUT std_logic;
          ciphertext : OUT std_logic_vector (63 DOWNTO 0));
END des_ecb_single;
ARCHITECTURE behav OF des_ecb_single IS
BEGIN
-- Your code goes here
END behav;
```

Use the results from **Homework Problems 5.1.7.3**, **5.1.7.4**, and **5.1.7.16** to validate your design. Specify the target technology used to implement the design and the maximum operating frequency as specified by your place-and-route tools. What is the throughput of your implementation? How does this compare to the throughputs calculated in **Homework Problems 5.1.7.19** and **5.1.7.23**? What is the ratio of throughput improvement versus the increased logic resources of **Homework Problem 5.1.7.19**?

5.2 The Advanced Encryption Standard

With the expiration of *DES* in 1998 [275], NIST initiated a process to develop a FIPS standard for the *Advanced Encryption Standard* (AES) so as to specify an *Advanced Encryption Algorithm*. In an effort to avoid the concerns associated with the *DES S-Box* design criteria detailed in Section 5.1.6, the *AES* selection process was kept open to public scrutiny. NIST solicited candidate algorithms for inclusion in *AES*, resulting in fifteen official candidate algorithms, of which five were selected as finalists. Unlike *DES*, which was designed specifically for hardware implementations, one of the design criteria for *AES* candidate algorithms was that they must be efficiently implemented in both hardware and software. Thus, NIST announced that both hardware and software performance measurements would be included in their efficiency testing. In addition, NIST required that *AES* be a block cipher that operates on 128-bit blocks and that supports key lengths of 128, 192, and 256 bits. In October of 2000, NIST chose *Rijndael* as the *Advanced Encryption Algorithm* [227].

5.2.1   Galois Field Mathematics

The *Ring* Z_m was defined in Section 2.4. Similarly, a *Field* is now defined as a *Ring* in which there exists an inverse for all elements except zero. A *Finite Field* is a *Field* with a finite number of elements and a *Prime Field* is a *Field* with a prime number of elements p such that the *Field* is defined as:

1. The set $Z_p = \{0, 1, 2, \ldots p - 1\}$ where p is prime.

2. An additive *Group* over Z_p.

3. A multiplicative *Group* over Z_p^*, guaranteeing the existence of an inverse for all elements. See Section 8.1 for more on the *Group* over Z_p^*.

A *Galois Field* is a *Finite Field* represented by the notation *GF(p)* where all arithmetic in the *Field* is performed modulo p and p is prime.

Example 5.4: Construct the addition and multiplication tables for the *Galois Field GF(5)*.

The *Galois Field GF(5)* has elements $\{0, 1, 2, 3, 4\}$.

		Addition		
+ mod 5	**0** **1**	**2**	**3**	**4**
0	0 1	2	3	4
1	1 2	3	4	0
2	2 3	4	0	1
3	3 4	0	1	2
4	4 0	1	2	3

		Multiplication		
× mod 5	**0** **1**	**2**	**3**	**4**
0	0 0	0	0	0
1	0 1	2	3	4
2	0 2	4	1	3
3	0 3	1	4	2
4	0 4	3	2	1

Example 5.5: Identify the additive and multiplicative inverses for each element in the *Galois Field GF(5)*.

The *Galois Field GF(5)* has elements $\{0, 1, 2, 3, 4\}$.

Element	Additive Inverse	Multiplicative Inverse
0	0	Does Not Exist
1	4	1
2	3	3
3	2	2
4	1	4

Galois Fields may be extended by exponentiating the prime p by an integer m, forming the *Extension Field $GF(p^m)$*. Elements within *Extension Fields* are typically represented as polynomials with m coefficients where each coefficient is an element of the *Galois Field GF(p)*.

Example 5.6: Give the generic polynomial representation for an element A of the *Extension Field $GF(2^4)$*.

The *Extension Field $GF(2^4)$* has elements represented as polynomials with four coefficients. These polynomials are generically represented as $A(x) = a_3x^3 + a_2x^2 + a_1x + a_0$, where each coefficient a_i is an element of $GF(2) = \{0, 1\}$.

Elements within the *Extension Field $GF(p^m)$* may be combined in a manner consistent with polynomial addition and subtraction. Coefficients are reduced modulo p, yielding a resultant polynomial that is an element in the *Extension Field $GF(p^m)$*. Note that for $p = 2$, addition and subtraction modulo 2 are the same operation. This characteristic is extremely useful when implementing *Extension Fields* in software, i.e. a binary computer. This characteristic is also useful in hardware implementations where addition and subtraction of coefficients modulo 2 are easily implemented as 2-input XOR gates.

Example 5.7: Given the polynomials $A(x)$ and $B(x)$, each contained in the *Extension Field $GF(2^4)$*:

$$A(x) = x^3 + x^2 + x + 1$$

$$B(x) \;=\; x^2 + x$$

Compute $C(x) \;=\; A(x) + B(x)$.

Coefficient addition is performed modulo 2:

$$A(x) \;=\; x^3 + x^2 + x + 1$$
$$B(x) \;=\; x^2 + x$$

$$C(x) \;=\; A(x) + B(x)$$
$$C(x) \;=\; x^3 + x^2 + x + 1 + x^2 + x$$
$$C(x) \;=\; x^3 + (2 \bmod 2)x^2 + (2 \bmod 2)x + 1$$
$$C(x) \;=\; x^3 + 1$$

Therefore $C(x) \;=\; x^3 + 1$ and $C(x)$ is an element in the *Extension Field GF(2^4)*.

Elements within the *Extension Field GF(p^m)* may be multiplied in a manner consistent with polynomial multiplication. Coefficients are reduced modulo p but the resultant polynomial is of degree $2m - 2$ and is therefore not an element in the *Extension Field GF(p^m)*. Therefore, the intermediate polynomial must be reduced from degree $2m - 2$ to degree $m - 1$ to yield a polynomial that is an element in the *Extension Field GF(p^m)*. This reduction requires an *Irreducible Polynomial*, i.e. a polynomial that cannot be factored into the product of other polynomials over $GF(p)$, and this *Irreducible Polynomial* must be of degree m.

Example 5.8: Given the polynomials $A(x)$ and $B(x)$, each contained in the *Extension Field GF(2^4)*:

$$A(x) = x^3 + x + 1$$
$$B(x) = x + 1$$

and the *Irreducible Polynomial* $P(x) = x^4 + x + 1$. Compute $C(x) = A(x) \times B(x) \bmod P(x)$.

Coefficient multiplication is performed modulo 2:

$$C(x) = A(x) \times B(x)$$
$$C(x) = x^4 + x^2 + x + x^3 + x + 1$$
$$C(x) = x^4 + x^3 + x^2 + (2 \bmod 2)x + 1$$
$$C(x) = x^4 + x^3 + x^2 + 1$$

Now x^4 must be reduced modulo $P(x)$. Note that:

$$P(x) = x^4 + x + 1$$
$$x^4 = P(x) - x - 1$$

However, as previously discussed, for $p = 2$, addition and subtraction modulo 2 are the same operation. This leads to:

$$x^4 = P(x) + x + 1$$
$$x^4 = (x + 1) \ mod \ P(x)$$

Substituting into the equation for $C(x)$ yields:

$$C(x) = x^4 + x^3 + x^2 + 1$$
$$C(x) = x + 1 + x^3 + x^2 + 1$$
$$C(x) = x^3 + x^2 + x + (2 \ mod \ 2)$$
$$C(x) = x^3 + x^2 + x$$

Therefore, $C(x) = x^3 + x^2 + x$ and $C(x)$ is an element in the *Extension Field GF(2⁴)*.

Based on the results of **Example 5.8**, the binary representation of the polynomial multiplication as it would be stored in a computer is easily derived. Each polynomial in the *Extension Field GF(2⁴)* may be represented as a 4-bit binary vector, where each bit in the vector represents the values of the coefficients of the polynomial. Therefore:

$$A(x) = x^3 + x + 1 = 1011_2$$
$$B(x) = x + 1 = 0011_2$$
$$C(x) = x^3 + x^2 + x = 1110_2$$

As a result, $C(x) = A(x) \times B(x) \mod P(x)$ may be represented as $C(x) = 1011_2 \times 0011_2 = 1110_2$.

A non-zero element within the *Extension Field GF(p^m)*, $A(x)$, may be inverted to yield a new polynomial, $A^{-1}(x)$, such that $A(x) \cdot A^{-1}(x) = 1 \mod P(x)$. This is because the non-zero elements of the *Extension Field GF(p^m)* form a *Cyclic Group*, as defined in Section 8.1, with $p^m - 1$ elements. As will be shown in Section 6.8, *Fermat's Little Theorem* states that $A(x)^{p^m - 1} \equiv 1 \mod P(x)$. Consider that $A(x) \cdot A^{-1}(x) \equiv 1 \mod P(x)$. Therefore, $A(x) \cdot A^{-1}(x) \mod P(x) \equiv A(x)^{p^m - 1} \mod P(x)$, leading to the conclusion that $A^{-1}(x) \equiv A(x)^{p^m - 2} \mod P(x)$. Alternatively, the *Extended Euclidean Algorithm*, discussed in Section 6.5, may also be used to compute $A^{-1}(x) \mod P(x)$. Two excellent resources for more discussion on *Galois Field* arithmetic are [57] and [180].

5.2.2   Cryptosystem

Rijndael was submitted as an *AES* candidate algorithm by Joan Daemen and Vincent Rijmen [57]. The choice of *Rijndael* as an *AES* candidate algorithm finalist (and as the *Advanced Encryption Algorithm*) was due to the algorithm's fast key setup, low memory requirements, straightforward design, and ability to take advantage of parallel processing [215].

Rijndael maps plaintext into a rectangular $4 \times Nb$ array of bytes, as shown in Figure 5.17. *Nb* is defined as the block size divided by 32; for *AES*, *Nb* is set to four. The most significant byte of plaintext is mapped to $a_{0,0}$, and the next significant byte is mapped to $a_{1,0}$. The mapping continues, as the arrows indicate, with the least significant byte being mapped to $a_{3,3}$. Within a given byte in the array, $a_{r,c}$, the first number, r, refers to the row number and the second number, c, refers to the column number. Similarly, the *Cipher Key* is mapped into a rectangular $4 \times Nk$ array of bytes, as per Figure 5.17. *Nk* is defined as the key length divided by 32; for *AES*, *Nk* may be four, six, or eight for key lengths of 128, 192, and 256 bits, respectively.

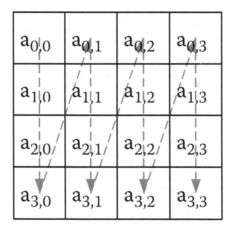

Figure 5.17: Rijndael Plaintext Mapping

The number of rounds required to encrypt or decrypt a 128-bit block, denoted as *Nr*, is based on the size of the *Cipher Key*. For key lengths of 128, 192, and 256 bits, *Nr* is set to ten, twelve, and fourteen rounds, respectively. Figure 5.18 details the *Rijndael* encryption round structure for a 128-bit *Cipher Key* and thus the number of rounds (*Nr*) is ten. For the first nine rounds, the round input passes through the *SubBytes*, *ShiftRows*, *MixColumns*, and *AddRoundKey* transformations. For round ten, the final round, the *MixColumns* transformation is eliminated.

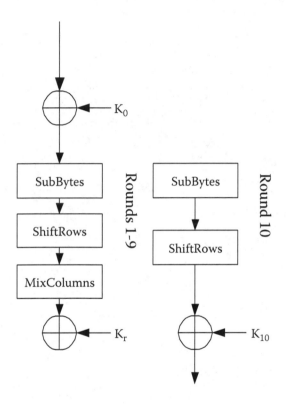

Figure 5.18: Rijndael Encryption Block Diagram

The input array is combined with K_0 via the XOR operation and then passed to the *SubBytes* transformation which performs a byte-wise substitution on each of the sixteen bytes of the array. The substitution is non-linear and invertible [57], and is also an example of Shannon's *Confusion* property. Each byte of the array is treated as an element of the *Extension Field GF(2^8)*. The *SubBytes* transformation performs an inversion of each byte $A(x)$

in the *Extension Field* $GF(2^8)$ using the *Irreducible Polynomial* $P(x) = x^8 + x^4 + x^3 + x + 1$, yielding $B(x) = A^{-1}(x) \bmod P(x)$. Note that 00_{16} is mapped to itself. The result of the inversion is then passed through the following affine transformation to produce the final output byte $C(x)$:

$$
\begin{pmatrix} c_0 \\ c_1 \\ c_2 \\ c_3 \\ c_4 \\ c_5 \\ c_6 \\ c_7 \end{pmatrix}
=
\begin{pmatrix}
1 & 1 & 1 & 1 & 1 & 0 & 0 & 0 \\
0 & 1 & 1 & 1 & 1 & 1 & 0 & 0 \\
0 & 0 & 1 & 1 & 1 & 1 & 1 & 0 \\
0 & 0 & 0 & 1 & 1 & 1 & 1 & 1 \\
1 & 0 & 0 & 0 & 1 & 1 & 1 & 1 \\
1 & 1 & 0 & 0 & 0 & 1 & 1 & 1 \\
1 & 1 & 1 & 0 & 0 & 0 & 1 & 1 \\
1 & 1 & 1 & 1 & 0 & 0 & 0 & 1
\end{pmatrix}
\begin{pmatrix} b_0 \\ b_1 \\ b_2 \\ b_3 \\ b_4 \\ b_5 \\ b_6 \\ b_7 \end{pmatrix}
+
\begin{pmatrix} 0 \\ 1 \\ 1 \\ 0 \\ 0 \\ 0 \\ 1 \\ 1 \end{pmatrix}. \quad (5.1)
$$

The *ShiftRows* transformation performs a byte-wise left rotation on the rows of the array output from the *SubBytes* transformation — see Figure 5.19. The first row, row 0, is not rotated, row 1 is rotated by one byte, row 2 by two bytes, and row 3 by three bytes, resulting in the values that were previously aligned by column now being aligned along a left diagonal. This operation is analogous to the data swapping characteristic of the Feistel structure found in other algorithms. However, it is important to note that *Rijndael* does not have a Feistel structure and thus one round of the cipher encrypts or decrypts the entire 128-bit block. As a result, *Rijndael* requires fewer rounds versus other block ciphers that do employ a Feistel structure.

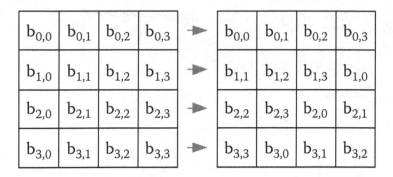

Figure 5.19: Rijndael ShiftRows Transformation

The *MixColumns* transformation operates on each column independently within the array output from the *ShiftRows* transformation. Within a given column, each byte is considered a polynomial over the *Extension Field* $GF(2^8)$. The *SubBytes* and *MixColumns* transformations are examples of Shannon's *Diffusion* property. Figure 5.20 depicts the *MixColumns* transformation with input column a and output column b.

$$
\begin{bmatrix} b_0 \\ b_1 \\ b_2 \\ b_3 \end{bmatrix} = \begin{bmatrix} 02 & 03 & 01 & 01 \\ 01 & 02 & 03 & 01 \\ 01 & 01 & 02 & 03 \\ 03 & 01 & 01 & 02 \end{bmatrix} \begin{bmatrix} a_0 \\ a_1 \\ a_2 \\ a_3 \end{bmatrix}
$$

Figure 5.20: Rijndael MixColumns Transformation

To illustrate the transformation, the output equation for b_0 is

$$ b_0 = (02 \times a_0) \oplus (03 \times a_1) \oplus (01 \times a_2) \oplus (01 \times a_3) $$

All multiplications and additions are in the *Extension Field* $GF(2^8)$. Addition within the *Extension Field* $GF(2^8)$ is defined as the bit-wise XOR of both arguments. As previously discussed in Section 5.2.1, multiplication in an *Extension Field* is dependent on the field polynomial. For *Rijndael*, the field polynomial is given as the *Irreducible Polynomial* [57]:

$$P(x) = x^8 + x^4 + x^3 + x + 1$$

Each constant matrix entry represents an element within the *Extension Field GF*(2^8); $01_{16} = 1$, $02_{16} = x$, and $03_{16} = x + 1$. The use of such small polynomials results in extremely efficient hardware implementations of the *MixColumns* transformation; for the *Extension Field GF*(2^8) with the *Irreducible Polynomial m*$(x) = x^8 + x^5 + x^3 + x^2 + 1$, the average optimized complexity of a constant multiplicr is 14.4 2-input XOR gates [240].

The final transformation, *AddRoundKey*, is the combination of the previous *MixColumns* or *ShiftRows* output with the round's associated sub-key via the XOR operation. The combination of the round ten output array with K_{10} via the XOR operation forms the final output array, i.e. the ciphertext.

Because *Rijndael* does not have a Feistel structure and thus one round of the cipher operates on the entire 128-bit block, each of the encryption transformations must be inverted as part of the decryption process. Figure 5.21 details the *Rijndael* decryption round structure for a 128-bit *Cipher Key* and thus the number of rounds (*Nr*) is once again ten. For the first round, the *InvMixColumns* function is eliminated, matching the functionality of round ten of encryption which does not use the *MixColumns* transformation. For rounds two through ten of decryption, the round input passes through the *AddRoundKey*, *InvMixColumns*, *InvShiftRows*, *InvSubBytes* transformations, once again matching the functionality of rounds two through nine of encryption.

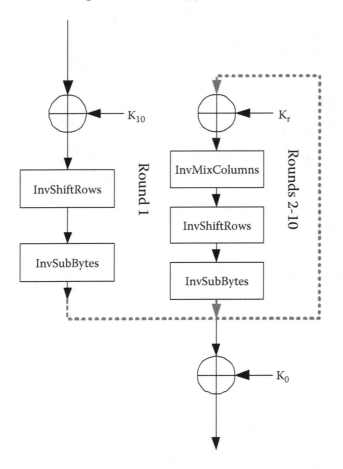

Figure 5.21: Rijndael Decryption Block Diagram

The *AddRoundKey* transformation for decryption is the same as for encryption, i.e. the combination of the previous *InvSubBytes* output with the round's associated sub-key via the XOR operation. *AddRoundKey* is its own inverse because $x_i \oplus z_i \oplus z_i = x_i$. This equation holds true because of the XOR properties $z_i \oplus z_i = 0$ and $x_i \oplus 0 = x_i$.

The *InvMixColumns* transformation operates on each column independently within the array output from the *AddRoundKey* transformation. Within a given column, each byte is considered a polynomial over the *Extension Field* $GF(2^8)$. Figure 5.22 depicts the *InvMixColumns* transformation with input column a and output column b.

$$\begin{bmatrix} b_0 \\ b_1 \\ b_2 \\ b_3 \end{bmatrix} = \begin{bmatrix} 0E & 0B & 0D & 09 \\ 09 & 0E & 0B & 0D \\ 0D & 09 & 0E & 0B \\ 0B & 0D & 09 & 0E \end{bmatrix} \begin{bmatrix} a_0 \\ a_1 \\ a_2 \\ a_3 \end{bmatrix}$$

Figure 5.22: Rijndael InvMixColumns Transformation

The same *Irreducible Polynomial* is used for both encryption and decryption:

$$P(x) = x^8 + x^4 + x^3 + x + 1$$

The *InvShiftRows* transformation performs a byte-wise right rotation on the rows of the array output from the *InvMixColumns* transformation — see Figure 5.23. The first row, row 0, is not rotated, row 1 is rotated by one byte, row 2 by two bytes, and row 3 by three bytes, resulting in the values that were previously aligned by column now being aligned along a right diagonal.

$b_{0,0}$	$b_{0,1}$	$b_{0,2}$	$b_{0,3}$	➡	$b_{0,0}$	$b_{0,1}$	$b_{0,2}$	$b_{0,3}$
$b_{1,1}$	$b_{1,2}$	$b_{1,3}$	$b_{1,0}$	➡	$b_{1,3}$	$b_{1,0}$	$b_{1,1}$	$b_{1,2}$
$b_{2,2}$	$b_{2,3}$	$b_{2,0}$	$b_{2,1}$	➡	$b_{2,2}$	$b_{2,3}$	$b_{2,0}$	$b_{2,1}$
$b_{3,3}$	$b_{3,0}$	$b_{3,1}$	$b_{3,2}$	➡	$b_{3,1}$	$b_{3,2}$	$b_{3,3}$	$b_{3,0}$

Figure 5.23: Rijndael InvShiftRows Transformation

The *InvSubBytes* transformation performs a byte-wise substitution on each of the sixteen bytes of the output from the *InvShiftRows* transformation. Each byte of the input array is treated as an element of the *Extension Field GF(2^8)*. The *InvSubBytes* transformation passes the input array through the inverse of the affine transformation performed as part of the *SubBytes* transformation during encryption. The result from the inverse affine transformation is then inverted in the *Extension Field GF(2^8)* using the *Irreducible Polynomial P(x)* $= x^8 + x^4 + x^3 + x + 1$ to produce the final output byte. The output from round ten is combined with K_0 via the XOR operation to form the final output array, i.e. the plaintext.

Key Expansion is used to expand the *Rijndael Cipher Key* into a *Key Schedule*, generating $Nb \cdot (Nr + 1)$ 4-byte words termed the *Expanded Key* as shown in Table 5.17.

Key Size in Bits	Nb	Nr	Nk	4-Byte Round Keys
128	4	10	4	11
192	4	12	6	13
256	4	14	8	15

Table 5.17: Rijndael Key Expansion Data

AES Key Expansion proceeds as follows [227]:

1. The *Cipher Key* is copied into the first *Nk* 4-byte words of the *Expanded Key*.

2. The *Round Constant Word Array*, denoted as *Rcon*, is indexed via an iteration counter variable, denoted as i, that is initialized to one. Each $Rcon[i] = 2^i \ mod \ P(x)$ where $P(x) = x^8 + x^4 + x^3 + x + 1$ is the *Rijndael Irreducible Polynomial*.

3. The following sequence of steps is repeated until the remaining $(Nb \cdot (Nr + 1)) - Nk$ 4-byte words of the *Expanded Key* have been filled:

   (a) To create the next 4-byte word of the *Expanded Key*, the previous 4-byte word of the *Expanded Key* is rotated one byte to the left.

   (b) The *SubBytes* transformation is applied to each byte of the 4-byte word output from Step 3a.

   (c) The least significant byte of the 4-byte word output from Step 3b is combined with *Rcon[i]* via the XOR operation.

   (d) The *Round Constant Word Array* index i is incremented.

(e) The 4-byte word $Nk \cdot 4$ bytes before the new 4-byte word of the *Expanded Key* is combined with the 4-byte word output from Step 3c via the XOR operation. The result is assigned to the next 4-byte word of the *Expanded Key*.

(f) The following sequence of steps is repeated three times:

    i. To create the next 4-byte word of the *Expanded Key*, the 4-byte word $Nk \cdot 4$ bytes before the new 4-byte word of the *Expanded Key* is combined with the previous 4-byte word of the *Expanded Key* via the XOR operation.

    ii. The output from Step 3f (i) is assigned to the next 4-byte word of the *Expanded Key*.

(g) If $Nk \cdot 32$ (the size of each round's sub-key) is 256, the following sequence of steps is performed to create the next 4-byte word of the *Expanded Key*:

    i. The *SubBytes* transformation is applied to the previous 4-byte word of the *Expanded Key*.

    ii. The 4-byte word 32 bytes before the new 4-byte word of the *Expanded Key* is combined with the 4-byte word output from Step 3g (i) via the XOR operation.

    iii. The output from Step 3g (ii) is assigned to the next 4-byte word of the *Expanded Key*.

(h) If $Nk \cdot 32$ (the size of each round's sub-key) is 256, the following sequence of steps is performed three times. If $Nk \cdot 32$ is 192, the following sequence of steps is performed twice.

i. To create the next 4-byte word of the *Expanded Key*, the 4-byte word $Nk \cdot 4$ bytes before the new 4-byte word of the *Expanded Key* is combined with the previous 4-byte word of the *Expanded Key* via the XOR operation.

ii. The output from Step 3h (i) is assigned to the next 4-byte word of the *Expanded Key*.

5.2.3   Modes of Operation

NIST has published its recommendations for *AES* (or any other block cipher) modes of operation, defining four specific categories [214]:

1. **Confidentiality Modes**: These modes are used to provide confidentiality via encryption and include *ECB*, *CBC*, *CFB*, *OFB*, and *CTR* modes [75], as discussed in Section 5.1.3.

2. **Authentication Mode**: This mode specifies a *Message Authentication Code* (MAC) that is block cipher based and is termed *CMAC* mode [77]. See Section 10.3 for a discussion of *Message Authentication Codes*.

3. **Authenticated Encryption Mode**: This mode employs *CTR* mode for confidentiality and uses *CBC* mode for message authentication and thus is termed *CCM* mode [76].

4. **Parallelizable Authenticated Encryption Mode**: This mode specifies *Galois/Counter* (GCM) mode for *AES*, using

CTR mode for confidentiality and a *Hash Function* for message authentication. Note that *GCM* mode is still in draft form and has not yet been fully approved by NIST [214]. See Section 10.2 for a discussion of *Hash Functions*.

5.2.3.1   Cipher-Based Message Authentication Code Mode

Cipher-Based Message Authentication Code (CMAC) mode is intended for use in systems where a NIST-approved block cipher is more readily available versus a NIST-approved *Hash Function*. *CMAC* mode is used to generate a *MAC* used to verify the integrity of the data being transmitted. *CMAC* mode operation is approved by NIST for use with two block ciphers, *AES* and *Triple-DES*, and is composed of three processes: *Sub-Key Generation*, *MAC Generation*, and *MAC Verification* [77].

Sub-Key Generation begins by using the master key k and an input block of zero to compute $y = e_k(0)$, where e is the encryption function of the block cipher. If the most significant bit of y is a zero, $k_1 = y << 1$, where the $<<$ operator is defined as a left shift by the number of bits specified by the value that follows the $<<$ operator, with emptied positions filled with zeros. If the most significant bit of y is a one, $k_1 = (y << 1) \oplus R_b$. When using *AES*, R_b is defined as a 128-bit value whose 120 most significant bits are set to zero and whose least significant bits are set to 10000111_2. When using *Triple-DES*, R_b is defined as a 64-bit value whose 59 most significant bits are set to zero and whose least significant bits are set to 11011_2. Once k_1 has been computed, it is then used to compute k_2. If the most significant bit of k_1 is a zero, $k_2 = k_1 << 1$. If the most significant bit of k_1 is a one, $k_2 = (k_1 << 1) \oplus R_b$.

Once the sub-keys k_1 and k_2 have been generated, *MAC Generation* begins by dividing the message M into n blocks where $n = \lceil \frac{M}{b} \rceil$ and b is the block size of the block cipher. Therefore, the message M is the concatenation of the n blocks M_i, i.e. $M = M_1 \| M_2 \| \ldots \| M_{n-1} \| M_n^*$. If M_n^* is a complete block, i.e. M is evenly divisible by b, $M_n = M_n^* \oplus k_1$. If M_n^* is not a complete block, i.e. M is not evenly divisible by b, it must be padded to form a complete block. This is achieved by concatenating M_n^* with a one followed by j zeros, i.e. $(M_n^* \| 100\ldots00_2)$, where $j = (M \bmod b) - 1$, and then $M_n = (M_n^* \| 100\ldots00_2) \oplus k_2$. Using the master key k and an initial value $C_0 = 0$, $C_i = e_k(C_{i-1} \oplus M_i)$ is then computed for each of the n blocks of M. The T most significant bits of C_n are then used as the *MAC* of M.

MAC Verification follows from *MAC Generation*. Upon receipt, the message M is used to generate the *MAC* T', following the process described above, and T' is compared to the received *MAC* T. If $T = T'$ then the *MAC* T is considered to be valid, verifying the integrity of the transmitted message M. If $T \neq T'$ then the *MAC* T is considered to be invalid, and the transmitted message M is not considered authentic and thus should be discarded.

The computation of $C_i = e_k(C_{i-1} \oplus M_i)$ applies *CBC* mode chaining to the message M to generate the *MAC* T as shown in Figures 5.24 and 5.25 for the cases where M_n^* is a complete block and M_n^* requires padding, respectively.

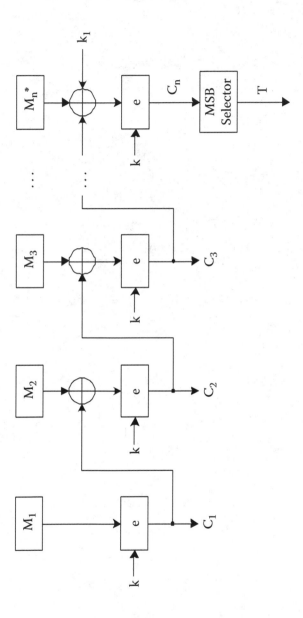

Figure 5.24: Message Authentication Code Generation — No Padding of M_n^*

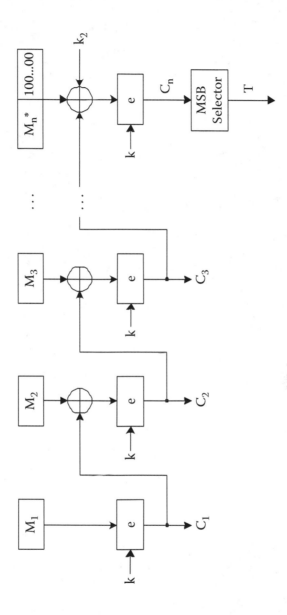

Figure 5.25: Message Authentication Code Generation — Padded M_n^*

The length of the *MAC T* impacts an attacker's ability to guess the correct value of T for a message M. Increasing the length of T increases the difficulty of performing a *Guessing* attack but also increases the storage requirements of the *MAC*. NIST recommends a minimum length of 64 bits for the *MAC T* to protect against *Guessing* attacks. NIST also states that the number of failed verification attempts for a master key k must be limited to prevent systematic guessing of the *MAC T* for a given message M. Whereas other system limitations, such as the duration of the session or the communication channel bandwidth, may prevent repeated *Guessing* attacks, the length of the *MAC T* should be computed based on two parameters:

1. The largest acceptable probability that a message M' that is not authentic will successfully verify, denoted by the parameter P_V.

2. The largest number of failed verification attempts for a master key k before k is retired from use, denoted by the parameter F.

From these two parameters, the length of the *MAC T* may be computed as:

$$T_L \;\geq\; log_2 \frac{F}{P_V}$$

Example 5.9: *AES* is used in *CMAC* mode. The system will retire a key after 32 failed verification attempts and is able to tolerate a false verification approximately once in a billion attempts. Compute the minimum length for the *MAC T*.

Based on the problem description, $P_V \approx 2^{-30}$ and $F = 2^5$. Therefore, the minimum length of the *MAC T* is computed as:

$$
\begin{aligned}
T_L &\geq log_2 \frac{F}{P_V} \\
T_L &\geq log_2(\frac{2^5}{2^{-30}}) \\
T_L &\geq log_2(2^{35}) \\
T_L &\geq 35
\end{aligned}
$$

Therefore, the minimum length of the *MAC T* is 35 bits.

Another concern that arises with the use of *CMAC* mode is that an attacker may find two messages, M and M', that yield the same C_n and thus the same *MAC*. This possibility exists because the size of the message space is significantly larger than the size of the *MAC* space and thus multiple messages must map to the same *MAC*. The existence of a multiple mapping therefore depends on the number of messages for which a *MAC* is generated using the same master key k relative to b, the block size of the block cipher.

Specifically, the existence of a multiple mapping is anticipated to occur if there are $2^{\frac{b}{2}}$ messages, i.e. 2^{32} messages if *Triple-DES* is used and 2^{64} messages if *AES* is used. As a result, NIST recommends that *CMAC* mode be applied to no more than 2^{21} messages when using *Triple-DES* and 2^{48} messages when using *AES* before retiring the master key k. These limits result in the probability of a multiple mapping occurring being less than 2^{-20} when *Triple-DES* is used and less than 2^{-30} when *AES* is used as the underlying block cipher. If even greater security is required, the limits may be applied to total message blocks instead of total messages.

It is important to note that *CMAC* mode does not protect against *Replay* attacks, where an attacker captures a message M with its valid *MAC* and then resends the message at some later time. Protection against such an attack must be provided at the protocol level by embedding information in the message M that uniquely identifies the message. Viable unique identifiers include sequence numbers, time-stamps, or nonces, each of which may be used by a message recipient to determine if a *Replay* attack has occurred.

5.2.3.2   Counter with Cipher Block Chaining-Message Authentication Code Mode

Counter with Cipher Block Chaining-Message Authentication Code (CCM) mode is intended for use in systems where all of the data is available prior to its use. *CCM* mode is only approved for use with block ciphers with 128-bit block sizes, and the only block cipher of that type that has been approved by NIST for use in *CCM* mode is *AES*. *CCM* mode accepts a three-part input [76]:

1. Data that will be authenticated and encrypted. This data is termed the *Payload*.

2. *Associated Information*, such as a header, that will only be authenticated, not encrypted.

3. A unique value assigned to the *Payload* and the *Associated Information*. This value is termed the *Nonce*.

CCM mode applies *CBC* mode with an *Initialization Vector* of zero to the *Payload, Associated Information*, and the *Nonce* to generate a *MAC*. This method of *MAC* generation for authentication is termed CBC-MAC and is only approved by NIST for use in *CCM* mode. Once the *MAC* has been generated, *CCM* mode then uses *CTR* mode to encrypt the *Payload* and the *MAC* to create the ciphertext, using the same key to create the *MAC* and the ciphertext. Upon receipt, the ciphertext is decrypted using *CTR* mode, and then *CBC* mode is applied to the decrypted *Payload, Associated Information*, and *Nonce* to generate a new *MAC* to compare with the decrypted *MAC*. If the two *MACs* match, then verification is successful; otherwise, the transmitted message is not considered authentic and thus should be discarded. Note that the *Associated Information* is optional and the *Nonce* must be non-repeating over the life of the key though it is not required to be random. Finally, NIST recommends that *CCM* mode be applied to no more than 2^{61} messages over the life of the key.

CCM mode formats the *Payload, Associated Information*, and the *Nonce* into a sequence of data blocks denoted as B_0, B_1, ..., B_r based on a formatting function which must adhere to the following three properties:

1. The *Nonce* is uniquely determined by the first block, B_0.

2. The first block, B_0, is distinct from any counter blocks used across all applications of *CCM* mode for a given key. Therefore, the formatting and counter generation functions should be co-designed due to their interdependence.

3. The *Payload* and *Associated Information* are uniquely determined by the formatted data such that no two blocks B_i and B_i' are the same if the same *Nonce* is used with two different *Payloads* and *Associated Information*.

The formatting function for *CCM* mode requires that the bit lengths of the *Payload, Associated Information*, and the *Nonce* be a multiple of eight bits. These bit lengths are denoted by the parameters p, a, and n. By extension, the *MAC T* must also be a multiple of eight bits in length and the length is denoted by the parameter t. p is represented within the first block of formatted data as the string Q which is also a multiple of eight bits whose length is denoted as q. Q is the binary representation of p in q 8-bit groupings. The parameter length requirements are:

1. t must be 4, 6, 8, 10, 12, 14, or 16, representing the number of bytes in the *MAC T*.

2. q must be 2, 3, 4, 5, 6, 7, or 8, representing the number of bytes in Q.

3. n must be 7, 8, 9, 10, 11, 12, or 13, representing the number of bytes in the *Nonce*.

4. $n + q = 15$.

5. $a < 2^{64}$.

q determines the maximum *Payload* length because $p < 2^{8q}$, resulting in $P < 2^{8q-4}$ 128-bit blocks. q also determines the length of the *Nonce* because $n = 15 - q$ and thus the number of unique *Nonce* values is 2^{8n}. As a result, a tradeoff must be made between the number of messages to which *CCM* mode is applied over the life of the key versus the maximum *Payload* length for these messages.

Example 5.10: If the size of the *Payload* in *CCM* mode is 2,048 bits and there are two 8-bit groupings used to represent Q, what is the value of Q?

If $P = 2,048$ then $p = 256$. Given that $q = 2$, the *Payload* is represented by $Q = 0000000100000000_2$.

The first byte of the first block, B_0, contains four control flags. Bit 7 is *Reserved* to enable future formatting extensions and must be set to zero. Bit 6 represents the *Adata* field and is set to one if $a > 0$ (the *Associated Information* is present); otherwise, it is set to zero. Bits 5-3 represent the encoded *MAC* length. The *MAC* length t is encoded as $\frac{t-2}{2}$. Because the maximum value of t is sixteen, the maximum value of the encoding is $\frac{16-2}{2} = 4$ which fits within the 3-bit field. Bits 2-0 represent the encoded value of q. q is encoded as $q - 1$, resulting in values between one and seven and thus fitting within the 3-bit field. The remaining bytes of B_0 are used to represent the *Nonce* and Q. Bytes 1-$(15 - q)$ are dedicated to the *Nonce* and bytes $(16 - q)$-16 are dedicated to Q. Therefore, the first block B_0 indicates if there will be *Associated Information*, the *MAC* length, the size of the *Payload*, and the *Nonce*.

If $a = 0$ is indicated by the *Adata* field in block B_0, then no formatted data blocks are assigned to the *Associated Information*. If $a > 0$ then a is encoded based on its size. If $0 < a < 2^{16} - 2^8$, then a is represented as a 2-byte binary value. If $2^{16} - 2^8 \leq a < 2^{32}$, then a is represented as a 6-byte value of the form $FFFE_{16}$ as the most significant bytes concatenated with a represented as a 4-byte binary value. Finally, if $2^{32} \leq a < 2^{64}$, then a is represented as a 10-byte value of the form $FFFF_{16}$ as the most significant bytes concatenated with a represented as an 8-byte binary value. The encoded a is then concatenated with the *Associated Information* followed by the minimum number of bits, all set to zero, necessary to partition the entire string into 16-byte blocks denoted as B_1, B_2, ..., B_u, where the value of u depends on a.

Example 5.11: What is the encoding of a for $a = 2^7$, 2^{18}, and 2^{35}?

If $a = 2^7$ then a is encoded as two bytes:

$$00000000 \ 10000000_2$$

If $a = 2^{18}$ then a is encoded as six bytes:

$$11111111 \ 11111110 \ 00000000 \ 00000100 \ 00000000 \ 00000000_2$$

If $a = 2^{35}$ then a is encoded as ten bytes:

$$11111111 \ 11111111 \ 00000000 \ 00000000 \ 00000000$$
$$00001000 \ 00000000 \ 00000000 \ 00000000 \ 00000000_2$$

For distinct values of a, the most significant bits of the encoding of a are distinct. If $0 < a < 2^{16} - 2^8$, then the first byte of the encoding of a cannot be FF_{16} as is the case if $2^{16} - 2^8 \leq a < 2^{32}$. If $2^{16} - 2^8 \leq a < 2^{32}$, then the first two bytes of the encoding of a cannot be $FFFF_{16}$ as is the case if $2^{32} \leq a < 2^{64}$. Encodings of a not specified by the three conditions (such as when the first two bytes are 0000_{16}, $FF00_{16}$, or $FF01_{16}$) are reserved.

The *Associated Information* (or, if no *Associated Information* is present, then B_0) is followed by the *Payload* blocks. The *Payload* is followed by the minimum number of bits, all set to zero, necessary to partition the entire string into 16-byte blocks denoted as B_{u+1}, B_{u+2}, $\ldots$, B_r, where $r = u + \lceil \frac{p}{16} \rceil$.

The first byte of the counter blocks, CTR_0, contains one control flag. Bits 7-6 are *Reserved* to enable future formatting extensions and must be set to zero. Bits 5-3 are also set to zero to ensure all counter blocks are distinct from B_0. Bits 2-0 represent the encoded value of q that is also contained in B_0. q is encoded as $q - 1$, resulting in values between one and seven and thus fitting within the 3-bit field. Bytes 1-$(15 - q)$ are dedicated to the *Nonce* and bytes $(16 - q)$-15 are dedicated to the counter index i.

CCM mode authentication determines if a ciphertext is legitimate, i.e. it is the output of the *MAC* generation process for the *Payload*, *Associated Information*, and *Nonce* for the key currently in use. The length of the *MAC T* impacts an attacker's ability to guess a value for a legitimate ciphertext. An attacker may be able to choose the ciphertext such that every bit of the corresponding

Payload can be controlled [259]. By definition, successful *CCM* mode verification assures that the *Payload* and *Associated Information* originated from a source with access to the key. However, because of the attack detailed in [259], it is critical to note that the *Payload* contents are not evidence of the authenticity of the *Payload*. Moreover, *CCM* mode does not protect against *Replay* attacks, where an attacker captures a legitimate ciphertext and then resends it at some later time. Protection against such an attack must be provided at the protocol level through methods such as sequentially numbering legitimate messages.

Increasing the length of T increases the difficulty of performing a *Guessing* attack but also increases the storage requirements of the ciphertext. NIST recommends a minimum length of 64 bits for the *MAC* T to protect against *Guessing* attacks unless the protocol limits the number of failed verification attempts for a given key. Although other system limitations, such as the duration of the session or the communication channel bandwidth, may prevent repeated *Guessing* attacks, the length of the *MAC* T should be computed based on two parameters:

1. The largest acceptable probability that a message that is not authentic will successfully verify, denoted by the parameter P_V.

2. The largest number of failed verification attempts for a key before the key is retired from use, denoted by the parameter F.

From these two parameters, the length of the *MAC T* may be computed as:

$$T_L \; \geq \; log_2 \frac{F}{P_V}$$

Example 5.12: *AES* is used in *CCM* mode. The system will retire a key after 2^{32} failed verification attempts and is able to tolerate a false verification approximately once in a billion attempts. Compute the minimum length for the *MAC T*.

Based on the problem description, $P_V \approx 2^{-30}$ and $F = 2^{32}$. Therefore, the minimum length of the *MAC T* is computed as:

$$T_L \; \geq \; log_2 \frac{F}{P_V}$$
$$T_L \; \geq \; log_2(\frac{2^{32}}{2^{-30}})$$
$$T_L \; \geq \; log_2(2^{62})$$
$$T_L \; \geq \; 62$$

Therefore, the minimum length of the *MAC T* is 62 bits.

5.2.4 Efficient Implementation

Rijndael software performance bottlenecks typically occur in the *SubBytes* and *MixColumns* transformations, one or both of which are usually implemented via 8-bit to 8-bit look-up tables. Often most of the *Rijndael* round transformations — *SubBytes*, *ShiftRows*, and *MixColumns* — are combined into large look-up tables termed *T tables*. Such implementations require up to three *T tables* whose size may be either 1 KB or 4 KB where the smaller tables require performing an additional rotation operation. The goal of the *T tables* is to avoid performing the *MixColumns* and *InvMixColumns* transformations because these operations perform *Galois Field* fixed field constant multiplication, an operation which maps poorly to general purpose processors. However, the use of *T tables* has significant disadvantages. The *T tables* significantly increase code size, their performance is dependent on the memory system architecture as well as cache size, and their use causes *Key Expansion* for *Rijndael* decryption to become significantly more complex. As an alternative to the *T tables* implementation method, it is also feasible to have the processor perform all of the *Rijndael* round transformations. Row-based implementations have been demonstrated to allow for greater efficiency in the implementation of the *MixColumns* and *InvMixColumns* transformations versus column-based implementations. However, the *SubBytes* transformation remains as a bottleneck, requiring separate 256-byte look-up tables for encryption and decryption [19, 27, 57, 58, 251, 263, 307].

Numerous co-processors have been developed to accelerate cryptographic algorithm implementations. The CryptoManiac VLIW co-processor was developed as a result of instruction set extensions designed to accelerate the performance of a number of the *AES* candidate algorithms. CryptoManiac features the execution of up to four instructions per cycle and the use of instructions with up to three operands to allow for the combination of short latency instructions for single cycle execution. Similarly, the Cryptonite co-processor is also VLIW based, with two 64-bit datapaths and special instructions combined with dedicated memories to support *Rijndael* implementations. Both co-processors improve the performance of *Rijndael* implementations versus implementations targeting general purpose processors. Other implementations couple FPGA co-processors with a LEON-2 processor core. The co-processors connect to the processor core either via a dedicated interface or as a memory-mapped peripheral and were able to significantly improve the performance of *Rijndael* implementations [39, 125, 234, 271, 331].

Multiple implementations of *Rijndael* have been presented targeting a wide range of hardware technologies. These implementations use specific *Galois Field* fixed field constant multipliers, resulting in either logic equations or look-up tables being generated to perform the multiplication. Implementations based on logic equations are optimized for area and require a moderate number of logic levels. Implementations based on look-up tables are optimized for speed at the cost of additional logic resources though the performance of these implementations, like the software implementations employing *T tables*, is highly dependent on the memory system and cache organization and size. In the case of the *Galois Field* fixed field constant multipliers used in the *Mix-Columns* transformation, the 8-bit to 8-bit look-up tables may be replaced by 8-bit × 8-bit mapping matrices, reducing the associated memory requirements by a factor of nearly 20 [83, 84]. Look-up tables may also be replaced with logic equation implementations for the *SubBytes* and *MixColumns* transformations, significantly reducing the hardware resource requirements. To illustrate the significant reduction in logic resource requirements, in the case of the *SubBytes* transformation, a reduction in gate count by as much as a factor 4.66 has been realized using logic equations in place of a look-up table. When performing sixteen *SubBytes* transformations in parallel in a single round of *Rijndael* (assuming a 128-bit implementation), this equates to a savings of over 38,000 gate equivalences. For a pipelined implementation of 128-bit *AES*, this savings increases to over 380,000 gate equivalences [263]. Encryption, decryption, and *Key Scheduling* are all easily pipelined in non-feedback modes of operation, whereas single-round implementations are typically used when operating in feedback modes. Depending on the implementation methodology, *Rijndael* throughputs as high as 70 Gbps when operating in non-feedback modes and 2.29 Gbps when operating in feedback modes have been reported [82, 85, 86, 102, 124, 126, 131, 144, 175, 179, 199, 245, 265, 299, 300, 325, 326, 334, 338].

An interesting alternative to implementations based on large look-up tables has been proposed in [82, 83, 84]. The goal of the *AES Galois Field* fixed field constant multiplication is to perform the *MixColumns* and *InvMixColumns* transformations over the representative *Galois Field* $\text{GF}(2^8)$. Note that $[A_3 : A_0]$ are the input bytes and $[B_3 : B_0]$ are the output bytes:

$$
\begin{pmatrix} B_0 \\ B_1 \\ B_2 \\ B_3 \end{pmatrix} = \begin{pmatrix} K_{00} & K_{01} & K_{02} & K_{03} \\ K_{10} & K_{11} & K_{12} & K_{13} \\ K_{20} & K_{21} & K_{22} & K_{23} \\ K_{30} & K_{31} & K_{32} & K_{33} \end{pmatrix} \begin{pmatrix} A_0 \\ A_1 \\ A_2 \\ A_3 \end{pmatrix} \tag{5.2}
$$

The core operation in this fixed field multiplication is an 8-bit inner product that must be performed sixteen times, four per row. The four inner products of each row are then combined via the XOR operation to form the final output word. For a known primitive polynomial $p(x)$, $k(x)$ (representing the 8-bit constant), and a generic input $a(x)$, we create a polynomial equation of the form $b(x) = a(x) \times k(x) \mod p(x)$ where each coefficient of $b(x)$ is a function of $a(x)$. This results in an 8-bit $\times$ 8-bit matrix representing the coefficients of $b(x)$ in terms of $a(x)$ [82]. To illustrate the creation of this matrix, the following example is provided. Let:

$$
\begin{aligned}
k(x) &= (02)_{16} = (00000010)_2 = x \\
p(x) &= x^8 + x^4 + x^3 + x + 1 \\
a(x) &= a_7 x^7 + a_6 x^6 + a_5 x^5 + a_4 x^4 + a_3 x^3 + a_2 x^2 + a_1 x + a_0
\end{aligned}
$$

Therefore, we see that:

$$b(x) = a_7x^8 + a_6x^7 + a_5x^6 + a_4x^5 + a_3x^4 + a_2x^3 + a_1x^2 + a_0x \ mod \ p(x)$$

Reducing modulo $p(x)$ results in:

$$b(x) = a_6x^7 + a_5x^6 + a_4x^5 + [a_7 + a_3]x^4 + [a_7 + a_2]x^3 + a_1x^2 + [a_7 + a_0]x + a_7$$

This yields the resultant mapping:

$$\begin{pmatrix} b_0 \\ b_1 \\ b_2 \\ b_3 \\ b_4 \\ b_5 \\ b_6 \\ b_7 \end{pmatrix} = \begin{pmatrix} 0 & 0 & 0 & 0 & 0 & 0 & 0 & 1 \\ 1 & 0 & 0 & 0 & 0 & 0 & 0 & 1 \\ 0 & 1 & 0 & 0 & 0 & 0 & 0 & 0 \\ 0 & 0 & 1 & 0 & 0 & 0 & 0 & 1 \\ 0 & 0 & 0 & 1 & 0 & 0 & 0 & 1 \\ 0 & 0 & 0 & 0 & 1 & 0 & 0 & 0 \\ 0 & 0 & 0 & 0 & 0 & 1 & 0 & 0 \\ 0 & 0 & 0 & 0 & 0 & 0 & 1 & 0 \end{pmatrix} \begin{pmatrix} a_0 \\ a_1 \\ a_2 \\ a_3 \\ a_4 \\ a_5 \\ a_6 \\ a_7 \end{pmatrix} \qquad (5.3)$$

An 8-bit $\times$ 8-bit matrix must be generated for each K_{xy}, resulting in a total of sixteen matrices. Note that this analysis holds true for *Galois Field* other than GF(2^8), with corresponding adjustments to the mapping matrix used to calculate $b(x) = a(x) \times k(x) \ mod \ p(x)$.

Based on this methodology, 8-bit $\times$ 8-bit mapping matrices may be constructed for the *Galois Field* fixed field constant multiplications performed as part of the *AES MixColumns* and *InvMixColumns* transformations. The resultant $b(x) = a(x) \times k(x) \ mod \ p(x)$, and the final 8-bit $\times$ 8-bit mapping matrices for the constants associated with the *MixColumns* transformation are:

$$
\begin{aligned}
k(x) &= (01)_{16} = (00000001)_2 = 1 \\
b(x) &= a_7 x^7 + a_6 x^6 + a_5 x^5 + a_4 x^4 + a_3 x^3 + a_2 x^2 + a_1 x + \\
&\quad a_0 \ mod \ p(x)
\end{aligned}
$$

$$
\begin{pmatrix} b_0 \\ b_1 \\ b_2 \\ b_3 \\ b_4 \\ b_5 \\ b_6 \\ b_7 \end{pmatrix}
=
\begin{pmatrix}
1 & 0 & 0 & 0 & 0 & 0 & 0 & 0 \\
0 & 1 & 0 & 0 & 0 & 0 & 0 & 0 \\
0 & 0 & 1 & 0 & 0 & 0 & 0 & 0 \\
0 & 0 & 0 & 1 & 0 & 0 & 0 & 0 \\
0 & 0 & 0 & 0 & 1 & 0 & 0 & 0 \\
0 & 0 & 0 & 0 & 0 & 1 & 0 & 0 \\
0 & 0 & 0 & 0 & 0 & 0 & 1 & 0 \\
0 & 0 & 0 & 0 & 0 & 0 & 0 & 1
\end{pmatrix}
\begin{pmatrix} a_0 \\ a_1 \\ a_2 \\ a_3 \\ a_4 \\ a_5 \\ a_6 \\ a_7 \end{pmatrix}
\qquad (5.4)
$$

$$k(x) = (03)_{16} = (00000011)_2 = x + 1$$

$$b(x) = [a_7 + a_6]x^7 + [a_6 + a_5]x^6 + [a_5 + a_4]x^5 + [a_7 + a_4 + a_3]x^4 +$$
$$[a_7 + a_3 + a_2]x^3 + [a_2 + a_1]x^2 + [a_7 + a_1 + a_0]x +$$
$$[a_7 + a_0]$$

$$
\begin{pmatrix} b_0 \\ b_1 \\ b_2 \\ b_3 \\ b_4 \\ b_5 \\ b_6 \\ b_7 \end{pmatrix}
=
\begin{pmatrix}
1 & 0 & 0 & 0 & 0 & 0 & 0 & 1 \\
1 & 1 & 0 & 0 & 0 & 0 & 0 & 1 \\
0 & 1 & 1 & 0 & 0 & 0 & 0 & 0 \\
0 & 0 & 1 & 1 & 0 & 0 & 0 & 1 \\
0 & 0 & 0 & 1 & 1 & 0 & 0 & 1 \\
0 & 0 & 0 & 0 & 1 & 1 & 0 & 0 \\
0 & 0 & 0 & 0 & 0 & 1 & 1 & 0 \\
0 & 0 & 0 & 0 & 0 & 0 & 1 & 1
\end{pmatrix}
\begin{pmatrix} a_0 \\ a_1 \\ a_2 \\ a_3 \\ a_4 \\ a_5 \\ a_6 \\ a_7 \end{pmatrix}
\qquad (5.5)
$$

Note that the matrix for $k(x) = (02)_{16} = (00000010)_2 = x$ was provided as part of the example. Similarly, for the values for each K_{xy} in the *InvMixColumns* transformation, the resultant $b(x) = a(x) \times k(x) \bmod p(x)$ and the final 8-bit $\times$ 8-bit mapping matrices are:

$$k(x) \;=\; (09)_{16} = (00001001)_2 = x^3 + 1$$

$$
\begin{aligned}
b(x) \;=\;& [a_7 + a_4]x^7 + [a_7 + a_6 + a_3]x^6 + [a_7 + a_6 + a_5 + a_2]x^5 + \\
& [a_6 + a_5 + a_4 + a_1]x^4 + [a_7 + a_5 + a_3 + a_0]x^3 + \\
& [a_7 + a_6 + a_2]x^2 + [a_6 + a_5 + a_1]x + [a_5 + a_0]
\end{aligned}
$$

$$
\begin{pmatrix}
b_0 \\ b_1 \\ b_2 \\ b_3 \\ b_4 \\ b_5 \\ b_6 \\ b_7
\end{pmatrix}
=
\begin{pmatrix}
1 & 0 & 0 & 0 & 0 & 1 & 0 & 0 \\
0 & 1 & 0 & 0 & 0 & 1 & 1 & 0 \\
0 & 0 & 1 & 0 & 0 & 0 & 1 & 1 \\
1 & 0 & 0 & 1 & 0 & 1 & 0 & 1 \\
0 & 1 & 0 & 0 & 1 & 1 & 1 & 0 \\
0 & 0 & 1 & 0 & 0 & 1 & 1 & 1 \\
0 & 0 & 0 & 1 & 0 & 0 & 1 & 1 \\
0 & 0 & 0 & 0 & 1 & 0 & 0 & 1
\end{pmatrix}
\begin{pmatrix}
a_0 \\ a_1 \\ a_2 \\ a_3 \\ a_4 \\ a_5 \\ a_6 \\ a_7
\end{pmatrix}
\tag{5.6}
$$

$$k(x) \;=\; (0B)_{16} = (00001011)_2 = x^3 + x + 1$$

$$
\begin{aligned}
b(x) \;=\;& [a_7 + a_6 + a_4]x^7 + [a_7 + a_6 + a_5 + a_3]x^6 + \\
& [a_7 + a_6 + a_5 + a_4 + a_2]x^5 + \\
& [a_7 + a_6 + a_5 + a_4 + a_3 + a_1]x^4 + [a_5 + a_3 + a_2 + a_0]x^3 + \\
& [a_7 + a_6 + a_2 + a_1]x^2 + \\
& [a_7 + a_6 + a_5 + a_1 + a_0]x + [a_7 + a_5 + a_0]
\end{aligned}
$$

$$\begin{pmatrix} b_0 \\ b_1 \\ b_2 \\ b_3 \\ b_4 \\ b_5 \\ b_6 \\ b_7 \end{pmatrix} = \begin{pmatrix} 1 & 0 & 0 & 0 & 0 & 1 & 0 & 1 \\ 1 & 1 & 0 & 0 & 0 & 1 & 1 & 1 \\ 0 & 1 & 1 & 0 & 0 & 0 & 1 & 1 \\ 1 & 0 & 1 & 1 & 0 & 1 & 0 & 0 \\ 0 & 1 & 0 & 1 & 1 & 1 & 1 & 1 \\ 0 & 0 & 1 & 0 & 1 & 1 & 1 & 1 \\ 0 & 0 & 0 & 1 & 0 & 1 & 1 & 1 \\ 0 & 0 & 0 & 0 & 1 & 0 & 1 & 1 \end{pmatrix} \begin{pmatrix} a_0 \\ a_1 \\ a_2 \\ a_3 \\ a_4 \\ a_5 \\ a_6 \\ a_7 \end{pmatrix} \qquad (5.7)$$

$$k(x) = (0D)_{16} = (00001101)_2 = x^3 + x^2 + 1$$

$$\begin{aligned} b(x) = \ & [a_7 + a_5 + a_4]x^7 + [a_7 + a_6 + a_4 + a_3]x^6 + \\ & [a_6 + a_5 + a_3 + a_2]x^5 + \\ & [a_7 + a_5 + a_4 + a_2 + a_1]x^4 + [a_7 + a_6 + a_5 + a_3 + a_1 + a_0]x^3 + \\ & [a_6 + a_2 + a_0]x^2 + [a_7 + a_5 + a_1]x + [a_6 + a_5 + a_0] \end{aligned}$$

$$\begin{pmatrix} b_0 \\ b_1 \\ b_2 \\ b_3 \\ b_4 \\ b_5 \\ b_6 \\ b_7 \end{pmatrix} = \begin{pmatrix} 1 & 0 & 0 & 0 & 0 & 1 & 1 & 0 \\ 0 & 1 & 0 & 0 & 0 & 1 & 0 & 1 \\ 1 & 0 & 1 & 0 & 0 & 0 & 1 & 0 \\ 1 & 1 & 0 & 1 & 0 & 1 & 1 & 1 \\ 0 & 1 & 1 & 0 & 1 & 1 & 0 & 1 \\ 0 & 0 & 1 & 1 & 0 & 1 & 1 & 0 \\ 0 & 0 & 0 & 1 & 1 & 0 & 1 & 1 \\ 0 & 0 & 0 & 0 & 1 & 1 & 0 & 1 \end{pmatrix} \begin{pmatrix} a_0 \\ a_1 \\ a_2 \\ a_3 \\ a_4 \\ a_5 \\ a_6 \\ a_7 \end{pmatrix} \qquad (5.8)$$

$$
\begin{aligned}
k(x) \;&=\; (0E)_{16} = (00001110)_2 = x^3 + x^2 + x \\
b(x) \;&=\; [a_6 + a_5 + a_4]x^7 + [a_7 + a_5 + a_4 + a_3]x^6 + \\
&\quad [a_6 + a_4 + a_3 + a_2]x^5 + \\
&\quad [a_5 + a_3 + a_2 + a_1]x^4 + [a_6 + a_5 + a_2 + a_1 + a_0]x^3 + \\
&\quad [a_6 + a_1 + a_0]x^2 + [a_5 + a_0]x + [a_7 + a_6 + a_5]
\end{aligned}
$$

$$
\begin{pmatrix} b_0 \\ b_1 \\ b_2 \\ b_3 \\ b_4 \\ b_5 \\ b_6 \\ b_7 \end{pmatrix}
=
\begin{pmatrix}
0 & 0 & 0 & 0 & 0 & 1 & 1 & 1 \\
1 & 0 & 0 & 0 & 0 & 1 & 0 & 0 \\
1 & 1 & 0 & 0 & 0 & 0 & 1 & 0 \\
1 & 1 & 1 & 0 & 0 & 1 & 1 & 0 \\
0 & 1 & 1 & 1 & 0 & 1 & 0 & 0 \\
0 & 0 & 1 & 1 & 1 & 0 & 1 & 0 \\
0 & 0 & 0 & 1 & 1 & 1 & 0 & 1 \\
0 & 0 & 0 & 0 & 1 & 1 & 1 & 0
\end{pmatrix}
\begin{pmatrix} a_0 \\ a_1 \\ a_2 \\ a_3 \\ a_4 \\ a_5 \\ a_6 \\ a_7 \end{pmatrix}
\tag{5.9}
$$

With $b(x)$ computed for each K_{xy} of the *AES MixColumns* and *InvMixColumns* transformations, the resultant 8-bit × 8-bit mapping matrices are easily constructed and the total number of storage bits per look-up table, 64, is significantly smaller than the number of storage bits required to implement a 2^8 × 8 look-up table, i.e. 1,024 bits. To perform the entire *Galois Field* fixed field constant multiplication requires sixteen look-up tables, resulting in a total of $64 \cdot 16 = 1,024$ storage bits for the matrix-based implementation versus a total of $1,024 \cdot 16 = 16,384$ storage bits for a look-up table implementation based on $2^8 \times 8$ look-up tables.

Instruction set extensions are an interesting implementation option that bridges the gap between hardware and software. Significantly improved performance of software implementations have been demonstrated as a result of adding functionality to a processor's datapath and corresponding control logic to decode new instructions. Instruction set extensions designed to accelerate the performance of software implementations of *Rijndael* have been proposed for a wide range of processors. These extensions minimize the number of memory accesses, usually by combining the *SubBytes* and *MixColumns* transformations into one *T table* look-up operation to speed up algorithm execution. Whereas *T table* performance is heavily dependent upon available cache size, these extensions have been shown to result in performance improvements of up to a factor of 3.68 versus *Rijndael* implementations without the use of the instruction set extensions [84, 125, 142, 212, 250, 307, 271].

5.2.5   Attacks Against AES

The use of different *Round Constants* to generate each round's sub-key eliminates symmetry in *Rijndael's* behavior. Unlike *DES*, because encryption and decryption use different components — *SubBytes*, *ShiftRows*, and *MixColumns* versus *InvSubBytes*, *InvShiftRows*, and *InvMixColumns* — there is little possibility for weak or semi-weak keys. Moreover, the non-linear *Key Expansion*, caused by the use of the *SubBytes* transformation, results in little possibility for equivalent keys. As a result, no weak, semi-weak, or equivalent keys have been identified for *Rijndael*. This same non-linearity, in combination with the *Key Schedule's* high *Diffusion*, results in *Rijndael* being highly resistant to *Related Key* attacks described in [30, 152]. Therefore, there are no restrictions on *Rijndael* key selection [57, 227].

Both *Differential Cryptanalysis* and *Linear Cryptanalysis*, described in Section 5.1.6.4, may be adapted for use against *Rijndael*. In the case of *Differential Cryptanalysis*, the attack relies on predictable difference propagations (composed of differential trails) with propagation ratios significantly larger than 2^{1-n} where n is the block size. In the case of *Rijndael* the propagation ratios must be significantly larger than 2^{-127} to be of concern. It has been proven for *Rijndael* that no 4-round differential trails exist with propagation ratios greater than 2^{-150} and no 8-round differential trails exist with propagation ratios greater than 2^{-300} for all block lengths. Thus, *Rijndael* has sufficient strength to resist *Differential Cryptanalysis* attacks. *Rijndael* was also found to be resistant to truncated differentials and clustering differential trails [55, 165] for implementations with six or more rounds, as is the case for *AES* regardless of key length [57].

In the case of *Linear Cryptanalysis*, the attack relies on predictable correlations between the plaintext and the ciphertext (composed of linear trails) significantly larger than $2^{\frac{n}{2}}$ where n is the block size. In the case of *Rijndael* the correlations must be significantly larger than 2^{64} to be of concern. It has been proven for *Rijndael* that no 4-round differential trails exist with propagation ratios greater than 2^{-75} and no 8-round differential trails exist with correlations greater than 2^{-150} for all block lengths [57]. Thus, *Rijndael* has sufficient strength to resist *Linear Cryptanalysis* attacks.

Rijndael shares many of the same features as the block cipher *Square*. An attack that exploits the structure of *Square* may also be applied to *Rijndael* and this attack, a *Chosen-Plaintext* attack known as the *Square* attack, is more effective than an *Exhaustive Key Search* attack for *Rijndael* implementations with fewer than seven rounds [56]. However, an *Exhaustive Key Search* attack is the fastest known attack for *Rijndael* implementations with seven or more rounds, as is the case for *AES* regardless of key length [57]. Extensions of the *Square* attack have been proposed [66, 95] that are capable of attacking 9-round implementations of *Rijndael* with 256-bit keys. However, the best of these *Chosen-Plaintext* attacks require $2^{128} - 2^{119}$ chosen plaintexts and thus are not practical. A *Related-Key Chosen-Plaintext* attack has also been presented, again targeting 9-round implementations of *Rijndael*. Such attacks are also not considered practical given the large number of chosen plaintexts required and these attacks have not been extended to 10-round implementations of *Rijndael*, the minimum number of rounds for *AES* [95].

Interpolation attacks construct polynomials using pairs of plaintext and ciphertext [143]. If the polynomials are of small degree, the polynomial's coefficients may be determined with only a few pairs of plaintext and ciphertext. However, *Rijndael's SubBytes* transformation, which is based on the *Extension Field* $GF(2^8)$, in combination with the *MixColumns* transformation (both of which provide *Diffusion*), prohibits this type of attack [57].

5.2.6   Homework Problems

Homework Problem 5.2.6.1: Compute $A(x) \cdot B(x) \bmod P(x)$ in the *Extension Field* $GF(2^4)$ with $P(x) = x^4 + x + 1$

   a) for $A(x) = x^2 + 1$ and $B(x) = x^3 + x^2 + 1$

   b) for $A(x) = x^2 + 1$ and $B(x) = x + 1$

Homework Problem 5.2.6.2: Compute $A(x) \cdot B(x) \bmod P(x)$ in the *Extension Field* $GF(3^3)$ with $P(x) = x^3 + 2x^2 + 1$

   a) for $A(x) = x^2 + 2$ and $B(x) = x + 1$

   b) for $A(x) = 2x^2 + x$ and $B(x) = 2x$

Homework Problem 5.2.6.3: Generate the multiplication table for the *Extension Field* $GF(2^3)$ for the case of the *Irreducible Polynomial* $P(x) = x^3 + x + 1$.

Homework Problem 5.2.6.4: Consider the *Extension Field* $GF(2^4)$ with the *Irreducible Polynomial* $P(x) = x^4 + x + 1$. Find the inverse of $A(x) = x^2 + x$ and $B(x) = x$.

Homework Problem 5.2.6.5: Compute $A(x) \cdot B(x) \bmod P(x)$ in the *Extension Field* $GF(2^4)$, assuming that $A(x) = x^3 + x^2 + x + 1$, $B(x) = x^2 + x + 1$, and $P(x) = x^4 + x + 1$.

Homework Problem 5.2.6.6: The minimum key length for the *AES* algorithm *Rijndael* is 128 bits. Assume that a special-purpose hardware key search machine can test one key in 10 *ns* on a single processor and that processors can be parallelized. Assume further that one such processor costs \$1 including overhead. Assume that *Moore's Law* holds, resulting in processor performance doubling every eighteen months. How many processors must be operating in parallel so that an *AES* key search machine can be built that breaks the algorithm on average in one day? How long must pass in years, assuming *Moore's Law* holds, so that the key-search machine does not cost more than \$100,000?

Homework Problem 5.2.6.7: What is the value of the 4×4 array of bytes representing the encrypted plaintext after the first round of *AES* is complete if the 128-bit input plaintext and the 128-bit round keys k_0 and k_1 are both all zeros?

Homework Problem 5.2.6.8: Assume the 128-bit input plaintext and the 128-bit *AES* round key k_1 are all zeros and the 128-bit round key:

$$k_0 = \text{0000 0000 0000 0000 0000 0000 0000 0001}_{16}$$

a) What is the value of the 4×4 array of bytes representing the encrypted plaintext after the first round of *AES* is complete?

b) How many S-Boxes get different inputs compared to the case considered in **Homework Problem 5.2.6.7**?

c) How many output bits have changed as compared to the case when the plaintext was all zero in **Homework Problem 5.2.6.7**?

Homework Problem 5.2.6.9: Assume that *Oscar* performs a *Known-Plaintext* attack against *AES* with one pair of plaintext and ciphertext. How many keys must be tested in a worst-case scenario if an *Exhaustive Key Search* attack is applied in a straightforward manner? How many keys must be tested on average if an *Exhaustive Key Search* attack is applied in a straightforward manner?

Homework Problem 5.2.6.10: Assume an *AES* implementation is used with a key length of 256 bits. Assume a special-purpose chip that searches $5 \cdot 10^{10}$ keys per second. Also assume that 100,000 of these chips are used in parallel. How long does an average key search take? Relate this time to the age of the universe, which is approximately 10^{10} years.

Homework Problem 5.2.6.11: How many years will pass before the key search machine described in **Homework Problem 5.2.6.10** can be built such that the average search time is twenty-four hours, assuming *Moore's Law* holds true?

Homework Problem 5.2.6.12: Compute the inverse of $A(x)$ *mod* $P(x)$ in the *Extension Field* $GF(2^4)$ using *Fermat's Little Theorem* assuming that $A(x) = x^3 + x + 1$ and $P(x) = x^4 + x + 1$.

Homework Problem 5.2.6.13: Write a VHDL architecture to implement the entire 128-bit *AES Key Scheduling* and encryption operating in *CBC* mode using a non-pipelined architecture. Your implementation must update the output ciphertext on every rising edge of the clock. Assume that the user will provide a *loadkey* signal to indicate that the master key is ready to be loaded from the *plaintext* bus on the next rising edge of the clock. Also assume that the user will provide a *loadiv* signal to indicate that the *Initialization Vector*, IV, is ready to be loaded on the next rising edge of the clock via the *plaintext* bus. Your system must output a *valid* signal to indicate when the output ciphertext is valid, i.e. an encryption has completed. Your system must also output a *keygendone* signal to indicate when round key generation has been completed after loading of the master key. Use the following entity declaration for your implementation:

```vhdl
LIBRARY ieee;
USE ieee.std_logic_1164.ALL;
USE ieee.std_logic_arith.ALL;
USE ieee.std_logic_unsigned.ALL;
ENTITY aes_128_cbc IS
  PORT ( plaintext  : IN  std_logic_vector (127 DOWNTO 0);
            clk        : IN  std_logic;
            rst        : IN  std_logic;
            loadkey    : IN  std_logic;
            loadiv     : IN  std_logic;
            valid      : OUT std_logic;
            keygendone : OUT std_logic;
            ciphertext : OUT std_logic_vector (127 DOWNTO 0));
END aes_128_cbc;
ARCHITECTURE behav OF aes_128_cbc IS
BEGIN
-- Your code goes here
END behav;
```

Use the results from **Homework Problem 5.2.6.8** to validate your design. Specify the target technology used to implement the design and the maximum operating frequency as specified by your place-and-route tools. What is the throughput of your implementation?

Homework Problem 5.2.6.14: Write a VHDL architecture to implement the entire 128-bit *AES Key Scheduling* and encryption in *ECB* mode using a pipelined architecture. Your implementation must update the output ciphertext on every rising edge of the clock. Assume that the user will provide a *loadkey* signal to indicate that the master key is ready to be loaded from the *plaintext* bus on the next rising edge of the clock and that a new key may be loaded while previous encryptions are still in progress. Your system must output a *valid* signal to indicate when the output ciphertext is valid, i.e. an encryption has completed. Your system must also output a *keygendone* signal to indicate when round key generation has been completed after loading of the master key. Use the following entity declaration for your implementation:

```
LIBRARY ieee;
USE ieee.std_logic_1164.ALL;
USE ieee.std_logic_arith.ALL;
USE ieee.std_logic_unsigned.ALL;
ENTITY aes_128_ecb IS
   PORT ( plaintext  : IN  std_logic_vector (127 DOWNTO 0);
          clk        : IN  std_logic;
          rst        : IN  std_logic;
          loadkey    : IN  std_logic;
          valid      : OUT std_logic;
          keygendone : OUT std_logic;
          ciphertext : OUT std_logic_vector (127 DOWNTO 0));
END aes_128_ecb;
ARCHITECTURE behav OF aes_128_ecb IS
BEGIN
-- Your code goes here
END behav;
```

Use the results from **Homework Problem 5.2.6.8** to validate your design. Specify the target technology used to implement the design and the maximum operating frequency as specified by your place-and-route tools. What is the throughput of your implementation?

Homework Problem 5.2.6.15: Compare the throughputs and logic resource requirements of **Homework Problems 5.2.6.13** and **5.2.6.14**. What is the ratio of throughput improvement versus the increased logic resources of **Homework Problem 5.2.6.13** versus **Homework Problem 5.2.6.14**?

Homework Problem 5.2.6.16: Write a C program to implement 128-bit *AES Key Scheduling* and encryption operating in *CBC* mode. Write a user interface that queries the user for an input file that contains the key, K, the *Initialization Vector*, IV, and five plaintexts $P_0 - P_4$, in hexadecimal notation. The program must output the five ciphertexts to the screen in hexadecimal notation and include code that measures the time required to encrypt each of the five ciphertexts, outputting this information to the screen. Specify the computer model used and the amount of available RAM.

Homework Problem 5.2.6.17: Compare the throughputs of **Homework Problems 5.2.6.13** and **5.2.6.16**. What is the ratio of throughput improvement for **Homework Problem 5.2.6.13** versus **Homework Problem 5.2.6.16**?

Homework Problem 5.2.6.18: Write a C program to implement 128-bit *AES Key Scheduling* and encryption operating in *ECB* mode. Write a user interface that queries the user for an input file that contains the key, K, and five plaintexts $P_0 - P_4$ in hexadecimal notation. The program must output the five ciphertexts to the screen in hexadecimal notation and include code that measures the time required to encrypt each of the five ciphertexts, outputting this information to the screen. Specify the computer model used and the amount of available RAM.

Homework Problem 5.2.6.19: Compare the throughputs of **Homework Problems 5.2.6.14** and **5.2.6.18**. What is the ratio of throughput improvement for **Homework Problem 5.2.6.14** versus **Homework Problem 5.2.6.18**?

Homework Problem 5.2.6.20: Write a VHDL architecture to implement 128-bit *AES Key Scheduling* and one round of encryption operating in *ECB* mode using a non-pipelined architecture that iterates ten times to perform a complete encryption. Assume that the user will provide a *loadkey* signal to indicate that the master key is ready to be loaded from the *plaintext* bus on the next rising edge of the clock. Your system must output a *valid* signal to indicate when the output ciphertext is valid, i.e. an encryption has completed. Your system must also output a *keygendone* signal to indicate when round key generation has been completed after loading of the master key. Use the following entity declaration for your implementation:

```
LIBRARY ieee;
USE ieee.std_logic_1164.ALL;
USE ieee.std_logic_arith.ALL;
USE icee.std_logic_unsigned.ALL;
ENTITY aes_128_ecb_single IS
   PORT ( plaintext  : IN   std_logic_vector (127 DOWNTO 0);
          clk        : IN   std_logic;
          rst        : IN   std_logic;
          loadkey    : IN   std_logic;
          valid      : OUT  std_logic;
          keygendone : OUT  std_logic;
          ciphertext : OUT  std_logic_vector (127 DOWNTO 0));
END aes_128_ecb_single;
ARCHITECTURE behav OF aes_128_ecb_single IS
BEGIN
-- Your code goes here
END behav;
```

Use the results from **Homework Problem 5.2.6.8** to validate your design. Specify the target technology used to implement the design and the maximum operating frequency as specified by your place-and-route tools. What is the throughput of your implemen-

tation? How does this compare to the throughputs calculated in
Homework Problems 5.2.6.14 and **5.2.6.18**? What is the ratio of throughput improvement versus the increased logic resources
of **Homework Problem 5.2.6.14**?

Homework Problem 5.2.6.21: Compare the C program implementations in **Homework Problem 5.1.7.23** and **Homework Problem 5.2.6.18**:

a) How many bytes of memory does each implementation require for data storage? Be sure to include the cost of sub-key
storage, intermediate round values, temporary variables, etc.

b) What is the code size of each implementation in bytes?

c) What is the throughput of each implementation? Be sure
to calculate throughput in terms of bits processed per clock cycle
instead of bits processed per second. Specify the computer model
used and the amount of available RAM.

Chapter 6

Public-Key Cryptography

6.1 Issues with Symmetric-Key Cryptosystems

As shown in Figure 2.1, symmetric-key cryptosystems require that the two parties attempting to communicate share the same key. This key is used for both encryption and decryption because the two operations are symmetric, i.e. almost identical, hence why such cryptosystems are known as symmetric-key cryptosystems. Such cryptosystems are analogous to securing a cabinet with a combination lock; anyone with the combination can either deposit or withdraw information from the cabinet.

Unfortunately, symmetric-key cryptosystems, by their very nature, introduce significant problems related to the shared key. In particular, the key must be securely distributed to the communicating parties, a non-trivial problem. Moreover, as shown in Figure 6.1, each user in a system must have a unique key for

195

every other user in the system if they are to communicate using a symmetric-key cryptosystem.

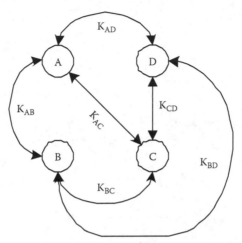

Figure 6.1: Symmetric-Key Cryptosystem Key Sharing

As shown in Figure 6.1, for a system with n users, each user must maintain $n - 1$ different keys, resulting in a total of $n \cdot \frac{n - 1}{2}$ different keys. Clearly this number of keys, approximately n^2, becomes unmanageable if n is large. Moreover, as discussed in **Homework Problem 4.5.12**, the real-world implications of such a system are significant when considering issues such as life cycle of the key, storage of the key both during and after the life cycle, key distribution, generation of the key, etc.

6.2   Public-Key Cryptosystem Overview

As discussed in Chapters 1 and 2, all cryptosystems were symmetric-key based prior to 1976. In 1976, Whitfield Diffie and Martin Hellman proposed a revolutionary key distribution methodology based on the idea that what was previously the master key, k, in a symmetric-key cryptosystem could be split into two parts. The first part, known as the *Public Key* (denoted as K_{PUB}), is used to encrypt information and the second part, known as the *Private Key* (denoted as K_{PR}), is used to decrypt information [70]. This idea transformed the symmetric-key cryptosystem locked cabinet analogy to the public-key cryptosystem analogy of a post office mailbox; anyone can deposit information into the mailbox, but only one party can unlock the mailbox and withdraw the information. Information deposits occur using the public key and information withdrawals occur using the private key. The basic public-key protocol for *Alice* to encrypt and transmit information to *Bob* is as follows:

1. *Alice* and *Bob* agree on a public-key cryptosystem.

2. *Bob* transmits his public key, denoted as K_{PUB_B}, to *Alice*.

3. *Alice* uses *Bob's* public key and the public-key cryptosystem encryption function, denoted as e, to encrypt the plaintext x, yielding the ciphertext $y = e_{K_{PUB_B}}(x)$.

4. *Alice* transmits the ciphertext y to *Bob*.

5. *Bob* decrypts the ciphertext y using his private key, denoted as K_{PR_B}, and the public-key cryptosystem decryption function, denoted as d, to yield the plaintext $x = d_{K_{PUB_B}}(y)$.

Public-key cryptosystems may be used for *key establishment*, *key transport*, *Digital Signatures*, and encryption. However, because symmetric-key algorithms tend to be significantly faster than public-key algorithms, they are typically used in bulk data encryption [275]. Modern cryptosystems tend to be hybrid systems that include both symmetric-key and public-key algorithms. In a typical session, a public-key algorithm will be used for the exchange of a session key, such as through the *Diffie-Hellman Key Agreement Protocol* discussed in Section 8.3, and to provide message authentication through *Digital Signatures*. The session key is then used in conjunction with a symmetric-key algorithm to transmit encrypted information.

Public-key cryptosystems are primarily classified as based on one of the following types of mathematical problems:

1. *Integer Factorization*

2. *Discrete Logarithms*

3. *Elliptic Curves*

Based on the strength of existing attacks, public-key cryptosystems based on either *Integer Factorization* or *Discrete Logarithms* require 1024-bit operands whereas public-key cryptosystems based on *Elliptic Curves* require only 256-bit operands. These operand lengths are considered to provide equivalent security to a 128-bit block cipher that may be successfully attacked via approximately 2^{128} computations. Clearly, the computations associated with public-key algorithms are significantly more complex versus those of symmetric-key algorithms in terms of memory size requirements, data management, and multi-precision arithmetic when targeting standard processors with word sizes ranging from 16 to 64 bits.

A number of standards have been developed targeting public-key cryptosystems. IEEE P1363 is a comprehensive standard for public-key cryptosystems based on *Integer Factorization*, *Discrete Logarithms*, and *Elliptic Curves*. This IEEE standard specifies *key establishment*, *key transport*, and *Digital Signature* algorithms, but it intentionally does not specify bit lengths or security levels [132, 133]. This is because such parameters must continuously adapt as computing power increases over time, following *Moore's Law*. Similarly, ANSI banking security standards have been developed to specify the proper use of public-key algorithms, targeting *Digital Signatures*, *Hash Functions*, and key management, while United States government FIPS standards have been developed to specify proper use of *Digital Signatures*, *Hash Functions*, and entity authentication [11, 12, 13, 14, 15, 16, 17, 224, 225, 226].

6.3   One-Way Functions

A function f is a *One-Way* function if its forward transformation $y = f(x)$ is easy to compute and its inverse transformation $x = f^{-1}(y)$ is very difficult to compute. Examples of *One-Way* functions include *Integer Factorization* and the *Discrete Logarithm* problem. In the case of *Integer Factorization*, $y = p \cdot q$ is easy to compute, while $x = p \cdot q$, where the goal is to determine the values of p and q (the factors of x) is difficult to compute. In the case of the *Discrete Logarithm* problem, $\beta = \alpha^i$ is easy to compute, while $i = log_\alpha\beta$ is difficult to compute. Often the inverse transformation becomes significantly easier to compute when a *Trap Door* is opened via the use of an additional parameter, i.e. the *Private Key*.

6.4   The Euclidean Algorithm

The goal of the *Euclidean Algorithm* is to compute the $gcd(r_0, r_1)$ for the integers r_0 and r_1 by representing the larger integer, r_0, in terms of multiples of r_1 and a remainder r_2. r_1 is then represented in terms of multiples of r_2 and a remainder r_3. This process continues until no remainder exists, resulting in termination of the *Euclidean Algorithm*. Therefore, we see that:

$$
\begin{aligned}
r_0 &= q_1 \cdot r_1 + r_2 & &\rightarrow & gcd(r_0, r_1) &= gcd(r_1, r_2) \\
r_1 &= q_2 \cdot r_2 + r_3 & &\rightarrow & gcd(r_1, r_2) &= gcd(r_2, r_3) \\
r_2 &= q_3 \cdot r_3 + r_4 & &\rightarrow & gcd(r_2, r_3) &= gcd(r_3, r_4) \\
&\;\;\vdots & & & &\;\;\vdots \\
r_{m-2} &= q_{m-1} \cdot r_{m-1} + r_m & &\rightarrow & gcd(r_{m-2}, r_{m-1}) &= gcd(r_{m-1}, r_m) \\
r_{m-1} &= q_m \cdot r_m + 0 & &\rightarrow & gcd(r_{m-1}, r_m) &= r_m = gcd(r_0, r_1)
\end{aligned}
$$

Upon termination of the *Euclidean Algorithm*, the $gcd(r_0, r_1) = r_m$.

Example 6.1: Compute the $gcd(39, 12)$ using the *Euclidean Algorithm*.

The *Euclidean Algorithm* yields:

$$39 = 3 \cdot 12 + 3 \; ; \; gcd(39, \; 12) = gcd(12, \; 3)$$

$$12 = 4 \cdot 3 + 0 \; ; \; gcd(12, \; 3) = 3$$

Therefore, the $gcd(39, \; 12)$ is 3.

Example 6.2: Compute the $gcd(586, \; 139)$ using the *Euclidean Algorithm*.

The *Euclidean Algorithm* yields:

$$586 = 4 \cdot 139 + 30 \; ; \; gcd(586, \; 139) = gcd(139, \; 30)$$

$$139 = 4 \cdot 30 + 19 \; ; \; gcd(139, \; 30) = gcd(30, \; 19)$$

$$30 = 1 \cdot 19 + 11 \; ; \; gcd(30, \; 19) = gcd(19, \; 11)$$

$$19 = 1 \cdot 11 + 8 \; ; \; gcd(19, \; 11) = gcd(11, \; 8)$$

$$11 = 1 \cdot 8 + 3 \; ; \; gcd(11, \; 8) = gcd(8, \; 3)$$

$$8 = 2 \cdot 3 + 2 \; ; \; gcd(8, \; 3) = gcd(3, \; 2)$$

$$3 = 1 \cdot 2 + 1 \; ; \; gcd(3, \; 2) = gcd(2, \; 1)$$

$$2 = 2 \cdot 1 + 0 \; ; \; gcd(2, \; 1) = 1 = gcd(586, \; 139)$$

Therefore, the $gcd(586, \; 139)$ is 1.

6.5   The Extended Euclidean Algorithm

The *Extended Euclidean Algorithm* is based on the theory that given two integers, r_0 and r_1, compute the $gcd(r_0, r_1) = r_m = s \cdot r_0 + t \cdot r_1$ in terms of the two integers s and t. The *Extended Euclidean Algorithm* extends the *Euclidean Algorithm* by representing each remainder r_j in terms of r_0 and r_1 as follows:

$$r_0 = q_1 \cdot r_1 + r_2 \qquad \rightarrow \qquad \begin{aligned} r_2 &= 1 \cdot r_0 + -q_1 \cdot r_1 \\ &= s_2 \cdot r_0 + t_2 \cdot r_1 \end{aligned}$$

$$r_1 = q_2 \cdot r_2 + r_3 \qquad \rightarrow \qquad \begin{aligned} r_3 &= r_1 - q_2 \cdot r_2 \\ &= r_1 - q_2(r_0 - q_1 \cdot r_1) \\ &= -q_2 \cdot r_0 + (1 + q_1 \cdot q_2) \cdot r_1 \\ &= s_3 \cdot r_0 + t_3 \cdot r_1 \end{aligned}$$

$$\vdots \qquad\qquad\qquad \vdots$$

$$r_{i-2} = q_{i-1} \cdot r_{i-1} + r_i \qquad \rightarrow \qquad r_i = s_i \cdot r_0 + t_i \cdot r_1$$

$$r_{i-1} = q_i \cdot r_i + r_{i+1} \qquad \rightarrow \qquad r_{i+1} = s_{i+1} \cdot r_0 + t_{i+1} \cdot r_1$$

$$r_i = q_{i+1} \cdot r_{i+1} + r_{i+2} \qquad \rightarrow \qquad r_{i+2} = s_{i+2} \cdot r_0 + t_{i+2} \cdot r_1$$

$$\vdots \qquad\qquad\qquad \vdots$$

$$r_{m-2} = q_{m-1} \cdot r_{m-1} + r_m \qquad \rightarrow \qquad r_m = s_m \cdot r_0 + t_m \cdot r_1$$

$$r_{m-1} = q_m \cdot r_m + 0 \qquad \rightarrow \qquad s = s_m, t = t_m$$

Upon termination of the *Extended Euclidean Algorithm*, the $gcd(r_0, r_1) = r_m = s_m \cdot r_0 + t_m \cdot r_1 = s \cdot r_0 + t \cdot r_1$. Moreover, it is evident that $s_i = s_{i-2} - q_{i-1} \cdot s_{i-1}$ and $t_i = t_{i-2} - q_{i-1} \cdot t_{i-1}$ with the initial conditions $s_0 = 1$, $s_1 = 0$, $t_0 = 0$, $t_1 = 1$. The significance of the *Extended Euclidean Algorithm* is demonstrated when attempting to determine the inverse of an element $a \in Z_m$. In order for $a^{-1} \bmod m$ to exist, a and m must be relatively prime to each other, i.e. the $gcd(a, m)$ must be one. The $gcd(a, m)$ may be determined via the *Extended Euclidean Algorithm*. Moreover, if $r_0 = m$ and $r_1 = a$ and the $gcd(a, m)$

is one, then $s \cdot m + t \cdot a = gcd(m, a) = 1$. Rearranging this equation yields:

$$s \cdot m + t \cdot a = 1$$
$$t \cdot a = (-s) \cdot m + 1$$

However, $t \cdot a = (-s) \cdot m + 1$ follows the definition of the *Modulo* operator from Section 2.2 such that $t \cdot a \equiv 1 \; mod \; m$. Using the definition of the multiplicative inverse from Section 2.4, i.e. that $a \times a^{-1} \equiv 1 \; mod \; m$, yields $a^{-1} = t \; mod \; m$. Therefore, the *Extended Euclidean Algorithm* yields the inverse of a via the parameter t assuming the $gcd(a, m)$ is one. In practice, only the t parameter is calculated when using the *Extended Euclidean Algorithm* to compute the inverse of a. Moreover, the value of t upon termination of the *Extended Euclidean Algorithm* may be negative. In this case, t is converted to a positive number within the *Ring Z_m* by adding the modulus m to t until $t > 0$.

Example 6.3: Compute the inverse of 139 *mod* 586 using the *Extended Euclidean Algorithm*.

The *Extended Euclidean Algorithm* yields:

$$
\begin{array}{llll}
586 = 4 \cdot 139 + 30 & t_2 = t_0 - q_1 \cdot t_1 & = 0 \text{-} 4 \cdot 1 = \text{-}4 \\
139 = 4 \cdot 30 + 19 & t_3 = t_1 - q_2 \cdot t_2 & = 1 \text{-} 4 \cdot \text{-}4 = 17 \\
30 = 1 \cdot 19 + 11 & t_4 = t_2 - q_3 \cdot t_3 & = \text{-}4 \text{-} 1 \cdot 17 = \text{-}21 \\
19 = 1 \cdot 11 + 8 & t_5 = t_3 - q_4 \cdot t_4 & = 17 \text{-} 1 \cdot \text{-}21 = 38 \\
11 = 1 \cdot 8 + 3 & t_6 = t_4 - q_5 \cdot t_5 & = \text{-}21 \text{-} 1 \cdot 38 = \text{-}59 \\
8 = 2 \cdot 3 + 2 & t_7 = t_5 - q_6 \cdot t_6 & = 38 \text{-} 2 \cdot \text{-}59 = 156 \\
3 = 1 \cdot 2 + 1 & t_8 = t_6 - q_7 \cdot t_7 & = \text{-}59 \text{-} 1 \cdot 156 = \text{-}215 \\
2 = 2 \cdot 1 + 0 & & \\
\end{array}
$$

Therefore, $t = -215 \equiv 371 \bmod 586 = 139^{-1} \bmod 586$.

The *Extended Euclidean Algorithm* does not map well to either hardware or software implementations. The associated modular reduction of the *Extended Euclidean Algorithm* is performed in a base-10 system whereas hardware and software, i.e. computer systems, operate in a binary (base-2) system. As described in Section 2.2, the computational aspects of performing the *Modulo* operation in a base-10 system must be considered when implementing the division that must be performed. Base-10 division in both software and hardware tends to be slow and resource intensive. As a result, implementations designed to compute the inverse of an element $a \in Z_m$ typically make use of the *Binary Extended Euclidean Algorithm* because this algorithm uses base-2 division instead of base-10 division. Base-2 division may be implemented as a right shift of the data by n bit positions when dividing by 2^n.

The *Binary Extended Euclidean Algorithm* may be used to compute the $gcd(r_1, r_0)$ and the inverse of r_1 if the $gcd(r_1, r_0)$ is one. The pseudo-code for the *Binary Extended Euclidean Algorithm* proceeds as follows [202]:

1. $g \leftarrow 1$

2. While r_0 and r_1 are even:

   (a) $r_0 \leftarrow r_0/2$

   (b) $r_1 \leftarrow r_1/2$

   (c) $g \leftarrow 2 \cdot g$

3. $u \leftarrow r_0, v \leftarrow r_1, A \leftarrow 1, B \leftarrow 0, C \leftarrow 0, D \leftarrow 1$

4. While u is even:

   (a) $u \leftarrow u/2$

   (b) If A and B are even Then

      i. $A \leftarrow A/2$

      ii. $B \leftarrow B/2$

   Else

      i. $A \leftarrow (A + r_1)/2$

      ii. $B \leftarrow (B - r_0)/2$

5. While v is even:

   (a) $v \leftarrow v/2$

   (b) If C and D are even Then

      i. $C \leftarrow C/2$

      ii. $D \leftarrow D/2$

   Else

    i. $C \leftarrow (C + r_1)/2$

    ii. $D \leftarrow (D - r_0)/2$

6. If $u \geq v$ Then

  (a) $u \leftarrow u - v$

  (b) $A \leftarrow A - C$

  (c) $B \leftarrow B - D$

Else

  (a) $v \leftarrow v - u$

  (b) $C \leftarrow C - A$

  (c) $D \leftarrow D - B$

7. If $u = 0$ Then

  (a) $gcd(r_1, r_0) = v \cdot g$

  (b) If the $gcd(r_1, r_0) = 1$ then $r_1^{-1} \bmod r_0 \equiv D \bmod r_0$

Else go to Step 4

Example 6.4: Use the *Binary Extended Euclidean Algorithm* to compute the $gcd(r_0 = 8, r_1 = 2)$. Does the inverse of 2 *mod* 8 exist? If so, what is the inverse of 2 *mod* 8?

Algorithm Step	Evaluation Result	Updated Values
1	N/A	$g \leftarrow 1$
2	r_0 and r_1 are even	$r_0 \leftarrow 4$
		$r_1 \leftarrow 1$
		$g \leftarrow 2$
3	N/A	$u \leftarrow 4$
		$v \leftarrow 1$
		$A \leftarrow 1$
		$B \leftarrow 0$
		$C \leftarrow 0$
		$D \leftarrow 1$
4	u is even, both A and B are not even	$u \leftarrow 2$
		$A \leftarrow 2$
		$B \leftarrow -2$
4	u is even, both A and B are even	$u \leftarrow 1$
		$A \leftarrow 1$
		$B \leftarrow -1$
6	$u \geq v$	$u \leftarrow 0$
		$A \leftarrow 1$
		$B \leftarrow -2$
7	$u = 0$	$gcd(r_0 = 8, r_1 = 2)$
		$= v \cdot g = 2$

Therefore, the $gcd(8, 2)$ is 2. Because the $gcd(8, 2) \neq 1$, the inverse of $2 \bmod 8$ does not exist.

Example 6.5: Use the *Binary Extended Euclidean Algorithm* to compute the $gcd(r_0 = 19, r_1 = 3)$. Does the inverse of $3 \bmod 19$ exist? If so, what is the inverse of $3 \bmod 19$?

Algorithm Step	Evaluation Result	Updated Values
1	N/A	$g \leftarrow 1$
3	N/A	$u \leftarrow 19$
		$v \leftarrow 3$
		$A \leftarrow 1$
		$B \leftarrow 0$
		$C \leftarrow 0$
		$D \leftarrow 1$
6	$u \geq v$	$u \leftarrow 16$
		$A \leftarrow 1$
		$B \leftarrow -1$
4	u is even, both A and B are not even	$u \leftarrow 8$
		$A \leftarrow 2$
		$B \leftarrow -10$
4	u is even, both A and B are even	$u \leftarrow 4$
		$A \leftarrow 1$
		$B \leftarrow -5$
4	u is even, both A and B are not even	$u \leftarrow 2$
		$A \leftarrow 2$
		$B \leftarrow -12$
4	u is even, both A and B are even	$u \leftarrow 1$
		$A \leftarrow 1$
		$B \leftarrow -6$
6	$u < v$	$v \leftarrow 2$
		$C \leftarrow -1$
		$D \leftarrow 7$
5	v is even, both C and D are not even	$v \leftarrow 1$
		$C \leftarrow 1$
		$D \leftarrow -6$
6	$u \geq v$	$u \leftarrow 0$
		$A \leftarrow 0$
		$B \leftarrow -12$
7	$u = 0$	$gcd(r_0 = 19, r_1 = 3)$
		$= v \cdot g = 1$
		$3^{-1} \bmod 19 = -6 \bmod 19$
		$\equiv 13 \bmod 19$

Therefore, the $gcd(19, 3)$ is 1. Because the $gcd(19, 3) = 1$, $3^{-1} \bmod 19 \equiv 13 \bmod 19$.

Example 6.6: Use the *Binary Extended Euclidean Algorithm* to compute the $gcd(r_0 = 18, r_1 = 3)$. Does the inverse of 3 *mod* 18 exist? If so, what is the inverse of 3 *mod* 18?

Algorithm Step	Evaluation Result	Updated Values
1	N/A	$g \leftarrow 1$
3	N/A	$u \leftarrow 18$
		$v \leftarrow 3$
		$A \leftarrow 1$
		$B \leftarrow 0$
		$C \leftarrow 0$
		$D \leftarrow 1$
4	u is even, both A and B are not even	$u \leftarrow 9$
	$A \leftarrow 2$	
	$B \leftarrow -9$	
6	$u \geq v$	$u \leftarrow 6$
		$A \leftarrow 2$
		$B \leftarrow -10$
4	u is even, both A and B are even	$u \leftarrow 3$
		$A \leftarrow 1$
		$B \leftarrow -5$
6	$u \geq v$	$u \leftarrow 0$
		$A \leftarrow 1$
		$B \leftarrow -6$
7	$u = 0$	$gcd(r_0 = 18, r_1 = 3)$
		$= v \cdot g = 3$

Therefore, the $gcd(18, 3)$ is 3. Because the $gcd(18, 3) \neq 1$, the inverse of 3 *mod* 18 does not exist.

Example 6.7: Use the *Binary Extended Euclidean Algorithm* to compute the $gcd(r_0 = 213, r_1 = 5)$. Does the inverse of 213 *mod* 5 exist? If so, what is the inverse of 5 *mod* 213?

Algorithm Step	Evaluation Result	Updated Values
1	N/A	$g \leftarrow 1$
3	N/A	$u \leftarrow 213$
		$v \leftarrow 5$
		$A \leftarrow 1$
		$B \leftarrow 0$
		$C \leftarrow 0$
		$D \leftarrow 1$
6	$u \geq v$	$u \leftarrow 208$
		$A \leftarrow 1$
		$B \leftarrow -1$
4	u is even, both A and B are not even	$u \leftarrow 104$
		$A \leftarrow 3$
		$B \leftarrow -107$
4	u is even, both A and B are not even	$u \leftarrow 52$
		$A \leftarrow 4$
		$B \leftarrow -160$
4	u is even, both A and B are even	$u \leftarrow 26$
		$A \leftarrow 2$
		$B \leftarrow -80$
4	u is even, both A and B are even	$u \leftarrow 13$
		$A \leftarrow 1$
		$B \leftarrow -40$
6	$u \geq v$	$u \leftarrow 8$
		$A \leftarrow 1$
		$B \leftarrow -41$
4	u is even, both A and B are not even	$u \leftarrow 4$
		$A \leftarrow 3$
		$B \leftarrow -127$
4	u is even, both A and B are not even	$u \leftarrow 2$
		$A \leftarrow 4$
		$B \leftarrow -170$
4	u is even, both A and B are even	$u \leftarrow 1$
		$A \leftarrow 2$
		$B \leftarrow -85$
6	$u < v$	$v \leftarrow 4$
		$C \leftarrow -2$
		$D \leftarrow 86$
5	v is even, both C and D are even	$v \leftarrow 2$
		$C \leftarrow -1$
		$D \leftarrow 43$
5	v is even, both C and D are not even	$v \leftarrow 1$
		$C \leftarrow -3$
		$D \leftarrow 128$
6	$u \geq v$	$u \leftarrow 0$
		$A \leftarrow 5$
		$B \leftarrow -213$
7	$u = 0$	$gcd(r_0 = 213, r_1 = 5)$
		$= v \cdot g = 1$
		$5^{-1} \bmod 213 = 128 \bmod 213$

Therefore, the $gcd(213,\ 5)$ is 1. Because the $gcd(213,\ 5)\ =\ 1$, $5^{-1}\ mod\ 213\ \equiv\ 128\ mod\ 19$.

6.6   Euler's Phi Function

Euler's Phi Function is used to determine the number of integers in the *Ring* Z_m that are relatively prime to m and is denoted as $\phi(m)$.

Example 6.8: Compute $\phi(7)$ for the *Ring* Z_7.

$$gcd(0,\ 7)\ =\ 7$$
$$gcd(1,\ 7)\ =\ 1$$
$$gcd(2,\ 7)\ =\ 1$$
$$gcd(3,\ 7)\ =\ 1$$
$$gcd(4,\ 7)\ =\ 1$$
$$gcd(5,\ 7)\ =\ 1$$
$$gcd(6,\ 7)\ =\ 1$$

Therefore, $\phi(7)$ is 6.

Example 6.9: Compute $\phi(8)$ for the *Ring Z_8*.

$$gcd(0,\ 8)\ =\ 8$$

$$gcd(1,\ 8)\ =\ 1$$

$$gcd(2,\ 8)\ =\ 2$$

$$gcd(3,\ 8)\ =\ 1$$

$$gcd(4,\ 8)\ =\ 4$$

$$gcd(5,\ 8)\ =\ 1$$

$$gcd(6,\ 8)\ =\ 2$$

$$gcd(7,\ 8)\ =\ 1$$

Therefore, $\phi(8)$ is 4.

When considering the number of integers in the *Ring Z_m* that are relatively prime to m, m may be represented as the product of prime numbers of the form $m = P_1^{e_1} \cdot P_2^{e_2} \cdot \ldots P_n^{e_n}$, where each P_i is a different prime number and each e_i is an integer. Using this notation, *Euler's Phi Function* may be calculated as $\phi(m) = \prod_{i=1}^{n} P_i^{e_i} - P_i^{e_i - 1}$. The usefulness of *Euler's Phi Function* to calculate $\phi(m)$ relies on the ability to factor the integer m. This fact will be exploited when examining the *RSA* cryptosystem in Chapter 7.

Example 6.10: Compute $\phi(8)$ for the *Ring* Z_8.

Factoring 8 into its prime components yields 2^3. Therefore, $\phi(8) = 2^3 - 2^2 = 8 - 4 = 4$.

Example 6.11: Compute $\phi(350)$ for the *Ring* Z_{350}.

Factoring 350 into its prime components yields $2 \cdot 5^2 \cdot 7$. Therefore:

$$\phi(350) = (2^1 - 2^0) \cdot (5^2 - 5^1) \cdot (7^1 - 7^0)$$
$$\phi(350) = (2 - 1) \cdot (25 - 5) \cdot (7 - 1)$$
$$\phi(350) = 1 \cdot 20 \cdot 6$$
$$\phi(350) = 120$$

Therefore, $\phi(350)$ is 120.

6.7 Euler's Theorem

Euler's Theorem states that if the $gcd(a, m) = 1$, then $a^{\phi(m)} \equiv 1 \ mod \ m$. The significance of *Euler's Theorem* is demonstrated when attempting to determine the inverse of an element $a \ \epsilon \ Z_m$.

a^{-1} mod m must exist because a and m are relatively prime to each other. Multiplying both sides of the equation by a^{-1} yields $a^{\phi(m)} \cdot a^{-1} \equiv a^{-1}$ mod m. Combining exponents results in $a^{-1} \equiv a^{\phi(m)-1}$ mod m. Therefore, the inverse of a may be calculated via exponentiation, and this process may be significantly faster than either the *Extended Euclidean Algorithm* or the *Binary Extended Euclidean Algorithm*. Fast exponentiation will be discussed in detail in Section 7.2.2.

Example 6.12: Prove that $a^{\phi(m)} \equiv 1$ mod m using *Euler's Theorem* for $a = 2$ and $m = 5$.

   Euler's Phi Function states that $\phi(5) = 5^1 - 5^0 = 5 - 1 = 4$. Using *Euler's Theorem*, 2^4 mod $5 = 16$ mod $5 \equiv 1$ mod 5. Therefore, *Euler's Theorem* holds true, i.e. $2^{\phi(5)}$ mod $5 \equiv 1$ mod 5.

6.8   Fermat's Little Theorem

Fermat's Little Theorem extends *Euler's Theorem* for the case where the modulus m is prime and thus is denoted as p. In such cases, $\phi(p) = p - 1$ and thus *Fermat's Little Theorem* states that $a^{p-1} \equiv 1$ mod p if the $gcd(a,\ p) = 1$. As in the case of *Euler's Theorem*, *Fermat's Little Theorem* may be used to determine the inverse of an element a in the *Ring* Z_p. Multiplying both sides of the equation by a^{-1} yields $a^{p-1} \cdot a^{-1} \equiv a^{-1} \bmod p$. Combining exponents results in $a^{-1} \equiv a^{p-2} \bmod p$.

As discussed in Section 5.2.1, *Fermat's Little Theorem* may be applied to a non-zero element $A(x)$ within the *Extension Field* $GF(p^m)$ to find its inverse, $A^{-1}(x)$, such that $A(x) \cdot A^{-1}(x) = 1 \bmod P(x)$. This is because the non-zero elements of the *Extension Field* $GF(p^m)$ form a *Cyclic Group*, as defined in Section 8.1, with $p^m - 1$ elements. In this case, *Fermat's Little Theorem* states that $A(x)^{p^m - 1} \equiv 1 \bmod P(x)$. Consider that $A(x) \cdot A^{-1}(x) \equiv 1 \bmod P(x)$. Therefore, $A(x) \cdot A^{-1}(x) \bmod P(x) \equiv A(x)^{p^m - 1} \bmod P(x)$, leading to the conclusion that $A^{-1}(x) \equiv A(x)^{p^m - 2} \bmod P(x)$.

Example 6.13: Calculate the inverse of $a = 7$ in the *Ring* Z_{11} using *Fermat's Little Theorem*.

Fermat's Little Theorem may be applied as follows because $p = 11$ is prime:

$$7^{-1} \bmod 11 \equiv 7^{11-2} \bmod 11$$

$$7^{11-2} \bmod 11 = 7^9 \bmod 11$$

$$7^9 \bmod 11 = 40,353,607 \bmod 11$$

$$40,353,607 \bmod 11 \equiv 8 \bmod 11$$

Therefore, $7^{-1} \bmod 11 \equiv 8 \bmod 11$ since $7 \cdot 8 \bmod 11 = 56 \bmod 11 \equiv 1 \bmod 11$.

6.9   Homework Problems

Homework Problem 6.9.1: Use the *Euclidean Algorithm* to compute the *Greatest Common Divisor* of:

a) 7,469 and 2,464

b) 2,689 and 4,001

c) 2,947 and 3,997

Show every iteration step of the algorithm and for every *gcd* provide the chain $gcd(r_0, r_1) = gcd(r_1, r_2) = \ldots$

Homework Problem 6.9.2: Use the *Extended Euclidean Algorithm* to compute the *Greatest Common Divisor* and the parameters s and t for:

a) 7,469 and 2,464

b) 2,689 and 4,001

c) 2,947 and 3,997

For each problem check if $s \cdot r_0 + t \cdot r_1 = gcd(r_0, r_1)$ is true. Show every iteration step of the algorithm and for every *gcd* provide the chain $gcd(r_0, r_1) = gcd(r_1, r_2) = \ldots$

Homework Problem 6.9.3: Find the inverses in Z_m for the following elements a *modulo* m using the *Euclidean Algorithm*:

a) $a = 7$, $m = 26$

b) $a = 19$, $m = 999$

Note that the inverses must be elements in Z_m.

Homework Problem 6.9.4: Write a C program that implements the *Extended Euclidean Algorithm*. Include the following features:

1. Write the program as a single function that has r_0 and r_1 as input parameters and returns the values for s, t, and $gcd(r_0, r_1)$.

2. At the start of the function, check whether $r_0 > r_1$. If the check fails, swap the values of r_0 and r_1.

3. The program must be able to perform all arithmetic with long type variables, i.e. signed 32-bit values. Make sure that you call the function using long type variables if the magnitude of either of the input parameters is greater than $2^{15} - 1 = 32,767$.

4. Write a user interface that queries the user for r_0 and r_1 and returns the values for s, t, and $gcd(r_0, r_1)$ after calling the function.

5. Include code that measures the time required to compute s, t, and $gcd(r_0, r_1)$, outputting this information to the screen. Specify the computer model used and the amount of available RAM.

a) Compute s, t, and the $gcd(r_0, r_1)$ for $r_0 = 92,204,805$ and $r_1 = 139,928,096$.

b) Compute s, t, and the $gcd(r_0, r_1)$ for $r_0 = 123,456,789$ and $r_1 = 987,644,322$.

Homework Problem 6.9.5: Modify your C program from **Homework Problem 6.9.4** to implement the *Binary Extended Euclidean Algorithm*. Specify the computer model used and the amount of available RAM.

a) Compare the execution times of the two programs when computing A, B, C, D, and the $gcd(r_0, r_1)$ for $r_0 = 92,204,805$ and $r_1 = 139,928,096$.

b) Compare the execution times of the two programs when computing A, B, C, D, and the $gcd(r_0, r_1)$ for $r_0 = 123,456,789$ and $r_1 = 987,644,322$.

Homework Problem 6.9.6: Determine $\phi(m)$ for $m = 12,\ 15,\ 26$ according to the definition of $\phi(m)$. Check for each positive integer $n < m$ whether the $gcd(n, m) = 1$.

Homework Problem 6.9.7: Develop formulae for $\phi(m)$ for the special cases where:

a) m is prime.

b) $m = p \cdot q$ where p and q are prime.

Verify your formulae for $m = 12, \ 15, \ 26$ with the results from **Homework Problem 6.9.6**.

Homework Problem 6.9.8: Using the program you wrote for **Homework Problem 6.9.4**, compute $\phi(m)$ according to its definition, i.e. without using the *Integer Factorization* of m, for:

a) $m = 12,111$

b) $m = 12,553$

c) $m = 10,000,017$

d) $m = 10,000,019$

Which of the numbers m are prime?

Homework Problem 6.9.9: Verify that *Euler's Theorem* holds in Z_m, $m = 5, \ 6, \ 9$ for all elements a for which the $gcd(a, \ m) = 1$. Also verify that the theorem does not hold true for all elements a for which the $gcd(a, \ m) \neq 1$.

Homework Problem 6.9.10: For the affine cipher, you were told that the multiplicative inverse of an element modulo 26 may be determined as $a^{-1} \equiv a^{11} \ mod \ 26$. Derive this relationship using *Euler's Theorem*.

Homework Problem 6.9.11: The *Extended Euclidean Algorithm* has the initial conditions $s_0 = 1$, $s_1 = 0$, $t_0 = 0$, and $t_1 = 1$. Derive these conditions.

Homework Problem 6.9.12: Use the *Extended Euclidean Algorithm* to compute the inverse of 769 *mod* 7, 835. Prove that the inverse of 769 *mod* 7, 835 must exist.

Homework Problem 6.9.13: Write a VHDL architecture to implement the *Binary Extended Euclidean Algorithm* for 16-bit input values r_0 and r_1. Assume that the user will provide a *load* signal to indicate that r_0 and r_1 are ready to be loaded on the next rising edge of the clock. Your system must output a *gvalid* signal to indicate when the output *gcd* is valid, i.e. computation of the $gcd(r_1, r_0)$ is completed, and a *ivalid* signal to indicate that the output inverse r_1^{-1} *mod* r_0 is valid. Use the following entity declaration for your implementation:

```
LIBRARY ieee;
USE ieee.std_logic_1164.ALL;
USE ieee.std_logic_arith.ALL;
USE ieee.std_logic_unsigned.ALL;
ENTITY bin_euc IS
   PORT ( r0, r1     : IN  std_logic_vector (15 DOWNTO 0);
          clk        : IN  std_logic;
          rst        : IN  std_logic;
          load       : IN  std_logic;
          gvalid     : OUT std_logic;
          ivalid     : OUT std_logic;
          gcd        : OUT std_logic_vector (15 DOWNTO 0);
          r1inverse  : OUT std_logic_vector (15 DOWNTO 0));
END bin_euc;
ARCHITECTURE behav OF bin_euc IS
BEGIN
-- Your code goes here
END behav;
```

Use the results from **Examples 6.4**, **6.5**, **6.6**, and **6.7** to validate your design. Specify the target technology used to implement the design and the maximum operating frequency as specified by your place-and-route tools. What is the execution time of your implementation for each of the four examples?

Homework Problem 6.9.14: Using the program you wrote for **Homework Problem 6.9.4**, compute the execution times for the inputs specified in **Examples 6.4**, **6.5**, **6.6**, and **6.7**. Compare these execution times to the results from **Homework Problem 6.9.13**. What is the speed-up of the hardware implementation versus the software implementation for each of the four examples?

Homework Problem 6.9.15: Using the program you wrote for **Homework Problem 6.9.5**, compute the execution times for the inputs specified in **Examples 6.4**, **6.5**, **6.6**, and **6.7**. Compare these execution times to the results from **Homework Problem 6.9.13**. What is the speed-up of the hardware implementation versus the software implementation for each of the four examples?

Homework Problem 6.9.16: Find the inverse of 17 *mod* 881 using *Fermat's Little Theorem*.

Homework Problem 6.9.17: Compute the *gcd*(204, 210) using the *Binary Extended Euclidean Algorithm*.

Chapter 7

Public-Key Cryptography: RSA

In 1977, the *RSA* cryptosystem was proposed by Ron Rivest, Adi Shamir, and Leonard Adleman of the Massachusetts Institute of Technology (MIT). *RSA* was patented in the United States by MIT on September 20, 1983. Although the patent for *RSA* expired September 21, 2000 [254], *RSA* has become the most popularly implemented public-key cryptosystem.

7.1 Cryptosystem

The *RSA* cryptosystem is composed of two stages: set-up and encryption/decryption. The set-up stage generates the private and public keys as follows:

1. Choose two large prime numbers, denoted as p and q.

2. Compute $n = p \cdot q$.

3. Compute $\phi(n) = (p - 1) \cdot (q - 1)$.

4. Select a random integer, denoted as b, such that $0 < b < \phi(n)$ and the $gcd(\phi(n),\ b) = 1$.

5. Compute $a = b^{-1} \ mod \ \phi(n)$.

where $\phi(n)$ is *Euler's Phi Function* as described in Section 6.6. Upon completion of the *RSA* set-up stage, the public key is denoted as $K_{PUB} = (n,\ b)$ and the private key is denoted as $K_{PR} = (p,\ q,\ a)$.

Once the private and public keys have been established, encryption of the plaintext x to form the ciphertext y is performed as follows:

$$y = e_{K_{PUB}}(x) = x^b \ mod \ n$$

where x is an element in the *Ring* Z_n. Decryption of the ciphertext y to form the plaintext x is performed as follows:

$$x = d_{K_{PR}}(y) = y^a \ mod \ n$$

Example 7.1: *Alice* wants to send the message $x = 13$ to *Bob*. *Bob* chooses $p = 5$ and $q = 17$. Show the process for *Bob* to calculate his private and public keys. Also show the result of *Alice's* encryption of x using *Bob's* public key and the result of *Bob's* decryption of y using his own private key.

Bob begins by computing his private and public keys:

1. $n = 5 \cdot 17 = 85$.

2. $\phi(n) = (5 - 1) \cdot (17 - 1) = 4 \cdot 16 = 64$.

3. *Bob* selects the random integer $b = 7$, noting that the $gcd(\phi(85), 7) = 1$.

4. $a = 7^{-1} \bmod 64 \equiv 55 \bmod 64$.

Bob publishes his public key $K_{PUB} = (85, 7)$ and keeps his private key $K_{PR} = (5, 17, 55)$ secret. *Alice* uses *Bob's* public key to encrypt x as follows:

$$y = e_{K_{PUB_{Bob}}}(13) = 13^7 \bmod 85 \equiv 72 \bmod 85$$

Alice then transmits $y = 72$ to *Bob*. *Bob* then uses his private key to decrypt y as follows:

$$x = d_{K_{PR_{Bob}}}(72) = 72^{55} \bmod 85 \equiv 13 \bmod 85$$

For *RSA* to function, $d_{K_{PR}}(e_{K_{PUB}}(x)) = x$, i.e. decryption must be the inverse of encryption. Substituting $x^b \bmod n$ into the decryption function yields:

$$d_{K_{PR}}(y) = y^a \bmod n$$
$$d_{K_{PR}}(y) = (x^b)^a \bmod n$$
$$d_{K_{PR}}(y) = x^{ab} \bmod n$$

However, the set-up phase dictates that $a \cdot b \equiv 1 \bmod \phi(n)$. This equation may be restated as $a \cdot b \equiv w \cdot \phi(n) + 1$ based on the definition of the *Modulo* operator from Section 2.2, where w is an integer. Substituting this result into the decryption function yields:

$$d_{K_{PR}}(y) = x^{w\phi(n) + 1} \bmod n$$
$$d_{K_{PR}}(y) = x^{w\phi(n)} \cdot x^1 \bmod n$$
$$d_{K_{PR}}(y) = (x^{\phi(n)})^w \cdot x \bmod n$$

If the $gcd(n, x) = 1$ then *Euler's Theorem* states that $x^{\phi(n)} \equiv 1 \bmod n$ and therefore:

$$d_{K_{PR}}(y) = 1^w \cdot x \bmod n$$
$$d_{K_{PR}}(y) = x \bmod n$$

If the $gcd(n, x) \neq 1$, then the $gcd(p \cdot q, x) \neq 1$ given that $n = p \cdot q$. Because p and q are the only factors of n, either p or q must be a multiple of x. Assume that $x = v \cdot q$, where v is an integer and thus the $gcd(p, x) = 1$. Decryption may now be expressed as:

$$d_{K_{PR}}(y) = (x^{(p-1) \cdot (q-1)})^w \cdot x \bmod n$$
$$d_{K_{PR}}(y) = (x^{\phi(p) \cdot (q-1)})^w \cdot x \bmod n$$
$$d_{K_{PR}}(y) = ((x^{\phi(p)})^{(q-1)})^w \cdot x \bmod n$$

Because the $gcd(p, x) = 1$ then *Euler's Theorem* states that $x^{\phi(p)} \equiv 1 \bmod p$. Therefore, $(x^{\phi(n)})^w \equiv 1 + s \cdot p \bmod n$, accounting for multiples of p that may be contained in $(x^{\phi(n)})^w$, where s is an integer. Substituting this result into the decryption function yields:

$$d_{K_{PR}}(y) = (1 + s \cdot p) \cdot x \bmod n$$
$$d_{K_{PR}}(y) = x + x \cdot s \cdot p \bmod n$$

Recalling that $x = v \cdot q$, the decryption function yields:

$$d_{K_{PR}}(y) = x + v \cdot q \cdot s \cdot p \bmod n$$
$$d_{K_{PR}}(y) = x + v \cdot s \cdot n \bmod n$$

However, $v \cdot s \cdot n \bmod n = 0$ based on the definition of the *Modulo* operator from Section 2.2. Therefore, $d_{K_{PR}}(y) = x \bmod n$. The same analysis holds true if $x = v \cdot p$, thus proving that $d_{K_{PR}}(e_{K_{PUB}}(x)) = x$ for all cases.

7.2   Efficient Implementation

7.2.1   Parameter Selection

RSA parameter selection significantly impacts the performance of the cryptosystem. The process of selecting values for p and q necessitates the application of a primality test to determine if a randomly chosen integer meets the cryptosystem requirements, i.e. is a prime number. This process is typically implemented via a *Monte Carlo* algorithm such as the *Miller-Rabin Algorithm*. The *Miller-Rabin Algorithm* determines whether or not an integer p is composite with respect to an arbitrary integer r. For 1000-bit prime numbers, the *Miller-Rabin Algorithm* is usually run three times with different integers r, whereas for shorter 150-bit prime numbers the algorithm is run up to twelve times with different integers r [202]. If the *Miller-Rabin Algorithm's* result is that p is not composite with respect to r for each r that is tested, then the probability that p is prime is extremely high.

Primality tests such as the *Miller-Rabin Algorithm* are considerably faster than *Integer Factorization* [301] and are thus used to find large prime numbers for use as the *RSA* parameters p

and q. The speed of a primality test is dependent upon the likelihood that a random integer p is prime, and this probability is $P(p \ is \ prime) \approx \frac{1}{ln \ p}$. Therefore, for a 1024-bit integer, $P(2^{1024} \ is \ prime) \approx \frac{1}{ln \ 2^{1024}} \approx \frac{1}{710}$, i.e. 1 of 710 1024-bit randomly selected integers will be prime. However, because all even numbers are composite (they have two as a factor) and such numbers are easily identified (their least significant bit is always a zero), these numbers are immediately discarded and are not passed through the primality test algorithm. By removing half of the search space, only 355 1024-bit randomly selected integers must be tested on average before a prime number is found. Thus, efficient primality tests such as the *Miller-Rabin Algorithm* are critical for finding large prime numbers to be used as the *RSA* parameters p and q.

The process of selecting a value for b must conform to the requirements that $0 < b < \phi(n)$ and the $gcd(\phi(n), \ b) = 1$. In practice, small values, termed *short exponents*, are often chosen for b in an effort to accelerate *RSA* encryption. Examples of such values include $b = 3$, $b = 17 = 10001_2$, and $b = 65,537 = 1 \ 0000 \ 0000 \ 0000 \ 0001_2$. Although small values of b minimize the number of exponentiations performed, choosing b such that its binary representation is composed primarily of zeros also significantly improves the performance of exponentiation algorithms, such as the *Square-and-Multiply Algorithm*, as will be shown in Section 7.2.2. Once b has been selected, a may be computed using either the *Extended Euclidean Algorithm* or the *Binary Extended Euclidean Algorithm*, both of which will also verify that the $gcd(\phi(n), b) = 1$. Note that the use of *short exponents* may only be applied to b because the resultant a will be of a bit length equivalent to the bit length of n even though b is a small value. Moreover, the public key, (b, n), is known because it is public, and knowledge of the public key does not provide an attacker with an advantage when attempting to determine the private key, (p, q, a), because the attacker must factor $\phi(n)$ to determine (p, q) and thus a. This technique is never used to accelerate decryption instead of encryption. Doing so implies choosing a small value for a, the exponent of the private key, and then calculating the corresponding value of b using either the *Extended Euclidean Algorithm* or the *Binary Extended Euclidean Algorithm*. This would allow an attacker to perform a simplified *Exhaustive Key Search* attack, focusing on small values and thus quickly yielding a and compromising the cryptosystem. The attacker would then be able to decrypt all messages sent to the owner of the keys even though p and q are not known.

7.2.2   Exponentiation

Exponentiation in *RSA* may be generalized as the repeated application of the *Group* operation, in this case multiplication, to an element x in the *Ring* Z_n. Two options are available to accelerate exponentiation:

1. Reduce the number of *Group* operations that must be performed.

2. Accelerate the *Group* operation.

Sections 7.2.3, 7.2.4, 7.2.4.4, and 7.2.5 will focus on accelerating the *RSA Group* operation, i.e. multiplication, while this Section will examine methods for reducing the number of *RSA Group* operations performed during exponentiation.

As will be discussed in Section 7.3, the *RSA* parameters n and a, the plaintext x, and the ciphertext y are typically on the order of 1,024 bits or more in length whereas b is usually selected to be a *short exponent*. Performing iterative exponentiation with 1024-bit exponents, i.e. of the form:

$$x^2 = x \cdot x$$
$$x^3 = x^2 \cdot x$$
$$x^4 = x^3 \cdot x$$
$$\vdots$$

is not feasible if the exponentiation is to be completed in a reasonable amount of time. In such an implementation, computing x^i requires $i - 1$ multiplications. A significantly faster exponentiation method is the *Square-and-Multiply Algorithm*. The *Square-and-Multiply Algorithm* evaluates the exponent i as a binary value and builds x^i in an iterative manner through squaring and multiplication operations. The algorithm begins with the value x^{1_2} and the exponent i is scanned from most significant bit to least significant bit (left to right) with the most significant bit assumed to be a one. The value x^{1_2} is squared, resulting in the value $x^{10_2} = x^2$. If the bit of the exponent i being evaluated is a one then the result from the squaring stage is multiplied by x, resulting in the value $x^{11_2} = x^3$; otherwise, no multiplication occurs. The algorithm repeats until all bits of the exponent i have been evaluated and x^i has been fully computed.

Example 7.2: Compute $z = x^{17}$ using the *Square-and-Multiply Algorithm* showing the intermediate values at each step. Compare the number of multiplications required versus iterative exponentiation.

The exponent $17 = 10001_2 = i_4 i_3 i_2 i_1 i_0$. Therefore, the *Square-and-Multiply Algorithm* proceeds as follows:

$$z = x \; ; \; i_4 = 1$$

$$z = x \cdot x = x^2 = x^{10_2} \; ; \; i_3 = 0$$

$$z = x^2 \cdot x^2 = x^4 = x^{100_2} \; ; \; i_2 = 0$$

$$z = x^4 \cdot x^4 = x^8 = x^{1000_2} \; ; \; i_1 = 0$$

$$z = x^8 \cdot x^8 = x^{16} = x^{10000_2}$$

$$z = x^{16} \cdot x = x^{17} = x^{10001_2} \; ; \; i_0 = 1$$

The *Square-and-Multiply Algorithm* requires four squarings and one multiplication to compute x^{17} versus sixteen multiplications required to compute x^{17} via iterative exponentiation.

Example 7.3: Compute $z = x^{23}$ using the *Square-and-Multiply Algorithm* showing the intermediate values at each step. Compare the number of multiplications required versus iterative exponentiation.

The exponent $23 = 10111_2 = i_4 i_3 i_2 i_1 i_0$. Therefore, the *Square-and-Multiply Algorithm* proceeds as follows:

$$z = x \; ; \; i_4 = 1$$
$$z = x \cdot x = x^2 = x^{10_2} \; ; \; i_3 = 0$$
$$z = x^2 \cdot x^2 = x^4 = x^{100_2}$$
$$z = x^4 \cdot x = x^5 = x^{101_2} \; ; \; i_2 = 1$$
$$z = x^5 \cdot x^5 = x^{10} = x^{1010_2}$$
$$z = x^{10} \cdot x = x^{11} = x^{1011_2} \; ; \; i_1 = 1$$
$$z = x^{11} \cdot x^{11} = x^{22} = x^{10110_2}$$
$$z = x^{22} \cdot x = x^{23} = x^{10111_2} \; ; \; i_0 = 1$$

The *Square-and-Multiply Algorithm* requires four squarings and three multiplications to compute x^{23} versus twenty-two multiplications required to compute x^{23} via iterative exponentiation.

Example 7.4: Compute $z = x^{91}$ using the *Square-and-Multiply Algorithm* showing the intermediate values at each step. Compare the number of multiplications required versus iterative exponentiation.

The exponent $91 = 1011011_2 = i_6 i_5 i_4 i_3 i_2 i_1 i_0$. Therefore, the *Square-and-Multiply Algorithm* proceeds as follows:

$$z = x \; ; \; i_6 = 1$$
$$z = x \cdot x = x^2 = x^{10_2} \; ; \; i_5 = 0$$
$$z = x^2 \cdot x^2 = x^4 = x^{100_2}$$
$$z = x^4 \cdot x = x^5 = x^{101_2} \; ; \; i_4 = 1$$
$$z = x^5 \cdot x^5 = x^{10} = x^{1010_2}$$
$$z = x^{10} \cdot x = x^{11} = x^{1011_2} \; ; \; i_3 = 1$$
$$z = x^{11} \cdot x^{11} = x^{22} = x^{10110_2}; \; i_2 = 0$$
$$z = x^{22} \cdot x^{22} = x^{44} = x^{101100_2}$$
$$z = x^{44} \cdot x = x^{45} = x^{101101_2} \; ; \; i_1 = 1$$
$$z = x^{45} \cdot x^{45} = x^{90} = x^{1011010_2}$$
$$z = x^{90} \cdot x = x^{91} = x^{1011011_2} \; ; \; i_0 = 1$$

The *Square-and-Multiply Algorithm* requires six squarings and four multiplications to compute x^{91} versus ninety multiplications required to compute x^{91} via iterative exponentiation.

The *Square-and-Multiply Algorithm* may be represented by the following pseudo-code to compute $x^i \; mod \; n$ where l represents the number of bits in the exponent i, thus resulting in i being represented as $i_{l-1}i_{l-2}\ldots i_1 i_0$:

1. $z = x$

2. For $k = (l - 2) \; Downto \; 0$

   (a) $z = z \cdot z \; mod \; n$

   (b) If $i_k = 1$ Then $z = z \cdot x \; mod \; n$

If the exponent i is assumed to have l bits, then the *Square-and-Multiply Algorithm* will require $l - 1$ squarings because x^1 requires no computation. The number of multiplications required will depend on the number of ones in the binary representation of the exponent i. The minimum number of multiplications will be zero (when only the most significant bit of i is a one) and the maximum number of multiplications will be $l - 1$ (when all of the bits of i are one). On average, $\frac{l-1}{2}$ multiplications will be required, resulting in the *Square-and-Multiply Algorithm* having a complexity of $l - 1 + \frac{l-1}{2} = 1.5 \cdot (l - 1)$ operations. This logarithmic complexity is a significant improvement versus iterative exponentiation, which demonstrates a linear complexity.

Example 7.5: Compute the average number of operations required to compute x^i using the *Square-and-Multiply Algorithm* versus iterative exponentiation for a 256-bit exponent.

For a 256-bit exponent, the *Square-and-Multiply Algorithm* will require $1.5 \cdot (256 - 1) = 382.5$ operations on average to compute x^i. The iterative exponentiation method will require $2^{256} - 1 \approx 1.16 \times 10^{77}$ operations to compute x^i.

Example 7.6: Compute the average number of operations required to compute x^i using the *Square-and-Multiply Algorithm* versus iterative exponentiation for a 1024-bit exponent.

For a 1024-bit exponent, the *Square-and-Multiply Algorithm* will require $1.5 \cdot (1024 - 1) = 1534.5$ operations on average to compute x^i. The iterative exponentiation method will require $2^{1024} - 1 \approx 1.80 \times 10^{308}$ operations to compute x^i.

It is critical to note that the pseudo-code for the *Square-and-Multiply Algorithm* applies reduction modulo n after every squaring and multiplication. Reducing each intermediate product modulo n ensures that intermediate products remain relatively small, reducing the complexity of future squarings and multiplications. However, recall that modular reduction performs division, which is slow and resource intensive in both software and hardware. Thus, the reduction in size of intermediate products must be balanced against the increased use of division. Section 7.2.4.4 will investigate methods of avoiding division by applying a transformation to a basis which results in division and multiplication becoming shifting operations. Also note that a squaring or multiplication using the *RSA* parameters with 1,024 bits or more in length requires many smaller multiplications when mapped to software implementations targeting general purpose processors whose word sizes range from 8 to 64 bits in length. Such multiplications generate numerous intermediate partial products that must be combined to form the final product of the multi-precision squaring or multiplication. Moreover, multi-precision arithmetic requires complex data structures and memory management to effectively manipulate the subcomponents of the data being operated on. These issues have a significant impact on the performance of squaring and multiplication operations and will be discussed in detail in Section 7.2.4.

The *Square-and-Multiply Algorithm* operates upon the exponent a single bit at a time. An improvement to the *Square-and-Multiply Algorithm*, termed the *k-ary Method*, evaluates the exponent i as a binary value and builds x^i by shifting the exponent i by more than one position, resulting in multiple squarings and one multiplication. The exponent i is represented as groupings of k bits, denoted as e_j, where each e_j ranges from zero to $2^k - 1$. The *k-ary Method* is composed of two stages: precomputation and exponentiation. The precomputation stage generates and stores the values x^0, x^1, x^2, x^3, ... $x^{2^k - 2}$, $x^{2^k - 1}$ (all reduced modulo n). Thus, the precomputation stage requires one squaring to compute $x^2 \ mod \ n$ and $2^k - 3$ multiplications because $x^0 = 1$ and $x^1 = x$ do not have to be computed.

The exponentiation stage of the *k-ary Method* evaluates the exponent i as a binary value in groupings of k bits and builds x^i in an iterative manner through squaring and multiplication operations. The algorithm begins with the value $x^{e_{t-1}}$, where $x^{e_{t-1}}$ is one of the precomputed values and e_{t-1} is the k most significant bits of the exponent i. i is then scanned from left to right in k-bit groupings denoted as $e_{t-1}e_{t-2}\dots e_1e_0$. The value $x^{e_{t-1}}$ is squared k times, resulting in the value $x^{e_{t-1}0000\dots0000_2}$, where the new exponent is e_{t-1} followed by k zeros. If the k-bit grouping of the exponent i being evaluated (denoted as e_j) is zero, then no multiplication is performed because $x^0 = 1$. If e_j is not zero, then multiplication by x^{e_j}, one of the precomputed values, is performed. The process repeats until all bits of the exponent i have been evaluated and x^i has been fully computed.

Example 7.7: Compute $z = x^{17}$ using the *k-ary Method* for $k = 3$, showing the intermediate values at each step. Compare the number of squarings and multiplications required versus the results of **Example 7.2** using the *Square-and-Multiply Algorithm*.

The exponent $17 = 010\ 001_2 = e_1 e_0$. Therefore, the k-ary $Method$ proceeds as follows. The precomputation stage computes and stores the values for x^0, x^1, $\ldots$ x^6, x^7, requiring a total of one squaring and five multiplications. Exponentiation then follows:

$$z = x^{010_2} = x^2$$

$$z = x^2 \cdot x^2 = x^4 = x^{010\ 0_2}$$

$$z = x^4 \cdot x^4 = x^8 = x^{010\ 00_2}$$

$$z = x^8 \cdot x^8 = x^{16} = x^{010\ 000_2}$$

$$z = x^{16} \cdot x^{001_2} = x^{17} = x^{010\ 001_2}$$

The k-ary $Method$ requires a total of four squarings and six multiplications to compute x^{17}. **Example 7.2** required four squarings and one multiplications to compute x^{17}. Therefore, in this case the $Square$-and-$Multiply$ $Algorithm$ performs better than the k-ary $Method$ for $k = 3$.

Example 7.8: Compute $z = x^{23}$ using the k-ary $Method$ for $k = 3$, showing the intermediate values at each step. Compare the number of squarings and multiplications required versus the results of **Example 7.3** using the $Square$-and-$Multiply$ $Algorithm$.

The exponent $23 = 010\ 111_2 = e_1 e_0$. Therefore, the k-ary $Method$ proceeds as follows. The precomputation stage computes and stores the values for x^0, x^1, ... x^6, x^7, requiring a total of one squaring and five multiplications. Exponentiation then follows:

$$z = x^{010_2} = x^2$$

$$z = x^2 \cdot x^2 = x^4 = x^{010\ 0_2}$$

$$z = x^4 \cdot x^4 = x^8 = x^{010\ 00_2}$$

$$z = x^8 \cdot x^8 = x^{16} = x^{010\ 000_2}$$

$$z = x^{16} \cdot x^{111_2} = x^{23} = x^{010\ 111_2}$$

The *k-ary Method* requires a total of four squarings and six multiplications to compute x^{23}. **Example 7.3** required four squarings and three multiplications to compute x^{23}. Therefore, in this case the *Square-and-Multiply Algorithm* performs better than the *k-ary Method* for $k = 3$.

Example 7.9: Compute $z = x^{91}$ using the *k-ary Method* for $k = 3$, showing the intermediate values at each step. Compare the number of squarings and multiplications required versus the results of **Example 7.4** using the *Square-and-Multiply Algorithm*.

The exponent $91 = 001\ 011\ 011_2 = e_2 e_1 e_0$. Therefore, the *k-ary Method* proceeds as follows. The precomputation stage computes and stores the values for x^0, x^1, ... x^6, x^7, requiring a total of one squaring and five multiplications. Exponentiation then follows:

$$z = x^{001_2} = x$$

$$z = x \cdot x = x^2 = x^{001\ 0_2}$$

$$z = x^2 \cdot x^2 = x^4 = x^{001\ 00_2}$$

$$z = x^4 \cdot x^4 = x^8 = x^{001\ 000_2}$$

$$z = x^8 \cdot x^{011_2} = x^{11} = x^{001\ 011_2}$$

$$z = x^{11} \cdot x^{11} = x^{22} = x^{001\ 011\ 0_2}$$

$$z = x^{22} \cdot x^{22} = x^{44} = x^{001\ 011\ 00_2}$$

$$z = x^{44} \cdot x^{44} = x^{88} = x^{001\ 011\ 000_2}$$

$$z = x^{88} \cdot x^{011_2} = x^{91} = x^{001\ 011\ 011_2}$$

The *k-ary Method* requires a total of seven squarings and seven multiplications to compute x^{91}. **Example 7.4** required six squarings and four multiplications to compute x^{91}. Therefore, in this case the *Square-and-Multiply Algorithm* performs better than the *k-ary Method* for $k = 3$.

Example 7.10: Compute $z = x^{1023}$ using the *k-ary Method* for $k = 2$ and $k = 3$, showing the intermediate values at each step.

The exponent $1023 = 11\ 11\ 11\ 11\ 11_2 = e_4 e_3 e_2 e_1 e_0$. Therefore, the *k-ary Method* proceeds as follows for $k = 2$. The precomputation stage computes and stores the values for x^0, x^1, x^2, x^3, requiring a total of one squaring and one multiplication. Exponentiation then follows:

$$z = x^{11_2} = x^3$$

$$z = x^3 \cdot x^3 = x^6 = x^{11\ 0_2}$$

$$z = x^6 \cdot x^6 = x^{12} = x^{11\ 00_2}$$

$$z = x^{12} \cdot x^{11_2} = x^{15} = x^{11\ 11_2}$$

$$z = x^{15} \cdot x^{15} = x^{30} = x^{11\ 11\ 0_2}$$

$$z = x^{30} \cdot x^{30} = x^{60} = x^{11\ 11\ 00_2}$$

$$z = x^{60} \cdot x^{11_2} = x^{63} = x^{11\ 11\ 11_2}$$

$$z = x^{63} \cdot x^{63} = x^{126} = x^{11\ 11\ 11\ 0_2}$$

$$z = x^{126} \cdot x^{126} = x^{252} = x^{11\ 11\ 11\ 00_2}$$

$$z = x^{252} \cdot x^{11_2} = x^{255} = x^{11\ 11\ 11\ 11_2}$$

$$z = x^{255} \cdot x^{255} = x^{510} = x^{11\ 11\ 11\ 11\ 0_2}$$

$$z = x^{510} \cdot x^{510} = x^{1020} = x^{11\ 11\ 11\ 11\ 00_2}$$

$$z = x^{1020} \cdot x^{11_2} = x^{1023} = x^{11\ 11\ 11\ 11\ 11_2}$$

The exponent $1023 = 001\ 111\ 111\ 111_2 = e_3 e_2 e_1 e_0$. Therefore, the *k-ary Method* proceeds as follows for $k = 3$. The precomputation stage computes and stores the values for x^0, x^1, $\ldots$ x^6, x^7, requiring a total of one squaring and five multiplications. Exponentiation then follows:

$$z = x^{001_2} = x$$

$$z = x \cdot x = x^2 = x^{001\ 0_2}$$

$$z = x^2 \cdot x^2 = x^4 = x^{001\ 00_2}$$

$$z = x^4 \cdot x^4 = x^8 = x^{001\ 000_2}$$

$$z = x^8 \cdot x^{111_2} = x^{15} = x^{001\ 111_2}$$

$$z = x^{15} \cdot x^{15} = x^{30} = x^{001\ 111\ 0_2}$$

$$z = x^{30} \cdot x^{30} = x^{60} = x^{001\ 111\ 00_2}$$

$$z = x^{60} \cdot x^{60} = x^{120} = x^{001\ 111\ 000_2}$$

$$z = x^{120} \cdot x^{111_2} = x^{127} = x^{001\ 111\ 111_2}$$

$$z = x^{127} \cdot x^{127} = x^{254} = x^{001\ 111\ 111\ 0_2}$$

$$z = x^{254} \cdot x^{254} = x^{508} = x^{001\ 111\ 111\ 00_2}$$

$$z = x^{508} \cdot x^{508} = x^{1016} = x^{001\ 111\ 111\ 000_2}$$

$$z = x^{1016} \cdot x^{111_2} = x^{1023} = x^{001\ 111\ 111\ 111_2}$$

The *k-ary Method* requires a total of nine squarings and five multiplications to compute x^{1023} for $k = 2$ and a total of ten squarings and eight multiplications for $k = 3$. The *Square-and-Multiply Algorithm* requires eight squarings and eight multiplications to compute x^{1023}. Therefore, in this case the *Square-and-Multiply Algorithm* performs better than the *k-ary Method* for $k = 3$, but the *k-ary Method* performs better than the *Square-and-Multiply Algorithm* for $k = 2$. In the latter case, if a squaring is considered equivalent to a multiplication, the *k-ary Method* outperforms the *Square-and-Multiply Algorithm* by two multiplications.

Examples 7.7, **7.8**, **7.9**, and **7.10** demonstrate that the performance of the *k-ary Method* versus the *Square-and-Multiply Algorithm* is dependent upon both the number of bits in the exponent i versus the value chosen for k and how many of the bits in the exponent i are one. Moreover, the additional squaring and multiplications incurred as part of the precomputation stage significantly impact the performance of the *k-ary Method* versus the *Square-and-Multiply Algorithm* for exponents with short bit lengths.

If the exponent i is assumed to have l bits, then the *k-ary Method* will divide the exponent i into $t = \frac{l}{k}$ k-bit groupings. Note that the most significant bits of e_{t-1} may require the addition of leading zeros so that e_{t-1} meets the requirements of being k bits in length. Because $x^{e_{t-1}}$ is obtained from the table of precomputed values, the exponentiation stage requires $(t-1) \cdot k$ squarings. The exponentiation stage performs a multiplication in $2^k - 1$ instances of the 2^k possible instances, resulting in a total of $(t-1) \cdot \frac{2^k-1}{2^k}$ multiplications on average. Combining the results of the precomputation and exponentiation stages yields a total of $k \cdot (t-1) + 1$ squarings and $2^k - 3 + (t-1) \cdot \frac{2^k-1}{2^k}$ multiplications on average for the *k-ary Method*.

It is possible to modify the *k-ary Method* to reduce the number of precomputations and thus improve the overall performance of exponentiation. This modified algorithm, termed the *Improved k-ary Method*, computes and stores only the values of x raised to odd exponents. Therefore the precomputation stage generates and stores the values x^1, x^3, ... x^{2^k-1}. Note that x^2 is generated as well and is used to compute the successive odd exponents of x, i.e. $x^3 = x \cdot x^2$, $x^5 = x^3 \cdot x^2$, etc. Thus the precomputation stage requires one squaring to compute $x^2 \bmod n$ and $\frac{2^k}{2} - 1 = 2^{k-1} - 1$ multiplications because $x^1 = x$ does not have to be computed.

The exponentiation stage of the *Improved k-ary Method* is similar to the exponentiation stage of the *k-ary Method* in that it evaluates the exponent i as a binary value in groupings of k bits and builds x^i in an iterative manner through squaring and multiplication operations. The algorithm begins with the value $x^{e_{t-1}}$, where $x^{e_{t-1}}$ is one of the precomputed values and e_{t-1} is the k most significant bits of the exponent i. i is then scanned from left to right in k-bit groupings denoted as $e_{t-1}e_{t-2}\ldots e_1 e_0$. However, there are now two possible situations when evaluating e_{t-1}. e_{t-1} may be odd, in which case $x^{e_{t-1}}$ is available from the precomputation stage and the *Improved k-ary Method* operates exactly the same as the *k-ary Method*, performing k squarings and then multiplying the result by $x^{e_{t-1}}$. The *Improved k-ary Method* differs from the *k-ary Method* when e_j is even. In this case, x^{e_j} is not available from the precomputation stage. However, when e_j is even, it may be represented as $e_{k-1}e_{k-2}\ldots e_h 0 \ldots 0$, an exponent with h trailing zeros and a non-zero bit pattern of length $k - h$ bits which must be odd because bit e_h must be a one. Therefore, in the case where e_j is even, the *Improved k-ary Method* will perform $k - h$ squarings and then multiply by $x^{e_k - 1 e_k - 2 \cdots e_h}$, a value that must be available from the precomputation stage because $e_{k-1} e_{k-2} \ldots e_h$ must be odd. Once the multiplication is completed, the *Improved k-ary Method* will perform h squarings, completing the processing of exponent e_j. As in the *k-ary Method*, the process repeats until all bits of the exponent i have been evaluated and x^i has been fully computed. The exponentiation stage of the *Improved k-ary Method* results in the same number of squarings and multiplications as the *k-ary Method*, i.e. $(t - 1) \cdot k$ squarings and $(t - 1) \cdot \frac{2^k - 1}{2^k}$ multiplications on average. Combining the results of the precomputation and exponentiation stages yields a total of $k \cdot (t - 1) + 1$ squarings and $2^{k-1} - 1 + (t - 1) \cdot \frac{2^k - 1}{2^k}$ multiplications on average for the *Improved k-ary Method*.

Example 7.11: How many squarings and multiplications are required to compute $z = x^{17}$ using the *Improved k-ary Method* for $k = 3$? Compare the number of squarings and multiplications required versus the results of **Example 7.8**.

The exponent $17 = 010\,001_2 = e_1 e_0$. Therefore, the *Improved k-ary Method* proceeds as follows. The precomputation stage computes the values for x^1, x^2, x^3, x^5, and x^7, storing all but x^2 and requiring a total of one squaring and three multiplications. Exponentiation requires three squarings and one multiplication for a total of four squarings and four multiplications, a reduction of two multiplications versus the *k-ary Method* and equivalent performance to the results seen when using the *Square-and-Multiply Algorithm*.

Example 7.12: How many squarings and multiplications are required to compute $z = x^{23}$ using the *Improved k-ary Method* for $k = 3$? Compare the number of squarings and multiplications required versus the results of **Example 7.9**.

The exponent $23 = 010\ 111_2 = e_1 e_0$. Therefore, the *Improved k-ary Method* proceeds as follows. The precomputation stage computes the values for x^1, x^2, x^3, x^5, and x^7, storing all but x^2 and requiring a total of one squaring and three multiplications. Exponentiation requires three squarings and one multiplication for a total of four squarings and four multiplications, a reduction of two multiplications versus the *k-ary Method* although the *Square-and-Multiply Algorithm* yields better performance, requiring one less multiplication than the *Improved k-ary Method*.

Example 7.13: How many squarings and multiplications are required to compute $z = x^{91}$ using the *Improved k-ary Method* for $k = 3$? Compare the number of squarings and multiplications required versus the results of **Example 7.10**.

The exponent $91 = 001\ 011\ 011_2 = e_2 e_1 e_0$. Therefore, the *Improved k-ary Method* proceeds as follows. The precomputation stage computes the values for x^1, x^2, x^3, x^5, and x^7, storing all but x^2 and requiring a total of one squaring and three multiplications. Exponentiation requires six squarings and two multiplications for a total of seven squarings and five multiplications, a reduction of two multiplications versus the *k-ary Method* although the *Square-and-Multiply Algorithm* yields better performance, requiring one less squaring and one less multiplication than the *Improved k-ary Method*.

Example 7.14: How many squarings and multiplications are required to compute $z = x^{1023}$ using the *Improved k-ary Method* for $k = 2$ and $k = 3$? Compare the number of squarings and multiplications required versus the results of **Example 7.10**.

The exponent $1023 = 11\ 11\ 11\ 11\ 11_2 = e_4 e_3 e_2 e_1 e_0$ for $k = 2$. Therefore, the *Improved k-ary Method* proceeds as follows. The precomputation stage computes the values for x^1, x^2, and x^3, storing all but x^2 and requiring a total of one squaring and one multiplication. Exponentiation requires eight squarings and four multiplications for a total of nine squarings and five multiplications, matching the performance of the *k-ary Method* and thus outperforming the *Square-and-Multiply Algorithm* by two multiplications if a squaring is considered equivalent to a multiplication.

The exponent $1023 = 001\ 111\ 111\ 111_2 = e_3 e_2 e_1 e_0$ for $k = 3$. Therefore, the *Improved k-ary Method* proceeds as follows. The precomputation stage computes the values for x^1, x^2, x^3, x^5, and x^7, storing all but x^2 and requiring a total of one squaring and three multiplications. Exponentiation requires nine squarings and three multiplications for a total of ten squarings and six multiplications, a reduction of two multiplications versus the *k-ary Method* while matching the performance of the *Square-and-Multiply Algorithm* if a squaring is considered equivalent to a multiplication.

Examples 7.11, **7.12**, **7.13**, and **7.14** demonstrate that the performance of the *Improved k-ary Method* is better than the performance of the *k-ary Method* versus the *Square-and-Multiply Algorithm*, with the improvement being a reduction of the computation and storage overhead associated with the precomputation stage. Once again, the additional squaring and multiplications incurred as part of the precomputation stage significantly impact the performance of the *Improved k-ary Method* versus the *Square-and-Multiply Algorithm* for exponents with short bit lengths.

In an effort to further optimize the performance of exponentiation, consider that significant inefficiencies are introduced by the *k-ary Method* and the *Improved k-ary Method* if the value k is poorly chosen. To mitigate this effect, k must be treated as a maximum window size, but the optimal window size must be determined on-the-fly based on the exponent's bit pattern. Therefore, the *Sliding Window Method* attempts to use windows of size k with the added requirement that the window must have a one as its least significant bit, guaranteeing that the window value is odd. If the window's least significant bit is a zero, the window size shrinks by one bit, *sliding* the right edge of the window one bit position to the left. This window evaluation process is repeated until the requirement that the window have a one as its least significant bit is met. Once the processing of a window has been completed, i.e. the necessary squarings and single multiplication have been performed, successive bits in the exponent that are zero result in continuous squarings until a non-zero bit is encountered, at which time the window evaluation process begins again. As in the *k-ary Method* and *Improved k-ary Method*, the process repeats until all bits of the exponent i have been evaluated and x^i has been fully computed. The *Sliding Window Method* both reduces the number of precomputed values (in the same manner as the *Improved k-ary Method*) and minimizes the number of windows, thus minimizing the number of multiplications.

The *Sliding Window Method* may be represented by the following pseudo-code to compute x^i where l represents the number of bits in the exponent i. Therefore, the exponent i is represented as $i_{l-1}i_{l-2}\ldots i_1i_0$:

1. Precompute all values of x raised to odd exponents ranging from 3 to $2^k - 1$

2. $j = l - 1$; Initialize loop to most significant bit of i (must be a 1)

3. $A = 1$

4. While $j \geq 0$:

    (a) If $i_j = 0$ Then

        i. $A = A^2$; Square until non-zero bit encountered

        ii. $j = j - 1$

    (b) Else

        i. Find the longest bit string $e_j e_{j-1} \ldots e_m$ of length $j - m + 1 \leq k$ with $e_m = 1$

        ii. $A = A^{2^{j-m+1}}$; Square $j - m + 1$ times

        iii. $A = A \cdot x^{e_j e_{j-1} \ldots e_m}$; Multiply by precomputed value

        iv. $i = m - 1$; Move one position to the right of the finished window

---

Example 7.15: Compute $z = x^{1023}$ using the *Sliding Window Method* for $k = 4$, showing the intermediate values at each step. Compare the number of squarings and multiplications required versus the results of **Example 7.14**.

The exponent $1023 = 11\ 1111\ 1111_2$. Therefore, the *Sliding Window Method* proceeds as follows for $k = 4$. The precomputation stage computes the value x^2 and precomputes and stores the values for x^i, $i = 1, 3, 5, 7, 9, 11, 13, 15$, requiring a total of one squaring and seven multiplications. Exponentiation then follows:

$$z = 1$$

$$Window\ Size = 4,\ Window = 1111_2$$

$$z = 1 \cdot x^{1111_2} = x^{15} = x^{1111_2}$$

$$z = x^{15} \cdot x^{15} = x^{30} = x^{1111\ 0_2}$$

$$z = x^{30} \cdot x^{30} = x^{60} = x^{1111\ 00_2}$$

$$z = x^{60} \cdot x^{60} = x^{120} = x^{1111\ 000_2}$$

$$z = x^{120} \cdot x^{120} = x^{240} = x^{1111\ 0000_2}$$

$$z = x^{240} \cdot x^{1111_2} = x^{255} = x^{1111\ 1111_2}$$

$$New\ Window\ Size = 2\ for\ LSBs,\ Window = 11_2$$

$$z = x^{255} \cdot x^{255} = x^{510} = x^{1111\ 11110_2}$$

$$z = x^{510} \cdot x^{510} = x^{1020} = x^{1111\ 111100_2}$$

$$z = x^{1020} \cdot x^{11_2} = x^{1023} = x^{1111\ 1111111_2}$$

The *Sliding Window Method* requires a total of six squarings and two multiplications for the exponentiation stage, resulting in a total of seven squarings and nine multiplications to compute x^{1023} for $k = 4$. This results in a reduction of two multiplications versus the *k-ary Method* while matching the performance of the *Square-and-Multiply Algorithm* and the *Improved k-ary Method* if a squaring is considered equivalent to a multiplication (see **Home-work Problem 7.4.26** for a detailed comparative analysis of the performance of exponentiation methods).

The *Square-and-Multiply Algorithm*, *k-ary Method*, *Improved k-ary Method*, and *Sliding Window Method* are all forms of *fixed exponent* exponentiation, where the exponent is fixed and the base is variable when computing x^i. Such methods map extremely well to *RSA*, where the exponent is either the public key b or the private key a, both of which are fixed once the set-up stage of the cryptosystem has been completed, and the base is either the plaintext x or the ciphertext y, both of which are variable. Although *fixed base* exponentiation methods, such as the *Fixed Base Windowing Method* [38], have also been proposed, these methods do not map as well to *RSA* and are therefore not considered here.

7.2.3   The Chinese Remainder Theorem

If the bit length of the *RSA* modulus n is denoted as l such that $l = \lceil log_2 n \rceil$, then the complexity of one modular multiplication or squaring is equivalent to $c \cdot l^2$, where c is a constant. Using the *Square-and-Multiply Algorithm* to perform exponentiation requires $1.5 \cdot (l - 1)$ operations for a total exponentiation complexity of $1.5 \cdot (l - 1) \cdot c \cdot l^2 \approx 1.5 \cdot c \cdot l^3$. This complexity may be adjusted for the use of other *fixed exponent* exponentiation methods described in Section 7.2.2. Based on the total number of operations required for each method and that $t = \frac{l}{k}$, the *k-ary Method* has a complexity of $(c \cdot l^2) \cdot (l - k + 2^k - 2 + (\frac{l}{k} - 1) \cdot \frac{2^k - 1}{2^k})$ while the *Improved k-ary Method* has a complexity of $(c \cdot l^2) \cdot (l - k + 2^{k-1} + (\frac{l}{k} - 1) \cdot \frac{2^k - 1}{2^k})$. Clearly, the complexity of these methods are highly dependent upon k, the window size of the groupings of bits of the exponent i.

The *Chinese Remainder Theorem* seeks to reduce the complexity of exponentiation by employing smaller sized operands. Assume a modulus $M = m_1 \cdot m_2 \cdot m_3 \cdot \ldots \cdot m_t$ where all of the m_i factors of M are pair-wise relatively prime, i.e. $gcd(m_i, m_j) = 1; 1 \le i, j \le t; i \ne j$. The *Chinese Remainder Theorem* states that if given a vector $x_1, x_2, x_3, \ldots x_t$ such that $x_i = X \bmod m_i$, then $X \bmod M$ may be uniquely reconstructed.

Example 7.16: Given a modulus $M = 143$ and $X = 15$, determine the vector x_i per the *Chinese Remainder Theorem*.

The modulus $M = 143 = 11 \cdot 13 = m_1 \cdot m_2$. Therefore, the vector x_i is computed as:

$$x_1 = X \bmod m_1 = 15 \bmod 11 \equiv 4 \bmod 11$$
$$x_2 = X \bmod m_2 = 15 \bmod 13 \equiv 2 \bmod 13$$

Assume that $M = m_1 \cdot m_2 \cdot m_3 \cdot \ldots \cdot m_t$, where all of the m_i factors of M are pair-wise relatively prime, and the vectors $x_1, x_2, x_3, \ldots x_t$ and $y_1, y_2, y_3, \ldots y_t$, where $x_i = X \bmod m_i$ and $y_i = Y \bmod m_i$. If $Z = X + Y \bmod M$ and $W = X \cdot Y \bmod M$, then $z_i = x_i + y_i \bmod m_i$ and $w_i = x_i \cdot y_i \bmod m_i$. Therefore, as evidenced by **Example 7.16**, when performing modulo M arithmetic, X may be viewed as either an integer of the form $0 \leq X < M$ or a vector of the form $x_1, x_2, x_3, \ldots x_t$; $0 \leq x_i < m_i$. The conversion of the integer X to the vector $x_1, x_2, x_3, \ldots x_t$ may be viewed as a forward transformation, T, while the conversion of the vector $x_1, x_2, x_3, \ldots x_t$ to the integer X may be viewed as the inverse transformation, T^{-1}. Figure 7.1 illustrates this relationship.

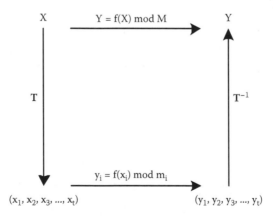

Figure 7.1: Chinese Remainder Theorem Transformation

The forward transformation is defined as $x_i = X \bmod m_i$; $1 \leq i \leq t$, and the inverse transformation is defined as $Y = \sum_{i=1}^{t} y_i \cdot M_i \cdot c_i \bmod M$, where $M_i = \frac{M}{m_i}$ and $c_i = M_i^{-1} \bmod m_i$ for

$1 \leq i \leq t$. $M_i^{-1} \bmod m_i$ must exist because $gcd(M_i, \; m_i) =$ $gcd(m_1 \cdot m_2 \cdot \ldots \cdot m_{i-1} \cdot m_{i+1} \cdot \ldots \cdot m_t, \; m_i) = 1$ as a result of the initial assumption that all of the m_i factors of M are pair-wise relatively prime. For the inverse transform to function, $Y = \sum_{i=1}^{t} y_i \cdot M_i \cdot c_i \bmod M$ and $Y = y_i \bmod m_i$ must be true for all i. Thus, consider the case of m_i:

$$Y = \sum_{i=1}^{t} y_i \cdot M_i \cdot c_i \bmod m_i$$

Expanding the summation yields $Y = (y_1 \cdot M_1 \cdot c_1 \bmod m_1) +$ $\ldots + (y_i \cdot M_i \cdot c_i \bmod m_i) + \ldots + (y_t \cdot M_t \cdot c_t \bmod m_t)$. However, because all of the m_i factors of M are pair-wise relatively prime, the $gcd(m_i, \; m_j) = 1; \; 1 \leq i, j \leq t; \; i \neq j$. Therefore, $y_j \cdot M_j \cdot c_j \bmod m_j = 0$ for all $i \neq j$, reducing the summation to:

$$Y = y_i \cdot M_i \cdot c_i \bmod m_i$$
$$Y = (y_i \bmod m_i) \cdot (M_i \cdot c_i \bmod m_i)$$

But $c_i = M_i^{-1} \bmod m_i$ and thus $M_i \cdot c_i \bmod m_i = M_i \cdot M_i^{-1} \bmod m_i \equiv 1 \bmod m_i$. Substituting this result into the summation yields:

$$Y = (y_i \bmod m_i) \cdot 1 \bmod m_i$$
$$Y = y_i \bmod m_i$$

Thus, because $Y = y_i\ mod\ m_i$ is true for all i, $Y = \sum_{i=1}^{t} y_i \cdot M_i \cdot c_i\ mod\ M$ must be true and the inverse transformation must also hold true.

The applicability of the *Chinese Remainder Theorem* to *RSA* is based on the fact that all arithmetic is performed modulo $n = p \cdot q$. Therefore the *Chinese Remainder Theorem* may be applied to *RSA* with $t = 2$ given that the $gcd(p,\ q) = 1$. This leads to the relationship shown in Figure 7.2.

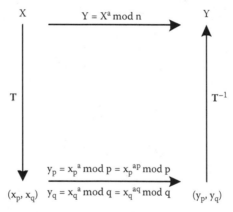

Figure 7.2: Chinese Remainder Theorem Transformation Applied to RSA

The *Chinese Remainder Theorem* is applied to *RSA* by performing the forward transformation on the plaintext x to yield the vector $(x_p,\ x_q)$, where $x_p = X\ mod\ p$ and $x_q = X\ mod\ q$. Arithmetic is then performed in either Z_p^* or Z_q^*. The goal is then to compute $x_p^a\ mod\ p$ and $x_q^a\ mod\ q$. However, it is possible to reduce the number of exponentiations that must be performed by reducing a. Note that:

$$x_p^a \bmod p \;=\; x_p^{i(p-1)+a_p}$$

and

$$x_q^a \bmod q \;=\; x_q^{j(q-1)+a_q}$$

implying that the exponent a may be represented as $a = i \cdot (p - 1) + a_p$ and $a = j \cdot (q - 1) + a_q$. Therefore, the equations may be rearranged, resulting in:

$$x_p^a \bmod p \;=\; x_p^{(p-1)^i} \cdot x_p^{a_p}$$

and

$$x_q^a \bmod q \;=\; x_q^{(q-1)^j} \cdot x_q^{a_q}$$

However, according to *Fermat's Little Theorem*, $a^{p-1} \equiv 1 \bmod p$ if the $gcd(a,\ p) = 1$, which must be the case if p is prime. Therefore, $x_p^a \bmod p \equiv x_p^{a_p} \bmod p$ and $x_q^a \bmod q \equiv x_q^{a_q} \bmod p$, where $a_p \equiv a \bmod (p - 1)$ and $a_q \equiv a \bmod (q - 1)$. $x_p^a \bmod p$ and $x_q^a \bmod q$ may be computed using the *Square-and-Multiply Algorithm* or any of the other *fixed exponent* exponentiation methods described in Section 7.2.2.

Once exponentiation has been completed, the inverse transformation must be applied to convert (y_p, y_q) to Y. This transformation is achieved by computing $Y = y_p \cdot M_p \cdot c_p + y_q \cdot M_q \cdot c_q \bmod M$, where:

$$M = n$$
$$M_p = n/p = q$$
$$M_q = n/q = p$$
$$c_p = M_p^{-1} \bmod p = q^{-1} \bmod p$$
$$c_q = M_q^{-1} \bmod q = p^{-1} \bmod q$$

Substituting these values into the equation used to compute Y yields $Y = y_p \cdot q \cdot c_p + y_q \cdot p \cdot c_q \bmod n$

The inverses $M_p^{-1} \bmod p$ and $M_q^{-1} \bmod q$ may be obtained by once again using *Fermat's Little Theorem*, noting that:

$$q^{p-1} \equiv 1 \bmod p$$

and

$$p^{q-1} \equiv 1 \bmod q$$

if the $gcd(q, p) = 1$, which must be the case because both p and q are prime numbers. Expanding on these relationships yields:

$$q \cdot q^{p-2} \equiv 1 \bmod p$$

and

$$p \cdot p^{q-2} \equiv 1 \bmod q$$

Using the definition of the multiplicative inverse from Section 2.4, i.e. that $a \times a^{-1} \equiv 1 \bmod m$, yields:

$$q^{-1} \bmod p \equiv q^{p-2} \bmod p = c_p$$

and

$$p^{-1} \bmod q \equiv p^{q-2} \bmod q = c_q$$

Both $q \cdot c_p$ and $p \cdot c_q$ may be precomputed because these values are only dependent on n, which is known.

Example 7.17: Given the *RSA* parameters $p = 17$, $q = 19$, $n = p \cdot q = 17 \cdot 19 = 323$, and $\phi(n) = (p-1) \cdot (q-1) = 16 \cdot 18 = 288$. The public key is chosen as the *short exponent* $b = 7$, resulting in $a = b^{-1} \bmod \phi(n) = 7^{-1} \bmod 288 \equiv 247 \bmod 288$. If the plaintext $x = 21$, use the *Chinese Remainder Theorem* to compute the ciphertext $y = x^b \bmod n$.

The plaintext x must first be transformed to the vector (x_p, x_q):

$$x_p = x \bmod p = 21 \bmod 17 \equiv 4 \bmod 17$$

$$x_q = x \bmod q = 21 \bmod 19 \equiv 2 \bmod 19$$

Prior to exponentiation, the reduced exponents b_p and b_q must be computed:

$$b_p = a \bmod (p - 1) = 7 \bmod 16$$

$$b_q = a \bmod (q - 1) = 7 \bmod 18$$

Exponentiation is then performed to compute the vector (y_p, y_q):

$$y_p = x_p^{b_p} \bmod p = 21^7 \bmod 17 \equiv 13 \bmod 17$$

$$y_q = x_q^{b_q} \bmod q = 21^7 \bmod 19 \equiv 14 \bmod 19$$

The vector (y_p, y_q) must then pass through the inverse transformation to yield the ciphertext y. The inverse transformation requires the precomputation of M_p, M_q, c_p, and c_q:

$$M_p = n/p = q = 19$$

$$M_q = n/q = p = 17$$

$$c_p = M_p^{-1} \bmod p = q^{-1} \bmod p = 19^{-1} \bmod 17 \equiv 9 \bmod 17$$

$$c_q = M_q^{-1} \bmod q = p^{-1} \bmod q = 17^{-1} \bmod 19 \equiv 9 \bmod 19$$

Therefore, $q \cdot c_p = 19 \cdot 9 = 171$ and $p \cdot c_q = 17 \cdot 9 = 153$. The ciphertext y may now be computed as:

$$y = y_p \cdot q \cdot c_p + y_q \cdot p \cdot c_q \bmod n$$
$$y = 13 \cdot 171 + 14 \cdot 153 \bmod 323$$
$$y = 2,223 + 2,142 \bmod 323$$
$$y = 166 \bmod 323$$

Therefore, the ciphertext $y = 166$ and this is confirmed by computing $y = 21^7 \bmod 323 \equiv 166 \bmod 323$.

Example 7.18: Given the *RSA* parameters $p = 17$, $q = 19$, $n = p \cdot q = 17 \cdot 19 = 323$, and $\phi(n) = (p-1) \cdot (q-1) = 16 \cdot 18 = 288$. The public key is chosen as the *short exponent* $b = 7$, resulting in $a = b^{-1} \bmod \phi(n) = 7^{-1} \bmod 288 \equiv 247 \bmod 288$. If the ciphertext $y = 166$, use the *Chinese Remainder Theorem* to compute the plaintext $x = y^a \bmod n$.

The ciphertext x must first be transformed to the vector (y_p, y_q):

$$y_p = y \bmod p = 166 \bmod 17 \equiv 13 \bmod 17$$
$$y_q = y \bmod q = 166 \bmod 19 \equiv 14 \bmod 19$$

Prior to exponentiation, the reduced exponents a_p and a_q must be computed:

$$a_p = a \bmod (p - 1) = 247 \bmod 16 \equiv 7 \bmod 16$$
$$a_q = a \bmod (q - 1) = 247 \bmod 18 \equiv 13 \bmod 16$$

Exponentiation is then performed to compute the vector (x_p, x_q):

$$x_p = y_p^{a_p} \bmod p = 13^7 \bmod 17 \equiv 4 \bmod 17$$
$$x_q = y_q^{a_q} \bmod q = 14^{13} \bmod 19 \equiv 2 \bmod 19$$

The vector (x_p, x_q) must then pass through the inverse transformation to yield the plaintext x. The inverse transformation requires the precomputation of M_p, M_q, c_p, and c_q:

$$M_p = n/p = q = 19$$
$$M_q = n/q = p = 17$$
$$c_p = M_p^{-1} \bmod p = q^{-1} \bmod p = 19^{-1} \bmod 17 \equiv 9 \bmod 17$$
$$c_q = M_q^{-1} \bmod q = p^{-1} \bmod q = 17^{-1} \bmod 19 \equiv 9 \bmod 19$$

Therefore, $q \cdot c_p = 19 \cdot 9 = 171$ and $p \cdot c_q = 17 \cdot 9 = 153$. The ciphertext y may now be computed as:

$$x = x_p \cdot q \cdot c_p + x_q \cdot p \cdot c_q \bmod n$$

$$x = 4 \cdot 171 + 2 \cdot 153 \bmod 323$$

$$x = 684 + 306 \bmod 323$$

$$x = 21 \bmod 323$$

Therefore, the plaintext $x = 21$ and this is confirmed by computing $x = 166^{247} \bmod 323 \equiv 21 \bmod 323$, the original plaintext
from **Example 7.17**.

Example 7.17 demonstrates that the use of a *short exponent*
for b accelerates *RSA* encryption such that use of the *Chinese
Remainder Theorem* is not necessary. However, **Example 7.18**
demonstrates that the use of the *Chinese Remainder Theorem*
significantly accelerates *RSA* decryption. The speed-up associated
with the use of the *Chinese Remainder Theorem* is the ratio of
the complexity of exponentiation without the *Chinese Remainder
Theorem* to the complexity of exponentiation using the *Chinese
Remainder Theorem*. The complexity of exponentiation using the
Chinese Remainder Theorem depends on the size of the operands
and the number of exponentiations performed. The bit widths of
the operands are computed as $\lceil log_2 x_p \rceil$, $\lceil log_2 x_q \rceil$, $\lceil log_2 a_p \rceil$, and
$\lceil log_2 a_q \rceil$, all of which are approximately $\frac{l}{2}$ bits in length if the
bit length of the *RSA* modulus n is denoted as l such that $l = \lceil log_2 n \rceil$. Therefore, the complexity of a multiplication or squaring

is $c \cdot (\frac{l}{2})^2 = c \cdot \frac{l^2}{4}$, where c is a constant. The *Square-and-Multiply Algorithm* requires $1.5 \cdot (\frac{l}{2} - 1)$ operations and two exponentiations must be performed to compute x_p and x_q, resulting in a total of $2 \cdot 1.5 \cdot (\frac{l}{2} - 1) \cdot c \cdot \frac{l^2}{4} \approx 1.5 \cdot c \cdot \frac{l^3}{4}$ operations. Exponentiation without the *Chinese Remainder Theorem* requires $1.5 \cdot c \cdot l^3$ operations. Therefore the speed-up associated with the use of the *Chinese Remainder Theorem* is $\frac{1.5 \cdot c \cdot l^3}{1.5 \cdot c \cdot \frac{l^3}{4}} = 4$.

This complexity analysis may be adjusted for the use of other *fixed exponent* exponentiation methods described in Section 7.2.2. Based on the operands having approximately $\frac{l}{2}$ bits in length and that two exponentiations must be performed to compute x_p and x_q, the *k-ary Method* has a complexity of $(c \cdot \frac{l^2}{4}) \cdot 2 \cdot (\frac{l}{2} - k + 2^k - 2 + (\frac{l}{2 \cdot k} - 1) \cdot \frac{2^k - 1}{2^k})$ while the *Improved k-ary Method* has a complexity of $(c \cdot \frac{l^2}{4}) \cdot 2 \cdot (\frac{l}{2} - k + 2^{k-1} + (\frac{l}{2 \cdot k} - 1) \cdot \frac{2^k - 1}{2^k})$. The complexity of these methods is highly dependent on k, the window size of the groupings of bits of the exponent i. However, the speed-up associated with the use of the *Chinese Remainder Theorem* for these methods approaches four, which is the speed-up when using the *Square-and-Multiply Algorithm*. To illustrate, consider the *k-ary Method* for $k = 1$. Without the use of the *Chinese Remainder Theorem*, the complexity of exponentiation is $(c \cdot l^2) \cdot [(l - 1) + (l - 1) \cdot (\frac{2^k - 1}{2^k})]$ operations. Using the *Chinese Remainder Theorem*, the complexity of exponentiation is $(c \cdot \frac{l^2}{4}) \cdot 2 \cdot [(\frac{l}{2} - 1) + (\frac{l}{2} - 1) \cdot (\frac{2^k - 1}{2^k})]$ operations. The ratio of the complexity of exponentiation without the *Chinese*

Remainder Theorem to the complexity of exponentiation using the *Chinese Remainder Theorem* using the *k-ary Method* for $k = 1$ is $2 \cdot \frac{l-1}{\frac{l}{2}-1} \approx 2 \cdot \frac{l}{\frac{l}{2}} \approx 4$. Similar analyses may be performed for the *Improved k-ary Method* and for different values of k.

7.2.4   Multi-Precision Arithmetic

As will be discussed in Section 7.3, the *RSA* parameters n and a, the plaintext x, and the ciphertext y are typically on the order of 1,024 bits or more in length. However, the processor word size in modern computers typically fails to exceed 64 bits. Therefore, representing multi-precision integers requires multiple processor words and such integers are stored in multiple memory locations. Figure 7.3 shows the representation of a multi-precision integer using multiple w-bit storage locations, where w is the processor word size. In this example, the multi-precision integer D requires $n + 1$ w-bit storage locations. Note that the bit length of D is likely not evenly divisible by w and thus the upper bits of D_n are padded with zeros to fill the most significant bits of the storage location.

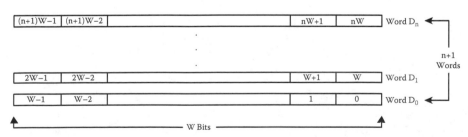

Figure 7.3: Storage Representation of a Multi-Precision Integer

D is represented mathematically in radix-b polynomial notation, where $b = 2^w$, and takes the form:

$$D = D_0 + D_1 \cdot 2^w + D_2 \cdot 2^{2w} + \ldots +$$
$$D_{n-1} \cdot 2^{(n-1)w} + D_n \cdot 2^{nw}$$

More succinctly, $D = (D_n, D_{n-1}, \ldots D_1, D_0)_b$ and algorithms may be constructed to perform different arithmetic operations using data structures of this type.

7.2.4.1 Addition

Consider the multi-precision addition of two integers X and Y:

$$X = (X_n, X_{n-1}, \ldots X_1, X_0)_b$$
$$Y = (Y_m, Y_{m-1}, \ldots Y_1, Y_0)_b$$

with $n \geq m$. The result of the addition is stored in:

$$Z = (Z_{n+1}, Z_n, Z_{n-1}, \ldots Z_1, Z_0)_b$$

Note that Z requires an additional storage word, Z_{n+1}, to hold an output carry that may result from the addition of the most significant words of X and Y. The multi-precision addition may be computed using the following pseudo-code [202]:

1. $C = 0$

2. For $i = 0\ To\ n$

   (a) $z_i = x_i + y_i + C\ mod\ b$

   (b) If $z_i = x_i + y_i + C < b$ Then $C = 0$

   (c) Else $C = 1$

3. $z_{n+1} = C$

Note that the reduction modulo b in Step 2a eliminates any over-flow bits from the addition of the most significant bits of x_i and y_i. The algorithm for multi-precision addition requires $n + 1$ iterations and thus has linear complexity in n.

7.2.4.2   Multiplication

Consider the multi-precision multiplication of two integers X and Y:

$$X = (X_n,\ X_{n-1},\ \ldots\ X_1,\ X_0)_b$$
$$Y = (Y_m,\ Y_{m-1},\ \ldots\ Y_1,\ Y_0)_b$$

with $n \geq m$. X and Y may also be represented using polynomial notation:

$$X = x_n \cdot b^n + x_{n-1} \cdot b^{n-1} + \ldots x_1 \cdot b + x_0$$
$$Y = y_m \cdot b^m + y_{m-1} \cdot b^{m-1} + \ldots y_1 \cdot b + y_0$$

Multiplication of the two polynomials yields a resultant polynomial of the form:

$$Z = X \cdot Y$$

$$Z = x_n \cdot y_m \cdot b^{n+m} +$$

$$(x_n \cdot y_{m-1} + x_{n-1} \cdot y_m) \cdot b^{n+m-1} + \ldots +$$

$$x_0 \cdot y_0$$

Example 7.19: Given the polynomials X and Y:

$$X = x_3 \cdot b^3 + x_2 \cdot b^2 + x_1 \cdot b + x_0$$

$$Y = y_3 \cdot b^3 + y_2 \cdot b^2 + y_1 \cdot b + y_0$$

Compute the product $Z = X \cdot Y$.

The product Z is computed as:

$$
\begin{aligned}
Z = \quad & X \cdot Y \\
Z = \quad & x_3 \cdot y_3 \cdot b^6 + x_3 \cdot y_2 \cdot b^5 + x_3 \cdot y_1 \cdot b^4 + x_3 \cdot y_0 \cdot b^3 + \\
& x_2 \cdot y_3 \cdot b^5 + x_2 \cdot y_2 \cdot b^4 + x_2 \cdot y_1 \cdot b^3 + x_2 \cdot y_0 \cdot b^2 + \\
& x_1 \cdot y_3 \cdot b^4 + x_1 \cdot y_2 \cdot b^3 + x_1 \cdot y_1 \cdot b^2 + x_1 \cdot y_0 \cdot b + \\
& x_0 \cdot y_3 \cdot b^3 + x_0 \cdot y_2 \cdot b^2 + x_0 \cdot y_1 \cdot b^1 + x_0 \cdot y_0 \\
Z = \quad & x_3 \cdot y_3 \cdot b^6 + (x_3 \cdot y_2 + x_2 \cdot y_3) \cdot b^5 + \\
& (x_3 \cdot y_1 + x_2 \cdot y_2 + x_1 \cdot y_3) \cdot b^4 + \\
& (x_3 \cdot y_0 + x_2 \cdot y_1 + x_1 \cdot y_2 + x_0 \cdot y_3) \cdot b^3 + \\
& (x_2 \cdot y_0 + x_1 \cdot y_1 + x_0 \cdot y_2) \cdot b^2 + \\
& (x_1 \cdot y_0 + x_0 \cdot y_1) \cdot b + x_0 \cdot y_0
\end{aligned}
$$

The multiplication of the polynomials X and Y results in the need to compute numerous *Inner Products* of the form $x_i \cdot y_j = u \cdot b + v = (u, v)_b$. These *Inner Products* are then combined to form the coefficients of each b^k of the resultant product polynomial Z, where $0 \leq k \leq i + j$. For the inputs:

$$X = (X_n, X_{n-1}, \ldots X_1, X_0)_b$$
$$Y = (Y_m, Y_{m-1}, \ldots Y_1, Y_0)_b$$

The multi-precision multiplication $W = X \cdot Y$, where $W = (w_{n+t+1}, w_{n+t}, \ldots w_1, w_0)_b$, may be computed using the following pseudo-code [202]:

1. $W = 0$

2. For $i = 0 \, To \, t$

    (a) $C = 0$

    (b) For $j = 0 \, To \, n$

        i. $(u, v)_b = x_j \cdot y_i + w_{i+j} + c$

        ii. $w_{i+j} = v$

        iii. $c = u$

    (c) $w_{i+j+1} = u$

The core operation in the multi-precision multiplication algorithm is the computation of $x_j \cdot y_i + w_{i+j} + c$, where x_j, y_i, w_{i+j}, and c are all single-precision integers stored in radix-b polynomial notation, where $b = 2^w$ and w is the processor word size. The value computed by $x_j \cdot y_i + w_{i+j} + c$ can always be stored in two processor words $(u, v)_b$. This is demonstrated by examining the maximum values of the operands in the expression to determine if the result is $\leq 2^{2w} - 1$, the maximum value that may be contained in a double word. Each operand has a maximum value of $2^w - 1$. Therefore, $x_j \cdot y_i + w_{i+j} + c$ may be represented as the combination of its maximum sized operands, taking the form:

$$Maximum\ Size = (2^w - 1) + (2^w - 1)^2 + (2^w - 1)$$
$$Maximum\ Size = 2 \cdot (2^w - 1) + (2^{2w} - 2 \cdot 2^w + 1)$$
$$Maximum\ Size = 2 \cdot 2^w - 2 + 2^{2w} - 2 \cdot 2^w + 1$$
$$Maximum\ Size = 2^{2w} - 1$$

Therefore, the maximum value of $x_j \cdot y_i + w_{i+j} + c$ fits exactly in a double word such that any non-zero value added to $x_j \cdot y_i + w_{i+j} + c$ results in the need for three processor words of storage space, as will be demonstrated in Section 7.2.4.3.

The algorithm for multi-precision multiplication requires the computation of $(n + 1) \cdot (t + 1)$ *Inner Products*. For equivalent sized operands X and Y, i.e. when $n = t$, the complexity of the multi-precision multiplication algorithm is $(n + 1)^2 \approx n^2$.

7.2.4.3 Squaring

Multi-precision squaring of an integer X, a special case of multi-precision multiplication, yields the resultant polynomial:

$$Z \; = \; X^2$$

$$Z \; = \; x_n \cdot x_n \cdot b^{2n} \; + \; (x_n \cdot x_{n-1} + x_{n-1} \cdot x_n) \cdot b^{2n-1} \; +$$
$$\ldots \; + \; x_0^2$$

Example 7.20: Given the polynomial X:

$$X \; = \; x_3 \cdot b^3 \; + \; x_2 \cdot b^2 \; + \; x_1 \cdot b \; + \; x_0$$

Compute $Z \; = \; X^2$.

Z is computed as:

$$
\begin{aligned}
Z = \quad & X^2 \\
Z = \quad & x_3 \cdot x_3 \cdot b^6 \; + \; x_3 \cdot x_2 \cdot b^5 \; + \; x_3 \cdot x_1 \cdot b^4 \; + \; x_3 \cdot x_0 \cdot b^3 \; + \\
& x_2 \cdot x_3 \cdot b^5 \; + \; x_2 \cdot x_2 \cdot b^4 \; + \; x_2 \cdot x_1 \cdot b^3 \; + \; x_2 \cdot x_0 \cdot b^2 \; + \\
& x_1 \cdot x_3 \cdot b^4 \; + \; x_1 \cdot x_2 \cdot b^3 \; + \; x_1 \cdot x_1 \cdot b^2 \; + \; x_1 \cdot x_0 \cdot b \; + \\
& x_0 \cdot x_3 \cdot b^3 \; + \; x_0 \cdot x_2 \cdot b^2 \; + \; x_0 \cdot x_1 \cdot b^1 \; + \; x_0 \cdot x_0 \\
Z = \quad & x_3^2 \cdot b^6 \; + \; (2 \cdot x_3 \cdot x_2) \cdot b^5 \; + \; (2 \cdot x_3 \cdot x_1 + x_2^2) \cdot b^4 \; + \\
& (2 \cdot x_3 \cdot x_0 + 2 \cdot x_2 \cdot x_1) \cdot b^3 \; + \; (2 \cdot x_2 \cdot x_0 + x_1^2) \cdot b^2 \; + \\
& (2 \cdot x_1 \cdot x_0) \cdot b \; + \; x_0^2
\end{aligned}
$$

The multi-precision squaring $W = X^2$, where

$$W = (w_{2n + 1}, w_{2n}, \ldots w_1, w_0)_b$$

may be computed using the following pseudo-code [202]:

1. $W = 0$

2. For $i = 0 \, To \, n$

    (a) $(u, v)_b = x_i \cdot x_i + w_{2i}$

    (b) $w_{2i} = v$

    (c) $c = u$

    (d) For $j = (i + 1) \, To \, n$

        i. $(r, u, v)_b = 2 \cdot x_j \cdot x_i + w_{i + j} + c$

        ii. $w_{i + j} = v$

        iii. $c = u$

    (e) $w_{i + n + 1} = u$

The core operation in the multi-precision squaring algorithm is the computation of $2 \cdot x_j \cdot x_i + w_{i + j} + c$ where x_i, x_j, $w_{i + j}$, and c are all single-precision integers stored in radix-b polynomial notation, where $b = 2^w$ and w is the processor word size. The value computed by $2 \cdot x_j \cdot x_i + w_{i + j} + c$ requires storage space greater than two processor words $(u, v)_b$. This is demonstrated by examining the maximum values of the operands in the expression to determine if the result is $\leq 2^{2w} - 1$, the maximum value that may be contained in a double word. Each operand has a maximum value of $2^w - 1$. Therefore, $2 \cdot x_j \cdot x_i + w_{i+j} + c$ may be represented as the combination of its maximum sized operands, taking the form:

$$Maximum\ Size \;=\; (2^w - 1) + 2 \cdot (2^w - 1)^2 + (2^w - 1)$$

$$Maximum\ Size \;=\; 2 \cdot (2^w - 1) + 2 \cdot (2^{2w} - 2 \cdot 2^w + 1)$$

$$Maximum\ Size \;=\; 2 \cdot 2^{2w} - 2 \cdot 2^w$$

$$Maximum\ Size \;=\; 2 \cdot 2^w \cdot (2^w - 1)$$

$$Maximum\ Size \;=\; 2^{w+1} \cdot (2^w - 1)$$

$$Maximum\ Size \;=\; 2^{2w+1} - 2^{w+1} > 2^{2w} - 1$$

Therefore, because the maximum value of $2 \cdot x_j \cdot x_i + w_{i+j} + c$ is $2^{2w+1} - 2^{w+1} > 2^{2w} - 1$, there is a need for three processor words of storage space, $(r,\ u,\ v)_b$.

The algorithm for multi-precision squaring requires the computation of $\frac{(n+1)^2 + (n+1)}{2} \approx \frac{n^2 + n}{2} \approx \frac{n^2}{2}$ *Inner Products*. Therefore, multi-precision squaring is approximately twice as fast as multi-precision multiplication.

7.2.4.4   Montgomery Arithmetic

Montgomery Arithmetic was proposed by Peter Montgomery in 1985 as a method for performing efficient modular arithmetic [210]. Although other methods, such as *Barrett Reduction* [20], have also been proposed, *Montgomery Arithmetic* remains the most popular method for performing efficient modular arithmetic. *Montgomery Arithmetic* addresses the issues associated with performing division to achieve modular reduction. To compute $x \equiv r \bmod m$ requires the computation of $q = x/m$ via integer division so that r may be computed as $r = x - q \cdot m$. However, base-10 division in both software and hardware tends to be slow and resource intensive. *Montgomery Arithmetic* therefore attempts to perform a transformation, similar to that of the *Chinese Remainder Theorem*, to a domain that does not require base-10 division.

Montgomery Arithmetic defines the *m-Residue* of an integer $a \in Z_m$ as $\tilde{a} = a \cdot R \bmod m$, where R is the *Radix*. The *m-Residue* may be viewed as a forward transformation whereas the inverse transformation is defined as $a = \tilde{a} \cdot R^{-1} \bmod m$. Figure 7.4 illustrates this relationship.

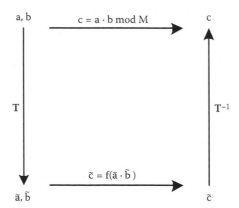

Figure 7.4: Montgomery Arithmetic Transformation

It is important to note that $\tilde{a} = a \cdot R \bmod m$; $0 \le i \le m - 1$ forms a *Complete Residue System* such that all possible values for a have a unique representation when transformed to the $\tilde{a}$ domain.

Example 7.21: Given $m = 11$ and $R = 16$. Compute the m-*Residues* for all possible values of $a \in Z_m$.

$$\tilde{a} = a \cdot R \bmod m = a \cdot 16 \bmod 11.$$

a	0	1	2	3	4	5	6	7	8	9	10
$\tilde{a}$	0	5	10	4	9	3	8	2	7	1	6

Having a *Complete Residue System* in place allows for the definition of the *Montgomery Reduction Algorithm*, denoted as *MRed(T)*, used for the efficient computation of $T \cdot R^{-1} \bmod m$ if $R = b^n$, where $b = 2^w$ and w is the processor word size. The *Montgomery Reduction Algorithm* employs T, the *Radix R*, and the modulus m, requiring that [202]:

1. $gcd(m, R) = 1$

2. $m' = -m^{-1} \bmod R$

3. $0 \leq T < R \cdot m$

The *Montgomery Reduction Algorithm* proceeds as follows:

1. $U \equiv T \cdot m' \bmod R$

2. $t = (T + U \cdot m)/R$

3. If $t \geq m$ Then $MRed(T) = t - m$

4. Else $MRed(T) = t$

The *Montgomery Reduction Algorithm* employs reduction modulo R in Step 1. This reduction is trivial to perform given that $R = b^n$. Once $T \cdot m' \equiv U = u_m u_{m-1} \ldots u_n u_{n-1} \ldots u_1 u_0$ is computed, reduction modulo R results in $U = u_{n-1} \ldots u_1 u_0$, i.e. the n least significant bits are saved and the most significant bits are discarded. Moreover, the division by R performed in Step 2 is also trivial given that $R = b^n = 2^{wn}$, resulting in a right shift of $(T + U \cdot m)$ by wn bits (or n digits).

To prove that $t = T \cdot R^{-1} \bmod m$, i.e. that the inverse transformation holds true, it first must be shown that $t = (T + U \cdot m)/R$ yields an integer. This may be demonstrated via Step 1 of the *Montgomery Reduction Algorithm*:

$$U \equiv T \cdot m' \bmod R$$
$$U \cdot m \equiv (T \cdot m') \cdot m \bmod R$$
$$U \cdot m \equiv (T \cdot -m^{-1}) \cdot m \bmod R$$
$$U \cdot m \equiv -T \bmod R$$
$$U \cdot m \equiv h \cdot R - T$$

where $h > 0$ is an integer. Therefore:

$$t = (T + U \cdot m)/R$$
$$t = (T + [h \cdot R - T])/R$$
$$t = [h \cdot R]/R$$
$$t = h$$

Thus t must be an integer. The inverse transformation may then be computed as:

$$t = (T + U \cdot m)/R$$

$$t \cdot R = T + U \cdot m$$

$$t \cdot R \equiv T \; mod \; m$$

Multiplying both sides of the equation by R^{-1} yields:

$$t \cdot R \cdot R^{-1} \equiv T \cdot R^{-1} \; mod \; m$$

$$t \equiv T \cdot R^{-1} \; mod \; m$$

Example 7.22: Given $T = 7$, $R = 100$, and $m = 97$. Compute *MRed(T)*.

To compute *MRed(T)* requires computation of:

$$m' = -97^{-1} \; mod \; 100$$

$$m' \equiv 3^{-1} \; mod \; 100$$

$$m' \equiv 67 \; mod \; 100$$

Knowing $m' = 67$, the three steps of the *Montgomery Reduction Algorithm* may be performed:

Step 1

$$U \equiv T \cdot m' \bmod R$$
$$U \equiv 7 \cdot 67 \bmod 100$$
$$U \equiv 469 \bmod 100$$
$$U \equiv 69 \bmod 100$$

Step 2

$$t = (T + U \cdot m)/R$$
$$t = (7 + 69 \cdot 97)/100$$
$$t = (7 + 6693)/100$$
$$t = 6700/100$$
$$t = 67$$

Step 3

Because $t < m$, $MRed(7) = 67$. This is verified by computing $t = T \cdot R^{-1} \bmod m$. $R^{-1} \bmod m = 100^{-1} \bmod 97 \equiv 65 \bmod 97$, resulting in:

$$t = T \cdot R^{-1} \bmod m$$
$$t = 7 \cdot 65 \bmod 97$$
$$t = 455 \bmod 97$$
$$t \equiv 67 \bmod 97$$

Having established the *Montgomery Reduction Algorithm MRed(T)*, when performing arithmetic where a, b, $c \in Z_m$ and $c = a \cdot b \bmod m$, then $MRed(\tilde{a} \cdot \tilde{b}) = \tilde{c}$. This statement is proved true by considering that:

$$\tilde{a} = a \cdot R \bmod m$$
$$\tilde{b} = b \cdot R \bmod m$$

Multiplying $\tilde{a}$ and $\tilde{b}$ yields:

$$\tilde{a} \cdot \tilde{b} = a \cdot b \cdot R^2 \bmod m$$
$$\tilde{a} \cdot \tilde{b} = c \cdot R^2 \bmod m$$

Applying the *Montgomery Reduction Algorithm MRed(T)* yields:

$$MRed(c \cdot R^2 \bmod m) = c \cdot R^2 \cdot R^{-1} \bmod m$$
$$MRed(c \cdot R^2 \bmod m) = c \cdot R \bmod m$$
$$MRed(c \cdot R^2 \bmod m) = \tilde{c}$$

Therefore, the transformation $f(\tilde{a} \cdot \tilde{b}) = \tilde{c}$ shown in Figure 7.4 must be $MRed(\tilde{a} \cdot \tilde{b})$. Figure 7.5 illustrates this relationship.

As shown in Figure 7.5, $\tilde{a}$ and $\tilde{b}$ are the *m-Residues* of a and b. The *m-Residues* are combined via a multi-precision multiplication

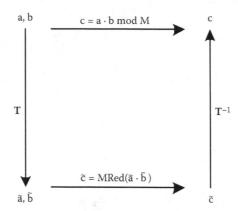

Figure 7.5: Montgomery Arithmetic Transformation with MRed

and then *MRed()* is applied to the product, resulting in $\tilde{c}$. Note that:

$$c \cdot R \ mod \ m \ = \ \tilde{c}$$
$$c \cdot R \cdot R^{-1} \ mod \ m \ = \ \tilde{c} \cdot R^{-1} \ mod \ m$$
$$c \ mod \ m \ = \ \tilde{c} \cdot R^{-1} \ mod \ m$$
$$c \ mod \ m \ = \ MRed(\tilde{c})$$

Therefore, the inverse transformation from $\tilde{c}$ to c is achieved by applying *MRed()* to the result of $MRed(\tilde{a} \cdot \tilde{b})$. This is significant in that the inverse transformation does not require base-10 division. However, the forward transformation requires two base-10 divisions to perform the modular reduction when computing $\tilde{a}$ and $\tilde{b}$. Therefore, use of the *Montgomery Reduction Algorithm* requires that multiple operations be performed in the $\tilde{a}$ domain to outweigh the performance overhead associated with the forward transformation to the $\tilde{a}$ domain. This requirement maps extremely well to exponentiation of the form $x^i \bmod n$, as shown in Figure 7.6. Any of the methods discussed in Section 7.2.2 may be used when performing exponentiation in the $\tilde{a}$ domain. When operating in the $\tilde{a}$ domain, the *Montgomery Reduction Algorithm, MRed()*, is used to reduce intermediate results versus the base-10 division required to reduce intermediate results modulo n in the original domain.

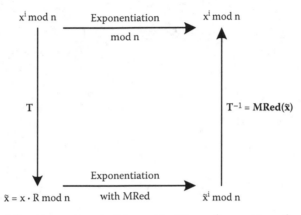

Figure 7.6: Montgomery Arithmetic Transformation for Exponentiation

The following pseudo-code presents a multi-precision implementation of the *Montgomery Reduction Algorithm, MRed()*, which computes the reduction of $T = (t_{2n-1}t_{2n-2}\ldots t_1 t_0)_b < m \cdot R$ for $m' = -m^{-1} \bmod b$ and $R = b^n$, where $b = 2^w$ and w is the processor word size [202]:

1. $A = T$

2. For $i = 0 \; To \; n - 1$

    (a) $u_i = a_i \cdot m' \bmod b$

    (b) $A = A + u_i \cdot m \cdot b^i$

3. $A = A/b^n$

4. If $A \geq m$ Then $A = A - m$

The algorithm for the multi-precision *Montgomery Reduction Algorithm, MRed()*, requires the computation of n *Inner Products* in Step 2a and n^2 *Inner Products* in Step 2b for a total of $n^2 + n \approx n^2$ *Inner Products*. Because *MRed()* must be performed twice, once to perform the modular reduction of $\tilde{a} \cdot \tilde{b}$ and once to convert $\tilde{c}$ to c, a total of $\approx 2 \cdot n^2$ *Inner Products* are required. Therefore, the complexity of the multi-precision *Montgomery Reduction Algorithm*, which requires $\approx 2n^2$ *Inner Products*, is roughly equivalent to the complexity of multi-precision multiplication, which requires $\approx n^2$ *Inner Products*.

7.2.4.5 Inversion

The *RSA* cryptosystem requires the computation of the private key $a = b^{-1} \bmod \phi(n)$, where $0 < b < \phi(n)$ and the $gcd(\phi(n), b) = 1$. In Section 6.7, *Euler's Theorem* was used to determine that $a^{-1} \equiv a^{\phi(m) - 1} \bmod m$, where m may be either prime or composite. The computation of the inverse was extended to $a^{-1} \equiv a^{p-2} \bmod p$ by *Fermat's Little Theorem* in Section 6.8 for the case where $m = p$ is prime, such as in *Discrete Logarithm* cryptosystems. Section 5.2.1 employed *Fermat's Little Theorem* to compute the inverse of a non-zero element $A(x)$ within

the *Extension Field $GF(p^m)$* as $A^{-1}(x) \equiv A(x)^{p^m - 2 \ mod \ P(x)}$.
The *Binary Extended Euclidean Algorithm*, an alternative method
for computing the inverse, was proposed in Section 6.5. The *Binary Extended Euclidean Algorithm* uses base-2 division instead of
base-10 division to compute the inverse, and base-2 division may
be implemented in a fast and efficient manner as a right shift of
the data by n bit positions when dividing by 2^n.

When m is composite, the computation of the inverse a^{-1} requires *Integer Factorization* of m to compute $\phi(m)$. As discussed
in Section 7.2.1, *Integer Factorization* is slow [301]. Moreover,
computing $a^{\phi(m)-1} \ mod \ m$, $a^{p-2} \ mod \ p$, or $A(x)^{p^m - 2} \ mod \ P(x)$
requires exponentiation with an average complexity of $\approx 1.5 \cdot l$
operations and a cost of $c \cdot l^2$ per modular multiplication when
using the *Square-and-Multiply Algorithm* for exponentiation. This
results in a total complexity of $1.5 \cdot l \cdot c \cdot l^2 = d \cdot l^3$,
where d is a constant and $l = \lceil log_2 n \rceil$ is the bit width of the
operands. Although this complexity may be improved by using
the enhanced exponentiation methods discussed in Section 7.2.2,
the *Binary Extended Euclidean Algorithm* is often a better implementation choice as a significantly faster method of computing the
inverse. As shown in Section 6.5, the pseudo-code for the *Binary
Extended Euclidean Algorithm* provides the inverse of r_1 in output
parameter D if the $gcd(r_1, r_0)$ is one and thus may be used to
compute $a = b^{-1} \ mod \ \phi(n)$, where $0 < b < \phi(n)$ and the
$gcd(\phi(n), b) = 1$ for the *RSA* cryptosystem.

7.2.5   The Karatsuba-Ofman Multiplication Algorithm

Consider the multiplication of two n-digit integers X and Y:

$$X = (X_{n-1}, X_{n-2}, \ldots X_1, X_0)_b$$
$$Y = (Y_{n-1}, Y_{n-2}, \ldots Y_1, Y_0)_b$$

X and Y may also be represented using polynomial notation:

$$X = x_{n-1} \cdot b^{n-1} + \ldots x_1 \cdot b + x_0$$
$$Y = y_{n-1} \cdot b^{n-1} + \ldots y_1 \cdot b + y_0$$

Multiplication of the two polynomials yields a resultant polynomial of the form:

$$Z = x_{n-1} \cdot y_{n-1} \cdot b^{2n-2} +$$
$$(x_{n-1} \cdot y_{n-2} + x_{n-2} \cdot y_{n-1}) \cdot b^{2n-3} + \ldots$$
$$+ x_0 \cdot y_0$$

The computation of Z via this method of multiplication requires n^2 *Inner Products*, denoted as $x_i \cdot y_j$. Consider the smaller polynomials A and B:

$$A \;=\; a_1 \cdot x + a_0$$
$$B \;=\; b_1 \cdot x + b_0$$

Multiplication of the two polynomials yields a resultant polynomial of the form:

$$C \;=\; a_1 \cdot b_1 \cdot x^2 + (a_1 \cdot b_0 + a_0 \cdot b_1) \cdot x + a_0 \cdot b_0$$

The computation of C via this straightforward method requires four multiplications and one addition. But C may be computed with fewer multiplications via the *Karatsuba-Ofman Multiplication Algorithm* by defining three intermediate products:

1. $D_0 \;=\; a_0 \cdot b_0$

2. $D_1 \;=\; (a_0 + a_1) \cdot (b_0 + b_1)$

3. $D_2 \;=\; a_1 \cdot b_1$

The product $C \;=\; A \cdot B$ is then computed using the three intermediate products as follows:

$$C \;=\; D_2 \cdot x^2 + (D_1 - D_0 - D_2) \cdot x + D_0$$

The computation of C via the *Karatsuba-Ofman Multiplication Algorithm* requires three multiplications and four additions, a decrease of one multiplication at the cost of three additional additions. The application of the *Karatsuba-Ofman Multiplication Algorithm* may be generalized for polynomials of higher degree. Consider the polynomial $A(x)$:

$$A(x) = a_{n-1} \cdot x^{n-1} + \ldots +$$
$$a_{\frac{n}{2}} \cdot x^{\frac{n}{2}} + a_{\frac{n}{2}-1} \cdot x^{\frac{n}{2}-1} + \ldots +$$
$$a_0$$

The polynomial $A(x)$ may be rewritten as the sum of two polynomials, $A_h(x)$ and $A_l(x)$, representing the upper and lower coefficients of $A(x)$. If $A_h(x)$ and $A_l(x)$ are defined as:

$$A_h(x) = a_{n-1} \cdot x^{\frac{n}{2}-1} + \ldots + a_{\frac{n}{2}}$$
$$A_l(x) = a_{\frac{n}{2}-1} \cdot x^{\frac{n}{2}-1} + \ldots + a_0$$

then $A(x) = A_h(x) \cdot x^{\frac{n}{2}} + A_l(x)$. $B(x)$ may be represented in a similar manner, resulting in:

$$C(x) = A(x) \cdot B(x)$$
$$C(x) = A_h(x) \cdot B_h(x) \cdot x^2 +$$
$$[A_l(x) \cdot B_h(x) + A_h(x) \cdot B_l(x)] \cdot x^{\frac{n}{2}} +$$
$$A_l(x) \cdot B_l(x)$$

The complexity of each multiplication is $(\frac{n}{2})^2 = \frac{n^2}{4}$. Using the straightforward method results in four multiplications for a total complexity of $4 \cdot \frac{n^2}{4} = n^2$. Using the *Karatsuba-Ofman Multiplication Algorithm* to compute $C(x)$ yields:

$$
\begin{aligned}
D_0(x) &= A_l(x) \cdot B_l(x) \\
D_1(x) &= (A_l(x) + A_h(x)) \cdot (B_l(x) + B_h(x)) \\
D_2(x) &= A_h(x) \cdot B_h(x)
\end{aligned}
$$

The product $C(x) = A(x) \cdot B(x)$ is then computed using the three intermediate products as follows:

$$
\begin{aligned}
C(x) &= D_2(x) \cdot x^n + \\
&\quad (D_1(x) - D_0(x) - D_2(x)) \cdot x^{\frac{n}{2}} + \\
&\quad D_0(x)
\end{aligned}
$$

The complexity of each multiplication is $(\frac{n}{2})^2 = \frac{n^2}{4}$. Using the *Karatsuba-Ofman Multiplication Algorithm* results in three multiplications for a total complexity of $3 \cdot \frac{n^2}{4}$. The *Karatsuba-Ofman Multiplication Algorithm* may be applied in a recursive manner to the three multiplications contained in each of the three intermediate values, $D_0(x)$, $D_1(x)$, and $D_2(x)$, resulting in each having a complexity of $3 \cdot (\frac{n}{4})^2 = \frac{3 \cdot n^2}{16}$. Therefore, the total complexity is $3 \cdot \frac{3 \cdot n^2}{16} = (\frac{3}{4})^2 \cdot n^2 \approx 0.56 \cdot n^2$. If $n = 2^i$, a likely characteristic when mapping to binary computers, then the number of

Inner Products for the *Karatsuba-Ofman Multiplication Algorithm* applied in a recursive manner is $n^{log_2 3} \approx n^{1.58}$.

Example 7.23: Given $n = 256$ (representing an n-digit number in base b) and two n-digit operands, denoted as A and B. To compute $C = A \cdot B$, how many *Inner Products* are required using the straightforward method? How many *Inner Products* are require using the *Karatsuba-Ofman Multiplication Algorithm*?

To compute $C = A \cdot B$ using the straightforward method requires $n^2 = 256^2 = (2^8)^2 = 2^{16} = 65,536$ *Inner Products*. To compute $C = A \cdot B$ using the *Karatsuba-Ofman Multiplication Algorithm* requires $n^{log_2 3} = 256^{log_2 3} = 6,561$ *Inner Products*. Therefore, using the *Karatsuba-Ofman Multiplication Algorithm* results in a reduction of the number of *Inner Products* required to compute C by a factor of 9.99 versus the number of *Inner Products* required to compute C using the straightforward method.

7.2.6 Performance

Multiple implementations of the *RSA* algorithm have been presented targeting a wide range of hardware technologies. These implementations take advantage of the optimization and acceleration methods described in Sections 7.2.1 through 7.2.5. The use of *short exponents* for encryption, fast exponentiation methods, the

Chinese Remainder Theorem, *Montgomery Arithmetic*, and the
Karatsuba-Ofman Multiplication Algorithm combine to form implementations that are fast and efficient. When considering 1024-
bit implementations of the *RSA* algorithm, numerous ASIC implementations have been published [1, 42, 123, 139, 161, 176, 333,
282, 335, 337], with reported decryption times as fast as 2.7 *ms*
[333], yielding a maximum decryption throughput of 379.3 Kbps.
Similarly, a wide variety of 1024-bit FPGA implementations of the
RSA algorithm exist in the literature [1, 35, 46, 97, 117, 160, 193,
196, 205, 207, 216, 221, 222, 223, 231, 264], with reported decryption times as low as 3.83 *ms* [207] and encryption times as low as
142.8 μs [97]. These values translate to a maximum decryption
throughput of 267.4 Kbps and a maximum encryption throughput
of 7.2 Gbps when considering FPGA targets. A comprehensive review of hardware architectures for the *RSA* algorithm (and other
public-key algorithms) is available in [23]. Software implementations of the *RSA* algorithm targeting processors such as the DEC
Alpha, Intel Pentium, and Digital Signal Processors such as the
Texas Instruments TMS320C6201 are also available in the literature. These implementations have yielded decryption times as low
as 36.5 *ms*, a full order of magnitude slower than the best hardware
implementations of the *RSA* algorithm [81, 172, 213, 241, 279].

When targeting either ASICs or FPGAs, even the best 1024-
bit implementations of the *RSA* algorithm are between one and
two orders of magnitude slower than equivalent implementations
of symmetric-key algorithms such as the block cipher *Rijndael*, as

discussed in Section 5.2.4. As a result, hybrid systems are typically used in practice. In such systems, slower public-key algorithms such as *RSA* are used for infrequently occurring operations, such as *key establishment* and the generation of *Digital Signatures*. *Key establishment* occurs only at the start of a communication session and a *Digital Signature* is generated only once for the entire stream of data being transmitted to provide message authentication and non-repudiation as discussed in Section 11.1. Frequently occurring operations, such as bulk data encryption, are performed by significantly faster symmetric-key algorithms, such as the block cipher *Rijndael*. As a result, hybrid systems combining public-key and symmetric-key algorithms exploit the best features of each type of algorithm to guarantee that the necessary security services are provided while also maintaining a high level of performance.

When combining the exponentiation and *Montgomery Arithmetic* techniques described in Sections 7.2.2 and 7.2.4.4, respectively, the computational complexity hinges on the addition of the inner products. Therefore, strategies for implementing high performance addition must be analyzed and evaluated for optimal performance. Typically, two strategies are used to implement high performance wide-operand modular addition: redundant representation and systolic arrays [34, 35].

Redundant representation number systems are used in conjunction with *Montgomery Arithmetic* to avoid carry propagation and are typically implemented as a redundant radix number system [87, 282, 306, 317]. In a redundant radix number system, the

operands are typically in binary representation while the intermediate partial products are in redundant representation. For iterative multiplication, the products of previous multiplications are
used as the operands to successive multiplications. This results
in the computational speed of iterative multiplication algorithms
being decreased due to conversions that require a carry-propagate
addition of long numbers at each multiplication stage [306]. The
conversion of the operands to non-redundant form may be avoided
by maintaining all operands in redundant form throughout the
multiplication process [306]. However, this results in a multiplier
that is nearly twice the length of a multiplier in non-redundant
form [282]. To avoid this increase in resources, the use of asynchronous carry completion circuits has been proposed [282]. An
asynchronous carry completion circuit detects the completion of
carry propagation and provides an indication to the multiplier
controller that the multiplication has completed. However, the associated cost of the asynchronous carry completion circuit is the
increase in the average number of cycles required to implement
modular multiplication. Another method of minimizing the propagation of carries by subtracting the modulus from intermediate
partial products has been proposed [282]. However, the cost of
this implementation is that an evaluation circuit is required to
compare the upper bits of the partial product with the upper bits
of the modulus, resulting in an increase in resources [317].

Other systems have been proposed to perform modular multiplication using *Montgomery Arithmetic* based on redundant repre-

sentation using a modified version of Brickell's multiplier [37]. System performance is enhanced by interleaving modular subtractions within the partial product calculations, pre-calculation of multiples of the modulus for use in the modular subtractions, and other speed-up techniques [87, 190]. Note that an overview of Ernest Brickell's multiplication algorithm (and other multiplication algorithms) may be found in [28]. Using similar techniques to the implementation in [87], an implementation where pre-computed modulus complements and the iterative Horner's rule are used to perform modular multiplication is presented in [146]. Based on a slightly modified carry-save adder structure, the implementation operates on the most significant bits first and evaluates the intermediate result to determine which multiples of the modulus to subtract [146].

The major hindrance of all of these implementations is that they require either a large number of clock cycles or a large amount of storage space to compute the modular multiplication [34, 35]. Additionally, if the modulus is to be dynamic, the stored values of the modulus multiples must be updated whenever the modulus is changed. Moreover, in the implementation in [146], the stored values of the modulus complements must also be updated whenever the modulus is changed. However, a speed-up factor of two has been demonstrated when comparing the implementation in [87] to other modular multiplication algorithms. Therefore, with sufficient storage space the implementation in [87] is a highly attractive solution, especially for systems with a dynamic modulus.

Systolic arrays [174] may be used to implement a multi-precision
RSA processor, and numerous systolic array approaches have been
proposed for implementing the modular arithmetic of the *RSA*
cryptosystem in conjunction with *Montgomery Arithmetic*. A
VLSI-based architecture to perform modular multiplication using
Montgomery Arithmetic is presented in [100]. The implementation
is physically realizable due to the limited number of processing elements and their simplicity of design. However, the architecture
requires approximately four times as many cycles to compute a
modular multiplication in comparison to more customary implementations [34, 35]. Two-dimensional systolic array architectures,
whose array size is based on the bit length of the modulus, have
been shown to achieve a throughput of one modular multiplication per clock cycle [34, 35, 138, 309, 318, 323]. This throughput is accomplished by performing multiple modular multiplication operations in parallel with each processing element operating on one bit, requiring n^2 processing elements, where n is the
number of bits in the modulus. The number of modular multiplication operations executed in parallel is equal to twice the bit
length of the modulus. Cryptographic algorithms such as *RSA*,
whose parameters are typically on the order of 1,024 bits or more
in length (as will be discussed in Section 7.3), result in an extremely large array size. However, the resource requirements of
two-dimensional systolic array architectures may be alleviated by
using larger processing elements that operate over multiple bits
[34, 35, 127, 150, 171, 182, 183, 185, 282, 316, 319, 328, 329].

Multiple systolic array implementations of the *RSA* algorithm have been presented targeting a wide range of hardware technologies. These implementations take advantage of optimization and acceleration techniques such as *Montgomery Arithmetic* and the *Chinese Remainder Theorem*. When considering ASIC implementations, numerous examples exist in the literature [1, 41, 113, 114, 136, 176, 178, 182, 183, 184, 185, 197, 239, 260, 284, 304, 318, 329, 332], yielding throughputs of up to 2.704 Mbps for 1024-bit implementations [185]. Similarly, a wide variety of FPGA implementations have been reported [1, 34, 35, 47, 59, 107, 117, 196, 197, 199, 203, 211, 231, 237, 313, 316, 318], yielding throughputs of up to 8.17 Mbps for 1024-bit implementations [107]. Note that the performance data assumes the worst case scenario of exponentiation using 1024-bit operands as opposed to exponentiation using *short exponents*, as is typically the case when performing encryption.

7.3   Attacks

The use of an *Exhaustive Key Search* to attack the *RSA* algorithm is performed by encrypting a plaintext x with the public key such that $y = x^b \, mod \, n$ and then trying all private keys $0 \leq a < \phi(n)$ to find the key that satisfies $x = y^a \, mod \, n$. Because the key space is a function of the size of $\phi(n)$, which is approximately the same size as the modulus n, the modulus must be chosen such that $n > 2^{500}$ to ensure that an *Exhaustive Key Search* attack is not feasible in practice.

With n chosen such that an *Exhaustive Key Search* attack is not practical, the only other known method for attacking the *RSA* algorithm is based on the *Integer Factorization* of n to determine $\phi(n)$ and thus a, the private key. Note that the following attacks are also possible:

1. Finding $\phi(n)$ given $y = x^b \bmod n$ and the public key. Once $\phi(n)$ is known, compute $a = b^{-1} \bmod \phi(n)$.

2. Finding a given $y = x^b \bmod n$ and the public key. Once a is known, the plaintext $x = y^a \bmod n$ is easily recovered.

However, the computation of $\phi(n)$ and the computation of a are both believed to be equivalent in complexity to the *Integer Factorization* of the modulus n. When performing *Integer Factorization* of the modulus n, the attacker must factor the modulus $n = p \cdot q$ to recover p and q and thus compute $\phi(n) = (p - 1) \cdot (q - 1)$. Once $\phi(n)$ is known, the attacker computes the private key $a = b^{-1} \bmod \phi(n)$ and is then able to recover all plaintexts $x = y^a \bmod n$.

Numerous *Integer Factorization* algorithms have been used to attack the *RSA* algorithm via the *Integer Factorization* of the modulus n. These include the *Quadratic Sieve*, the *Generalized Number Field Sieve*, and the *Lattice Sieve*. RSA Laboratories issued *RSA Factoring Challenges* in 1977 to both encourage research efforts and track the state of factoring capabilities [261]. The results of these challenges are shown in Table 7.1. The challenges were originally named based on the number of base-10 digits in the modulus n. In 2001, the challenges were renamed based on the number of binary bits in the modulus n. To date, the largest challenge that has been solved is **RSA-200**, where the modulus n has 200 base-10 digits, representing a 663-bit number. Note that the times required to complete the **RSA-160** and **RSA-576** challenges were not made available by the research groups that submitted the factored solutions that were verified as correct by RSA Laboratories. Also note that the times listed to complete the **RSA-640** and **RSA-200** challenges are for implementations targeting a 2.2 GHz Opteron CPU and that the **RSA-200** challenge was solved in a total of approximately three months using a cluster of 80 2.2 GHz Opterons [261].

Challenge	Modulus Digits	Date Factored	Time	Algorithm
RSA-100	100	April 1991	7 MIPS Years	Quadratic Sieve
RSA-110	110	April 1992	75 MIPS Years	Quadratic Sieve
RSA-120	120	June 1993	830 MIPS Years	Quadratic Sieve
RSA-129	129	April 1994	5000 MIPS Years	Quadratic Sieve
RSA-130	130	April 1996	500 MIPS Years	Generalized Number Field Sieve
RSA-140	140	February 1999	1500 MIPS Years	Generalized Number Field Sieve
RSA-155	155	August 1999	8000 MIPS Years	Generalized Number Field Sieve
RSA-160	160	April 2003	-	Lattice Sieve
RSA-576	174	December 2003	-	Lattice Sieve
RSA-640	193	November 2005	30 CPU Years	Lattice Sieve
RSA-200	200	May 2005	55 CPU Years	Lattice Sieve

Table 7.1: RSA Integer Factorization Challenge Results

Based on the results of the *RSA Factoring Challenges*, it is generally held that based on current computing technology, 1024-bit moduli, equivalent to numbers with approximately 310 base-10 digits, cannot be factored. Thus, the *RSA* parameters n and a, the plaintext x, and the ciphertext y are typically on the order of 1,024 bits in length while b is usually selected to be a *short exponent*. However, based on *Moore's Law* and potential advances in *Integer Factorization* algorithms, it is recommended that 2048-bit moduli be used with the *RSA* algorithm to ensure long-term security.

7.4   Homework Problems

Homework Problem 7.4.1: Compute the result of the exponentiation x^e *mod* m by applying the *Square-and-Multiply Algorithm* to:

a) $x = 2$, $e = 79$, $m = 101$

b) $x = 3$, $e = 197$, $m = 101$

After each iteration, show the exponent of the intermediate result in binary notation.

Homework Problem 7.4.2: Encrypt and decrypt using the *RSA* cryptosystem with the parameters:

a) $p = 3$, $q = 11$, $a = 7$, $x = 5$

b) $p = 5$, $q = 11$, $b = 3$, $x = 9$

Apply the *Square-and-Multiply Algorithm* whenever possible.

Homework Problem 7.4.3: Assume *Bob* has a pair of public/private keys for the *RSA* cryptosystem. Develop a simple protocol using the *RSA* cryptosystem that will allow the two parties, *Alice* and *Bob*, to agree on a shared secret key. Who determines the key in this protocol — *Alice*, *Bob*, or both?

Homework Problem 7.4.4: Develop a protocol similar to the one developed in **Homework Problem 7.4.3** in which both parties influence the key. Assume that both *Alice* and *Bob* have a pair of public/private keys for the *RSA* cryptosystem.

Homework Problem 7.4.5: Assume *Bob* has a pair of 1024-bit public/private keys for the *RSA* cryptosystem. *Alice* transmits a message to *Bob* by encrypting individual ASCII characters represented as integers between 0 and 127.

a) Describe how *Oscar* can easily decrypt any message sent by *Alice* to *Bob*.

b) Decrypt the ciphertext 182, 67, 67, 182, 84, 147 encrypted using the *RSA* cryptosystem with $n = 221$ and $b = 5$ without factoring the modulus n.

Homework Problem 7.4.6: One way of thwarting the attack described in **Homework Problem 7.4.5** is to encrypt several characters at once. However, there are a number of scenarios in which it is of interest to encrypt a single letter with a full-size *RSA* cryptosystem implementation, i.e. 1,024-bit modulus. What must be done to thwart the attack described in **Homework Problem 7.4.5**?

Homework Problem 7.4.7: The size of the modulus of RSA cryptosystem implementations has been increased over the years to thwart dramatically improved attacks, resulting in slower implementations as the word length increases. The performance of RSA implementations is dependent on how fast modular exponentiation of large numbers can be performed.

a) Assume that one modular multiplication or squaring of k-bit numbers takes $c \cdot k^2$ clock cycles, where c is a constant. How much slower is RSA encryption/decryption using a 1,024-bit modulus as compared to RSA encryption/decryption using a 512-bit modulus? Only consider the encryption/decryption itself with an exponent of full length and the *Square-and-Multiply Algorithm*.

b) In practice, the Karatsuba-Ofman Multiplication Algorithm, which has a complexity of $O(k^{log_2 3})$, is often used for multi-precision multiplication. Assume that this more advanced technique requires $c' \cdot k^{log_2 3} = c' \cdot k^{1.585}$ clock cycles for multiplication or squaring where c' is a constant. What is the ratio of RSA encryption/decryption using a 1,024-bit modulus to RSA encryption/decryption using a 512-bit modulus if the *Karatsuba-Ofman Multiplication Algorithm* is used in both cases? Again, assume that full length exponents are being used.

Homework Problem 7.4.8: For an RSA cryptosystem, $p = 97$, $q = 101$, and $b = 1,003$. Compute the plaintext for the ciphertext $y = 2,709$.

Homework Problem 7.4.9: Many practical cryptosystems use both symmetric-key algorithms and public-key algorithms. What is the advantage of using such a hybrid system?

Homework Problem 7.4.10: For an *RSA* cryptosystem, $p = 17$ and $q = 19$.

a) Which of the two values, $b_1 = 33$ and $b_2 = 35$, can be used as the parameter b?

b) Use the valid b from part (a) and provide the public key $K_{PUB} = (n, b)$ and the private key $K_{PR} = (p, q, a)$.

Homework Problem 7.4.11: Assume an implementation of the *RSA* cryptosystem such that a modular multiplication takes twice as much time as a modular squaring. How much quicker is one encryption on average if instead of a 1024-bit public key the *short exponent* $b = 17$ is used? Assume that the *Square-and-Multiply Algorithm* is used in both cases.

Homework Problem 7.4.12: Assume an *RSA* cryptosystem with the parameters $p = 5$, $q = 11$, $b = 3$, $x = SECURITY$. Convert the word *SECURITY* to a numerical representation for each letter, assuming that A through Z map to 0 through 25. Encrypt all of the letters of x and convert the result back to letters using the same mapping. Apply the *Square-and-Multiply Algorithm* whenever possible.

Homework Problem 7.4.13: Assume an *RSA* cryptosystem with the parameters $p = 97, q = 101, b = 17$. Compute the plaintext for the ciphertext

$$y = 5219\ 6736\ 5906\ 7685\ 5149\ 7563\ 7563\ 5149\ 0\ 6996\ 8069$$

by converting y back to letters using the mapping that A through Z map to 0 through 25.

Homework Problem 7.4.14: Assume an *RSA* cryptosystem with the parameters $p = 13, q = 11, b = 7$.

a) Is 7 a valid choice for b?

b) Compute the plaintext for the ciphertext

$$y = 138\ 46\ 82\ 109\ 82\ 85\ 30\ 53\ 85\ 0\ 117$$

by converting y back to letters using the mapping that A through Z map to 0 through 25.

Homework Problem 7.4.15: Modular multiplication or squaring of multi-precision integers takes $c \cdot l^2$ steps or clock cycles, where c is a constant and l is the bit length of each operand. By using the *Karatsuba-Ofman Multiplication Algorithm*, the complexity of the multiplication or squaring may be reduced to $k \cdot l^{log_2 3} = k \cdot l^{1.58}$ steps.

a) What is the speed-up factor of a standard *RSA* cryptosystem implementation with a *short exponent* if the *Karatsuba-Ofman*

Multiplication Algorithm is applied to the elementary multiplications?

b) What is the speed-up factor of an *RSA* cryptosystem implementation which exploits the *Chinese Remainder Theorem* if the *Karatsuba-Ofman Multiplication Algorithm* is applied to the elementary multiplications?

Homework Problem 7.4.16: Let $M = 3 \times 5 \times 7 = 105$ be a modulus. Find the modular representation of $A = 17$ and $B = 24$. Show also the inverse transformation from the modular representation to the radix representation.

Homework Problem 7.4.17: The *Chinese Remainder Theorem* can be used for efficient integer multiplication.

a) Solve $A \times B \bmod M$ for $M = 3 \times 5 \times 7 = 105$ and $A = 17$ and $B = 24$ using the *Chinese Remainder Theorem*.

b) Solve $A \times B \bmod M$ for $M = 3 \times 5 \times 7 = 105$ and $A = 93$ and $B = 104$ using the *Chinese Remainder Theorem*.

Homework Problem 7.4.18: For the set-up stage of an *RSA* cryptosystem, find the private key using *Euler's Theorem* assuming the parameters $p = 29$, $q = 31$, and the public key $b = 17$.

Homework Problem 7.4.19: How many single-digit multiplications are required to multiply two 2-digit numbers, $(xy)_{10}$ and $(uv)_{10}$, in a straightforward manner? Develop formulae to multiply two such numbers with three single-digit multiplications using the

Karatsuba-Ofman Multiplication Algorithm. Express each number as a polynomial with 10 as the independent variable.

Homework Problem 7.4.20: Multiply 89×74 using the *Karatsuba-Ofman Multiplication Algorithm.* You should only use three single-digit multiplications. Show each step of the computation.

Homework Problem 7.4.21: The product of two complex numbers is $C = A \times B$, where A and B are complex numbers $a_r + i \cdot a_i$ and $b_r + i \cdot b_i$ and $i = \sqrt{(-1)}$. A straightforward computation of C requires four *Inner Products*. Develop an explicit formula for the computation of the real and imaginary parts of C, denoted as c_r and c_i, which requires only three multiplications using the *Karatsuba-Ofman Multiplication Algorithm.*

Homework Problem 7.4.22: Assume that arithmetic is performed using 1024-bit variables and that the processor word size is 32 bits. How many *Inner Products* are needed if two variables are multiplied using:

a) The straightforward method?

b) The *Karatsuba-Ofman Multiplication Algorithm* with 1, 2, 3, 4, and 5 iterations?

Provide a table that shows the number of *Inner Products* for each of the five cases as a percentage relative to the straightforward method. Why is it not possible for more than five iterations of the *Karatsuba-Ofman Multiplication Algorithm* to be used?

Homework Problem 7.4.23: To multiply two polynomials of degree three:

$$A(x) = a_3 \cdot x^3 + a_2 \cdot x^2 + a_1 \cdot x + a_0$$
$$B(x) = b_3 \cdot x^3 + b_2 \cdot x^2 + b_1 \cdot x + b_0$$

a) How many *Inner Products* are needed for the multiplication using the straightforward method?

b) How many *Inner Products* are needed for the multiplication using the *Karatsuba-Ofman Multiplication Algorithm* with one or two iterations?

c) Develop an explicit formula for computing the product polynomial $C(x) = A(x) \times B(x)$ using the *Karatsuba-Ofman Multiplication Algorithm* with two iterations.

Homework Problem 7.4.24: To compute A^e where e is a 31-bit exponent:

a) How many squarings and multiplications does the *Square-and-Multiply Algorithm* require on average?

b) What is the optimum number of k for the k *ary Method*?

c) How many squarings and multiplications are required using the *k-ary Method*? What is the improvement versus part (a)?

d) Redo parts (b) and (c) considering exponents with 256 bits and exponents with 1,024 bits.

Homework Problem 7.4.25: Consider an exponent with 24 bits:

$$e \; = \; 101 \; 110 \; 001 \; 100 \; 101 \; 010 \; 111 \; 100$$

a) How many squarings and multiplications are required for computing A^e using the *Square-and-Multiply Algorithm*?

b) How many squarings and multiplications are required if the *Sliding Window Method* is used with $k \; = \; 3$? Assume that the precomputation requires one squaring and three multiplications. Show the windows in the binary representation of e that are generated by the algorithm.

Homework Problem 7.4.26: Analyze the performance of the following exponentiation methods:

1. The *Square-and-Multiply Algorithm*

2. The *k-ary Method*

3. The *Improved k-ary Method*

4. The *Sliding Window Method*

Implement all four exponentiation methods in a C program using the GNU MP long number library. The file *gmp.h*, the GNU MP long number library header file, is available on the CD included with this book and should be incorporated into your program. Documentation for the GNU MP long number library functions is available on-line [98]. The file *HW7-4-26-Parameters.htm* contains the modulus parameters required for the implementations and is also available on the CD included with this book. Investigate the performance of your implementations for the exponentiation of 1024-bit numbers with both 256-bit and 1024-bit exponents. Your program must include code that measures the time required to perform the exponentiation. Specify the computer model used and the amount of available RAM. You should average your results over a large number of exponentiations with pseudo-random exponents. Construct two identical tables, one for 256-bit exponents and one for 1024-bit exponents. The tables should be of the form:

Method	$k =$			$k =$			$k =$			$k =$			k_{opt}
	S	M	t	S	M	t	S	M	t	S	M	t	
Sq-and-Mul													
k-ary													
Imp k-ary													
Slid Win													

For each value of k (note that there is no k for the *Square-and-Multiply Algorithm*), your program must count the number of squarings (S), the number of multiplications (M), and the absolute time for exponentiation (t). Make sure that you provide the units for time and that you specify how many exponentiations were used for obtaining the averaged results (the number of runs).

In each column of the table, identify the fastest algorithm. Also identify the fastest overall algorithm.

Homework Problem 7.4.27: Since all computers are binary, it is natural to choose $R = b^n = 2^{wn}$ for the *Montgomery Reduction Algorithm*, where w is the processor word size. Is it possible that R and the modulus of the cryptosystem are not relatively prime (which is a necessary condition for the *Montgomery Reduction Algorithm* in the case of the *RSA* cryptosystem)?

Homework Problem 7.4.28: Verify that $MRed(\tilde{a} \cdot \tilde{b}) = \tilde{c}$, where $c = a \cdot b \bmod m$, for the values $a = 7, b = 8, m = 97$, and $R = 100$. First compute $\tilde{c}$ directly from c and then compute $\tilde{c}$ using the *Montgomery Reduction Algorithm*.

Homework Problem 7.4.29: Given an *RSA* cryptosystem with the parameters $p = 29, q = 31$, and the *short exponent* $b = 3$ as the public key. Encrypt $x = 47$ using the *Montgomery Reduction Algorithm* with $R = 1,000$.

Homework Problem 7.4.30: Assume the use of the *Montgomery Reduction Algorithm* for exponentiation of the form $x^i \bmod n$. Assume that $m < b^n$, where $b = 2^w$, and w is the processor word size. Always perform one reduction using *MRed()* after every squaring or multiplication. What is the condition on the size of R so that the *Montgomery Reduction Algorithm*, *MRed()*, can always be applied?

Homework Problem 7.4.31: Using the results from **Homework Problem 7.4.26**, add a new column to each of the tables that estimates the performance of the different implementations, assuming that the *Chinese Remainder Theorem* is used to accelerate exponentiation.

Homework Problem 7.4.32: Write a VHDL architecture to implement *RSA* encryption for 4-bit plaintext input values x using the *RSA* public-key parameters n and b. Assume that the user will provide a *pload* signal to indicate that n and b are ready to be loaded on the next rising edge of the clock. Similarly, assume that the user will provide an *xload* signal to indicate that x is ready to be loaded on the next rising edge of the clock. Use the *Square-and-Multiply Algorithm* to perform the exponentiation. Your system must output a *valid* signal to indicate when the output y is valid, i.e. computation of $y = x^b \bmod n$ is completed. Use the following entity declaration for your implementation:

```
LIBRARY ieee;
USE ieee.std_logic_1164.ALL;
USE ieee.std_logic_arith.ALL;
USE ieee.std_logic_unsigned.ALL;
ENTITY rsa_4 IS
  PORT ( n, b, x : IN  std_logic_vector (3 DOWNTO 0);
         clk      : IN  std_logic;
         rst      : IN  std_logic;
         pload    : IN  std_logic;
         xload    : IN  std_logic;
         valid    : OUT std_logic;
         y        : OUT std_logic_vector (3 DOWNTO 0));
END rsa_4;
ARCHITECTURE behav OF rsa_4 IS
BEGIN
-- Your code goes here
END behav;
```

Use the parameters $n = 15$ and $b = 3$ and validate your design for all possible values of x. Specify the target technology used to implement the design and the maximum operating frequency as specified by your place-and-route tools. What is the execution time of your implementation? What is the gate count of your implementation?

Homework Problem 7.4.33: Expand your VHDL architecture from **Homework Problem 7.4.32** to implement *RSA* encryption for 8-bit plaintext input values x using the *RSA* public-key parameters n and b. Use the following entity declaration for your implementation:

```
LIBRARY ieee;
USE ieee.std_logic_1164.ALL;
USE ieee.std_logic_arith.ALL;
USE ieee.std_logic_unsigned.ALL;
ENTITY rsa_8 IS
   PORT ( n, b, x : IN  std_logic_vector (7 DOWNTO 0);
          clk     : IN  std_logic;
          rst     : IN  std_logic;
          pload   : IN  std_logic;
          xload   : IN  std_logic;
          valid   : OUT std_logic;
          y       : OUT std_logic_vector (7 DOWNTO 0));
END rsa_8;
ARCHITECTURE behav OF rsa_8 IS
BEGIN
-- Your code goes here
END behav;
```

Use the parameters $n = 85$ and $b = 7$ and validate your design for all possible values of x. Specify the target technology used to implement the design and the maximum operating frequency as specified by your place-and-route tools. What is the execution time of your implementation? How does this execution time compare to the execution time of **Homework Problem 7.4.32**? What is the gate count of your implementation? How does this gate count compare to the gate count of **Homework Problem 7.4.32**?

Chapter 8

Public-Key Cryptography: Discrete Logarithms

The *Discrete Logarithm* problem is the underlying *One-Way* function for almost all public-key cryptosystems other than *RSA*, including the *Diffie-Hellman Key Agreement Protocol*, *Elliptic Curve* cryptosystems, *ElGamal* encryption, and *ElGamal Digital Signatures*.

8.1 Cyclic Groups

A *Group* is defined as consisting of:

1. A set of elements.

2. A binary operation, denoted as $\bigcirc$, with the following properties:

   (a) **Closure:** $a \bigcirc b = c$ results in element c contained in the set of elements.

(b) **Associativity**: $(a \bigcirc b) \bigcirc c = a \bigcirc (b \bigcirc c)$ for all elements a, b, and c contained in the set of elements.

(c) **Identity**: e is the identity element such that $e \bigcirc a = a \bigcirc e = a$ for a contained in the set of elements.

(d) **Inverse**: $\bar{a}$ is the inverse of a such that $\bar{a} \bigcirc a = e$ for a contained in the set of elements.

Example 8.1: If the set of all integers and the binary operation $\bigcirc = +$, i.e. addition, are used, does the set of all integers and $\bigcirc = +$ form a *Group*?

The set of all integers and the binary operation $\bigcirc = +$ demonstrate the properties of closure and associativity. The identity element $e = 0$ because $a + 0 = a$. The inverse of element a is $\bar{a} = -a$ because $a + (-a) = 0$, i.e. the identity element e. Therefore, the set of all integers and the binary operation $\bigcirc = +$ do form a *Group*.

Example 8.2: If the set of all integers and the binary operation $\bigcirc = \times$, i.e. multiplication, are used, does the set of all integers and $\bigcirc = \times$ form a *Group*?

The set of all integers and the binary operation $\bigcirc = \times$ demonstrate the properties of closure and associativity. The identity element $e = 1$ because $a \times 1 = a$. However, the inverse of element a is $\bar{a} = \frac{1}{a}$ and the element $\frac{1}{a}$ is not guaranteed to be contained in the set of all integers. Therefore, the set of all integers and the binary operation $\bigcirc = \times$ do not form a *Group*.

Example 8.3: If the set Z_n and the binary operation $\bigcirc = \times$, i.e. multiplication, are used, does the set Z_n and $\bigcirc = \times$ form a *Group*?

The set of all integers and the binary operation $\bigcirc = \times$ demonstrate the properties of closure and associativity. The identity element $e = 1$ because $a \times 1 = a$. The inverse of element a is $a = a^{-1} \bmod n$. However, the element $a^{-1} \bmod n$ is not guaranteed to exist unless the $gcd(a, n) = 1$. Therefore, the set Z_n and the binary operation $\bigcirc = \times$ do not form a *Group*.

As shown in **Example 8.3**, the set Z_n may contain elements that are not relatively prime to n and therefore an inverse will not exist. To form a *Group*, all elements within the set of elements must have an inverse. Thus the set Z_n^* is defined as the set of integers i, $0 \leq i < n$, that are relatively prime to n, i.e. the $gcd(i, n) = 1$.

Example 8.4: If the set Z_n^* and the binary operation $\bigcirc$ $=$ $\times$, i.e. multiplication, are used, does the set Z_n^* and $\bigcirc$ $=$ $\times$ form a *Group*?

The set of all integers and the binary operation $\bigcirc$ $=$ $\times$ demonstrate the properties of closure and associativity. The identity element e $=$ 1 because $a \times 1 = a$. The inverse of element a is $\bar{a} = a^{-1}\ mod\ n$. Because the definition of Z_n^* guarantees that the *gcd* of all elements i, $0 \leq i < n$, of Z_n^* are relatively prime to n, the inverse of a, $a^{-1}\ mod\ n$, must exist. Therefore, the set Z_n^* and the binary operation $\bigcirc$ $=$ $\times$ do form a *Group*.

Example 8.5: What are the elements of Z_{15}^*?

$$Z_{15}^* = \{1,\ 2,\ 4,\ 7,\ 8,\ 11,\ 13,\ 14\}$$

Example 8.6: What are the elements of Z_{17}^*?

$$Z_{17}^* = \{1,\ 2,\ 3,\ 4,\ 5,\ 6,\ 7,\ 8,\ 9,\ 10,\ 11,\ 12,\ 13,\ 14,\ 15,\ 16\}$$

Example 8.7: Construct the multiplication table of Z_{15}^*.

× mod 15	1	2	4	Multiplication 7	8	11	13	14
1	1	2	4	7	8	11	13	14
2	2	4	8	14	1	7	11	13
4	4	8	1	13	2	14	7	11
7	7	14	13	4	11	2	1	8
8	8	1	2	11	4	13	14	7
11	11	7	14	2	13	1	8	4
13	13	11	7	1	14	8	4	2
14	14	13	11	8	7	4	2	1

A *Group* is *Finite* if it has a finite number of elements, denoted as g. The *cardinality* of a *Finite Group* G is the number of elements in the *Finite Group* and is denoted as $|G| = g$.

Example 8.8: What is the *cardinality* of the *Finite Group* formed by the set Z_{15}^* and the multiplication operation?

$$|(Z_{15}^*, \times)| = 8$$

Example 8.9: What is the *cardinality* of the *Finite Group* formed by the set Z_p^*, where p is prime, and the multiplication operation?

$$|(Z_p^*, \times)| = p - 1$$

The *order* of an element a contained in a *Finite Group* with a binary operation denoted as $\bigcirc$ is the smallest positive integer θ such that $\underbrace{a \bigcirc a \bigcirc \ldots \bigcirc a}_{\theta \ times} = e$. When a *Finite Group* is formed by the set Z_p^*, where p is prime, then the maximum *order* of an element a contained in the *Finite Group* is $p - 1$.

Example 8.10: What is the *order* of the element 5 contained in the *Finite Group* formed by the set Z_7^* and the multiplication operation?

The *order* of the element 5 is obtained via repeated application of the multiplication operation, noting that $e = 1$:

$$5^1 \ mod \ 7 \ = \ 5 \ mod \ 7$$
$$5^2 \ mod \ 7 \ = \ 5 \cdot 5 \ mod \ 7 \ = \ 25 \ mod \ 7 \ \equiv \ 4 \ mod \ 7$$
$$5^3 \ mod \ 7 \ = \ 5 \cdot 4 \ mod \ 7 \ = \ 20 \ mod \ 7 \ \equiv \ 6 \ mod \ 7$$
$$5^4 \ mod \ 7 \ = \ 5 \cdot 6 \ mod \ 7 \ = \ 30 \ mod \ 7 \ \equiv \ 2 \ mod \ 7$$
$$5^5 \ mod \ 7 \ = \ 5 \cdot 2 \ mod \ 7 \ = \ 10 \ mod \ 7 \ \equiv \ 3 \ mod \ 7$$
$$5^6 \ mod \ 7 \ = \ 5 \cdot 3 \ mod \ 7 \ = \ 15 \ mod \ 7 \ \equiv \ 1 \ mod \ 7$$

Therefore, the *order* of the element 5 contained in the *Finite Group* formed by the set Z_7^* and the multiplication operation is 6.

A *Finite Group* G containing elements α with maximum *order*, i.e. the *order* of α is $|G| = g$, is said to be *Cyclic*. Elements with maximum *order* are termed *generators* or *primitive elements* of the *Cyclic Group*. Such elements generate all elements of the set through repeated application of the binary operation.

Example 8.11: Based on the results of **Example 8.10**, is the *Finite Group* formed by the set Z_7^* and the multiplication operation a *Cyclic Group*?

The *order* of the element 5 contained in the *Finite Group* formed by the set Z_7^* and the multiplication operation is 6 and this is the maximum *order* of the *Finite Group*. The element 5 generates all of the elements within the *Finite Group*. Therefore, the *Finite Group* formed by the set Z_7^* and the multiplication operation is a *Cyclic Group*.

By extending the results of **Example 8.11**, the *Finite Group* formed by the set Z_p^* and the multiplication operation is a *Cyclic Group*. *Cyclic Groups* have a number of properties of note:

- The number of *primitive elements* in a *Cyclic Group* is $\phi(|G|)$, where $\phi(|G|)$ is *Euler's Phi Function* applied to the *cardinality* of the *Cyclic Group*.

- For every element a contained in the *Cyclic Group* G, $a^{|G|} = 1$.

- For every element a contained in the *Cyclic Group* G, the *order* of a evenly divides $|G|$.

Example 8.12: How many *primitive elements* are in the *Cyclic Group* formed by the set Z_{17}^* and the multiplication operation?

Based on the first property of *Cyclic Groups* and $|G| = 16$, the number of *primitive elements* in the *Cyclic Group* is $\phi(16) = \phi(2^4) = 2^4 - 2^3 = 16 - 8 = 8$.

Example 8.13: Show that $a^{|G|} = 1$ for every element in the *Cyclic Group* formed by the set Z_5^* and the multiplication operation?

Based on the second property of *Cyclic Groups* and $|G| = 4$,

$$1^4 = 1 \bmod 5$$

$$2^4 = 16 \bmod 5 \equiv 1 \bmod 5$$

$$3^4 = 81 \bmod 5 \equiv 1 \bmod 5$$

$$4^4 \;=\; 256 \; mod \; 5 \;\equiv\; 1 \; mod \; 5$$

Example 8.14: What are the possible *orders* of elements in the *Cyclic Group* formed by the set Z_{17}^* and the multiplication operation?

Based on the third property of *Cyclic Groups* and $|G| \;=\; 16$, the possible *orders* of elements in the *Cyclic Group* are $\{1, \; 2, \; 4, \; 8, \; 16\}$.

A subset of a *Cyclic Group* is termed a *Subgroup* if the elements of the subset form a *Cyclic Group* using the binary operation of the original *Cyclic Group*. Moreover, a *Subgroup* of a *Cyclic Group* must also be a *Cyclic Group*. Therefore, an element δ of a *Cyclic Group* that has an *order* of θ must generate a *Subgroup* that is a *Cyclic Group* with θ elements. Finally, based on the third property of *Cyclic Groups*, θ must evenly divide $|G|$, the *cardinality* of the original *Cyclic Group*.

Example 8.15: Consider the *Cyclic Group* formed by the set Z_{17}^* and the multiplication operation. Determine the elements of the *Subgroup* formed by repeatedly applying the multiplication operation to the element 2.

$$2^1 \bmod 17 = 2 \bmod 17$$

$$2^2 \bmod 17 = 2 \cdot 2 \bmod 17 = 4 \bmod 17$$

$$2^3 \bmod 17 = 2 \cdot 4 \bmod 17 = 8 \bmod 17$$

$$2^4 \bmod 17 = 2 \cdot 8 \bmod 17 = 16 \bmod 17$$

$$2^5 \bmod 17 = 2 \cdot 16 \bmod 17 = 32 \bmod 17 \equiv 15 \bmod 17$$

$$2^6 \bmod 17 = 2 \cdot 15 \bmod 17 = 30 \bmod 17 \equiv 13 \bmod 17$$

$$2^7 \bmod 17 = 2 \cdot 13 \bmod 17 = 26 \bmod 17 \equiv 9 \bmod 17$$

$$2^8 \bmod 17 = 2 \cdot 9 \bmod 17 = 18 \bmod 17 \equiv 1 \bmod 17$$

Therefore, the *Subgroup* of the *Cyclic Group* formed by the set Z_{17}^* and the multiplication operation formed by repeatedly applying the multiplication operation to the element 2 is {1, 2, 4, 8, 9, 13, 15, 16} and thus the element 2 is a *primitive element* of the *Subgroup*. Because the element 2 has an *order* of eight, there are eight elements in the *Subgroup*.

Example 8.16: Construct the multiplication table for the *Subgroup* formed in **Example 8.15**.

× mod 17	1	2	4	Multiplication 8	9	13	15	16
1	1	2	4	8	9	13	15	16
2	2	4	8	16	1	9	13	15
4	4	8	16	15	2	1	9	13
8	8	16	15	13	4	2	1	9
9	9	1	2	4	13	15	16	8
13	13	9	1	2	15	16	8	4
15	15	13	9	1	16	8	4	2
16	16	15	13	9	8	4	2	1

Example 8.17: Consider the *Cyclic Group* formed by the set Z_{17}^* and the multiplication operation. Determine the elements of the *Subgroup* formed by repeatedly applying the multiplication operation to the element 16.

$16^1 \ mod \ 17 \ = \ 16 \ mod \ 17$

$16^2 \ mod \ 17 \ = \ 16 \cdot 16 \ mod \ 17 \ = \ 256 \ mod \ 17 \ \equiv \ 1 \ mod \ 17$

Therefore, the *Subgroup* of the *Cyclic Group* formed by the set Z_{17}^* and the multiplication operation formed by repeatedly applying the multiplication operation to the element 16 is $\{1, \ 16\}$ and thus the element 16 is a *primitive element* of the *Subgroup*. Because the element 16 has an *order* of two, there are two elements in the *Subgroup*.

Example 8.18: Construct the multiplication table for the *Subgroup* formed in **Example 8.17**.

× mod 17	Multiplication 1	16
1	1	16
16	16	1

8.2 The Discrete Logarithm Problem

Assume the existence of a *Cyclic Group* (or a *Subgroup*) denoted as $(G, \bigcirc)$ and a *primitive element* α. Let $\beta = \underbrace{a \bigcirc a \bigcirc \cdots \bigcirc a}_{i\ times}$ $= e$. Therefore, if the binary operation $\bigcirc = +$, then $\beta = i \times \alpha$. If the binary operation $\bigcirc = \times$, then $\beta = \alpha^i$ and this is the case of primary interest. When $\bigcirc = \times$, the *Discrete Logarithm* problem states that given G, α, and $\beta = \alpha^i$, find $i = log_\alpha\beta$. When the *Cyclic Group* $(G, \bigcirc)$ is based on the set Z_p^* and the binary operation $\bigcirc = \times$, then the *Discrete Logarithm* problem states that given G, α, and $\beta = \alpha^i \bmod p$, find $i = log_\alpha\beta \bmod p$.

Example 8.19: Given the *Cyclic Group* formed by the set Z_{17} and the addition operation, the *primitive element* $\alpha = 3$, and $\beta = i \times \alpha \bmod 17 = 16$. Solve the *Discrete Logarithm* problem for i.

When the binary operation is addition, the *Discrete Logarithm* problem states that $i = \alpha^{-1} \times \beta \bmod p = 3^{-1} \times 16 \bmod 17$. $3^{-1} \bmod 17$ may be computed using either the *Extended Euclidean Algorithm* or the *Binary Extended Euclidean Algorithm*, both of which yield $3^{-1} \bmod 17 = 6 \bmod 17$. Therefore, i is computed as $i = 6 \times 16 \bmod 17 = 96 \bmod 17 \equiv 11 \bmod 17$.

Based on the results of **Example 8.19**, it is clear that *Cyclic Groups* based on the addition operation are not secure given that a fast and efficient algorithm, i.e. the *Binary Extended Euclidean Algorithm*, may be used to solve for i.

Example 8.20: Given the *Cyclic Group* formed by the set Z_{17}^{*} and the multiplication operation, the *primitive element* $\alpha = 3$, and $\beta = \alpha^{i} \bmod 17 = 7$. Solve the *Discrete Logarithm* problem for the exponent i.

The *Discrete Logarithm* problem states that $i = log_{\alpha}\beta \bmod p = log_{3}7 \bmod 17$. Therefore, through repeated application of the multiplication operation to α, i.e. trial and error, i may be determined as:

$$3^{1} \bmod 7 = 3 \bmod 17$$
$$3^{2} \bmod 7 = 3 \cdot 3 \bmod 17 = 9 \bmod 17$$
$$3^{3} \bmod 7 = 3 \cdot 9 \bmod 17 = 27 \bmod 17 \equiv 10 \bmod 17$$

$$3^4 \bmod 7 = 3 \cdot 10 \bmod 17 = 30 \bmod 17 \equiv 13 \bmod 17$$

$$3^5 \bmod 7 = 3 \cdot 13 \bmod 17 = 39 \bmod 17 \equiv 5 \bmod 17$$

$$3^6 \bmod 7 = 3 \cdot 5 \bmod 17 = 15 \bmod 17$$

$$3^7 \bmod 7 = 3 \cdot 15 \bmod 17 = 45 \bmod 17 \equiv 11 \bmod 17$$

$$3^8 \bmod 7 = 3 \cdot 11 \bmod 17 = 33 \bmod 17 \equiv 16 \bmod 17$$

$$3^9 \bmod 7 = 3 \cdot 16 \bmod 17 = 48 \bmod 17 \equiv 14 \bmod 17$$

$$3^{10} \bmod 7 = 3 \cdot 14 \bmod 17 = 42 \bmod 17 \equiv 8 \bmod 17$$

$$3^{11} \bmod 7 = 3 \cdot 8 \bmod 17 = 24 \bmod 17 \equiv 7 \bmod 17$$

Therefore, $i = 11$ because $\beta = \alpha^i \bmod 17 = 3^{11} \bmod 17 = 7 \bmod 17$.

Example 8.20 demonstrates that *Cyclic Groups* based on the multiplication operation are secure — this *Discrete Logarithm* problem is a computationally intensive and difficult problem to solve, and thus meets the definition of a *One-Way* function, as stated in Section 6.3, i.e. that the forward transformation is easy to compute and the inverse transformation is very difficult to compute.

8.3 Diffie-Hellman Key Agreement Protocol

In 1976, Whitfield Diffie and Martin Hellman proposed a revolutionary key distribution methodology [70]. The *Diffie-Hellman*

Key Agreement Protocol may be based on any *Discrete Logarithm* problem and is used in many cryptographic protocols. The most common usages of the *Diffie-Hellman Key Agreement Protocol* are:

1. The *Cyclic Group* formed by Z_p^*, where p is prime, and the multiplication operation.

2. The *Group* of an *Elliptic Curve* cryptosystem.

Chapter 9 will discuss *Elliptic Curve* cryptosystems and will examine the use of the *Diffie-Hellman Key Agreement Protocol* in such cryptosystems. This Section will focus on the use of the *Diffie-Hellman Key Agreement Protocol* in the *Cyclic Group* formed by Z_p^* and the multiplication operation. In this case, the *Diffie-Hellman Key Agreement Protocol* is composed of two stages: set-up and key establishment.

For the *Cyclic Group* formed by Z_p^* and the multiplication operation, the set-up stage proceeds as follows:

1. Choose a large prime number, denoted as p. This process is typically implemented via a *Monte Carlo* algorithm such as the *Miller-Rabin Algorithm*, as discussed in Section 7.2.1.

2. Choose a *primitive element* α in Z_p^*.

where α and p are made publicly known.

The key establishment stage, shown in Figure 8.1, is used to establish a shared secret between two parties, *Alice* and *Bob*, who wish to communicate.

Step	Alice	Bob
1	Choose a random integer $K_{PR_A} = a_A$ where $a_A \in \{2,\ 3,\ 4,\ \ldots\ p\ -\ 1\}$	Choose a random integer $K_{PR_B} = a_B$ where $a_B \in \{2,\ 3,\ 4,\ \ldots\ p\ -\ 1\}$
2	Compute $K_{PUB_A} = b_A = \alpha^{a_A} \bmod p$	Compute $K_{PUB_B} = b_B = \alpha^{a_B} \bmod p$
3	Send b_A to $Bob \longrightarrow$	$\longleftarrow$ Send b_B to $Alice$
4	Compute $K_{AB} = b_B^{a_A} \bmod p$ $= (\alpha^{a_B})^{a_A} \bmod p = \alpha^{a_A a_B} \bmod p$	Compute $K_{AB} = b_A^{a_B} \bmod p$ $= (\alpha^{a_A})^{a_B} \bmod p = \alpha^{a_A a_B} \bmod p$

Figure 8.1: Diffie-Hellman Key Agreement Protocol Key Establishment Stage in Z_p^*

Note that for the *Diffie-Hellman Key Agreement Protocol* in the *Cyclic Group* formed by the *Extension Field* $GF(2^k)^*$ and the multiplication operation, the *Irreducible Polynomial* is $P(x)$, the *primitive element* $\alpha(x) \in GF(2^k)^*$, the private keys a_A, $a_B \in \{2,\ 3,\ 4,\ \ldots\ 2^k\ -\ 1\}$, the public keys are computed as $b_A = \alpha(x)^{a_A} \bmod P(x)$ and $b_B = \alpha(x)^{a_B} \bmod P(x)$, and the session key is computed as $K_{AB} = \alpha(x)^{a_A a_B} \bmod P(x)$.

At the completion of the key establishment stage, *Alice* and *Bob* share the session key $K_{AB} = \alpha^{a_A a_B} \bmod p$. *Alice* and *Bob* have both contributed to the computation of K_{AB} without being able to extract information regarding the other party's private key K_{PR}. This is because for *Bob* to extract *Alice's* private key, K_{PR_A}, he must solve the *Discrete Logarithm* problem $a_A = log_\alpha b_A \bmod p$.

The same holds true for *Alice*, as she must solve the *Discrete Logarithm* problem $a_B = log_\alpha b_B \bmod p$ to extract *Bob's* private key K_{PR_B}. This *Discrete Logarithm* problem has been shown to be computationally intensive and difficult to solve. As will be discussed in Section 8.6, the *Discrete Logarithm* problem parameters p and α, the plaintext x, and the ciphertext y are typically on the order of 1,024 bits or more in length to ensure the computational complexity of the *Discrete Logarithm* problem.

When considering the security of the *Diffie-Hellman Key Agreement Protocol*, it is important to note exactly what information is available to an attacker. For the *Cyclic Group* formed by Z_p^* and the multiplication operation, the publicly available information as part of the protocol includes the prime p, the *primitive element* α, and the parameters b_A and b_B. Therefore, the *Diffie-Hellman* problem states that given $b_A = \alpha^{a_A} \bmod p$, $b_B = \alpha^{a_B} \bmod p$, and the *primitive element* α, find $\alpha^{a_A a_B} \bmod p$. One method of solving the *Diffie-Hellman* problem is to solve one of the *Discrete Logarithm* problems for either $a_A = log_\alpha b_A \bmod p$ or $a_B = log_\alpha b_B \bmod p$. Once either a_A or a_B is known, computing $\alpha^{a_A a_B} \bmod p$ may be accomplished by computing either $b_B^{a_A} \bmod p$ or $b_A^{a_B} \bmod p$, both of which are equivalent to $\alpha^{a_A a_B} \bmod p$. Therefore, as will be shown in Section 8.6, p must be on the order of 1,024 bits or more in length to ensure the computational complexity of the *Discrete Logarithm* problem and thus the computational complexity of the *Diffie-Hellman* problem. Although it is generally held that solving the *Discrete Logarithm* problem is the only means of solving the *Diffie-Hellman* problem, there is no proof of this and it is possible that other as yet unidentified solutions exist.

8.4 Efficient Implementation

Implementation of the *Discrete Logarithm* problem in Z_p^* requires the following steps:

1. Selection of a large prime number, denoted as p.

2. Selection of a *primitive element* α in Z_p^*.

3. Exponentiation operations to compute $\beta = \alpha^i \bmod p$.

Per Section 8.2, the *Cyclic Group* $(G, \bigcirc)$ based on the set Z_p^* and the binary operation $\bigcirc = \times$ is the primary *Discrete Logarithm* problem of interest, where $\beta = \alpha^i \bmod p$. Moreover, implementation of the *Diffie-Hellman Key Agreement Protocol* based on the *Discrete Logarithm* problem requires an additional two exponentiation operations to compute $\alpha^{a_A} \bmod p$ and $K_{AB} = (\alpha^{a_A})^{a_B} \bmod p$. Sections 7.2.3, 7.2.4, 7.2.4.4, and 7.2.5 discussed methods for accelerating the *Group* operation, multiplication (multi-precision multiplication in particular), and Section 7.2.2 examined methods for reducing the number of *Group* operations performed during exponentiation.

Selection of a large prime number via a *Monte Carlo* algorithm such as the *Miller-Rabin Algorithm* was discussed in Section 7.2.1.

However, as will be shown in Section 8.6.3, an additional constraint must be placed on the large prime number, denoted as p. Due to an attack known as the *Pohlig-Hellman Algorithm*, $\phi(p) = p - 1$ must have a large prime factor $q_k \geq 2^{256}$. Therefore, the process of selection of a large prime number requires the *Integer Factorization* of $\phi(p) = p - 1$ to determine if $p - 1$ has a large prime factor that meets the minimum system requirements in terms of bit length, i.e. that the large prime factor $q_k \geq 2^{256}$. Section 7.3 discussed *Integer Factorization* algorithms such as the *Quadratic Sieve*, the *Generalized Number Field Sieve*, and the *Lattice Sieve*.

Once the *Integer Factorization* of $p - 1$ has been performed, $p - 1$ may be represented as the product of its prime factors such that $p - 1 = q_1^{e_1} \cdot q_2^{e_2} \cdot q_3^{e_3} \cdot \ldots \cdot q_k^{e_k}$, where $q_1 < q_2 < q_3 < \ldots < q_k$ with q_k being the largest prime factor of $p - 1$. Once a valid prime number p has been selected, the following pseudo-code may be used to find a *primitive element* α in Z_p^* [202]:

1. Choose a random element α of the *Cyclic Group G* whose *order* is $\phi(p) = p - 1$.

2. For $i = 0\ To\ k$

   (a) $b = \alpha^{\frac{p-1}{q_i}}\ mod\ p$

   (b) If $b = 1$ Then go to Step 1

3. Return α

As indicated by the pseudo-code, finding a *primitive element* α in Z_p^* requires exponentiation to compute $b = \alpha^{\frac{p-1}{q_i}}\ mod\ p$, leading back to the aforementioned Sections for multi-precision multiplication acceleration methods and reducing the number of *Group* operations performed during exponentiation. With a fast and efficient method for the selection of a *primitive element* α in Z_p^*, fast and efficient methods have been identified for implementing each of the three steps required of the *Discrete Logarithm* problem and the *Diffie-Hellman Key Agreement Protocol* based on the *Discrete Logarithm* problem. However, as discussed in Section 7.2.1, *Integer Factorization* is slow [301]. As a result, *Integer Factorization* is nearly always the bottleneck in implementations of the *Diffie-Hellman Key Agreement Protocol* based on the *Discrete Logarithm* problem.

8.5 ElGamal Encryption

ElGamal encryption was proposed in 1985 by Taher El Gamal and is an extension of the *Diffie-Hellman Key Agreement Protocol* based on the *Discrete Logarithm* problem in either Z_p^* or $GF(2^k)$ [103]. *ElGamal* encryption is composed of two stages: set-up and encryption/decryption. The set-up stage generates the private and public keys as follows:

1. Choose a large prime number, denoted as p.

2. Choose a *primitive element* α contained in the set Z_p^*.

3. Choose a secret key $a \in \{2, 3, 4, \ldots p - 2\}$. Note that $a = p - 1$ is not a useful choice because $\alpha^{p-1} \equiv 1 \bmod p$ per *Fermat's Little Theorem*.

4. Compute $\beta = \alpha^a \bmod p$.

Upon completion of the *ElGamal* encryption set-up stage, the public key is denoted as $K_{PUB} = (\beta, \alpha, p)$ and the private key is denoted as $K_{PR} = (a)$.

Once the private and public keys have been established, encryption of the plaintext x to form the ciphertext y is performed as follows:

1. Choose $k \in \{2, 3, 4, \ldots p - 2\}$.

2. Compute $y_1 = \alpha^k \bmod p$.

3. Compute $y_2 = \beta^k \cdot x \bmod p$.

where the plaintext x is contained in the set Z_p and the ciphertext is the pair (y_1, y_2) such that $e_{K_{PUB}}(x) = (y_1, y_2)$. Decryption of the ciphertext (y_1, y_2) to form the plaintext x is performed as follows:

$$x = d_{K_{PR}}(y_1, y_2) = (y_1^a)^{-1} \cdot y_2 \bmod p$$

Therefore, *ElGamal* encryption is an extension of the *Diffie- Hellman Key Agreement Protocol*, where $\beta^k \bmod p$ corresponds to the mutually determined session key K_{AB}. For *ElGamal* encryption to function, $d_{K_{PR}}(e_{K_{PUB}}(x)) = x$, i.e. decryption must be the inverse of encryption. Substituting into the decryption function yields:

$$d_{K_{PR}}(y_1,\ y_2) = (y_1^a)^{-1} \cdot y_2 \ mod \ p$$

$$d_{K_{PR}}(y_1,\ y_2) = ((\alpha^k)^a)^{-1} \cdot \beta^k \cdot x \ mod \ p$$

$$d_{K_{PR}}(y_1,\ y_2) = ((\alpha^k)^a)^{-1} \cdot (\alpha^a)^k \cdot x \ mod \ p$$

$$d_{K_{PR}}(y_1,\ y_2) = \alpha^{-ak} \cdot \alpha^{ak} \cdot x \ mod \ p$$

$$d_{K_{PR}}(y_1,\ y_2) = \alpha^{ak \ - \ ak} \cdot x \ mod \ p$$

$$d_{K_{PR}}(y_1,\ y_2) = \alpha^0 \cdot x \ mod \ p$$

$$d_{K_{PR}}(y_1,\ y_2) = 1 \cdot x \ mod \ p$$

$$d_{K_{PR}}(y_1,\ y_2) = x \ mod \ p$$

Example 8.21: Compute the encryption and decryption of $x = 3$ with the *ElGamal* encryption algorithm using the parameters $p = 31$, $\alpha = 17$, $a = 4$, and $k = 6$.

ElGamal encryption begins with the computation of β:

$$\beta = \alpha^a \ mod \ p$$

$$\beta = 17^4 \ mod \ 31$$

$$\beta = 83,521 \; mod \; 31$$

$$\beta \equiv 7 \; mod \; 31$$

Encryption is then performed by computing the pair $(y_1, \; y_2)$:

$$y_1 = \alpha^k \; mod \; p$$

$$y_1 = 17^6 \; mod \; 31$$

$$y_1 = 24,137,569 \; mod \; 31$$

$$y_1 \equiv 8 \; mod \; 31$$

$$y_2 = \beta^k \cdot x \; mod \; p$$

$$y_2 = 7^6 \cdot 3 \; mod \; 31$$

$$y_2 = 117,649 \cdot 3 \; mod \; 31$$

$$y_2 = 352,947 \; mod \; 31$$

$$y_2 \equiv 12 \; mod \; 31$$

Therefore, the ciphertext is (8, 12). Decryption is then performed as follows:

$$x = (y_1^a)^{-1} \cdot y_2 \; mod \; p$$

$$x = (8^4)^{-1} \cdot 12 \; mod \; 31$$

$$x = (4,096)^{-1} \cdot 12 \; mod \; 31$$

$$x \equiv 4^{-1} \cdot 12 \; mod \; 31$$

$$x \equiv 8 \cdot 12 \ mod \ 31$$

$$x \equiv 96 \ mod \ 31$$

$$x \equiv 3 \ mod \ 31$$

Therefore, as expected, the decrypted ciphertext results in the plaintext $x = 3$.

It is critical to note that a new value for k must be chosen for every plaintext x_i to be encrypted via the *ElGamal* encryption algorithm and thus *ElGamal* encryption is non-deterministic. If the same value for k is used, *Oscar* can recover the entire plaintext with a *Known-Plaintext* attack (see **Homework Problem 8.7.29**). Moreover, *ElGamal* encryption causes *message expansion*, generating the ciphertext pair (y_1, y_2) for each plaintext x. Because x, y_1, and y_2 are all contained in the set Z_p, the *message expansion* factor of *ElGamal* encryption is $\frac{\lceil log_2 p \rceil + \lceil log_2 p \rceil}{\lceil log_2 p \rceil} = 2$. Therefore, each plaintext x_i of $\lceil log_2 p \rceil$ bits in length requires the transmission of $2 \cdot \lceil log_2 p \rceil$ ciphertext bits, reducing the transmission rate throughput by a factor of two.

When considering efficient implementation of *ElGamal* encryption, Section 8.4 discussed efficient methods for choosing a large prime, denoted as p, as well as finding a *primitive element* α in Z_p^* [202]. *ElGamal* encryption requires the computation of two exponentiations, $\alpha^k \ mod \ p$ and $\beta^k \ mod \ p$, and one multiplication, $\beta^k \cdot x \ mod \ p$. Sections 7.2.3, 7.2.4, 7.2.4.4, and 7.2.5

discussed methods for accelerating the *Group* operation, multiplication (multi-precision multiplication in particular), and Section 7.2.2 examined methods for reducing the number of *Group* operations performed during exponentiation. *ElGamal* decryption requires the computation of one inverse, $(y_1^a)^{-1} \bmod p$, and one multiplication, $y_2 \cdot (y_1^a)^{-1} \bmod p$. The inverse $(y_1^a)^{-1} \bmod p$ may be efficiently computed by taking advantage of *Fermat's Little Theorem*, which states that $f^{p-1} \equiv 1 \bmod p$ if the $gcd(f, p) = 1$. Because p is prime, $gcd(f, p) = 1$ must hold true. Therefore, the exponent of $(y_1^a)^{-1} \bmod p$ may be reduced modulo $p - 1$, resulting in $y_1^{-a \bmod p - 1} \bmod p$. However, $-a \bmod p - 1 = p - 1 - a$. Therefore, $y_1^{-a \bmod p - 1} \bmod p = y_1^{p-1-a} \bmod p$, and this may be computed via the aforementioned fast and efficient exponentiation methods.

When evaluating the security of *ElGamal* encryption, *Oscar* has two options for attacking the system. *Oscar* can attempt to recover the private key a by solving the *Discrete Logarithm* problem $a = log_\alpha \beta \bmod p$ in Z_p^*. Alternatively, *Oscar* can attempt to recover the randomly chosen exponent k by solving the *Discrete Logarithm* problem $k = log_\alpha y_1 \bmod p$ in Z_p^*. In both cases, once either *Discrete Logarithm* problem is solved the plaintext x is easily recovered. The best attack against the *Discrete Logarithm* problem is the *Index Calculus Method*. As will be shown in Section 8.6.4, the parameters of the *Discrete Logarithm* problem must be chosen to be 1024-bit values to ensure that the *Index Calculus Method* is not computationally feasible in practice.

8.6 Attacks

Similar to the discussion of Section 7.3, when considering attacks against the *Discrete Logarithm* problem in Z_p^*, an *Exhaustive Key Search* attack may be performed to determine the exponent i such that $\beta = \alpha^i \bmod p$. The *Exhaustive Key Search* attack proceeds by choosing a value for i from the set of possible values $i \in \{2, 3, 4, \ldots p - 1\}$, exponentiating $\alpha^i \bmod p$, and then comparing the result to β. The *Exhaustive Key Search* attack has a complexity based on $|G|$, the *cardinality* of the *Cyclic Group*. However, $|G|$ of Z_p^* is $\approx p - 1$, and thus the complexity of the *Exhaustive Key Search* attack is $\frac{p-1}{2}$ on average. Therefore $p - 1$ must be chosen such that $|G| \geq 2^{128}$, i.e. equivalent security to a 128-bit block cipher, to ensure long-term security such that an *Exhaustive Key Search* attack is not feasible in practice.

8.6.1 Shank's Algorithm

Shank's Algorithm, also known as the *Baby-Step Giant-Step Algorithm*, attempts to solve the *Discrete Logarithm* problem $\beta = \alpha^i \bmod p$, where $|G| = n$ by exploiting the *generator* property of the *primitive element* α. Because α generates the *Cyclic Group*, the *Cyclic Group* may be represented as $G = \{\alpha^0, \alpha^1, \alpha^2, \ldots \alpha^{n-1}\}$. The exponent i of the *Discrete Logarithm* problem may be represented as $i = (s \cdot m) + t = (st)_m$, where $0 \leq s, t < m = \lceil \sqrt{n} \rceil$. Therefore, the *Discrete Logarithm* problem may be represented as:

$$\beta \;=\; \alpha^i \; mod \; p$$

$$\beta \;=\; \alpha^{sm \,+\, t} \; mod \; p$$

$$\beta \;=\; \alpha^{sm} \;\cdot\; \alpha^t \; mod \; p$$

The equation may now be rearranged such that:

$$(\alpha^{sm})^{-1} \;\cdot\; \beta \; mod \; p \;=\; \alpha^t \; mod \; p$$

$$\alpha^{-sm} \;\cdot\; \beta \; mod \; p \;=\; \alpha^t \; mod \; p$$

Shank's Algorithm attempts to solve the *Discrete Logarithm* problem by finding the pair of integers $(s,\ t)$ that satisfy the equation $\alpha^{-sm} \;\cdot\; \beta \;=\; \alpha^t \; mod \; p$ and then recovering the exponent $i \;=\; (s \cdot m) + t$. This is achieved via a two-stage process. In the first stage, all possible values for α^t are precomputed and stored as a pair, $(\alpha^{t_k},\ t_k)$, forming a table with m entries of the form:

Value	Index
α^{t_0}	t_0
α^{t_1}	t_1
α^{t_2}	t_2
$\vdots$	$\vdots$
$\alpha^{t_{m\,-\,1}}$	$t_{m\,-\,1}$

where the table entries are sorted such that $\alpha^{t_0} \;<\; \alpha^{t_1} \;<\; \alpha^{t_2} \ldots \alpha^{t_{m\,-\,1}}$. Such a table may be searched in $\lceil log_2 m \rceil$ steps using a *Binary Search Algorithm*.

In the second stage of *Shank's Algorithm*, the goal is to find a *collision* such that $\alpha^{-sm} \cdot \beta \bmod p = \alpha^t \bmod p$. This is accomplished in an iterative manner by initially defining $\mu = \alpha^{-m} \bmod p = (\alpha^m)^{-1} \bmod p$. As a result, $\alpha^{-sm} \cdot \beta \bmod p = \mu^s \cdot \beta \bmod p = y_s$. Once μ has been precomputed, each successive computation of y may be computed simply by multiplying the previous value of y by μ. Therefore:

$$
\begin{aligned}
y_0 &= \beta \bmod p \\
y_1 &= \alpha^{-m} \cdot \beta \bmod p = \mu \cdot \beta \bmod p \\
y_2 &= \alpha^{-2m} \cdot \beta \bmod p = \mu^2 \cdot \beta \bmod p = y_1 \cdot \mu \bmod p \\
y_3 &= \alpha^{-3m} \cdot \beta \bmod p = \mu^3 \cdot \beta \bmod p = y_2 \cdot \mu \bmod p \\
&\vdots
\end{aligned}
$$

If y_{s_c} is in the table of all possible values for α^t at entry t_c, then $y_{s_c} = \alpha^{-s_c m} \cdot \beta \bmod p = \alpha^{t_c}$, resulting in $\beta = \alpha^{s_c m + t_c} \bmod p = \alpha^i \bmod p$ and thus $i = (s_c \cdot m) + t_c$.

The complexity of *Shank's Algorithm* is computed as a function of the number of binary operations within the *Cyclic Group* that must be performed. The first stage of *Shank's Algorithm* requires m computations to build the table of all possible values for α^t. The second stage of *Shank's Algorithm* requires $\frac{m}{2}$ computations on average to find the *collision*, resulting in a total of $m + \frac{m}{2} = 1.5 \cdot m \approx 1.5 \cdot \sqrt{n}$ computations. Therefore, $|G| \approx p - 1$ must be chosen for long-term security such that $|G| \geq 2^{256}$ to ensure a complexity of $\approx 2^{128}$, i.e. equivalent security to a 128-bit block cipher, so that an attack using *Shank's Algorithm* is not computationally feasible in practice. Note, however, that if the *primitive element* α is used over many *Discrete Logarithm* problems, then the computational cost associated with the first stage of *Shank's Algorithm*, m computations, is incurred only once. In such cases, the same table of all possible values for α^t may be reused and thus the computational cost associated with the first stage of *Shank's Algorithm* is effectively zero, i.e. it is treated as overhead if the *primitive element* α is used over many *Discrete Logarithm* problems.

The final aspect of *Shank's Algorithm* that must be considered is the cost of data storage. The table of all possible values for α^t has m entries of the form (α^{t_k}, t_k). The index t_k is of size $log_2 m$ whereas the entry α^{t_k} is of size $log_2 n = 2 \cdot log_2 m$ for a total of $log_2 m + 2 \cdot log_2 m = 3 \cdot log_2 m$ storage bits per table entry. Therefore, the total storage requirements for the table of all possible values for α^t is $m \cdot 3 \cdot log_2 m \approx \sqrt{n} \cdot 3 \cdot log_2\sqrt{n} = 1.5 \cdot \sqrt{n} \cdot log_2 n$ bits. Note that values y_{s_c} computed as part of the second stage of *Shank's Algorithm* that are not in the table of all possible values for α^t are discarded and thus the second stage of *Shank's Algorithm* requires negligible storage. As a result, $|G| \geq 2^{256} \approx n$ equates to approximately 2^{134} bytes of total storage required to implement *Shank's Algorithm*. This amount of storage far exceeds the capacity of current computing technology, making an attack based on *Shank's Algorithm* not feasible in practice.

8.6.2 Pollard's Rho Method

A new *Integer Factorization* algorithm was introduced by John Pollard in 1978 to solve the *Discrete Logarithm* problem [247]. This attack, known as *Pollard's Rho Method*, is a *collision* search method where a set S with elements x_i, where $|S| = n$ is given and the goal is to find a *collision* of the form $f(x_i) = f(x_j)$, $i \neq j$ where $f(x)$ is a pseudo-random function. To find a *collision*, a table may be constructed with entries of the form $(x_1, f(x_1))$, $(x_2, f(x_2))$, $(x_3, f(x_3))$, ... $(x_k, f(x_k))$. Each new entry is compared to all other entries in the table to determine if a *collision* has occurred, i.e. that $f(x_{k+1})$ matches some other $f(x_i)$ in the table. When constructing such a table, the probability that there is no *collision* is based on k. For the case where $k = 2$, the $P(no\ collision) = 1 - \frac{1}{n}$. For the case where $k = 3$, the $P(no\ collision) = [1 - \frac{1}{n}] \cdot [1 - \frac{2}{n}]$. For the general case, $P(no\ collision) = \prod_{u=1}^{k-1} 1 - \frac{u}{n} \approx e^{\frac{-k^2}{2n}}$. As will be shown in Section 10.2.1 when discussing the *Birthday Paradox*, for a *collision* to occur, the expected number of entries $(x_i, f(x_i))$ in the table is $k = \sqrt{\frac{n\pi}{2}} \approx 1.25 \cdot \sqrt{n}$. However, as discussed in Section 8.6.1, the amount of storage required to implement such a table would result in an attack based on *Pollard's Rho Method* to be not feasible in practice. Therefore, it is imperative that the table be eliminated.

In an effort to eliminate the table of output values of the pseudo-random function $f(x_i)$, *Pollard's Rho Method* defines a pseudo-random sequence $x_{i+1} = f(x_i)$. The pseudo-random sequence takes the form:

$$x_0 = Initial\ Value$$

$$x_1 = f(x_0)$$

$$x_2 = f(x_1)$$

$$x_3 = f(x_2)$$

$$\vdots$$

$$x_{i+1} = f(x_i)$$

It is critical to note that because the set S is finite, the pseudo-random sequence must partially repeat. Therefore, the pseudo-random sequence must take the form shown in Figure 8.2.

The values x_0, x_1, x_2, ... $x_{\mu-1}$ form the μ tail of the ρ shaped diagram for the pseudo-random sequence and is of length μ. The values x_μ, $x_{\mu+1}$, ... $x_{\mu+\lambda-1}$ form the λ cycle of the ρ shaped diagram for the pseudo-random sequence and is of length λ. As demonstrated in Figure 8.2, a *collision* has occurred at x_μ because $f(x_\mu) = f(x_{\mu+\lambda-1})$ and $x_\mu \neq x_{\mu+\lambda-1}$. The *collision* is expected to occur when $\mu + \lambda = \sqrt{\frac{n\pi}{2}}$.

Example 8.22: Show the pseudo-random sequence generated by the function $f(x_i) = x_i^2 + 9\ mod\ 19$. Identify the μ tail, the λ cycle, and x_μ where the *collision* occurs if $x_0 = 5$.

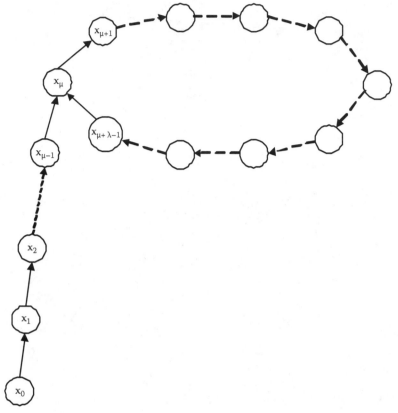

Figure 8.2: Pollard's Rho Sequence Diagram

For an initial value of $x_0 = 5$, the pseudo-random sequence generated by the function $f(x_i) = x_i^2 + 9 \bmod 19$ is:

$$x_0 = 5$$

$$x_1 = 5^2 + 9 \bmod 19 = 34 \bmod 19 \equiv 15 \bmod 19$$

$$x_2 = 15^2 + 9 \bmod 19 = 234 \bmod 19 \equiv 6 \bmod 19$$

$$x_3 = 6^2 + 9 \bmod 19 = 45 \bmod 19 \equiv 7 \bmod 19$$

$$x_4 = 7^2 + 9 \bmod 19 = 58 \bmod 19 \equiv 1 \bmod 19$$

$$x_5 = 1^2 + 9 \bmod 19 = 10 \bmod 19$$

$$x_6 = 10^2 + 9 \bmod 19 = 109 \bmod 19 \equiv 14 \bmod 19$$

$$x_7 = 14^2 + 9 \bmod 19 = 205 \bmod 19 \equiv 15 \bmod 19$$

Therefore, $x_1 = x_7 = x_\mu$, the μ tail is x_0, and the λ cycle is $x_1, x_2, \ldots x_6$.

Example 8.23: Show the pseudo-random sequence generated by the function $f(x_i) = x_i^2 + 9 \bmod 19$. Identify the μ tail, the λ cycle, and x_μ where the *collision* occurs if $x_0 = 3$.

For an initial value of $x_0 = 3$, the pseudo-random sequence generated by the function $f(x_i) = x_i^2 + 9 \bmod 19$ is:

$$x_0 = 3$$

$$x_1 = 3^2 + 9 \bmod 19 = 18 \bmod 19$$

$$x_2 = 18^2 + 9 \bmod 19 = 333 \bmod 19 \equiv 10 \bmod 19$$

$$x_3 = 10^2 + 9 \bmod 19 = 109 \bmod 19 \equiv 14 \bmod 19$$

$$x_4 = 14^2 + 9 \bmod 19 = 205 \bmod 19 \equiv 15 \bmod 19$$

$$x_5 = 15^2 + 9 \bmod 19 = 234 \bmod 19 \equiv 6 \bmod 19$$

$$x_6 = 6^2 + 9 \bmod 19 = 45 \bmod 19 \equiv 7 \bmod 19$$

$$x_7 = 7^2 + 9 \bmod 19 = 58 \bmod 19 \equiv 1 \bmod 19$$

$$x_8 = 1^2 + 9 \bmod 19 = 10 \bmod 19$$

Therefore, $x_2 = x_8 = x_\mu$, the μ tail is x_0, x_1, and the λ cycle is x_2, x_3, ... x_7.

As demonstrated in **Examples 8.22** and **8.23**, the length of the μ tail and the λ cycle may vary significantly for the same pseudo-random function $f(x_i)$ depending on the randomly chosen initial value x_0. However, neither example has eliminated the table of values for the pseudo-random function $f(x_i)$. Eliminating the table will require the use of *Floyd's Cycle Detecting Algorithm*. *Floyd's Cycle Detecting Algorithm* defines two sequences, $\sigma_1 : x_{i+1} = f(x_i)$ and $\sigma_2 : x_{2(i+1)} = f(f(x_{2i}))$, for $i \geq 0$. Therefore, σ_1 generates x_0, x_1, x_2, x_3, ... and σ_2 generates x_0, x_2, x_4, x_6, ... When used in conjunction with *Pollard's Rho Method*, *Floyd's Cycle Detecting Algorithm* exhibits three properties of interest:

1. Both the σ_1 and σ_2 sequences will eventually enter and begin cycling around the λ cycle.

2. σ_2 cycles at twice the rate of σ_1.

3. σ_1 and σ_2 will eventually collide within the λ cycle.

Example 8.24: Show the pseudo-random sequences generated by the function $f(x_i) = x_i^2 + 9 \bmod 19$ using *Floyd's Cycle Detecting Algorithm*. Identify where the *collision* occurs if $x_0 = 5$.

For an initial value of $x_0 = 5$, the pseudo-random sequences σ_1 and σ_2 generated by the function $f(x_i) = x_i^2 + 9 \bmod 19$ using *Floyd's Cycle Detecting Algorithm* are:

σ_1:	5	15	6	7	1	10	14	15
Value	x_0	x_1	x_2	x_3	x_4	x_5	x_6	x_7
σ_2:	5	6	1	14	6	1	14	1
Value	x_0	x_2	x_4	x_6	x_8	x_{10}	x_{12}	x_{14}

The μ tail of σ_1 and σ_2 is $\{5\}$. The λ cycle of σ_1 is $\{15, 6, 7, 1, 10, 14\}$. The λ cycle of σ_2 is $\{6, 1, 14\}$. The *collision* occurs at $\sigma_1 : x_6 = 14$ and $\sigma_2 : x_{12} = 14$.

Example 8.25: Show the pseudo-random sequences generated by the function $f(x_i) = x_i^2 + 9 \bmod 19$ using *Floyd's Cycle Detecting Algorithm*. Identify where the *collision* occurs if $x_0 = 3$.

For an initial value of $x_0 = 3$, the pseudo-random sequences σ_1 and σ_2 generated by the function $f(x_i) = x_i^2 + 9 \bmod 19$ using *Floyd's Cycle Detecting Algorithm* are:

σ_1:	3	18	10	14	15	6	7	1	10
Value	x_0	x_1	x_2	x_3	x_4	x_5	x_6	x_7	x_8
σ_2:	3	10	15	7	10	15	7	10	15
Value	x_0	x_2	x_4	x_6	x_8	x_{10}	x_{12}	x_{14}	x_{16}

The μ tail of σ_1 is $\{3, 18\}$. The μ tail of σ_2 is $\{3\}$. The λ cycle of σ_1 is $\{10, 14, 15, 6, 7, 1\}$. The λ cycle of σ_2 is $\{10, 15, 7\}$. The *collision* occurs at $\sigma_1 : x_6 = 7$ and $\sigma_2 : x_{12} = 7$.

As demonstrated in **Examples 8.24** and **8.25**, *Floyd's Cycle Detecting Algorithm* finds the *collision* between the two pseudo-random sequences while only requiring the storage of the current values of σ_1 and σ_2. The *collision* will always occur when x_i of σ_1 is in the λ cycle, i.e. that $\mu \leq i \leq \mu + \lambda - 1$ where $\mu + \lambda - 1 = \sqrt{\frac{n\pi}{2}}$, the expected value of i.

With *Floyd's Cycle Detecting Algorithm*, *Pollard's Rho Method* may now be used to solve the *Discrete Logarithm* problem. To review, the *Discrete Logarithm* problem states that given the *Cyclic Group* $(G, \bigcirc)$ based on the set Z_p^* and the binary operation $\bigcirc = \times$, a *primitive element* α whose *order* is $n = p - 1$, and $\beta = \alpha^i \bmod p$, find $i = \log_\alpha \beta \bmod p$. To solve the *Discrete Logarithm* problem, *Pollard's Rho Method* is used to find a *collision* $f(x_i) = f(x_j)$, where $f(x_i) = \alpha^a \cdot \beta^b \bmod p$ and $f(x_j) = \alpha^{a'} \cdot \beta^{b'} \bmod p$. Once the *collision* has been identified, the exponent i is identified by manipulating the equations associated with $f(x_i) = f(x_j)$:

$$f(x_i) = f(x_j)$$
$$\alpha^a \cdot \beta^b \bmod p = \alpha^{a'} \cdot \beta^{b'} \bmod p$$
$$\alpha^a \cdot (\alpha^i)^b \bmod p = \alpha^{a'} \cdot (\alpha^i)^{b'} \bmod p$$
$$\alpha^{a + ib} \bmod p = \alpha^{a' + ib'} \bmod p$$

Because the *order* of α is known to be n, the exponents may be used to solve for i:

$$a + (i \cdot b) \bmod n = a' + (i \cdot b') \bmod n$$
$$a - a' \bmod n = (i \cdot b') - (i \cdot b) \bmod n$$
$$a - a' \bmod n = i \cdot (b' - b) \bmod n$$
$$i = (a - a') \cdot (b' - b)^{-1} \bmod n$$

What remains is to generate the pseudo-random sequences σ_1 : $x_t = \alpha^{a_t} \cdot \beta^{b_t} \bmod p$ and $\sigma_2 : x_{2t} = \alpha^{a_{2t}} \cdot \beta^{b_{2t}} \bmod p$ through the functions $x_{t+1} = f(x_t)$ and $x_{2(t+1)} = f(f(x_{2t}))$ using *Floyd's Cycle Detecting Algorithm*. At each step t, if $x_t = x_{2t}$ then $i = (a_t - a_{2t}) \cdot (b_{2t} - b_t)^{-1} \bmod n$. A wide range of functions may be used to compute $f(x_t)$; as part of *Pollard's Rho Method*, John Pollard proposed the following function for computing $f(x_t)$ [247]:

$$f(x_t) = x_{t+1} = \begin{cases} \beta \cdot x_t \bmod p & \text{for } x_t \in S_1 \\ x_t^2 \bmod p & \text{for } x_t \in S_2 \\ \alpha \cdot x_t \bmod p & \text{for } x_t \in S_3 \end{cases} \qquad (8.1)$$

where x_t is an integer and

1. S_1 is the set of all integers such that $x_t \equiv 1 \bmod 3$.

2. S_2 is the set of all integers such that $x_t \equiv 0 \bmod 3$.

3. S_3 is the set of all integers such that $x_t \equiv 2 \bmod 3$.

This method of dividing the set of all integers results in $|S_1| \approx |S_2| \approx |S_3|$. Note that this function for computing $f(x_t)$ is not necessarily optimal. Similarly, functions are required to compute $a_{t+1} = f_a(a_t)$ and $b_{t+1} = f_b(b_t)$. If $x_t \in S_1$, then:

$$x_{t+1} = \beta \cdot x^t$$
$$x_{t+1} = \beta \cdot \alpha^{a_t} \cdot \beta^{b_t}$$
$$x_{t+1} = \alpha^{a_t} \cdot \beta^{b_t+1}$$
$$x_{t+1} = \alpha^{a_t+1} \cdot \beta^{b_t+1}$$

Therefore, $a_{t+1} = a_t \bmod n$ and $b_{t+1} = b_t + 1 \bmod n$. If $x_t \in S_2$, then:

$$x_{t+1} = x^t \cdot x^t$$
$$x_{t+1} = \alpha^{a_t} \cdot \beta^{b_t} \cdot \alpha^{a_t} \cdot \beta^{b_t}$$
$$x_{t+1} = \alpha^{2a_t} \cdot \beta^{2b_t}$$
$$x_{t+1} = \alpha^{a_t+1} \cdot \beta^{b_t+1}$$

Therefore, $a_{t+1} = 2 \cdot a_t \bmod n$ and $b_{t+1} = 2 \cdot b_t \bmod n$. If $x_t \in S_3$, then:

$$x_{t+1} = \alpha \cdot x^t$$
$$x_{t+1} = \alpha \cdot \alpha^{a_t} \cdot \beta^{b_t}$$

$$x_{t+1} = \alpha^{a_t + 1} \cdot \beta^{b_t}$$

$$x_{t+1} = \alpha^{a_t + 1} \cdot \beta^{b_t + 1}$$

Therefore, $a_{t+1} = a_t + 1 \bmod n$ and $b_{t+1} = b_t \bmod n$. As a result of this analysis, the functions to compute $a_{t+1} = f_a(a_t)$ and $b_{t+1} = f_b(b_t)$ are:

$$f_a(x_t, a_t) = a_{t+1} = \begin{cases} a_t \bmod n & \text{for } x_t \in S_1 \\ 2 \cdot a_t \bmod n & \text{for } x_t \in S_2 \\ a_t + 1 \bmod n & \text{for } x_t \in S_3 \end{cases} \quad (8.2)$$

$$f_b(x_t, b_t) = b_{t+1} = \begin{cases} b_t + 1 \bmod n & \text{for } x_t \in S_1 \\ 2 \cdot b_t \bmod n & \text{for } x_t \in S_2 \\ b_t \bmod n & \text{for } x_t \in S_3 \end{cases} \quad (8.3)$$

Having established functions for computing $f(x_t)$, $f_a(a_t)$, and $f_b(b_t)$, *Pollard's Rho Method* may be implemented via the following pseudo-code:

1. a_0 and b_0 are assigned random values from the set $\{0, 1, 2, \ldots n - 1\}$

2. $x_0 = \alpha^{a_0} \cdot \beta^{b_0} \bmod p$

3. $t = 1$

4. While $x_t \neq x_{2t}$:

    (a) $x_t = f(x_{t-1})$

    (b) $a_t = f_a(a_{t-1}, x_{t-1})$

(c) $b_t = f_b(b_{t-1}, x_{t-1})$

(d) $x_{2t} = f(f(x_{2t-2}))$

(e) $a_{2t} = f_a(f(x_{2t-2}), f_a(x_{2t-2}, a_{2t-2}))$

(f) $b_{2t} = f_b(f(x_{2t-2}), f_b(x_{2t-2}, b_{2t-2}))$

5. If $b_t - b_{2t} = 0$ Then go to Step 1 Else $i = (b_t - b_{2t})^{-1} \cdot (a_{2t} - a_t) \bmod n$

Note that Steps 4a, 4b, and 4c compute the pseudo-random sequence σ_1 whereas Steps 4d, 4e, and 4f compute the pseudo-random sequence σ_2. The output of the algorithm solves the *Discrete Logarithm* problem, where the output $i = \log_\alpha \beta \bmod p$. Although a *collision* is expected to occur when $\mu + \lambda = \sqrt{\frac{n\pi}{2}}$, i.e. after $\sqrt{\frac{n\pi}{2}}$ steps, the original table associated with the computation of $(x_i, f(x_i))$ has been eliminated. As a result, the complexity of *Pollard's Rho Method* used in conjunction with *Floyd's Cycle Detecting Algorithm* matches the complexity of *Shank's Algorithm* with minimal storage requirements. Only the variables associated with the computation of the pseudo-random sequences σ_1 and σ_2 must be stored, i.e. $x_t, a_t, b_t, x_{2t}, a_{2t}$, and b_{2t}. The implementation of *Pollard's Rho Method* is thus feasible in practice. Therefore, as was the case when using *Shank's Algorithm*, $|G| \approx p - 1$ must be chosen for long-term security such that $|G| \geq 2^{256}$ to ensure a complexity of $\approx 2^{128}$, i.e. equivalent security to a 128-bit block cipher, so that an attack using *Pollard's Rho Method* is not computationally feasible in practice.

It is possible to parallelize implementations of *Pollard's Rho Method* in an attempt to achieve linear speed-up. Such implementations define a set of v *distinguished points*, denoted as $S_d = \{x_{d_0}, x_{d_1}, x_{d_2}, \ldots x_{d_{v-1}}\}$, and each processor computes a pseudo-random sequence σ beginning with a random initial value x_0 until a *distinguished point* is reached, i.e. $\sigma = x_0, x_1, x_2, \ldots x_{d_j}$. Once a processor computes a *distinguished point*, the point, x_{d_j}, and its associated values, a_{d_j} and b_{d_j}, are reported to a central database. The reporting process continues until a *collision* occurs in the database such that $x_{d_j} = x_{d_k}$ and thus $\alpha^{a_j} \cdot \beta^{b_j} \bmod p = \alpha^{a_k} \cdot \beta^{b_k} \bmod p$, at which point the *Discrete Logarithm* problem is solved via the standard *Pollard's Rho Method*, where $i = (a_k - a_j) \cdot (b_j - b_k)^{-1} \bmod n$. Note that n is the *order* of the *primitive element* α. Normally a *collision* is expected to occur after $\sqrt{\frac{n\pi}{2}}$ steps when using the non-parallelized *Pollard's Rho Method*. When m processors are used in parallel, a *collision* is expected to occur after $\frac{\sqrt{\frac{n\pi}{2}}}{m}$ steps performed in parallel by each of the m processors. The time associated with finding a *collision* is a function of the number of steps, the size of the set S versus the size of the set of *distinguished points* S_d, and the time associated with computing an iteration of *Floyd's Cycle Detecting Algorithm*. Therefore, the time required to find a *collision* using the parallelized implementation of *Pollard's Rho Method* may be expressed as $t_P = \left(\frac{\sqrt{\frac{n\pi}{2}}}{m} + \frac{|S|}{|S_d|}\right) \cdot t_{iteration}$.

8.6.3   The Pohlig-Hellman Algorithm

The *Pohlig-Hellman Algorithm*, developed in 1978 [246], takes advantage of the fact that the *Discrete Logarithm* for a cryptosystem may be determined by computing the *Discrete Logarithm* modulo each of the prime factors of the group *order*. These smaller *Discrete Logarithms* are then combined via the *Chinese Remainder Theorem* to determine the cryptosystem's *Discrete Logarithm*. Recall that when the *Cyclic Group* $(G, \bigcirc)$ is based on the set Z_p^* and the binary operation $\bigcirc = \times$, then the *Discrete Logarithm* problem states that given G, α, and $\beta = \alpha^i \bmod p$, find $i = log_\alpha \beta \bmod p$. The *Pohlig-Hellman Algorithm* assumes that the *order* and the prime factors of the *order* of the *Cyclic Group*, denoted as $\{p_1, p_2, p_3, \ldots p_t\}$, are known and then solves the *Discrete Logarithm* problem via $i \bmod p - 1 = p_1^{e_1} \cdot p_2^{e_2} \cdot p_3^{e_3} \cdot \ldots \cdot p_t^{e_t}$. This is achieved by recognizing that the *order* of $\alpha^{\frac{p-1}{p_s^{e_s}}}$ is $p_s^{e_s}$ (where p_s is one of the prime factors of $p - 1$) and that for an element z in the *Cyclic Group*, $z^{\frac{p-1}{p_s^{e_s}}}$ has a maximum *order* of $p_s^{e_s}$. The *Discrete Logarithm* $i_{p_s^{e_s}} = log_{\alpha^{\frac{p-1}{p_s^{e_s}}}} z^{\frac{p-1}{p_s^{e_s}}} \bmod p_s^{e_s}$ may then be computed using an algorithm such as *Pollard's Rho Method* e_s times. This yields a complexity of $e_t \cdot \sqrt{p_t}$ (where p_t is the largest prime factor of $p - 1$) for computing the cryptosystem's *Discrete Logarithm* $i = log_\alpha z \bmod p - 1$ [303].

The initial goal of the *Pohlig-Hellman Algorithm* is to determine:

$$i_{p1} \equiv i \bmod p_1^{e_1}$$

$$i_{p2} \equiv i \bmod p_2^{e_2}$$

$$i_{p3} \equiv i \bmod p_3^{e_3}$$

$$\vdots$$

$$i_{pt} \equiv i \bmod p_t^{e_t}$$

Each i_s is represented as a number $mod\ p_s^{e_s}$ as follows:

$$i_{p1} = c_{0_{p1}} + c_{1_{p1}} \cdot p_1 + c_{2_{p1}} \cdot p_1^2 + \ldots + c_{(e_1-1)_{p1}} \cdot p_1^{e_1-1}$$

$$i_{p2} = c_{0_{p2}} + c_{1_{p2}} \cdot p_2 + c_{2_{p2}} \cdot p_2^2 + \ldots + c_{(e_2-1)_{p2}} \cdot p_2^{e_2-1}$$

$$i_{p3} = c_{0_{p3}} + c_{1_{p3}} \cdot p_3 + c_{2_{p3}} \cdot p_3^2 + \ldots + c_{(e_3-1)_{p3}} \cdot p_3^{e_3-1}$$

$$\vdots$$

$$i_{pt} = c_{0_{pt}} + c_{1_{pt}} \cdot p_t + c_{2_{pt}} \cdot p_t^2 + \ldots + c_{(e_t-1)_{pt}} \cdot p_t^{e_t-1}$$

where each $c_{s_{p_s}} \in \{0, 1, 2, \ldots p_s - 1\}$.

Example 8.26: Generate the equations for each i_s for use in attacking the *Discrete Logarithm* problem in Z_{13}^* using the *Pohlig-Hellman Algorithm*.

Z_{13}^* has an *order* of $12 = 2^2 \cdot 3$. Therefore, the equations for each i_s are:

$$i_2 = c_{0_2} + c_{1_2} \cdot 2$$
$$i_3 = c_{0_3}$$

Once the equations for each i_s have been generated, the individual *Discrete Logarithm* problems must be solved and then the results combined via the *Chinese Remainder Theorem* to determine the cryptosystem's *Discrete Logarithm*. However, if the prime factors of $p - 1$ are small, then the individual *Discrete Logarithm* problems may be quickly computed.

Example 8.27: Using the equations from **Example 8.26**, solve the *Discrete Logarithm* problem using the *Pohlig-Hellman Algorithm* with $\alpha = 2$ and having an *order* of $12 = 2^2 \cdot 3$ and $\beta = \alpha^i \bmod p = 11$ in Z_{13}^*.

Z_{13}^* has an *order* of $12 = 2^2 \cdot 3$. Therefore, the equations for each i_s are:

$$i_2 = c_{0_2} + c_{1_2} \cdot 2$$
$$i_3 = c_{0_3}$$

Examining the equation for i_2, note that:

$$\alpha^{\frac{p-1}{p_2^2}} \mod p = 2^{\frac{12}{2^2}} \mod 13$$

$$\alpha^{\frac{p-1}{p_2^2}} \mod p = 2^{12/4} \mod 13$$

$$\alpha^{\frac{p-1}{p_2^2}} \mod p = 2^3 \mod 13$$

$$\alpha^{\frac{p-1}{p_2^2}} \mod p = 8 \mod 13$$

and that:

$$\beta^{\frac{p-1}{p_2^2}} \mod p = 11^{\frac{12}{2^2}} \mod 13$$

$$\beta^{\frac{p-1}{p_2^2}} \mod p = 11^{12/4} \mod 13$$

$$\beta^{\frac{p-1}{p_2^2}} \mod p = 11^3 \mod 13$$

$$\beta^{\frac{p-1}{p_2^2}} \mod p = 1,331 \mod 13$$

$$\beta^{\frac{p-1}{p_2^2}} \mod p \equiv 5 \mod 13$$

Finally, note that:

$$(\alpha^{\frac{p-1}{p_2^2}})^{p_2} \mod p = 8^2 \mod 13$$

$$(\alpha^{\frac{p-1}{p_2^2}})^{p_2} \mod p = 64 \mod 13$$

$$(\alpha^{\frac{p-1}{p_2^2}})^{p_2} \mod p \equiv 12 \mod 13$$

Knowing $\beta = \alpha^i \mod p$ leads to the conclusion that:

$$\beta^{\frac{p-1}{p_2^2}} \bmod p \equiv (\alpha^{\frac{p-1}{p_2^2}})^{(c_{0_2} + c_{1_2} \cdot p_2)} \bmod p$$

$$(\beta^{\frac{p-1}{p_2^2}})^{p_2} \bmod p \equiv ((\alpha^{\frac{p-1}{p_2^2}})^{p_2})^{(c_{0_2} + c_{1_2} \cdot p_2)} \bmod p$$

$$(\beta^{\frac{p-1}{p_2^2}})^{p_2} \bmod p \equiv ((\alpha^{\frac{p-1}{p_2^2}})^{p_2})^{c_{0_2}} \cdot ((\alpha^{\frac{p-1}{p_2^2}})^{p_2^2})^{c_{1_2}} \bmod p$$

$$(\beta^{\frac{p-1}{p_2^2}})^{p_2} \bmod p \equiv ((\alpha^{\frac{p-1}{p_2^2}})^{p_2})^{c_{0_2}} \cdot (\alpha^{p-1})^{c_{1_2}} \bmod p$$

$$(\beta^{\frac{p-1}{p_2^2}})^{p_2} \bmod p \equiv ((\alpha^{\frac{p-1}{p_2^2}})^{p_2})^{c_{0_2}} \cdot (1)^{c_{1_2}} \bmod p$$

$$(\beta^{\frac{p-1}{p_2^2}})^{p_2} \bmod p \equiv ((\alpha^{\frac{p-1}{p_2^2}})^{p_2})^{c_{0_2}} \bmod p$$

Substituting into this final equation yields:

$$(\beta^{\frac{p-1}{p_2{}^2}})^{p_2} \bmod p \equiv ((\alpha^{\frac{p-1}{p_2{}^2}})^{p_2})^{c_{0_2}} \bmod p$$

$$5^2 \bmod 13 \equiv 12^{c_{0_2}} \bmod 13$$

$$25 \bmod 13 \equiv 12^{c_{0_2}} \bmod 13$$

$$12 \bmod 13 \equiv 12^{c_{0_2}} \bmod 13$$

Therefore, $c_{0_2} = 1$. Substituting this value into the original equation yields:

$$\beta^{\frac{p-1}{p_2^2}} \bmod p \equiv (\alpha^{\frac{p-1}{p_2^2}})^{(c_{0_2} + c_{1_2} \cdot p_2)} \bmod p$$

$$\beta^{\frac{p-1}{p_2^2}} \bmod p \equiv (\alpha^{\frac{p-1}{p_2^2}})^{(1 + c_{1_2} \cdot p_2)} \bmod p$$

$$\beta^{\frac{p-1}{p_2^2}} \bmod p \equiv (\alpha^{\frac{p-1}{p_2^2}}) \cdot (\alpha^{\frac{p-1}{p_2^2}})^{(c_{1_2} \cdot p_2)} \bmod p$$

$$5 \bmod 13 \equiv 8 \cdot 8^{(c_{1_2} \cdot 2)} \bmod 13$$

Noting that $8^{-1} \bmod 13 \equiv 5 \bmod 13$ yields:

$$8^{-1} \cdot 5 \bmod 13 \equiv 8^{-1} \cdot 8 \cdot 8^{(c_{1_2} \cdot 2)} \bmod 13$$
$$5 \cdot 5 \bmod 13 \equiv 8^{(c_{1_2} \cdot 2)} \bmod 13$$
$$25 \bmod 13 \equiv 8^{(c_{1_2} \cdot 2)} \bmod 13$$
$$12 \bmod 13 \equiv 8^{(c_{1_2} \cdot 2)} \bmod 13$$

Therefore, $c_{1_2} = 1$ and $i_2 = c_{0_2} + c_{1_2} \cdot 2 = 1 + 1 \cdot 2 = 3$.

Examining the equation for i_3, note that:

$$\alpha^{\frac{p-1}{p_3}} \bmod p = 2^{12/3} \bmod 13$$
$$\alpha^{\frac{p-1}{p_3}} \bmod p = 2^4 \bmod 13$$
$$\alpha^{\frac{p-1}{p_3}} \bmod p = 16 \bmod 13$$
$$\alpha^{\frac{p-1}{p_3}} \bmod p \equiv 3 \bmod 13$$

and that:

$$\beta^{\frac{p-1}{p_3}} \bmod p = 11^{12/3} \bmod 13$$
$$\beta^{\frac{p-1}{p_3}} \bmod p = 11^4 \bmod 13$$
$$\beta^{\frac{p-1}{p_3}} \bmod p = 14,641 \bmod 13$$
$$\beta^{\frac{p-1}{p_3}} \bmod p \equiv 3 \bmod 13$$

Knowing $\beta = \alpha^i \bmod p$ leads to the conclusion that:

$$\beta^{\frac{p-1}{p_3}} \bmod p \equiv (\alpha^{\frac{p-1}{p_3}})^{(c_{0_3})} \bmod p$$

Substituting into this equation yields:

$$(\beta^{\frac{p-1}{p_2^2}})^{p_2} \bmod p \equiv ((\alpha^{\frac{p-1}{p_2^2}})^{p_2})^{c_{0_2}} \bmod p$$

$$3 \bmod 13 \equiv 3^{c_{0_3}} \bmod 13$$

Therefore, $c_{0_3} = 1 = i_3$. What remains is the use of the *Chinese Remainder Theorem* to determine the final solution for i. Knowing:

$$i = i_2 \bmod p_2^{e_2}$$
$$i = 3 \bmod 2^2$$
$$i = 3 \bmod 4$$

and:

$$i = i_3 \bmod p_3$$
$$i = 1 \bmod 3$$

yields:

$$M_2 = \frac{p - 1}{p_2^{e_2}} = 12/4 = 3$$

$$M_3 = \frac{p - 1}{p_3} = 12/3 = 4$$

Computing the inverses of M_2 and M_3 yields:

$$M_2^{-1} \bmod p_2^{e_2} = 3^{-1} \bmod 4 \equiv 3 \bmod 4 = y_2$$

$$M_3^{-1} \bmod p_3 = 4^{-1} \bmod 3 \equiv 1 \bmod 3 = y_3$$

Therefore, the final value for the exponent i is reconstructed as:

$$i = (y_2 \cdot M_2 \cdot i_2) + (y_3 \cdot M_3 \cdot i_3) \bmod p - 1$$

$$i = (3 \cdot 3 \cdot 3) + (1 \cdot 4 \cdot 1) \bmod 12$$

$$i = 27 + 4 \bmod 12$$

$$i = 31 \bmod 12$$

$$i \equiv 7 \bmod 12$$

Therefore, $i = 7$ and this is verified by computing $\alpha^i \bmod p$ and comparing the result to β:

$$\alpha^i \bmod p = 2^7 \bmod 13$$

$$\alpha^i \bmod p \ = \ 128 \bmod 13$$

$$\alpha^i \bmod p \ \equiv \ 11$$

$$\alpha^i \bmod p \ = \ \beta$$

As previously discussed, the complexity of the *Pohlig-Hellman Algorithm* is $e_t \cdot \sqrt{p_t}$, where p_t is the largest prime factor of $p - 1$. Therefore, p_t must be chosen for long-term security such that $p_t \geq 2^{256}$ to ensure a complexity of $\approx 2^{128}$, i.e. equivalent security to a 128-bit block cipher, so that an attack using the *Pohlig-Hellman Algorithm* is not computationally feasible in practice.

8.6.4   The Index Calculus Method

The *Index Calculus Method* is by far the most powerful attack against *Discrete Logarithm* cryptosystems. However, as will be discussed in Chapter 9, the *Index Calculus Method* has not been successfully applied to the *Discrete Logarithm* problem in the *Group* of an *Elliptic Curve* cryptosystem. The *Index Calculus Method* may be applied to the *Discrete Logarithm* problem in the *Cyclic Group* formed by Z_p^*, where p is prime, and the multiplication operation. Note that the *Index Calculus Method* may also be applied to the *Discrete Logarithm* problem in the *Cyclic Group* formed by the *Extension Field* $GF(2^k)^*$ and the multiplication operation.

The *Discrete Logarithm* problem states that given the *Cyclic Group* $(G, \bigcirc)$ based on the set Z_p^* and the binary operation $\bigcirc = \times$, a *primitive element* α whose *order* is $n = p - 1$, and $\beta = \alpha^i \bmod p$, find $i = log_\alpha\beta \bmod p$. Solving the *Discrete Logarithm* problem using the *Index Calculus Method* is achieved in four stages:

1. Set-up.

2. Collecting linear equations.

3. Solving the system of linear equations.

4. Computing the *Discrete Logarithm* of $\beta = \alpha^i \bmod p$.

The set-up stage begins with the selection of a *Factor Base*, denoted as S, where $S = \{p_1, p_2, p_3, \ldots p_t\}$ and each p_s is a prime number contained in the *Cyclic Group*. The elements p_s of S are chosen such that a significant number of the elements contained in the *Cyclic Group* may be represented as the product of the elements of the *Factor Base*.

Example 8.28: For the *Cyclic Group* based on the set Z_{229}^* and the *Factor Base* $S = \{2, 3, 5, 7, 11\}$, determine if the *Cyclic Group* element 216 can be represented via the elements of the *Factor Base* S.

The *Integer Factorization* of 216 yields $216 = 2^3 \cdot 3^3$. Therefore, the prime factors of 216 are all contained in the *Factor Base* S and the element 216 can be represented via the elements of the *Factor Base S*.

Example 8.29: For the *Cyclic Group* based on the set Z_{229}^* and the *Factor Base* $S = \{2, 3, 5, 7, 11\}$, determine if the *Cyclic Group* element 136 can be represented via the elements of the *Factor Base S*.

The *Integer Factorization* of 136 yields $136 = 2^3 \cdot 17$. Therefore, the prime factors of 136 are not all contained in the *Factor Base S* and the element 136 cannot be represented via the elements of the *Factor Base S*.

A *Factor Base* of small prime numbers is termed *Smooth-X*, where X is the largest prime number in the *Factor Base*.

Example 8.30: For the *Factor Base* $S = \{2, 3, 5, 7, 11\}$, what is the *Smoothness* of the *Factor Base*?

Because the largest prime number in the *Factor Base S* is 11, the *Factor Base S* is termed *Smooth-11*.

Once the *Factor Base* has been established, the goal is to find the *Discrete Logarithm* of all elements p_s in the *Factor Base S*. Therefore, for each element p_s in the *Factor Base S*, $p_s = \alpha^{l_s} \bmod p$ and thus $l_s = log_\alpha p_s \bmod p$ for $1 \le s \le t$, i.e. for all elements p_s in the *Factor Base*. This is achieved by expressing arbitrary elements contained in the *Cyclic Group* with a known *Discrete Logarithm* as a function of the elements in the *Factor Base S*. The elements p_s are thus represented as:

$$p_1 = \alpha^{l_1} \bmod p$$
$$p_2 = \alpha^{l_2} \bmod p$$
$$p_3 = \alpha^{l_3} \bmod p$$
$$\vdots$$
$$p_t = \alpha^{l_t} \bmod p$$

Once the set-up stage has been completed, the collection of linear equations begins. For a random exponent k, $1 \le k \le p - 2$, $\alpha^k = g_k \bmod p$ is computed and then *Integer Factorization* is performed in an attempt to represent g_k in terms of the elements in the *Factor Base S*. If g_k cannot be represented in terms of the elements in the *Factor Base S*, then the value for the exponent k is discarded, a new value is chosen for k, and the process is repeated. Note that $k = p - 1$ is not a useful choice because $\alpha^{p-1} \equiv 1 \bmod p$ per *Fermat's Little Theorem*.

If g_k can be represented in terms of the elements in the *Factor Base S*, then g_k takes the form of:

$$\alpha^k \bmod p = g_k \bmod p$$
$$\alpha^k \bmod p = (\alpha^{l_1})^{m_1} \cdot (\alpha^{l_2})^{m_2} \cdot (\alpha^{l_3})^{m_3} \cdot \ldots \cdot (\alpha^{l_t})^{m_t} \bmod p$$

where each exponent m_s is an integer ≥ 0. Knowing that the *order* of the *Cyclic Group* is $n = p - 1$ results in the linear equation:

$$k = (m_1 \cdot l_1) + (m_2 \cdot l_2) + (m_3 \cdot l_3) + \ldots$$
$$+ (m_t \cdot l_t) \bmod p - 1$$

The process of equation generation is repeated until $t + c$ linear equations have been constructed, where $c \leq 10$ in practice.

Example 8.31: For the *Cyclic Group* based on the set Z_{229}^* and the *primitive element* $\alpha = 6$, the *Factor Base S* = {2, 3, 5, 7, 11} is chosen for use in an attack based on the *Index Calculus Method*. If $k = 100$ and $6^{100} \bmod 229 \equiv 180 \bmod 229$, generate the associated linear equation for use in the *Index Calculus Method* attack.

The elements p_s of the *Factor Base* are represented as:

$$2 = 6^{l_1} \bmod 229$$

$$3 = 6^{l_2} \bmod 229$$

$$5 = 6^{l_3} \bmod 229$$

$$7 = 6^{l_4} \bmod 229$$

$$11 = 6^{l_5} \bmod 229$$

Integer Factorization of 180 yields $180 = 2^2 \cdot 3^2 \cdot 5^1$, and all of the prime factors of 180 are in the *Factor Base S*. Therefore, $6^{100} \bmod 229 \equiv 2^2 \cdot 3^2 \cdot 5^1 \bmod 229$, and thus the associated linear equation for use in the *Index Calculus Method* attack is:

$$100 = (2 \cdot l_1) + (2 \cdot l_2) + (1 \cdot l_3) +$$
$$(0 \cdot l_4) + (0 \cdot l_5) \bmod 228$$

Once the process of equation generation is completed, the system of linear equations must be solved to yield equations of the form $l_s = log_\alpha p_s$ for $1 \leq s \leq t$, i.e. for all elements p_s in the *Factor Base*. The system of linear equations must be solved in the *mod p − 1* domain. Consider the two equations:

$$a \cdot l_1 + b \cdot l_2 \equiv c \bmod p - 1$$

$$d \cdot l_1 + e \cdot l_2 \equiv f \bmod p - 1$$

To solve for l_1 requires that the first equation be multiplied by $b^{-1} \bmod p - 1$ and the second equation be multiplied by $e^{-1} \bmod p - 1$, resulting in the modified equations:

$$b^{-1} \cdot a \cdot l_1 + l_2 \equiv b^{-1} \cdot c \bmod p - 1$$
$$e^{-1} \cdot d \cdot l_1 + l_2 \equiv e^{-1} \cdot f \bmod p - 1$$

Now l_2 may be eliminated by subtracting the second equation from the first equation, resulting in the final modified equation:

$$b^{-1} \cdot a \cdot l_1 - e^{-1} \cdot d \cdot l_1 \equiv b^{-1} \cdot c - e^{-1} \cdot f \bmod p - 1$$
$$l_1 \cdot (b^{-1} \cdot a - e^{-1} \cdot d) \equiv b^{-1} \cdot c - e^{-1} \cdot f \bmod p - 1$$

In this manner the system of linear equations may be solved to determine the values for each l_s in the *Factor Base*.

Having solved the system of linear equations, determining the values for each l_s in the *Factor Base*, the *Discrete Logarithm* of $\beta = \alpha^i \bmod p$ may now be computed. Once again, a random exponent k is selected, where $1 \leq k \leq p - 2$, and then $\beta \cdot \alpha^k \bmod p$ is computed. *Integer Factorization* is then performed in an attempt to represent $\beta \cdot \alpha^k \bmod p$ in terms of the elements in the *Factor Base S*. If $\beta \cdot \alpha^k \bmod p$ cannot be represented in terms of the elements in the *Factor Base S*, then the value for the exponent k is discarded, a new value is chosen for k, and the process is repeated.

If $\beta \cdot \alpha^k \bmod p$ can be represented in terms of the elements in the *Factor Base S*, then $\beta \cdot \alpha^k \bmod p$ takes the form of:

$$\beta \cdot \alpha^k \bmod p = p_1^{d_1} \cdot p_2^{d_2} \cdot p_3^{d_3} \cdot \ldots \cdot p_t^{d_t} \bmod p$$

$$\beta \cdot \alpha^k \bmod p = (\alpha^{l_1})^{d_1} \cdot (\alpha^{l_2})^{d_2} \cdot (\alpha^{l_3})^{d_3} \cdot \ldots$$
$$\cdot (\alpha^{l_t})^{d_t} \bmod p$$

$$\alpha^i \cdot \alpha^k \bmod p = (\alpha^{l_1})^{d_1} \cdot (\alpha^{l_2})^{d_2} \cdot (\alpha^{l_3})^{d_3} \cdot \ldots$$
$$\cdot (\alpha^{l_t})^{d_t} \bmod p$$

where each exponent d_s is an integer ≥ 0. Knowing that the *order* of the *Cyclic Group* is $n = p - 1$ results in the linear equation:

$$i + k = (d_1 \cdot l_1) + (d_2 \cdot l_2) + (d_3 \cdot l_3) + \ldots$$
$$+ (d_t \cdot l_t) \bmod p - 1$$

$$i = (d_1 \cdot l_1) + (d_2 \cdot l_2) + (d_3 \cdot l_3) + \ldots$$
$$+ (d_t \cdot l_t) - k \bmod p - 1$$

The values for each l_s in the *Factor Base* are known from having solved the system of linear equations. The values for each d_s

in the *Factor Base* are known from the *Integer Factorization* of $\beta \cdot \alpha^k \bmod p$. The exponent k is known because it was chosen when computing $\beta \cdot \alpha^k \bmod p$. Therefore, all values necessary for computing the exponent i are known and thus the the *Discrete Logarithm* problem has been solved using the *Index Calculus Method*.

Example 8.32: Given a *Discrete Logarithm* cryptosystem in Z_p of the form $\alpha^i = \beta \bmod p$. The parameters are $p = 89$, $\alpha = 3$, and $\beta = 61$. α is a *generator* of Z_{89}^*. Compute i using the *Index Calculus Method*. Use the factor base $S = \{2, 3, 5, 7, 11\}$. Show all steps of your algorithm.

The elements p_s of the *Factor Base* are represented as:

$$2 = 3^{l_1} \bmod 89$$
$$3 = 3^{l_2} \bmod 89$$
$$5 = 3^{l_3} \bmod 89$$
$$7 = 3^{l_4} \bmod 89$$
$$11 = 3^{l_5} \bmod 89$$

Begin by choosing $k = 1$, resulting in $\alpha^k \bmod p = 3^1 \bmod 89$. Therefore, the first linear equation is:

$$1 = (0 \cdot l_1) + (1 \cdot l_2) + (0 \cdot l_3) + (0 \cdot l_4) +$$
$$(0 \cdot l_5) \ mod \ 88$$
$$1 = l_2 \ mod \ 88$$

To generate the second linear equation, choose $k = 5$, resulting in:

$$\alpha^k \ mod \ p = 3^5 \ mod \ 89$$
$$\alpha^k \ mod \ p = 243 \ mod \ 89$$
$$\alpha^k \ mod \ p \equiv 65 \ mod \ 89$$
$$\alpha^k \ mod \ p \equiv 5 \cdot 13 \ mod \ 89$$

Because 13 is not in the *Factor Base S*, $k = 5$ is discarded. Choosing $k = 9$ yields:

$$\alpha^k \ mod \ p = 3^9 \ mod \ 89$$
$$\alpha^k \ mod \ p = 19,683 \ mod \ 89$$
$$\alpha^k \ mod \ p \equiv 14 \ mod \ 89$$
$$\alpha^k \ mod \ p \equiv 2 \cdot 7 \ mod \ 89$$

All of the prime factors of 14 are in the *Factor Base S*. Therefore, the associated linear equation is:

$$9 = (1 \cdot l_1) + (0 \cdot l_2) + (0 \cdot l_3) + (1 \cdot l_4) +$$
$$(0 \cdot l_5) \bmod 88$$
$$9 = l_1 + l_4 \bmod 88$$

To generate the third linear equation, choose $k = 12$, resulting in:

$$\alpha^k \bmod p = 3^{12} \bmod 89$$
$$\alpha^k \bmod p = 531,441 \bmod 89$$
$$\alpha^k \bmod p \equiv 22 \bmod 89$$
$$\alpha^k \bmod p \equiv 2 \cdot 11 \bmod 89$$

All of the prime factors of 22 are in the *Factor Base S*. Therefore, the associated linear equation is:

$$12 = (1 \cdot l_1) + (0 \cdot l_2) + (0 \cdot l_3) + (0 \cdot l_4) +$$
$$(1 \cdot l_5) \bmod 88$$
$$12 = l_1 + l_5 \bmod 88$$

To generate the fourth linear equation, choose $k = 14$, resulting in:

$$\alpha^k \ mod \ p \ = \ 3^{14} \ mod \ 89$$

$$\alpha^k \ mod \ p \ = \ 4,782,969 \ mod \ 89$$

$$\alpha^k \ mod \ p \ \equiv \ 20 \ mod \ 89$$

$$\alpha^k \ mod \ p \ \equiv \ 2^2 \cdot 5 \ mod \ 89$$

All of the prime factors of 20 are in the *Factor Base S*. Therefore, the associated linear equation is:

$$14 \ = \ (2 \cdot l_1) + (0 \cdot l_2) + (1 \cdot l_3) + (0 \cdot l_4) +$$
$$(0 \cdot l_5) \ mod \ 88$$
$$14 \ = \ 2 \cdot l_1 + l_3 \ mod \ 88$$

To generate the fifth linear equation, choose $k = 16$, resulting in:

$$\alpha^k \ mod \ p \ = \ 3^{16} \ mod \ 89$$

$$\alpha^k \ mod \ p \ = \ 43,046,721 \ mod \ 89$$

$$\alpha^k \ mod \ p \ \equiv \ 2 \ mod \ 89$$

Therefore, the associated linear equation is:

$$16 = (1 \cdot l_1) + (0 \cdot l_2) + (0 \cdot l_3) + (0 \cdot l_4) +$$
$$(0 \cdot l_5) \bmod 88$$
$$16 = l_1 \bmod 88$$

Substituting the value of $l_1 = 16$ into the second linear equation yields:

$$9 = l_1 + l_4 \bmod 88$$
$$9 = 16 + l_4 \bmod 88$$
$$-7 = l_4 \bmod 88$$
$$81 \equiv l_4 \bmod 88$$

Substituting the value of $l_1 = 16$ into the third linear equation yields:

$$12 = l_1 + l_5 \bmod 88$$
$$12 = 16 + l_5 \bmod 88$$
$$-4 = l_5 \bmod 88$$
$$84 \equiv l_5 \bmod 88$$

Substituting the value of $l_1 = 16$ into the fourth linear equation yields:

$$14 \; = \; 2 \cdot l_1 \; + \; l_3 \; mod \; 88$$

$$14 \; = \; 2 \cdot 16 \; + \; l_3 \; mod \; 88$$

$$14 \; = \; 32 \; + \; l_3 \; mod \; 88$$

$$-18 \; = \; l_3 \; mod \; 88$$

$$70 \; \equiv \; l_3 \; mod \; 88$$

Therefore:

$$l_1 \; = \; 16 \; mod \; 89$$

$$l_2 \; = \; 1 \; mod \; 89$$

$$l_3 \; = \; 70 \; mod \; 89$$

$$l_4 \; = \; 81 \; mod \; 89$$

$$l_5 \; = \; 84 \; mod \; 89$$

Having solved the system of linear equations, determining the values for each l_s in the *Factor Base*, the *Discrete Logarithm* of $\beta = \alpha^i \; mod \; p$ may now be computed. Choosing $k = 20$ yields:

$$\beta \cdot \alpha^k \; mod \; p \; = \; 61 \cdot 3^{20} \; mod \; 89$$

$$\beta \cdot \alpha^k \; mod \; p \; = \; 61 \cdot 3,486,784,401 \; mod \; 89$$

$$\beta \cdot \alpha^k \; mod \; p \; \equiv \; 61 \cdot 73 \; mod \; 89$$

$$\beta \cdot \alpha^k \ mod \ p \ = \ 4,453 \ mod \ 89$$

$$\beta \cdot \alpha^k \ mod \ p \ \equiv \ 3 \ mod \ 89$$

$\beta \ = \ \alpha^i \ mod \ p$ may be represented by the prime factors in the *Factor Base S* via the linear equation:

$$\beta \cdot \alpha^k \ mod \ p \ = \ 3 \ mod \ 89$$

$$\beta \cdot \alpha^k \ mod \ p \ = \ (\alpha^{l_2})^{d_2} \ mod \ 89$$

where $d_2 \ = \ 1$.

Therefore, the *Discrete Logarithm* is computed as:

$$i \ + \ k \ = \ (d_1 \cdot l_1) + (d_2 \cdot l_2) + (d_3 \cdot l_3) + (d_4 \cdot l_4) +$$
$$(d_5 \cdot l_5) \ mod \ 88$$

$$i \ = \ (d_1 \cdot l_1) + (d_2 \cdot l_2) + (d_3 \cdot l_3) + (d_4 \cdot l_4) +$$
$$(d_5 \cdot l_5) \ - \ k \ mod \ 88$$

$$i \ = \ (0 \cdot l_1) + (1 \cdot l_2) + (0 \cdot l_3) + (0 \cdot l_4) +$$
$$(0 \cdot l_5) \ - \ 20 \ mod \ 88$$

$$i \ = \ 1 \cdot l_2 \ - \ 20 \ mod \ 88$$

$$i \ = \ 1 \cdot 1 \ - \ 20 \ mod \ 88$$

$$i \ = \ 1 - \ 20 \ mod \ 88$$

$$i \ = \ -19 \ mod \ 88$$

$$i \ \equiv \ 69 \ mod \ 88$$

The value $i = 69$ may be verified as follows:

$$\beta = \alpha^i \bmod p$$
$$61 = 3^{69} \bmod 89$$
$$61 = (3^{20})^3 \cdot 3^9 \bmod 89$$
$$61 = (3,486,784,401)^3 \cdot 19,683 \bmod 89$$
$$61 \equiv (73)^3 \cdot 14 \bmod 89$$
$$61 = 389,017 \cdot 14 \bmod 89$$
$$61 \equiv 87 \cdot 14 \bmod 89$$
$$61 = 1,218 \bmod 89$$
$$61 \equiv 61 \bmod 89$$

Thus, the *Discrete Logarithm* problem has been solved using the *Index Calculus Method*.

It is interesting to note that choosing a new exponent i does not fully restore a *Discrete Logarithm* cryptosystem that has been successfully attacked via the *Index Calculus Method* such that *Oscar* has determined the value of i. Choosing a new exponent, i_{new}, results in the computation of a new $\beta = \alpha^{i_{new}} \bmod p$. However, if the modulus p does not change, then the *Factor Base* from the previous attack based on the *Index Calculus Method* and the corresponding solutions to the system of linear equations may be reused because the computations performed in these stages are all independent of i. Therefore, *Oscar* may skip the first three stages of the *Index Calculus Method* when attacking the *Discrete Logarithm* cryptosystem based on the new exponent i_{new}. All that remains is for *Oscar* to compute the *Discrete Logarithm* via the final stage of the *Index Calculus Method* and the new exponent i_{new} will be recovered.

For a *Discrete Logarithm* cryptosystem, the *Index Calculus Method* is the best attack for computing the *Discrete Logarithm* in Z_p^*. The complexity of the *Index Calculus Method* does not depend on the size of the exponent i; rather, it is related to the group size and is computed as $e^{[1 + \vartheta(1)]\sqrt{log\ (p)\ \cdot\ log(log\ p)}}$ as p approaches infinity, where $\vartheta(1)$ is a small constant [51]. The complexity of the *Index Calculus Method* depends on the *Integer Factorization* algorithm used, typically a sieving algorithm, as discussed in Section 7.3, and this complexity is subexponential in the bit length of p; however, it is not polynomial in the bit length of p [189]. More recently, a complexity of $e^{[\frac{64}{9}^{\frac{1}{3}} + \vartheta(1)][log\ (p)^{\frac{1}{3}} \cdot\ log(log\ p)^{\frac{2}{3}}]}$ as p approaches infinity (and $\vartheta(1)$ is a small constant) was achieved using the *Generalized Number Field Sieve Integer Factorization* algorithm [273]. Based on these complexities, the parameters α, β, and p are chosen to be 1024-bit values to ensure that the *Index Calculus Method* is not computationally feasible in practice. However, as with *RSA* cryptosystems, based on *Moore's Law* it is recommended that 2048-bit moduli be used with the *Discrete Logarithm* problem to ensure long-term security. Finally, *Discrete*

Logarithm cryptosystems exhibit similar performance versus *RSA* cryptosystems using equivalent (1024-bit) sized parameter values. This is a result of *Integer Factorization* being the performance bottleneck in both cryptosystems, as discussed in Sections 7.2 and 8.4.

8.7 Homework Problems

Homework Problem 8.7.1: Determine the *order* of all elements of the *Cyclic Groups*:

a) Z_5^*

b) Z_{11}^*

c) Z_{13}^*

Create a table with two columns for every *Cyclic Group*. Each row should contain a *Cyclic Group* element a and the *order* of element a, denoted as *ord(a)*. Compute all *orders*.

Homework Problem 8.7.2:

a) How many elements are in each of the three *Cyclic Groups* described in **Homework Problem 8.7.1**?

b) Do all *orders* of the three *Cyclic Groups* described in **Homework Problem 8.7.1** evenly divide the number of elements in the corresponding *Cyclic Group*?

c) Which of the elements of the three *Cyclic Groups* described in **Homework Problem 8.7.1** are *primitive elements*?

d) Verify for the three *Cyclic Groups* described in **Homework Problem 8.7.1** that the number of *primitive elements* is given by $\phi(|Z_p^*|)$.

e) Verify for all elements a of Z_p^* that $a^{|Z_p^*|} \equiv 1 \bmod p$ for $p = 7$, i.e. prove that *Fermat's Little Theorem* holds true.

Homework Problem 8.7.3:

a) How many *Subgroups* are there for each of the three *Cyclic Groups* described in **Homework Problem 8.7.1**? Exclude the trivial *Subgroup*, which consists of only the element 1. What is the *cardinality* of each *Subgroup*?

b) For each of the *Subgroups* identified in part (a), give the complete multiplication table, i.e. the table which describes the multiplication of all *Subgroup* elements with each other.

c) For each of the *Subgroups* identified in part (a), list all of the *primitive elements*. Under what conditions are all elements of a *Subgroup*, with the exception of 1, *primitive elements*?

Homework Problem 8.7.4: Write a C program that determines the *order* of an element in Z_p^*. The program should notify the user if an element is a *primitive element*. The inputs to the program are the *Field* element, a, and the prime, p. Remember to perform modular reduction after every arithmetic operation. Determine the *order* of the following elements a in Z_p^*:

a) $p = 3,571$, $a = 2, 4$, and $2,048$

b) $p = 12,553$, $a = 2, 5$, and $5,300$

Which elements are *primitive elements*?

Homework Problem 8.7.5: It is important to be able to find *primitive elements* for the *Diffie-Hellman Key Agreement Protocol* as well as many other public-key schemes based on the *Discrete Logarithm* problem.

a) What is the complexity (given by the average number of steps or using O notation) for the program implemented in **Homework Problem 8.7.4**? Is this approach feasible for reale *Diffie-Hellman Key Agreement Protocol* implementations?

b) Is there any way to dramatically improve the tests that need to be performed? Describe an idea upon which an improved algorithm can be based.

Homework Problem 8.7.6: Compute the two public keys and the session key for the *Diffie-Hellman Key Agreement Protocol* with the parameters $p = 467$, $\alpha = 2$, and:

a) $a_A = 98$, $a_B = 17$

b) $a_A = 287$, $a_B = 134$

c) $a_A = 9$, $a_B = 17$

In all cases, perform the computation of the common key for *Alice* and *Bob*.

Homework Problem 8.7.7: Use a *Diffie-Hellman Key Agreement Protocol* with $p = 467$ and $\alpha = 4$. The element 4 has order 233 and therefore generates a *Subgroup* with 233 elements. Compute K_{AB} for:

a) $a_A = 310, \ a_B = 107$

b) $a_A = 77, \ a_B = 107$

Why are the session keys identical?

Homework Problem 8.7.8: Consider a *Diffie-Hellman Key Agreement Protocol* with a modulus p that has 1,024 bits and with α a *generator* of a *Subgroup*, where $ord(\alpha) \approx 2^{160}$.

a) How long does the computation of a session key take on average if one modular multiplication takes 950 μs and one modular squaring takes 475 μs? Assume that the public keys have already been computed.

b) One well known acceleration technique for *Discrete Logarithm* cryptosystems uses short *primitive elements*. Assume that α is a *short element* (e.g. an 8-bit integer). Assume that the modular multiplication with α takes only 10 μs. How long does the computation of the session key take? Why is the time for one modular squaring still the same as in part (a) if the *Square-and-Multiply Algorithm* is applied?

Homework Problem 8.7.9: Consider Z_{17}^*:

a) How many *Subgroups*, excluding the trivial *Subgroup* which consists of the element 1, exist? What is the *cardinality* of each *Subgroup*?

b) For each *Subgroup* found in part (a), give the complete multiplication table as a square table which describes the multiplication of all *Subgroup* elements with each other.

c) For each *Subgroup* found in part (a), determine all *primitive elements*.

Homework Problem 8.7.10: Compute the *Discrete Logarithms* in Z_{109}^*, $\alpha = 6$, using *Shank's Algorithm* for:

a) $\beta = 76$

b) $\beta = 77$

Homework Problem 8.7.11: Consider $(Z_m, +)$, where Z_m is the set of all integers and α is a *primitive element* in the *Cyclic Group*.

a) State the *Discrete Logarithm* problem for this case.

b) Show that the $gcd(\alpha, m) = 1$ if α is a *primitive element* in $(Z_m, +)$.

c) Show that the *Discrete Logarithm* problem is not a *One-Way* function by providing an efficient algorithm for computing the secret exponent i.

Homework Problem 8.7.12: Show that the choice of $m =$ $\lceil \sqrt{n} \rceil$ is optimum for *Shank's Algorithm* if s and t are to have the same range. Be sure to consider the maximum value that must be represented by $(s \cdot m) + t$.

Homework Problem 8.7.13: Develop an algorithm that is closely related to *Shank's Algorithm* but whose number of storage locations is restricted to $n^{\frac{1}{3}}$, where n is the *Cyclic Group order*. Provide an exact description of this algorithm. How many steps must be performed on average before a *Discrete Logarithm* problem is solved?

Homework Problem 8.7.14: Generalize the algorithm from **Homework Problem 8.7.13** such that the number of storage locations may be chosen arbitrarily. Use the variable r for the number of storage locations available. How many steps must be performed on average before a *Discrete Logarithm* problem is solved?

Homework Problem 8.7.15: Given the pseudorandom function $f(x_i) = x_i^2 + 7 \ mod \ 29$. Write a C program that generates the *Pollard's Rho Method* sequence that follows from the start value $x_0 = 7$. The program must output the sequence to the screen and include code that measures the time required to compute the sequence, outputting this information to the screen. Specify the computer model used and the amount of available RAM. Draw the ρ shaped diagram for the sequence and mark the μ tail and λ cycle.

Show how the sequences σ_1 and σ_2 of *Floyd's Cycle Detecting Algorithm* find a *collision*.

Homework Problem 8.7.16: Repeat **Homework Problem 8.7.15** with the start value $x_0 = 5$. Show how the sequences σ_1 and σ_2 of *Floyd's Cycle Detecting Algorithm* find a *collision*.

Homework Problem 8.7.17: Given a *Discrete Logarithm* cryptosystem in Z_p^* of the form $\alpha^i = \beta \bmod p$. The parameters are $p = 47, \alpha = 25, \beta = 6$, and $ord(\alpha) = 23$. Note that α generates a *Subgroup* of *order* 23. Compute i using *Pollard's Rho Method*. As start values, use $a_0 = b_0 = 3$ and $x_0 = \alpha^{a_0} \cdot \beta^{b_0} \bmod p$. What is the expected number of iterations after which a *collision* should be found? How many iterations were actually used in this specific example? Count the computation of x_i and x_{2i} as one iteration although three *Cyclic Group* operations are actually performed

Homework Problem 8.7.18: Use all of the values computed in **Homework Problem 8.7.17** and draw the ρ shaped diagram with all points of the x_i sequence. Also mark the points that are used by the x_{2i} sequence and show where the *collision* occurs.

Homework Problem 8.7.19: Given a *Discrete Logarithm* cryptosystem in Z_p^* of the form $\alpha^i = \beta \bmod p$. The parameters are $p = 467, \alpha = 2$, and $\beta = 278$. α is a *generator* of Z_{467}^*. Compute i using the *Index Calculus Method*. Use the factor base $S = \{2, 3, 5, 7, 11\}$. Show all steps of your algorithm.

Homework Problem 8.7.20: Repeat **Homework Problem 8.7.19** using $\beta = 165$.

Homework Problem 8.7.21: Assume that a large population of users makes use of the same *Diffie-Hellman Key Agreement Protocol* for establishing session keys between each other. Such a system only makes sense if α and p are the same for all users. Discuss the implications for other users if the private key of one user is broken with the *Index Calculus Method*. What would you recommend for the choice of p?

Homework Problem 8.7.22: Consider a cryptosystem based on the *Discrete Logarithm* problem in Z_p^*. Name two conditions for the choice of p. Which attacks cause the two conditions?

Homework Problem 8.7.23: *Shank's Algorithm* and *Pollard's Rho Method* have asymptotically the same computational complexity. Why is *Pollard's Rho Method* preferred in practice?

Homework Problem 8.7.24: Assume *Discrete Logarithm* cryptosystems in Z_p^* of the form $\beta \equiv \alpha^x \bmod p$, where α, β, and p are given. In addition, the *order* n of α in the *Cyclic Group* of Z_p^* is known. The file *HW8-7-24-Parameters.htm* contains these parameters for implementations of the *Discrete Logarithm* cryptosystems for different sizes of p and is available on the CD included with this book. Note that n is a prime number in all cases.

a) Starting with the smallest problem, write a C program try to break as many *Discrete Logarithm* cryptosystems as possible using an *Exhaustive Key Search* attack and the GNU MP long number library. The file *gmp.h*, the GNU MP long number library header file, is available on the CD included with this book and should be incorporated into your program. Documentation for the GNU MP long number library functions is available on-line [98]. Specify the computer model used and the amount of available RAM. Provide the solution x to each *Discrete Logarithm* cryptosystem, the number of iterations your attack required (which may be equal to the value of x), and the time it took to break each *Discrete Logarithm* cryptosystem.

b) Implement the non-parallelized *Pollard's Rho Method*. For the 30-bit *Discrete Logarithm* cryptosystem, run 1,000 different instances of *Pollard's Rho Method*. For each instance, select a new random start point by selecting $0 < a_0$ and $b_0 < n$ at random. Determine the minimum, maximum, and average number of iterations required to find the solution to the *Discrete Logarithm* cryptosystem. Note that the solution x must be the same in all cases and that the computation of one new element x_i together with the computation of x_{2i} is considered to be one iteration, even though three *Cyclic Group* operations are performed. Compute the expected number of iterations of *Pollard's Rho Method* and compare the result with the maximum number of iterations required by your implementation to find the solution to the *Discrete Logarithm* cryptosystem.

c) Starting with the smallest problem, try to break as many *Discrete Logarithm* cryptosystems as possible using *Pollard's Rho*

Method. Note that *Pollard's Rho Method* is non-deterministic. As a result, your program should terminate an unsuccessful search after a while and restart the algorithm with a different initial value. Specify the computer model used and the amount of available RAM. Provide the solution x to each *Discrete Logarithm* cryptosystem, the number of iterations your attack required (which may be equal to the value of x), and the time it took to break each *Discrete Logarithm* cryptosystem.

d) Compare for each *Discrete Logarithm* cryptosystem the run time of the *Exhaustive Key Search* attack, the square root of the run time of the *Exhaustive Key Search* attack, and the run time of *Pollard's Rho Method*. How close is the actual execution time of *Pollard's Rho Method* to the estimated time?

e) Compare the number of iterations of the *Exhaustive Key Search* attack, the expected number of iterations of *Pollard's Rho Method*, and the actual number of iterations of *Pollard's Rho Method*.

Homework Problem 8.7.25: Write a VHDL architecture to implement the computation of $\beta = \alpha^i \bmod p$ for 4-bit input values i using the public-key parameters *alpha* and *p*. Assume that the user will provide a *pload* signal to indicate that *alpha*, *p*, and i are ready to be loaded on the next rising edge of the clock. Use the *Square-and-Multiply Algorithm* to perform the exponentiation. Your system must output a *valid* signal to indicate when the output *beta* is valid, i.e. computation of $\beta = \alpha^i \bmod p$ is

completed. Use the following entity declaration for your implementation:

```
LIBRARY ieee;
USE ieee.std_logic_1164.ALL;
USE ieee.std_logic_arith.ALL;
USE ieee.std_logic_unsigned.ALL;
ENTITY dl_4 IS
  PORT ( i     : IN  std_logic_vector (3 DOWNTO 0);
         p     : IN  std_logic_vector (3 DOWNTO 0);
         alpha : IN  std_logic_vector (3 DOWNTO 0);
         clk   : IN  std_logic;
         rst   : IN  std_logic;
         pload : IN  std_logic;
         valid : OUT std_logic;
         beta  : OUT std_logic_vector (3 DOWNTO 0));
END dl_4;
ARCHITECTURE behav OF dl_4 IS
BEGIN
-- Your code goes here
END behav;
```

Use the parameters $p = 13$ and $\alpha = 2$ and validate your design
for all possible values of i. Specify the target technology used to
implement the design and the maximum operating frequency as
specified by your place-and-route tools. What is the execution
time of your implementation? What is the gate count of your
implementation?

Homework Problem 8.7.26: Expand your VHDL architecture
from **Homework Problem 8.7.25** to implement the computa-
tion of $\beta = \alpha^i \bmod p$ for 8-bit input values x using the public-key
parameters *alpha* and *p*. Use the following entity declaration for
your implementation:

```
LIBRARY ieee;
USE ieee.std_logic_1164.ALL;
USE ieee.std_logic_arith.ALL;
USE ieee.std_logic_unsigned.ALL;
ENTITY dl_8 IS
    PORT ( i     : IN  std_logic_vector (7 DOWNTO 0);
           p     : IN  std_logic_vector (7 DOWNTO 0);
           alpha : IN  std_logic_vector (7 DOWNTO 0);
           clk   : IN  std_logic;
           rst   : IN  std_logic;
           pload : IN  std_logic;
           valid : OUT std_logic;
           beta  : OUT std_logic_vector (7 DOWNTO 0));
END dl_8;
ARCHITECTURE behav OF dl_8 IS
BEGIN
-- Your code goes here
END behav;
```

Use the parameters $p = 89$ and $\alpha = 3$ and validate your design for all possible values of i. Specify the target technology used to implement the design and the maximum operating frequency as specified by your place-and-route tools. What is the execution time of your implementation? How does this execution time compare to the execution time of **Homework Problem 8.7.25**? What is the gate count of your implementation? How does this gate count compare to the gate count of **Homework Problem 8.7.25**?

Homework Problem 8.7.27: Compute the encryption and decryption with the *ElGamal* encryption algorithm for:

a) $p = 31$, $\alpha = 17$, $a = 11$, $k = 8$

b) $p = 7$, $\alpha = 5$, $a = 5$, $k = 6$

c) $p = 7$, $\alpha = 5$, $a = 6$, $k = 6$

For each of the problems, assume a message of $x = 4$.

Homework Problem 8.7.28: The *ElGamal* encryption algorithm can be easily broken if the encrypting party does not change the random parameter k for every new message x. Assume *Alice* encrypts a string of data:

$$(x_1, \ x_2, \ \ldots \ , x_n)$$

into the ciphertext:

$$((y_{11}, \ y_{12}), \ (y_{21}, \ y_{22}), \ \ldots \ , \ (y_{n1}, \ y_{n2}))$$

Alice keeps the same k for all encryptions. Show how *Oscar* can recover the entire plaintext with a *Known-Plaintext* attack. Assume *Oscar* has knowledge of a single piece of plaintext, x_1, all ciphertext, and the public key.

Homework Problem 8.7.29: You receive the message:

$$(620, \ 308), \ (620, \ 537), \ (620, \ 455), \ (620, \ 862),$$
$$(620, \ 667), \ (620, \ 667), \ (620, \ 113)$$

which was encrypted using the *ElGamal* encryption algorithm with $p = 1,009$, $\alpha = 11$, and $\beta = 798$. Each encryption encrypts a single letter. The mapping from letters to numbers is $A \Leftrightarrow 1, \ldots , Z \Leftrightarrow 26$. It is known that the same secret parameter k was used for all encryptions and that the first letter is Y. What is the plaintext?

Homework Problem 8.7.30: An attack similar to the one performed in **Homework Problem 8.7.29** is possible even if k changes for every encryption when a very weak update function for computing the new k is used. Assume that *Bob* generates a new k_i for each encryption using the rule $k_i = k_{i-1} + 1$; $i \geq 1$, where k_0 is a true random value that cannot be guessed by *Oscar*. Show how *Bob's* encryption scheme can be broken if x_1 is known.

Homework Problem 8.7.31: A cryptosystem is said to be non-deterministic if there are many possible valid ciphertexts for a given plaintext with a fixed public key.

a) Why is encryption with the *ElGamal* encryption algorithm non-deterministic?

b) How many valid ciphertexts are there for each message x (general expression)?

c) Is the *RSA* cryptosystem non-deterministic once the public key has been selected?

d) What is the consequence of this behavior for the *ElGamal* and *RSA* schemes if the goal is to encrypt short messages individually, e.g. 8-bit ASCII values?

Homework Problem 8.7.32: *Bob* sends a message to *Alice* that is encrypted with the *ElGamal* encryption algorithm and he keeps the parameter k the same for all encryption processes. *Oscar* knows that *Bob's* first message is always his terminal number so that $x_1 = 17$. *Oscar* observes the two ciphertext messages $(y_{11} = 26, y_{12} = 22)$ and $(y_{21} = 26, y_{22} = 1)$. The cryptosystem parameters are $p = 31$, $\alpha = 3$, and $\beta = 18$. *Oscar* can now determine x_2. What is the second piece of plaintext (x_2) that *Bob* has sent to *Alice*?

Homework Problem 8.7.33: Encrypt the message $x = HELLO$ $WORLD$ with the *ElGamal* encryption algorithm with parameters $p = 31$, $\alpha = 17$, $a = 8$, and $k = 3$. Assume the correspondence $A \Leftrightarrow 1, \dots, Z \Leftrightarrow 26$. Why is this encryption method not secure?

Homework Problem 8.7.34: Compute the secret session key between *Alice* and *Bob* which was established using the *Diffie-Hellman Key Agreement Protocol*. The parameters of the protocol are the *Extension Field* $GF(2^5)^*$, with $P(x) = x^5 + x^2 + 1$ being the *Irreducible Polynomial* and $\alpha = x$ being the *primitive element*. *Alice's* public key is $b_A = x^4 + x^2$. Find *Alice's* private key by applying *Shank's Algorithm*. Show how the session key can be computed from this point.

Homework Problem 8.7.35: Consider a *Diffie-Hellman Key Agreement Protocol* in *Galois Fields*. All arithmetic is done in the *Extension Field* $GF(2^5)^*$, with $P(x) = x^5 + x^2 + 1$ being the *Irreducible Polynomial*. The *primitive element* for the *Diffie-Hellman Key Agreement Protocol* is $\alpha = x^2$. The private keys are $a_A = 3$ and $a_B = 12$. What is the session key K_{AB}?

Homework Problem 8.7.36: Consider the *Extension Field*

$$GF(2^4)^*$$

with the *Irreducible Polynomial* $P(x) = x^4 + x + 1$.

a) What is the *order* of the *Cyclic Group* of $GF(2^4)^*$?

b) What are the possible *orders* of the *Field* elements?

c) Find the *order* of the elements $A(x) = x^2 + x$ and $B(x) = x$.

d) Is either $A(x)$ or $B(x)$ a *primitive element*?

Chapter 9

Public-Key Cryptography: Elliptic Curves

Elliptic Curve cryptosystems were independently proposed by Victor Miller of IBM in 1985 [209] and Neal Koblitz in 1987 [167]. *Elliptic Curve* cryptosystems are believed to be as secure as *RSA* and the *Discrete Logarithm* problem in Z_p^*. Moreover, as will be discussed in Section 9.5, because the *Index Calculus Method* has not been successfully applied to the *Discrete Logarithm* problem in the *Group* of an *Elliptic Curve*, such cryptosystems require significantly smaller operands to achieve equivalent security versus cryptosystems such as *RSA* and the *Discrete Logarithm* problem in Z_p^*.

9.1 Cryptosystem

The definition of an *Elliptic Curve* over the set Z_p for $p > 3$ is the set of all coordinate pairs (x, y) (where x and y are contained in the set Z_p) such that:

$$y^2 \equiv x^3 + a \cdot x + b \bmod p$$

where a and b are contained in the set Z_p and:

$$4 \cdot a^3 + 27 \cdot b^2 \neq 0 \bmod p$$

Figure 9.1 shows the coordinate mapping of the equation for an *Elliptic Curve*. P_1 and P_2 are points on the *Elliptic Curve* represented by the coordinates (x_1, y_1) and (x_2, y_2), respectively. The point P_3 is the result of the addition of points P_1 and P_2 and is represented by the coordinates (x_3, y_3). Point addition, where $P_1 \neq P_2$, is achieved geometrically via the following steps:

1. Draw the line between points P_1 and P_2.

2. Extend the line between points P_1 and P_2 such that the line intersects the parabola.

3. From the point of intersection on the parabola, draw a vertical line perpendicular to the x-*axis* that intersects the parabola at the mirror of the original point of intersection on the parabola. This intersection point, P_3, represents the sum of the points P_1 and P_2 on the *Elliptic Curve*.

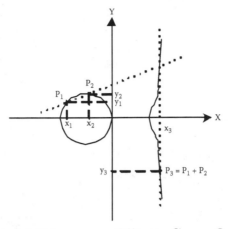

Figure 9.1: Point Addition on an Elliptic Curve Over Z_p for $p > 3$ where $P_1 \neq P_2$

Figure 9.2 shows the coordinate mapping of the equation for an *Elliptic Curve* with the addition of two points on the *Elliptic Curve* that are the same. The point P_2 is the result of the addition of point $P_1 = (x_1, y_1)$ with itself and is represented by the coordinates (x_2, y_2). In this case, point addition is achieved geometrically via the following steps:

1. Draw the line tangent to the circle passing through the point P_1.

2. Extend the line through the point P_1 such that the line intersects the parabola.

3. From the point of intersection on the parabola, draw a vertical line perpendicular to the *x-axis* that intersects the parabola at the mirror of the original point of intersection on the parabola. This intersection point, P_2, represents the sum of two points on the *Elliptic Curve* that are the same, i.e. $P_1 + P_1$.

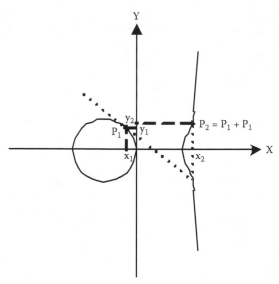

Figure 9.2: Point Addition on an Elliptic Curve Over Z_p for $p > 3$ where $P_1 = P_2$

As described in Section 8.1, a *Group* consists of a set of elements and a binary operation, denoted as $\bigcirc$. A *Cyclic Group* requires the existence of at least one element α with maximum *order*, i.e. a *generator* or *primitive elements* of the *Cyclic Group*, that generates all elements of the set through repeated application of the binary operation. The *order* of an *Elliptic Curve* is denoted as $\#E$ and the set of elements is made up of the coordinate points that fulfill the *Elliptic Curve* equation. The binary operation, denoted as $\bigcirc$, is the addition of points on the *Elliptic Curve* such that $P_1 + P_2 = P_3$, which may also be represented as $(x_1,\ y_1) + (x_2,\ y_2) = (x_3,\ y_3)$. Point addition is therefore defined as:

$$x_3 \equiv \lambda^2 - x_2 - x_1 \bmod p$$

$$y_3 \equiv \lambda \cdot (x_1 - x_3) - y_1 \ mod \ p$$

where the intermediate term λ is defined as:

$$\lambda = \begin{cases} \frac{y_2 - y_1}{x_2 - x_1} \ mod \ p & P_1 \neq P_2 \\ \frac{3x_1^2 + a}{2y_1} \ mod \ p & P_1 = P_2 \end{cases}$$

where division is performed by finding the inverse *mod* p of the denominator of λ, depending on whether or not $P_1 = P_2$, and then multiplying that inverse by the associated numerator to compute the final result for λ. If $P_2 = -P_1$, i.e. $P_2 = (x_1, -y_1)$, then the addition of P_1 and P_2 results in the denominator of $\lambda = 0$. Such an occurrence yields the *Point of Infinity*, denoted as ϑ, which is the identity element of the *Cyclic Group*. Therefore, if the *Point of Infinity* is added to a point P_1, the result is P_1, i.e. $P_1 + \vartheta = P_1$. Therefore, the set of elements of coordinate points that fulfill the *Elliptic Curve* equation together with the *Point of Infinity* and the binary operation of point addition form a *Cyclic Group* as long as there exists at least one element α, a point on the *Elliptic Curve*, with maximum *order*.

Example 9.1: The *Elliptic Curve* cryptosystem defined as $y^2 \equiv x^3 + x + 6 \ mod \ 11$ has a total of 13 points, i.e. the *order* of the *Elliptic Curve* $\#E = 13$. Is the point $(7, 9)$ a point on the *Elliptic Curve*?

If the point $(7, 9)$ is a point on the *Elliptic Curve*, then it must satisfy the curve equation:

$$y^2 \equiv x^3 + x + 6 \bmod 11$$
$$9^2 \equiv 7^3 + 7 + 6 \bmod 11$$
$$81 \bmod 11 \equiv 343 + 7 + 6 \bmod 11$$
$$4 \bmod 11 \equiv 356 \bmod 11$$
$$4 \bmod 11 \equiv 4 \bmod 11$$

Because the point $(7, 9)$ satisfies the curve equation, it is a point on the *Elliptic Curve* defined as $y^2 \equiv x^3 + x + 6 \bmod 11$.

Example 9.2: The *Elliptic Curve* cryptosystem defined as $y^2 \equiv x^3 + x + 6 \bmod 11$ has a total of 13 points, i.e. the *order* of the *Elliptic Curve* $\#E = 13$. Is the point $(7, 9)$ a *generator* of the *Cyclic Group* formed by the points on the *Elliptic Curve* and the *Point of Infinity*?

To determine if the point $(7, 9)$ is a point on the *Elliptic Curve*, repeated application of the binary operation of the *Cyclic Group*, i.e. point addition, must be performed using the point $(7, 9)$ to determine if all of the points on the *Elliptic Curve* are generated:

$$\alpha = (7, 9)$$

$$2 \cdot \alpha = (7, 9) + (7, 9)$$

$$\lambda = \frac{3x_1^2 + a}{2y_1} \ mod \ p$$

$$\lambda = \frac{3 \cdot 7^2 + 1}{2 \cdot 9} \ mod \ 11$$

$$\lambda = \frac{3 \cdot 49 + 1}{18} \ mod \ 11$$

$$\lambda = \frac{148}{18} \ mod \ 11$$

$$\lambda \equiv \frac{5}{7} \ mod \ 11$$

$$\lambda \equiv 5 \cdot 7^{-1} \ mod \ 11$$

$$\lambda \equiv 5 \cdot 8 \ mod \ 11$$

$$\lambda \equiv 40 \ mod \ 11$$

$$\lambda \equiv 7 \ mod \ 11$$

$$x_3 \equiv \lambda^2 - x_2 - x_1 \ mod \ p$$

$$x_3 \equiv 7^2 - 7 - 7 \ mod \ 11$$

$$x_3 \equiv 49 - 7 - 7 \ mod \ 11$$

$$x_3 \equiv 35 \ mod \ 11$$

$$x_3 \equiv 2 \ mod \ 11$$

$$y_3 \equiv \lambda \cdot (x_1 - x_3) - y_1 \ mod \ p$$

$$y_3 \equiv 7 \cdot (7 - 2) - 9 \ mod \ 11$$

$$y_3 \equiv 7 \cdot 5 - 9 \ mod \ 11$$

$$y_3 \equiv 35 - 9 \ mod \ 11$$

$$y_3 \equiv 26 \ mod \ 11$$

$$y_3 \equiv 4 \ mod \ 11$$

$$2 \cdot \alpha = (2, 4)$$

$$3 \cdot \alpha = (2, 4) + (7, 9)$$

$$\lambda = \frac{y_2 - y_1}{x_2 - x_1} \bmod p$$

$$\lambda = \frac{9 - 4}{7 - 2} \bmod 11$$

$$\lambda = \frac{5}{5} \bmod 11$$

$$\lambda \equiv 5 \cdot 5^{-1} \bmod 11$$

$$\lambda \equiv 5 \cdot 9 \bmod 11$$

$$\lambda \equiv 45 \bmod 11$$

$$\lambda \equiv 1 \bmod 11$$

$$x_3 \equiv \lambda^2 - x_2 - x_1 \bmod p$$

$$x_3 \equiv 1^2 - 7 - 2 \bmod 11$$

$$x_3 \equiv 1 - 7 - 2 \bmod 11$$

$$x_3 \equiv -8 \bmod 11$$

$$x_3 \equiv 3 \bmod 11$$

$$y_3 \equiv \lambda \cdot (x_1 - x_3) - y_1 \bmod p$$

$$y_3 \equiv 1 \cdot (2 - 3) - 4 \bmod 11$$

$$y_3 \equiv 1 \cdot -1 - 4 \bmod 11$$

$$y_3 \equiv -1 - 4 \bmod 11$$

$$y_3 \equiv -5 \bmod 11$$

$$y_3 \equiv 6 \bmod 11$$

$$3 \cdot \alpha = (3, 6)$$

$$4 \cdot \alpha = (3, 6) + (7, 9)$$

$$\lambda = \frac{y_2 - y_1}{x_2 - x_1} \bmod p$$

$$\lambda = \frac{9 - 6}{7 - 3} \bmod 11$$

$$\lambda = \frac{3}{4} \bmod 11$$

$$\lambda \equiv 3 \cdot 4^{-1} \bmod 11$$

$$\lambda \equiv 3 \cdot 3 \bmod 11$$

$$\lambda \equiv 9 \bmod 11$$

$$x_3 \equiv \lambda^2 - x_2 - x_1 \bmod p$$

$$x_3 \equiv 9^2 - 7 - 3 \bmod 11$$

$$x_3 \equiv 81 - 7 - 3 \bmod 11$$

$$x_3 \equiv 71 \bmod 11$$

$$x_3 \equiv 5 \bmod 11$$

$$y_3 \equiv \lambda \cdot (x_1 - x_3) - y_1 \bmod p$$

$$y_3 \equiv 9 \cdot (3 - 5) - 6 \bmod 11$$

$$y_3 \equiv 9 \cdot -2 - 6 \bmod 11$$

$$y_3 \equiv -18 - 6 \bmod 11$$

$$y_3 \equiv -24 \bmod 11$$

$$y_3 \equiv 9 \bmod 11$$

$$4 \cdot \alpha = (5, 9)$$

$$5 \cdot \alpha = (5, 9) + (7, 9)$$

$$\lambda = \frac{y_2 - y_1}{x_2 - x_1} \bmod p$$

$$\lambda = \frac{9 - 9}{7 - 5} \bmod 11$$

$$\lambda = \frac{0}{2} \bmod 11$$

$$\lambda \equiv 0 \cdot 2^{-1} \bmod 11$$

$$\lambda \equiv 0 \cdot 6 \bmod 11$$

$$\lambda \equiv 0 \bmod 11$$

$$x_3 \equiv \lambda^2 - x_2 - x_1 \bmod p$$

$$x_3 \equiv 0^2 - 7 - 5 \bmod 11$$

$$x_3 \equiv 0 - 7 - 5 \bmod 11$$

$$x_3 \equiv -12 \bmod 11$$

$$x_3 \equiv 10 \bmod 11$$

$$y_3 \equiv \lambda \cdot (x_1 - x_3) - y_1 \bmod p$$

$$y_3 \equiv 0 \cdot (5 - 10) - 9 \bmod 11$$

$$y_3 \equiv 0 \cdot -5 - 9 \bmod 11$$

$$y_3 \equiv 0 - 9 \bmod 11$$

$$y_3 \equiv -9 \bmod 11$$

$$y_3 \equiv 2 \bmod 11$$

$$5 \cdot \alpha = (10, 2)$$

$$6 \cdot \alpha = (10, \ 2) + (7, \ 9)$$

$$\lambda = \frac{y_2 - y_1}{x_2 - x_1} \ mod \ p$$

$$\lambda = \frac{9 - 2}{7 - 10} \ mod \ 11$$

$$\lambda = \frac{7}{-3} \ mod \ 11$$

$$\lambda \equiv \frac{7}{8} \ mod \ 11$$

$$\lambda \equiv 7 \cdot 8^{-1} \ mod \ 11$$

$$\lambda \equiv 7 \cdot 7 \ mod \ 11$$

$$\lambda \equiv 49 \ mod \ 11$$

$$\lambda \equiv 5 \ mod \ 11$$

$$x_3 \equiv \lambda^2 - x_2 - x_1 \ mod \ p$$

$$x_3 \equiv 5^2 - 7 - 10 \ mod \ 11$$

$$x_3 \equiv 25 - 7 - 10 \ mod \ 11$$

$$x_3 \equiv 8 \ mod \ 11$$

$$y_3 \equiv \lambda \cdot (x_1 - x_3) - y_1 \ mod \ p$$

$$y_3 \equiv 5 \cdot (10 - 8) - 2 \ mod \ 11$$

$$y_3 \equiv 5 \cdot 2 - 2 \ mod \ 11$$

$$y_3 \equiv 10 - 2 \ mod \ 11$$

$$y_3 \equiv 8 \ mod \ 11$$

$$6 \cdot \alpha = (8, \ 8)$$

$$7 \cdot \alpha = (8, \ 8) + (7, \ 9)$$

$$\lambda = \frac{y_2 - y_1}{x_2 - x_1} \ mod \ p$$

$$\lambda = \frac{9 - 8}{7 - 8} \ mod \ 11$$

$$\lambda = \frac{1}{-1} \ mod \ 11$$

$$\lambda \equiv \frac{1}{10} \ mod \ 11$$

$$\lambda \equiv 1 \cdot 10^{-1} \ mod \ 11$$

$$\lambda \equiv 1 \cdot 10 \ mod \ 11$$

$$\lambda \equiv 10 \ mod \ 11$$

$$x_3 \equiv \lambda^2 - x_2 - x_1 \ mod \ p$$

$$x_3 \equiv 10^2 - 7 - 8 \ mod \ 11$$

$$x_3 \equiv 100 - 7 - 8 \ mod \ 11$$

$$x_3 \equiv 85 \ mod \ 11$$

$$x_3 \equiv 8 \ mod \ 11$$

$$y_3 \equiv \lambda \cdot (x_1 - x_3) - y_1 \ mod \ p$$

$$y_3 \equiv 10 \cdot (8 - 8) - 8 \ mod \ 11$$

$$y_3 \equiv 10 \cdot 0 - 8 \ mod \ 11$$

$$y_3 \equiv 0 - 8 \ mod \ 11$$

$$y_3 \equiv -8 \ mod \ 11$$

$$y_3 \equiv 3 \ mod \ 11$$

$$7 \cdot \alpha = (8, \ 3)$$

$$8 \cdot \alpha = (8, 3) + (7, 9)$$

$$\lambda = \frac{y_2 - y_1}{x_2 - x_1} \; mod \; p$$

$$\lambda = \frac{9 - 3}{7 - 8} \; mod \; 11$$

$$\lambda = \frac{6}{-1} \; mod \; 11$$

$$\lambda \equiv \frac{6}{10} \; mod \; 11$$

$$\lambda \equiv 6 \cdot 10^{-1} \; mod \; 11$$

$$\lambda \equiv 6 \cdot 10 \; mod \; 11$$

$$\lambda \equiv 60 \; mod \; 11$$

$$\lambda \equiv 5 \; mod \; 11$$

$$x_3 \equiv \lambda^2 - x_2 - x_1 \; mod \; p$$

$$x_3 \equiv 5^2 - 7 - 8 \; mod \; 11$$

$$x_3 \equiv 25 - 7 - 8 \; mod \; 11$$

$$x_3 \equiv 10 \; mod \; 11$$

$$y_3 \equiv \lambda \cdot (x_1 - x_3) - y_1 \; mod \; p$$

$$y_3 \equiv 5 \cdot (8 - 10) - 3 \; mod \; 11$$

$$y_3 \equiv 5 \cdot -2 - 3 \; mod \; 11$$

$$y_3 \equiv -10 - 3 \; mod \; 11$$

$$y_3 \equiv -13 \; mod \; 11$$

$$y_3 \equiv 9 \; mod \; 11$$

$$8 \cdot \alpha = (10, 9)$$

$$9 \cdot \alpha = (10,\ 9) + (7,\ 9)$$

$$\lambda = \frac{y_2 - y_1}{x_2 - x_1} \bmod p$$

$$\lambda = \frac{9 - 9}{7 - 10} \bmod 11$$

$$\lambda = \frac{0}{-3} \bmod 11$$

$$\lambda \equiv \frac{0}{8} \bmod 11$$

$$\lambda \equiv 0 \cdot 8^{-1} \bmod 11$$

$$\lambda \equiv 0 \cdot 7 \bmod 11$$

$$\lambda \equiv 0 \bmod 11$$

$$x_3 \equiv \lambda^2 - x_2 - x_1 \bmod p$$

$$x_3 \equiv 0^2 - 7 - 10 \bmod 11$$

$$x_3 \equiv 0 - 7 - 10 \bmod 11$$

$$x_3 \equiv -17 \bmod 11$$

$$x_3 \equiv 5 \bmod 11$$

$$y_3 \equiv \lambda \cdot (x_1 - x_3) - y_1 \bmod p$$

$$y_3 \equiv 0 \cdot (10 - 5) - 9 \bmod 11$$

$$y_3 \equiv 0 \cdot 5 - 9 \bmod 11$$

$$y_3 \equiv 0 - 9 \bmod 11$$

$$y_3 \equiv -9 \bmod 11$$

$$y_3 \equiv 2 \bmod 11$$

$$9 \cdot \alpha = (5,\ 2)$$

$$10 \cdot \alpha = (5, \ 2) + (7, \ 9)$$

$$\lambda = \frac{y_2 - y_1}{x_2 - x_1} \ mod \ p$$

$$\lambda = \frac{9 - 2}{7 - 5} \ mod \ 11$$

$$\lambda = \frac{7}{2} \ mod \ 11$$

$$\lambda \equiv 7 \cdot 2^{-1} \ mod \ 11$$

$$\lambda \equiv 7 \cdot 6 \ mod \ 11$$

$$\lambda \equiv 42 \ mod \ 11$$

$$\lambda \equiv 9 \ mod \ 11$$

$$x_3 \equiv \lambda^2 - x_2 - x_1 \ mod \ p$$

$$x_3 \equiv 9^2 - 7 - 5 \ mod \ 11$$

$$x_3 \equiv 81 - 7 - 5 \ mod \ 11$$

$$x_3 \equiv 69 \ mod \ 11$$

$$x_3 \equiv 3 \ mod \ 11$$

$$y_3 \equiv \lambda \cdot (x_1 - x_3) - y_1 \ mod \ p$$

$$y_3 \equiv 9 \cdot (5 - 3) - 2 \ mod \ 11$$

$$y_3 \equiv 9 \cdot 2 - 2 \ mod \ 11$$

$$y_3 \equiv 18 - 2 \ mod \ 11$$

$$y_3 \equiv 16 \ mod \ 11$$

$$y_3 \equiv 5 \ mod \ 11$$

$$10 \cdot \alpha = (3, \ 5)$$

$$11 \cdot \alpha \ = \ (3, \ 5) \ + \ (7, \ 9)$$

$$\lambda \ = \ \frac{y_2 \ - \ y_1}{x_2 \ - \ x_1} \ mod \ p$$

$$\lambda \ = \ \frac{9 \ - \ 5}{7 \ - \ 3} \ mod \ 11$$

$$\lambda \ = \ \frac{4}{4} \ mod \ 11$$

$$\lambda \ \equiv \ 4 \cdot 4^{-1} \ mod \ 11$$

$$\lambda \ \equiv \ 4 \cdot 3 \ mod \ 11$$

$$\lambda \ \equiv \ 12 \ mod \ 11$$

$$\lambda \ \equiv \ 1 \ mod \ 11$$

$$x_3 \ \equiv \ \lambda^2 \ - \ x_2 \ - \ x_1 \ mod \ p$$

$$x_3 \ \equiv \ 1^2 \ - \ 7 \ - \ 3 \ mod \ 11$$

$$x_3 \ \equiv \ 1 \ - \ 7 \ - \ 3 \ mod \ 11$$

$$x_3 \ \equiv \ -9 \ mod \ 11$$

$$x_3 \ \equiv \ 2 \ mod \ 11$$

$$y_3 \ \equiv \ \lambda \cdot (x_1 \ - \ x_3) \ - \ y_1 \ mod \ p$$

$$y_3 \ \equiv \ 1 \cdot (3 \ - \ 2) \ - \ 5 \ mod \ 11$$

$$y_3 \ \equiv \ 1 \cdot 1 \ - \ 5 \ mod \ 11$$

$$y_3 \ \equiv \ 1 \ - \ 5 \ mod \ 11$$

$$y_3 \ \equiv \ -4 \ mod \ 11$$

$$y_3 \ \equiv \ 7 \ mod \ 11$$

$$11 \cdot \alpha \ = \ (2, \ 7)$$

$$12 \cdot \alpha = (2, 7) + (7, 9)$$

$$\lambda = \frac{y_2 - y_1}{x_2 - x_1} \; mod \; p$$

$$\lambda = \frac{9 - 7}{7 - 2} \; mod \; 11$$

$$\lambda = \frac{2}{5} \; mod \; 11$$

$$\lambda \equiv 2 \cdot 5^{-1} \; mod \; 11$$

$$\lambda \equiv 2 \cdot 9 \; mod \; 11$$

$$\lambda \equiv 18 \; mod \; 11$$

$$\lambda \equiv 7 \; mod \; 11$$

$$x_3 \equiv \lambda^2 - x_2 - x_1 \; mod \; p$$

$$x_3 \equiv 7^2 - 7 - 2 \; mod \; 11$$

$$x_3 \equiv 49 - 7 - 2 \; mod \; 11$$

$$x_3 \equiv 40 \; mod \; 11$$

$$x_3 \equiv 7 \; mod \; 11$$

$$y_3 \equiv \lambda \cdot (x_1 - x_3) - y_1 \; mod \; p$$

$$y_3 \equiv 7 \cdot (2 - 7) - 7 \; mod \; 11$$

$$y_3 \equiv 7 \cdot -5 - 7 \; mod \; 11$$

$$y_3 \equiv -35 - 7 \; mod \; 11$$

$$y_3 \equiv -42 \; mod \; 11$$

$$y_3 \equiv 2 \; mod \; 11$$

$$12 \cdot \alpha = (7, 2)$$

$$13 \cdot \alpha = (7,\ 2) + (7,\ 9)$$
$$\lambda = \frac{y_2 - y_1}{x_2 - x_1} \ mod \ p$$
$$\lambda = \frac{9 - 2}{7 - 7} \ mod \ 11$$
$$\lambda = \frac{7}{0} \ mod \ 11$$
$$13 \cdot \alpha = Point \ of \ Infinity$$

Because the point $(7,\ 9)$ generates all of the 13 points on the *Elliptic Curve*, it must be a *generator* of the *Cyclic Group* formed by the points on the *Elliptic Curve* and the *Point of Infinity*.

It is important to note that in **Example 9.2**, the number of points on the *Elliptic Curve*, $\#E$, was given. As will be discussed in Section 9.5, the most powerful attack that may be applied to the *Discrete Logarithm* problem in the *Group* of an *Elliptic Curve* cryptosystem is the *Pohlig-Hellman Algorithm*. The complexity of the *Pohlig-Hellman Algorithm* applied to this *Discrete Logarithm* problem is $e_t \cdot \sqrt{p_t}$, where p_t is the largest prime factor of $\#E$, resulting in $p_t \geq 2^{256}$ to ensure a complexity of $\approx 2^{128}$. Therefore, for *Elliptic Curves* where $p_t \geq 2^{256}$, determining the *order* $\#E$ of the *Cyclic Group* formed by the points on the *Elliptic Curve* and the *Point of Infinity* becomes computationally intensive if repeated application of the binary operation of the *Cyclic Group*, i.e. point addition, is the method used, as in **Example 9.2**. Similarly, finding a secure *Elliptic Curve* with appropriately sized parameters, specifically where $p_t \geq 2^{256}$, is also computationally intensive.

9.2 Diffie-Hellman Key Agreement Protocol

This Section will focus on the use of the *Diffie-Hellman Key Agreement Protocol* in the *Cyclic Group* formed by the points on the *Elliptic Curve* and the *Point of Infinity* using point addition as defined in Section 9.1 as the binary operation. In this case, the *Diffie-Hellman Key Agreement Protocol* is composed of two stages: set-up and key establishment. The set-up stage proceeds as follows:

1. Choose an *Elliptic Curve* of the form $y^2 \equiv x^3 + a \cdot x + b \bmod p$.

2. Choose a *primitive element* α, a point on the *Elliptic Curve*, denoted as $\alpha = (x_\alpha, y_\alpha)$.

where α and the *Elliptic Curve* are made publicly known.

The key establishment stage, shown in Figure 9.3, is used to establish a shared secret between two parties, *Alice* and *Bob*, who wish to communicate.

At the completion of the key establishment stage, *Alice* and *Bob* share the session key, $K_{AB} = (x_k, y_k)$. In practice, $K_{AB} = x_k$

Step	Alice	Bob
1	Choose a random integer $K_{PR_A} = a_A$ where $a_A \in \{2, 3, 4, \ldots \#E - 1\}$	Choose a random integer $K_{PR_B} = a_B$ where $a_B \in \{2, 3, 4, \ldots \#E - 1\}$
2	Compute $K_{PUB_A} = b_A$ $= a_A \cdot \alpha$ $= (x_A, y_A)$	Compute $K_{PUB_B} = b_B$ $= a_B \cdot \alpha$ $= (x_B, y_B)$
3	Send b_A to Bob $\longrightarrow$	$\longleftarrow$ Send b_B to $Alice$
4	Compute $K_{AB} = a_A \cdot b_B$ $= a_A \cdot (a_B \cdot \alpha)$ $= a_A \cdot a_B \cdot \alpha$ $= (x_k, y_k)$	Compute $K_{AB} = a_B \cdot b_A$ $= a_B \cdot (a_A \cdot \alpha)$ $= a_A \cdot a_B \cdot \alpha$ $= (x_k, y_k)$

Figure 9.3: Diffie-Hellman Key Agreement Protocol Key Establishment Stage for Elliptic Curves

because for a given x_k there are only two possible values for y and therefore only one variable is required for use as the key. Both *Alice* and *Bob* have contributed to the computation of K_{AB} without being able to extract information regarding the other party's private key, K_{PR}. This is because for *Bob* to extract *Alice's* private key, K_{PR_A}, he must solve the *Discrete Logarithm* problem for a_A based on the equation $b_A = a_A \cdot \alpha$. The same holds true for *Alice*, as she must solve the *Discrete Logarithm* problem for a_B based on the equation $b_B = a_B \cdot \alpha$ to extract *Bob's* private key, K_{PR_B}. The *Discrete Logarithm* problem has been shown to be computationally intensive and difficult to solve. As will be discussed in Section 9.5, the *Discrete Logarithm* problem parameters p, $\#E$, and α, the plaintext x, and the ciphertext y are typically on the order of 256 bits or more in length to ensure the computational complexity of the *Discrete Logarithm* problem.

When considering the security of the *Diffie-Hellman Key Agreement Protocol*, it is important to note exactly what information is available to an attacker. For the *Cyclic Group* formed by the points on the *Elliptic Curve* and the *Point of Infinity* using point addition as the binary operation, the publicly available information as part of the protocol includes the *Elliptic Curve*, the *primitive element* α, and the parameters b_A and b_B. Therefore, the *Diffie-Hellman* problem states that given $b_A = a_A \cdot \alpha$, $b_B = a_B \cdot \alpha$, and the *primitive element* α, find $K_{AB} = a_A \cdot a_B \cdot \alpha$. One method of solving the *Diffie-Hellman* problem is to solve one of the *Discrete Logarithm* problems for either a_A or a_B. Once either a_A or a_B is known, computing K_{AB} may be accomplished by computing either $a_A \cdot b_B$ or $a_B \cdot b_A$, both of which are equivalent to $K_{AB} = a_A \cdot a_B \cdot \alpha$. Therefore, as will be shown in Section 9.5, the parameters p, $\#E$, and α must be on the order of 256 bits or more in length to ensure the computational complexity of the *Discrete Logarithm* problem and thus the computational complexity of the *Diffie-Hellman* problem. Although it is generally held that solving the *Discrete Logarithm* problem is the only means of solving the *Diffie-Hellman* problem, there is no proof of this and it is possible that other as yet unidentified solutions exist.

9.3   Efficient Implementation

Multiple implementations of an *Elliptic Curve* cryptosystem have been presented targeting a wide range of hardware technologies. In most cases, *Elliptic Curve* cryptosystem implementations in hardware focus on the addition of points on the *Elliptic Curve*, also known as scalar multiplication [62]. Moreover, most implementations target *Extension Fields* of the form $GF(2^m)$ (as opposed to *Extension Fields* of the form $GF(p)$) because of the hardware advantages associated with performing arithmetic in the *Extension Field*.

The choice of a coordinate system is relevant in that the computation of the intermediate term λ requires the computation of an inverse *mod p* (the denominator) whose value depends on whether or not $P_1 = P_2$. The computation of an inverse is costly and is usually performed via either *Fermat's Little Theorem* or the *Extended Euclidean Algorithm* [62]. Moreover, an inverse must be computed every time a point doubling or a point addition occurs. Other coordinate systems may be used that eliminate the need for the computation of an inverse during the repeated application of the binary operation of the *Cyclic Group*, though the computation of an inverse is required during the forward and inverse transformations between coordinate systems. This is significant because the computation of an inverse is significantly more complex versus the computation of a multiplication [45]. Potential coordinate systems include Jacobian projective coordinates [33],

Lopez-Dahab coordinates [186], and mixed projective coordinates [48, 62]. When using an affine coordinate system as described in Section 9.1, the addition of points on the *Elliptic Curve* requires the computation of one inversion, one squaring, and two multiplications (note that additions are considered to have little impact on the overall computation time). Alternatively, the use of Jacobian projective coordinates requires the computation of four squarings and eleven multiplications [33].

It is critical that multipliers be fully utilized to minimize idle cycles and thus maximize performance when considering the scheduling of scalar multiplications. Moreover, to take advantage of hardware pipelining, implemented to increase the performance of multiplier units, data dependencies between successive multiplication operations must be identified to eliminate potential pipeline stalls. As a result, software implementations of scalar multiplication are often manually optimized based on the available hardware units to ensure that idle cycles and data dependencies are minimized. For *Extension Fields* of the form $GF(2^m)$, the *Montgomery Ladder* in combination with the *Lopez-Dahab Algorithm* is the fastest known scalar multiplication algorithm [147, 187]. In the case of *Extension Fields* of the form $GF(p)$, the *Binary Non-Adjacent Form Algorithm* using mixed projective coordinates is the fastest known scalar multiplication algorithm [62].

When considering implementations of *Elliptic Curve* cryptosystems over the *Extension Fields* $GF(2^m)$ and $GF(p)$, numerous ASIC implementations have been published [2, 9, 22, 40, 61, 93,

109, 120, 159, 173, 177, 204, 238, 272, 295, 320], with reported point addition times as fast as 21 μs [9] for 163-bit *Irreducible Polynomials* and 734 μs [61] for up to 256-bit *Irreducible Polynomials*. Similarly, a wide variety of FPGA implementations of *Elliptic Curve* cryptosystems over the *Extension Fields* $GF(2^m)$ and $GF(p)$ exist in the literature [9, 18, 24, 25, 78, 92, 93, 111, 115, 79, 130, 145, 157, 188, 195, 220, 233, 235, 236, 257, 266, 267, 286, 315], with reported point addition times as fast as 41 μs [9] for 163-bit *Irreducible Polynomials*, 56 μs [267] for 191-bit *Irreducible Polynomials*, 89 μs [286] for 233-bit *Irreducible Polynomials*, and 144 μs [79] for up to 256-bit *Irreducible Polynomials*. A comprehensive review of hardware implementations of *Elliptic Curve* cryptosystems over the *Extension Field* $GF(2^m)$ is available in [62]. Software implementations of *Elliptic Curve* cryptosystems over the *Extension Fields* $GF(2^m)$ and $GF(p)$ are available, targeting processors such as the CalmRISC and Digital Signal Processors such as the Texas Instruments TMS320C6201 are also available in the literature [44, 137]. These implementations have yielded point addition times as fast as 3.09 ms [137] for 160-bit *Irreducible Polynomials* over $GF(p)$, two full orders of magnitude slower than the best hardware implementations. Implementations targeting 64-bit dual-field processors exhibit better performance [80, 269], with point addition times as fast as 190 μs for 160-bit *Irreducible Polynomials* over the *Extension Field* $GF(2^m)$ and 1.21 ms for 160-bit *Irreducible Polynomials* over $GF(p)$ [269].

Instruction set extensions have been proposed to accelerate the performance of software implementations by improving the performance of arithmetic over the *Extension Field* $GF(2^m)$ targeting *Elliptic Curve* cryptosystems. Word-level polynomial multiplication was shown in [21] to be the time-critical operation when targeting an ARM processor, and a special *Galois Field* multiplication instruction resulted in significant performance improvement. Instruction set extensions targeting a SPARC V8 processor core were used to accelerate the multiplication of binary polynomials for arithmetic in $GF(2^m)$ in [262], resulting in almost double the performance for the *Extension Field* $GF(2^{191})$ and a fixed reduction polynomial. Similar results were shown in [141] using the same instruction set extensions retargeted to a 16-bit RISC processor core. The implementation in [140] targets a MIPS32 architecture and also attempts to accelerate word-level polynomial multiplication through the use of *Comba's Method* of handling the inner loops of the multiplication operation, resulting in a performance improvement by a factor of six. Numerous generalized *Galois Field* multipliers have also been proposed for use in *Elliptic Curve* cryptosystems. These implementations focus on accelerating exponentiation and inversion in *Extension Fields* of the form $GF(2^m)$, where $m \approx 160 - 256$ [60, 119, 163, 164, 191, 248].

As discussed in Section 7.2.6, frequently occurring operations, such as bulk data encryption, are performed by significantly faster symmetric-key algorithms such as the block cipher *Rijndael*. Hybrid systems combining public-key and symmetric-key algorithms exploit the best features of each type of algorithm to guarantee that the necessary security services are provided while also maintaining a high level of performance. Therefore, *Elliptic Curve* cryptosystems are typically used for infrequently occurring operations, such as *key establishment* and the generation of *Digital Signatures*. *Key establishment* occurs only at the start of a communication session, and a *Digital Signature* is generated only once for the entire stream of data being transmitted to provide message authentication and non-repudiation, as discussed in Section 11.1.

9.4   Menezes-Vanstone Encryption

Menezes-Vanstone encryption was proposed in 1993 by Alfred Menezes and Scott Vanstone [201] and is based on the *Discrete Logarithm* problem in the *Group* of an *Elliptic Curve* cryptosystem. *Menezes-Vanstone* encryption is composed of two stages: set-up and encryption/decryption. The set-up stage generates the private and public keys as follows:

1. Choose an *Elliptic Curve*, denoted as E, of the form $y^2 \equiv x^3 + a \cdot x + b \bmod p$.

2. Choose a *primitive element* α, a point on the *Elliptic Curve*, denoted as $\alpha = (x_\alpha, y_\alpha)$.

3. Choose a secret key $a \in \{2, 3, 4, \ldots \#E - 1\}$.

4. Compute $\beta = a \cdot \alpha = (x_\beta, y_\beta)$.

Upon completion of the *Menezes-Vanstone* encryption set-up stage, the public key is denoted as $K_{PUB} = (E, \beta, \alpha, p)$ and the private key is denoted as $K_{PR} = (a)$.

Once the private and public keys have been established, encryption of the plaintext x to form the ciphertext y is performed as follows:

1. Choose $k \in \{2, 3, 4, \ldots \#E - 1\}$.

2. Compute $y_0 = k \cdot \alpha$.

3. Compute $y_1 = c_1 \cdot x_1 \bmod p$.

4. Compute $y_2 = c_2 \cdot x_2 \bmod p$.

where the plaintext x is contained in the set Z_p and the ciphertext is the triplet (y_0, y_1, y_2) such that $e_{K_{PUB}}(x, k) = (y_0, y_1, y_2)$. Note that y_0 is a point on the *Elliptic Curve E* and y_1 and y_2 are integers in the set Z_p. Decryption of the ciphertext (y_0, y_1, y_2) to form the plaintext x is performed by first computing c_1 and c_2:

$$(c_1, c_2) = a \cdot y_0$$

Note that $(c_1, c_2) = a \cdot k \cdot \alpha$. Decryption then proceeds as follows:

$$(x_1, x_2) = d_{K_{PR}}(y_0, y_1, y_2)$$

$$(x_1, \ x_2) \ = \ (y_1 \cdot c_1^{-1} \ mod \ p, \ y_2 \cdot c_2^{-1} \ mod \ p)$$

For *Menezes-Vanstone* encryption to function, $d_{K_{PR}}(e_{K_{PUB}}(x)) = x$, i.e. decryption must be the inverse of encryption. Substituting into the decryption function yields:

$$(c_1, \ c_2) \ = \ a \cdot y_0$$

$$d_{K_{PR}}(y_0, \ y_1, \ y_2) \ = \ (y_1 \cdot c_1^{-1} \ mod \ p, \ y_2 \cdot c_2^{-1} \ mod \ p)$$
$$d_{K_{PR}}(y_0, \ y_1, \ y_2) \ = \ (c_1 \cdot x_1 \cdot c_1^{-1} \ mod \ p, \ c_2 \cdot x_2 \cdot c_2^{-1} \ mod \ p)$$
$$d_{K_{PR}}(y_0, \ y_1, \ y_2) \ = \ (x_1 \ mod \ p, \ x_2 \ mod \ p)$$

Example 9.3: Compute the encryption and decryption of $x = (4, \ 4)$ with the *Menezes-Vanstone* encryption algorithm using the *Elliptic Curve* $y^2 \equiv x^3 + x + 6 \ mod \ 11$ and the parameters $a = 2, \ k = 1$, and $\alpha = (3, \ 5)$.

Menezes-Vanstone encryption begins with the computation of β:

$$\beta \ = \ a \cdot \alpha$$
$$\beta \ = \ 2 \cdot (3, \ 5)$$

$$\beta \;=\; (3,\,5) \;+\; (3,\,5)$$

$$\lambda \;=\; \frac{3x_1^2 \;+\; a}{2y_1}\; mod\; p$$

$$\lambda \;=\; \frac{3\,\cdot\,3^2 \;+\; 1}{2\,\cdot 5}\; mod\; 11$$

$$\lambda \;=\; \frac{3\,\cdot\,9 \;+\; 1}{10}\; mod\; 11$$

$$\lambda \;-\; \frac{28}{10}\; mod\; 11$$

$$\lambda \;=\; \frac{6}{10}\; mod\; 11$$

$$\lambda \;=\; 6\,\cdot 10^{-1}\; mod\; 11$$

$$\lambda \;=\; 6\,\cdot 10\; mod\; 11$$

$$\lambda \;=\; 60\; mod\; 11$$

$$\lambda \;=\; 5\; mod\; 11$$

$$x_3 \;\equiv\; \lambda^2 \;-\; x_2 \;-\; x_1\; mod\; p$$

$$x_3 \;\equiv\; 5^2 \;-\; 3 \;-\; 3\; mod\; 11$$

$$x_3 \;\equiv\; 25 \;-\; 3 \;-\; 3\; mod\; 11$$

$$x_3 \;\equiv\; 19\; mod\; 11$$

$$x_3 \;\equiv\; 8\; mod\; 11$$

$$y_3 \;\equiv\; \lambda \,\cdot\, (x_1 \;-\; x_3) \;-\; y_1\; mod\; p$$

$$y_3 \;\equiv\; 5 \,\cdot\, (3 \;-\; 8) \;-\; 5\; mod\; 11$$

$$y_3 \;\equiv\; 5 \,\cdot\, -5 \;-\; 5\; mod\; 11$$

$$y_3 \;\equiv\; -25 \;-\; 5\; mod\; 11$$

$$y_3 \;\equiv\; -30\; mod\; 11$$

$$y_3 \;\equiv\; 3\; mod\; 11$$

$$\beta \;=\; (8,\,3)$$

Encryption is then performed by computing the triplet (y_0, y_1, y_2):

$$
\begin{aligned}
(c_1, c_2) &= k \cdot \beta \\
(c_1, c_2) &= 1 \cdot (8, 3) \\
(c_1, c_2) &= (8, 3)
\end{aligned}
$$

$$
\begin{aligned}
y_0 &= k \cdot \alpha \\
y_0 &= 1 \cdot (3, 5) \\
y_0 &= (3, 5)
\end{aligned}
$$

$$
\begin{aligned}
y_1 &= c_1 \cdot x_1 \bmod p \\
y_1 &= 8 \cdot 4 \bmod 11 \\
y_1 &= 32 \bmod 11 \\
y_1 &= 10 \bmod 11
\end{aligned}
$$

$$
\begin{aligned}
y_2 &= c_2 \cdot x_2 \bmod p \\
y_2 &= 3 \cdot 4 \bmod 11 \\
y_2 &= 12 \bmod 11 \\
y_2 &= 1 \bmod 11
\end{aligned}
$$

Therefore, the ciphertext is $((3,\ 5),\ 10,\ 1)$. Decryption is then performed as follows:

$$(c_1,\ c_2)\ =\ a\ \cdot\ y_0$$

$$(c_1,\ c_2)\ =\ 2\ \cdot\ (3,\ 5)$$

$$(c_1,\ c_2)\ =\ (3,\ 5)\ +\ (3,\ 5)$$

$$\lambda\ =\ \frac{3x_1^2\ +\ a}{2y_1}\ mod\ p$$

$$\lambda\ =\ \frac{3\ \cdot\ 3^2\ +\ 1}{2\ \cdot\ 5}\ mod\ 11$$

$$\lambda\ =\ \frac{3\ \cdot\ 9\ +\ 1}{10}\ mod\ 11$$

$$\lambda\ =\ \frac{28}{10}\ mod\ 11$$

$$\lambda\ =\ \frac{6}{10}\ mod\ 11$$

$$\lambda\ =\ 6\ \cdot\ 10^{-1}\ mod\ 11$$

$$\lambda\ =\ 6\ \cdot\ 10\ mod\ 11$$

$$\lambda\ =\ 60\ mod\ 11$$

$$\lambda\ =\ 5\ mod\ 11$$

$$x_3\ \equiv\ \lambda^2\ -\ x_2\ -\ x_1\ mod\ p$$

$$x_3\ \equiv\ 5^2\ -\ 3\ -\ 3\ mod\ 11$$

$$x_3\ \equiv\ 25\ -\ 3\ -\ 3\ mod\ 11$$

$$x_3\ \equiv\ 19\ mod\ 11$$

$$x_3\ \equiv\ 8\ mod\ 11$$

$$y_3\ \equiv\ \lambda\ \cdot\ (x_1\ -\ x_3)\ -\ y_1\ mod\ p$$

$$y_3\ \equiv\ 5\ \cdot\ (3\ -\ 8)\ -\ 5\ mod\ 11$$

$$y_3 \equiv 5 \cdot -5 - 5 \bmod 11$$

$$y_3 \equiv -25 - 5 \bmod 11$$

$$y_3 \equiv -30 \bmod 11$$

$$y_3 \equiv 3 \bmod 11$$

$$(c_1, \ c_2) = (8, \ 3)$$

$$c_1^{-1} \bmod p = 8^{-1} \bmod 11$$

$$c_1^{-1} \bmod p = 7 \bmod 11$$

$$c_2^{-1} \bmod p = 3^{-1} \bmod 11$$

$$c_2^{-1} \bmod p = 4 \bmod 11$$

$$(x_1, \ x_2) = (y_1 \cdot c_1^{-1} \bmod p, \ y_2 \cdot c_2^{-1} \bmod p)$$

$$(x_1, \ x_2) = (10 \cdot 7 \bmod 11, \ 1 \cdot 4 \bmod 11)$$

$$(x_1, \ x_2) = (70 \bmod 11, \ 4 \bmod 11)$$

$$(x_1, \ x_2) = (4 \bmod 11, \ 4 \bmod 11)$$

$$(x_1, \ x_2) = (4, \ 4)$$

Therefore, as expected, the decrypted ciphertext results in the plaintext $(x_1, \ x_2) = (4, \ 4)$.

Menezes-Vanstone encryption causes *message expansion*, generating the ciphertext triplet $(y_0, \ y_1, \ y_2)$ for each plaintext $(x_1, \ x_2)$.

Because x_1, x_2, y_1, y_2, and the two integer coordinates of y_0 are all contained in the set Z_p, the *message expansion* factor of *Menezes-Vanstone* encryption is $\frac{\lceil log_2 p \rceil + \lceil log_2 p \rceil + \lceil log_2 p \rceil + \lceil log_2 p \rceil}{\lceil log_2 p \rceil + \lceil log_2 p \rceil} =$ 2. Therefore, each plaintext (x_1, x_2) of $2 \cdot \lceil log_2 p \rceil$ bits in length requires the transmission of $4 \cdot \lceil log_2 p \rceil$ ciphertext bits, reducing the transmission rate throughput by a factor of two.

Obviously, computing $\beta = a \cdot \alpha$ and $y_0 = k \cdot \alpha$ cannot be done in a straightforward manner, i.e. by performing a (or k) point additions of the form $\alpha + \alpha + \alpha + \ldots + \alpha$. However, the *Square-and-Multiply Algorithm* can be directly adapted to address this problem. A new *Double-and-Add Algorithm* will rely entirely on the operations of point doubling and point addition to compute $i \cdot P$, where P is a point on the *Elliptic Curve* and i is a scalar multiplier representing the number of point additions to be applied to P. The *Double-and-Add Algorithm* evaluates the scalar multiplier as a binary value and builds the result in an iterative manner through point doubling and point addition operations. The algorithm begins with $1 \cdot P$, and the scalar multiplier i is scanned from most significant bit to least significant bit (left to right) with the most significant bit assumed to be a one. The value $1 \cdot P$ is doubled, i.e. $P + P$ is performed, resulting in the value $10_2 \cdot P = 2 \cdot P$. If the bit of the scalar multiplier i being evaluated is a one, then the point P is added to the result from the doubling stage, resulting in the value $11_2 \cdot P = 3 \cdot P$; otherwise, no point addition occurs. The algorithm repeats until all bits of the scalar multiplier i have been evaluated and $i \cdot P$ has been fully computed.

As described in Section 7.2.2, the efficiency of the *Square-and-Multiply Algorithm* may be extended via the *k-ary Method*, the *Improved k-ary Method*, and the *Sliding Window Method*. These same improvements may also be applied to the *Double-and-Add Algorithm*. Moreover, the complexities calculated in Section 7.2.2 for each of these methods applies to the *Double-and-Add Algorithm* and improvements made by the *k-ary Method*, the *Improved k-ary Method*, and the *Sliding Window Method*.

9.5   Attacks

The best known attack against *Elliptic Curve* cryptosystems combines the *Pohlig-Hellman Algorithm* with either *Shank's Algorithm* or *Pollard's Rho Method*. As discussed in Section 8.6, the complexity of the *Pohlig-Hellman Algorithm* is $e_t \cdot \sqrt{p_t}$, where p_t is the largest prime factor of $\#E$. Therefore, p_t must be chosen for long-term security such that $p_t \geq 2^{256}$ to ensure a complexity of $\approx 2^{128}$, i.e. equivalent security to a 128-bit block cipher, so that an attack using the *Pohlig-Hellman Algorithm* is not computationally feasible in practice. Note that the *Index Calculus Method* has not been successfully applied to the *Discrete Logarithm* problem in the *Group* of an *Elliptic Curve* cryptosystem. As a result, *Elliptic Curve* cryptosystems with 256-bit parameters are believed to be as secure as both *RSA* and *Discrete Logarithm* in Z_p^* cryptosystems with 1024-bit parameters.

9.6   Homework Problems

Homework Problem 9.6.1: Show that the condition $4a^3 + 27b^2 \neq 0 \bmod p$ is fulfilled for the *Elliptic Curve* $y^2 \equiv x^3 + x + 6 \bmod 11$.

Homework Problem 9.6.2: Perform the point additions:

a) $(2, 7) + (5, 2)$

b) $(3, 6) + (3, 6)$

in the *Group* of the *Elliptic Curve* from **Homework Problem 9.6.1**.

Homework Problem 9.6.3: Write a C program that generates a list of all thirteen elements in the group of points of the *Elliptic Curve* from **Homework Problem 9.6.1** from the *primitive element* $\delta = (5, 2)$. The list should look as follows:

$$\delta = (5, 2)$$
$$2\delta = \ldots$$
$$3\delta = \ldots$$
$$\vdots$$
$$13\delta = \ldots$$
$$14\delta = \ldots$$

Verify that the last element, 13δ, is the *point at infinity* and that $14\delta = \delta$.

Homework Problem 9.6.4: Verify that δ, 2δ, and 3δ are actually points on the *Elliptic Curve* from **Homework Problem 9.6.1**.

Homework Problem 9.6.5: In the group of points for the *Elliptic Curve* specified in **Homework Problem 9.6.1**, all elements are *primitive elements*. Why is this true?

Homework Problem 9.6.6: Write a C program that performs the operation $i \cdot P$ on an *Elliptic Curve*, where i is an integer and P is a point on the *Elliptic Curve*. This scalar multiplication can only be realized by repeated addition of the point P. Initially, the user should enter the *Elliptic Curve* parameters a and p (b is not required for the arithmetic). Once initialized, the user should be asked to enter a point P, specified by two integers, and i. The program should compute and display the resultant output of $i \cdot P$ and then ask the user if they want to compute another point multiplication (avoiding the need to reenter a and p) or exit. Your program must include code that measures the time required to perform the operation $i \cdot P$. Use the *Elliptic Curve* from **Homework Problem 9.6.1** and the *primitive element* $\delta = (5, 2)$ with test values of $i = 3$, $i = 7$, and $i = 13$. Verify your results against the results of **Homework Problem 9.6.3**.

Homework Problem 9.6.7: Write a C program to encrypt and decrypt with the *Menezes-Vanstone* cryptosystem using:

a) $a = 7$, $x = (9, 1)$, $k = 6$, $\alpha = (7, 2)$

b) $a = 7$, $x = (4, 4)$, $k = 6$, $\alpha = (7, 2)$

c) $a = 7$, $x = (9, 1)$, $k = 1$, $\alpha = (3, 5)$

Note that a denotes the public key, not the *Elliptic Curve* coefficient. Use the *Elliptic Curve* from **Homework Problem 9.6.1** as the underlying structure. For each example, compute β, (c_1, c_2), and (y_0, y_1, y_2). Also, for each example perform the decryption operation. This will require writing a function that computes the multiplicative inverse modulo p.

Homework Problem 9.6.8: In practice, a and k are both in the range of $p \approx 2^{160} - 2^{256}$.

a) Provide a pseudo-code description of the *Double-and-Add Algorithm*. Assume there is a function *ellc_add* that performs adding and doubling of points.

b) Illustrate how the *Double-and-Add Algorithm* works for $a = 19$ and for $a = 160$. Do not perform the *Elliptic Curve* operations — keep a variable α.

c) How many point additions and point doublings are required on average for one multiplication? Assume that all integers have $n = \lceil log_2 p \rceil$ bits.

d) Assume that all integers have $n = 256$ bits, i.e. that p is a 256-bit prime. Assume one *Group* operation (point addition or point doubling) requires 20 μs. What is the time required for one *Double-and-Add* operation? What is the encryption data throughput in bits per second if the *Menezes-Vanstone* cryptosystem is being used?

Homework Problem 9.6.9: Let E be the *Elliptic Curve* $y^2 \equiv x^3 + x + 13$ defined over Z_{31}. It can be shown that $\#E = 34$ and $(9, 10)$ is an element of *order* 34 in E. The *Menezes-Vanstone* cryptosystem defined on E will have as its plaintext space $Z_{34}^* \times Z_{34}^*$. Suppose *Bob's* secret exponent is $a = 25$.

a) Compute $\beta = a \cdot \alpha$.

b) Decrypt the following string of ciphertext:

((16, 8), 14, 5), ((6, 24), 17, 18), ((5, 22), 15, 4)

c) Assuming that each plaintext represents two alphabetic characters, convert the plaintext into an English word using the correspondence $A \Leftrightarrow 1, \ldots, Z \Leftrightarrow 26$ since 0 is not allowed in a plaintext ordered pair.

Homework Problem 9.6.10: Consider a cryptosystem based on the *Elliptic Curve* $y^2 \equiv x^3 + x + 6 \bmod 11$. The public key is $K_{PUB} = (\alpha, \beta) = ((8, 3), (2, 4))$. The private key $K_{PR} = a = 4$.

a) What are the coefficients a and b of the *Elliptic Curve*?

b) You receive the ciphertext $(y_0, y_1, y_2) = ((3, 5), 2, 10)$. Determine the plaintext values (x_1, x_2) assuming the use of the *Menezes-Vanstone* cryptosystem.

Homework Problem 9.6.11: Consider a cryptosystem based on the *Elliptic Curve* $y^2 \equiv x^3 + x + 6 \bmod 11$. Your private key is $a_A = 6$ and you receive *Bob's* public key $b_B = (5, 9)$. Compute a session key via the *Diffie-Hellman Key Agreement Protocol* so that you can securely communicate with *Bob*.

Homework Problem 9.6.12: Consider an *Elliptic Curve* cryptosystem with a prime modulus $p \approx 2^{200}$. The cryptosystem is used for a *Diffie-Hellman Key Agreement Protocol*. Assume that the private keys have already been established and that the time for a point addition and the time for a point doubling is 250 μs. What is the average time required to compute the session key in the *Diffie-Hellman Key Agreement Protocol* for one party?

Homework Problem 9.6.13: *Elliptic Curve* cryptosystems with $\#E \approx 2^m$ points are considered to be roughly as secure as block ciphers with $\frac{m}{2}$ key bits. Why is this assumption made?

Homework Problem 9.6.14: Estimate the cost of an attack machine for an *Elliptic Curve* cryptosystem with $\#E \approx 2^{256}$ points if *Shank's Algorithm* is used. Assume that for each *Group* element (point on the curve) only the x coordinate must be stored and that one Gbyte $= 2^{30}$ bytes and that one Tbyte $= 2^{40}$ bytes.

a) Why is it of interest to study the security of *Elliptic Curve* cryptosystems with $\#E \approx 2^{256}$ points?

b) How much storage capacity (in Tbytes) is needed for an attack using *Shank's Algorithm*?

c) What are the costs assuming that one Gbyte of hard-disk costs $20?

d) Assume that the cost for hard-disks decreases by a factor of two every eighteen months per *Moore's Law*. How long does it take until the cost for attacking the *Elliptic Curve* cryptosystem is $1 million?

Homework Problem 9.6.15: Write a VHDL architecture to implement the computation of $i \cdot P$ on an *Elliptic Curve*, where i is an integer and P is a point on the *Elliptic Curve*. This scalar multiplication can only be realized by repeated addition of the point P. Let E be the *Elliptic Curve* $y^2 \equiv x^3 + x + 13$ defined over Z_{31}. Assume that the user will provide a *pload* signal to indicate that P (denoted by the signals xp and yp) and i are ready to be loaded on the next rising edge of the clock. Use the algorithm developed in **Homework Problem 9.6.8** to perform the point doublings and point additions. Your system must output a *valid* signal to indicate when the output point (denoted by the signals $xout$ and $yout$) is valid, i.e. computation of $i \cdot P$ is completed. Use the following entity declaration for your implementation:

```
LIBRARY ieee;
USE ieee.std_logic_1164.ALL;
USE ieee.std_logic_arith.ALL;
USE ieee.std_logic_unsigned.ALL;
ENTITY ecc_31 IS
   PORT ( xp    : IN  std_logic_vector (4 DOWNTO 0);
          yp    : IN  std_logic_vector (4 DOWNTO 0);
          i     : IN  std_logic_vector (5 DOWNTO 0);
          clk   : IN  std_logic;
          rst   : IN  std_logic;
          pload : IN  std_logic;
          valid : OUT std_logic;
          xout  : OUT std_logic_vector (4 DOWNTO 0);
          yout  : OUT std_logic_vector (4 DOWNTO 0));
END ecc_31;
ARCHITECTURE behav OF ecc_31 IS
BEGIN
-- Your code goes here
END behav;
```

Using the point $(9, 10)$, generate all points on the *Elliptic Curve*. Demonstrate that the *order* of the point $(9, 10)$ is $\#E = 34$. Specify the target technology used to implement the design and the maximum operating frequency as specified by your place-and-route tools. What is the execution time of your implementation? What is the gate count of your implementation?

Homework Problem 9.6.16: Using the VHDL architecture of **Homework Problem 9.6.15**, assume that the *Menezes-Vanstone* cryptosystem is used and that *Bob's* secret exponent is $a = 25$ and that $\alpha = (9, 10)$.

a) Compute $\beta = a \cdot \alpha$.

b) Use your C program from **Homework Problem 9.6.6** to compute $\beta = a \cdot \alpha$.

c) Compare the results of parts (a) and (b).

Chapter 10

Cryptographic Components

Previous discussions of both symmetric-key and public-key cryptographic algorithms have focused on encryption and decryption. Such operations provide the confidentiality security service. However, other cryptographic components are required if security services such as data integrity, message authentication, and non-repudiation are also to be provided.

10.1   Digital Signatures

Digital Signatures are the electronic equivalent of physical signatures and are based on public-key cryptosystems. *Digital Signatures* were first proposed by Whitfield Diffie and Martin Hellman in 1976 [70]. As in the case of physical signatures, a *Digital Signature* is used to validate the authenticity of a message. This message authentication holds true if the only person capable of generating

437

a valid *Digital Signature* is the originator of the message. *Digital Signatures* must also change with each new message. Therefore, to meet both of these requirements, *Digital Signatures* must be a function of both the sender's private key and the message being sent. Such a structure allows two communicating parties, *Alice* and *Bob*, to prove that the sender generated a given message because only the sender has access to his or her private key. It is desirable that the *Digital Signature* verification process may be performed by *any* party. Therefore, *Digital Signature* verification must be a function of the sender's public key. As a result, *Digital Signature* schemes require two functions:

1. A *Digital Signature* signing function, denoted as

$$y \;=\; sig_{K_{PR}}(x)$$

2. A *Digital Signature* verification function, denoted as

$$ver_{K_{PUB}}(x, \; y) \;=\; true \; or \; false$$

For a given message x, the protocol for transmitting a message between two communicating parties, *Alice* and *Bob*, using *Digital Signatures* is as follows:

1. *Alice* and *Bob* agree on a *Digital Signature* scheme.

2. *Bob* transmits his public key, denoted as K_{PUB_B}, to *Alice*.

3. *Bob* uses his private key and the *Digital Signature* signing function to sign the message x, yielding the *Digital Signature* $y = sig_{K_{PR_B}}(x)$.

4. *Bob* transmits the message x and the *Digital Signature* y to *Alice*.

5. *Alice* verifies the *Digital Signature* y for the message x via the *Digital Signature* verification function $ver_{K_{PUB}}(x, y)$, yielding a value of *true* (indicating successful verification) or *false* (indicating failed verification).

Based on this protocol, *Digital Signatures* exhibit the following properties:

- *Digital Signatures* generate a fixed length signature for a fixed length message x.

- Only the sender of a message can sign the message because signing requires the use of the sender's private key.

- Everyone with access to the sender's public key can verify the signature of a message allegedly signed by the sender.

- Message authentication is guaranteed because the recipient is sure that the sender generated the message.

- Data integrity is guaranteed because any alteration of either the message x or the *Digital Signature* y will cause the *Dig-*

ital Signature verification function to yield a value of *false*, indicating that verification has failed.

- Non-repudiation is guaranteed because the sender cannot deny sending the message x if the associated *Digital Signature* y is valid, i.e. the *Digital Signature* verification function yields a value of *true*, indicating that verification has succeeded.

10.1.1   RSA

The *RSA Digital Signature* scheme is composed of two stages: set-up and signing/verification. The set-up stage generates the private and public keys in the same manner as is done in the *RSA* cryptosystem:

1. Choose two large prime numbers, denoted as p and q.

2. Compute $n = p \cdot q$.

3. Compute $\phi(n) = (p - 1) \cdot (q - 1)$.

4. Select a random integer, denoted as b, such that $0 < b < \phi(n)$ and the $gcd(\phi(n), b) = 1$.

5. Compute $a = b^{-1} \bmod \phi(n)$.

where $\phi(n)$ is *Euler's Phi Function* as described in Section 6.6. Upon completion of the set-up stage, the public key is denoted as $K_{PUB} = (n, b)$ and the private key is denoted as $K_{PR} = (p, q, a)$.

Once the private and public keys have been established, signing of the message x to form the signature y is performed as follows:

$$y = sig_{K_{PR}}(x) = x^a \ mod \ n$$

where x is an element in the *Ring* Z_n. Verification of the signature y is achieved by computing $ver_{K_{PUB}}(x, \ y) = y^b \ mod \ n$ and comparing the result to the message x. If $y^b \ mod \ n \equiv x$, then verification is successful; otherwise, verification fails.

Example 10.1: Using the *RSA Digital Signature* scheme with the parameters $p = 3$, $q = 11$, and $a = 3$, sign the message $x = 3$ and then verify the signature.

Based on the parameters p and q, the *RSA* modulus $n = p \cdot q = 3 \cdot 11 = 33$. The parameter $b = a^{-1} \ mod \ \phi(n) = 3^{-1} \ mod \ 20 = 7 \ mod \ 20$. Therefore, the *RSA Digital Signature* for the message x is:

$$y = x^a \ mod \ n$$
$$y = 3^3 \ mod \ 33$$
$$y = 27 \ mod \ 33$$

Verification of the signature y is achieved by computing:

$$ver_{K_{PUB}}(x,\ y)\ =\ y^b\ mod\ n$$

$$ver_{K_{PUB}}(3,\ 27)\ =\ 27^7\ mod\ 33$$

$$ver_{K_{PUB}}(3,\ 27)\ =\ 10,460,353,203\ mod\ 33$$

$$ver_{K_{PUB}}(3,\ 27)\ \equiv\ 3\ mod\ 33$$

Because $y^b\ mod\ n\ \equiv\ x$, verification is successful.

It is possible for an attacker, *Oscar*, to construct a message and *Digital Signature* pair $(x,\ y)$ that would appear to have been sent by another party, *Alice*. This is achieved by choosing a *Digital Signature* y and computing its associated message $x\ =\ y^b\ mod\ n$, where $K_{PUB}\ =\ (n,\ b)$ is *Alice's* public key. The *Digital Signature* y will pass the verification function because $y^b\ mod\ n\ \equiv\ x$. However, this attack is of little use in practice because the value of the resultant message x will be a random bit pattern that cannot be controlled by *Oscar*. This attack may be thwarted by imposing format requirements on the message x. An example of such a requirement would be that the 100 least significant bits of the message x must be a specific bit pattern, such as all zeros or all ones. It is highly unlikely that a randomly generated message x from a chosen *Digital Signature* y will meet such requirements. However, the recipient *Bob* must now also verify the validity of the message x in addition to the validity of the signature y.

A significant drawback to the *RSA Digital Signature* scheme (and all other *Digital Signature* schemes) is that the size of the message x to be signed is limited based on the size of the modulus n. Therefore, messages that are larger than the modulus n must be broken into blocks whose size is smaller than the size of the modulus n, forming the message grouping $\{x_0, x_1, x_2, \ldots x_k\}$ where each block x_i must be digitally signed prior to transmission. Such a process would require the computation of numerous *Digital Signatures* for a given message, which is not desirable due to the addition of considerable computation overhead while also imposing padding requirements on messages whose sizes are not evenly divisible by the size of the modulus n. Recall the parallel of *Digital Signatures* to physical signatures. Only one physical signature is required to validate the authenticity of a physical document, regardless of its size, and the same should hold true for a *Digital Signature* used to validate the authenticity of an electronic message. To address this problem, *Hash Functions* are used to generate a message digest whose size matches the size of the modulus n. It is this message digest that is digitally signed, resulting in the generation of a single *Digital Signature* for a message regardless of the size of the message. *Hash Functions* will be examined in greater detail in Section 10.2.

As discussed in Section 7.3, the *RSA* parameters n and a are typically on the order of 1,024 bits in length while b is usually selected to be a *short exponent*, although 2048-bit moduli are recommended to ensure long-term security. As a result, verification is accelerated by the use of the *short exponent* b whereas signing is significantly slower.

FIPS Standard 186-2, the *Digital Signature Standard* (DSS), specifies algorithms for use in generating *Digital Signatures*, including the *RSA Digital Signature* scheme [225], though the scheme itself is described in ANSI standard X9.31 [13]. The *DSS* requires that the modulus n be at least 1,024 bits and that p and q, the large prime numbers used to compute $n = p \cdot q$, be approximately half the bit length of n. Moreover, ANSI standard X9.31 also recommends using strong prime numbers in addition to placing other restrictions on p and q. Note that the *DSS* also includes the use of the *Hash Function SHA-1* to generate a message digest which is then used as the input to all of the *Digital Signature* algorithms, including the *RSA Digital Signature* scheme [225]. The *SHA-1 Hash Function* will be discussed in Section 10.2.2.4.

10.1.2   ElGamal

The *ElGamal Digital Signature* scheme was proposed in 1985 by Taher El Gamal and is based on the *Discrete Logarithm* problem in either Z_p^* or $GF(2^k)$, though it is different from *ElGamal* encryption [103]. The *ElGamal Digital Signature* scheme is composed of two stages: set-up and signing/verification. The set-up stage generates the private and public keys as follows:

1. Choose a large prime number, denoted as p.

2. Choose a *primitive element* α contained in the set Z_p^*.

3. Choose a secret key $a \in \{2, 3, 4, \ldots p - 2\}$. Note that $a = p - 1$ is not a useful choice because $\alpha^{p-1} \equiv 1 \bmod p$ per *Fermat's Little Theorem*.

4. Compute $\beta = \alpha^a \bmod p$.

Upon completion of the set-up stage, the public key is denoted as $K_{PUB} = (\beta, \alpha, p)$ and the private key is denoted as $K_{PR} = (a)$.

Once the private and public keys have been established, signing of the message x to form the *ElGamal Digital Signature* is performed as follows:

1. Choose $k \in \{2, 3, 4, \ldots p - 2\}$ such that the $gcd(k, p - 1) = 1$.

2. Compute $\gamma = \alpha^k \bmod p$.

3. Compute $\delta = (x - a \cdot \gamma) \cdot k^{-1} \bmod p - 1$.

where the plaintext x is contained in the set Z_p and the *ElGamal Digital Signature* is the pair $sig_{K_{PR}}(x, k) = (\gamma, \delta)$. Verification of the signature is achieved by computing $ver_{K_{PUB}}(x, (\gamma, \delta)) = \beta^\gamma \cdot \gamma^\delta \bmod p$ and comparing the result to $\alpha^x \bmod p$. If $\beta^\gamma \cdot \gamma^\delta \bmod p \equiv \alpha^x \bmod p$, then verification is successful; otherwise, verification fails. This equality is demonstrated to hold true for successful signature verification by substituting into the verification function:

$$\beta^{\gamma} \cdot \gamma^{\delta} \bmod p = (\alpha^a)^{\gamma} \cdot (\alpha^k)^{(x - a \cdot \gamma) \cdot k^{-1} \bmod p - 1} \bmod p$$

$$\beta^{\gamma} \cdot \gamma^{\delta} \bmod p = \alpha^{a \cdot \gamma} \cdot \alpha^{k \cdot (x - a \cdot \gamma) \cdot k^{-1} \bmod p - 1} \bmod p$$

$$\beta^{\gamma} \cdot \gamma^{\delta} \bmod p = \alpha^{a \cdot \gamma} \cdot \alpha^{k \cdot x \cdot k^{-1} - k \cdot a \cdot \gamma \cdot k^{-1} \bmod p - 1} \bmod p$$

$$\beta^{\gamma} \cdot \gamma^{\delta} \bmod p = \alpha^{a \cdot \gamma} \cdot \alpha^{x - a \cdot \gamma \bmod p - 1} \bmod p$$

$$\beta^{\gamma} \cdot \gamma^{\delta} \bmod p = \alpha^{a \cdot \gamma} \cdot \alpha^{x} \cdot \alpha^{-a \cdot \gamma \bmod p - 1} \bmod p$$

$$\beta^{\gamma} \cdot \gamma^{\delta} \bmod p = \alpha^{a \cdot \gamma - a \cdot \gamma \bmod p - 1} \cdot \alpha^{x} \bmod p$$

$$\beta^{\gamma} \cdot \gamma^{\delta} \bmod p = 1 \cdot \alpha^{x} \bmod p$$

$$\beta^{\gamma} \cdot \gamma^{\delta} \bmod p = \alpha^{x} \bmod p$$

Note that $k \cdot k^{-1} \equiv 1 \bmod p - 1$ because k was chosen such that $gcd(k, p - 1) = 1$ and δ is computed modulo $p - 1$.

Example 10.2: Using the *ElGamal Digital Signature* scheme with the parameters $p = 467$, $\alpha = 2$, $a = 127$, and $k = 39$, sign the message $x = 3$ and then verify the signature.

Based on the *ElGamal Digital Signature* scheme parameters, the *ElGamal Digital Signature* for the message x is:

$$\gamma = \alpha^k \bmod p$$
$$\gamma = 2^{39} \bmod 467$$
$$\gamma = 549,755,813,888 \bmod 467$$
$$\gamma \equiv 118 \bmod 467$$

$$\delta = (x - a \cdot \gamma) \cdot k^{-1} \bmod p - 1$$

$$\delta = (3 - 127 \cdot 118) \cdot 39^{-1} \bmod 466$$

$$\delta = (3 - 14{,}986) \cdot 239 \bmod 466$$

$$\delta \equiv -14{,}983 \cdot 239 \bmod 466$$

$$\delta \equiv 395 \cdot 239 \bmod 466$$

$$\delta \equiv 94{,}405 \bmod 466$$

$$\delta \equiv 273 \bmod 466$$

$$sig_{K_{PR}}(x, \ k) = (\gamma, \ \delta)$$

$$sig_{127}(3, \ 39) = (118, \ 273)$$

Verification of the signature $(\gamma, \ \delta)$ is achieved by computing:

$$\beta = \alpha^a \bmod p$$

$$\beta = 2^{127} \bmod 467$$

$$\beta = 2^{60} \cdot 2^{60} \cdot 2^7 \bmod 467$$

$$\beta = 1{,}152{,}921{,}504{,}606{,}846{,}976 \cdot 1{,}152{,}921{,}504{,}606{,}846{,}976 \cdot$$

$$128 \bmod 467$$

$$\beta \equiv 169 \cdot 169 \cdot 128 \bmod 467$$

$$\beta \equiv 3{,}655{,}808 \bmod 467$$

$$\beta \equiv 132 \bmod 467$$

$$ver_{K_{PUB}}(x, \ (\gamma, \delta)) \ = \ \beta^\gamma \ \cdot \ \gamma^\delta \ mod \ p$$

$$ver_{K_{PUB}}(3, \ (118, \ 80)) \ = \ 132^{118} \ \cdot \ 118^{273} \ mod \ 467$$

$$ver_{K_{PUB}}(3, \ (118, \ 80)) \ = \ (132^5)^{23} \ \cdot \ 132^3 \ \cdot \ (118^5)^{54}$$
$$\cdot \ 118^3 \ mod \ 467$$

$$ver_{K_{PUB}}(3, \ (118, \ 80)) \ = \ (40,074,642,432)^{23}$$
$$\cdot \ 2,299,968 \ \cdot \ (22,877,577,568)^{16}$$
$$\cdot \ 1,643,032 \ mod \ 467$$

$$ver_{K_{PUB}}(3, \ (118, \ 80)) \ \equiv \ 386^{23} \ \cdot \ 460 \ \cdot \ 372^{54} \ \cdot \ 126 \ mod \ 467$$

$$ver_{K_{PUB}}(3, \ (118, \ 80)) \ \equiv \ (386^4)^5 \ \cdot \ 386^3 \ \cdot \ 57,960 \ \cdot \ (372^4)^{13}$$
$$\cdot \ 372^2 \ mod \ 467$$

$$ver_{K_{PUB}}(3, \ (118, \ 80)) \ \equiv \ (22,199,808,016)^5 \ \cdot \ 57,512,456 \ \cdot \ 52$$
$$\cdot \ (19,150,131,456)^{13} \ \cdot \ 138,384 \ mod \ 467$$

$$ver_{K_{PUB}}(3, \ (118, \ 80)) \ \equiv \ 62^5 \ \cdot \ 5 \ \cdot \ 52 \ \cdot \ 221^{13} \ \cdot \ 152 \ mod \ 467$$

$$ver_{K_{PUB}}(3, \ (118, \ 80)) \ \equiv \ 916,132,832 \ \cdot \ 39,520 \ \cdot \ (221^4)^3$$
$$\cdot \ 221 \ mod \ 467$$

$$ver_{K_{PUB}}(3, \ (118, \ 80)) \ \equiv \ 252 \ \cdot \ 292 \ \cdot \ (2,385,443,281)^3$$
$$\cdot \ 221 \ mod \ 467$$

$$ver_{K_{PUB}}(3, \ (118, \ 80)) \ \equiv \ 16,262,064 \ \cdot \ 276^3 \ mod \ 467$$

$$ver_{K_{PUB}}(3, \ (118, \ 80)) \ \equiv \ 190 \ \cdot \ 21,024,576 \ mod \ 467$$

$$ver_{K_{PUB}}(3, \ (118, \ 80)) \ \equiv \ 190 \ \cdot \ 236 \ mod \ 467$$

$$ver_{K_{PUB}}(3, \ (118, \ 80)) \ \equiv \ 44,840 \ mod \ 467$$

$$ver_{K_{PUB}}(3, \ (118, \ 80)) \ \equiv \ 8 \ mod \ 467$$

$$\alpha^x \bmod p \;=\; 2^3 \bmod 467$$

$$\alpha^x \bmod p \;=\; 8 \bmod 467$$

Because $\beta^\gamma \cdot \gamma^\delta \bmod p \;=\; \alpha^x \bmod p$, verification is successful.

The security of the *ElGamal Digital Signature* scheme relies on the security of the *Discrete Logarithm* problem. As discussed in Section 8.6, the modulus p is typically chosen to be a 1024-bit value to ensure that the *Index Calculus Method* is not computationally feasible in practice. Moreover, $p - 1$ must have a large prime factor p_t such that $p_t \geq 2^{256}$ to ensure a complexity of $\approx 2^{128}$, i.e. equivalent security to a 128-bit block cipher, so that an attack using the *Pohlig-Hellman Algorithm* is not computationally feasible in practice.

As discussed in Section 10.1.1, the *DSS* specifies algorithms for use in generating *Digital Signatures*, including the *Digital Signature Algorithm* (DSA), which is a modified version of the *ElGamal Digital Signature* scheme [225]. The *DSA* specifies the use of a prime modulus, denoted as p, and requires that $2^{1023} < p < 2^{1024}$. The *DSA* also specifies the parameter denoted as q, a prime factor of $p - 1$, where $2^{159} < q < 2^{160}$. The parameter g, analogous to the *primitive element* α of the *ElGamal Digital Signature* scheme, is defined as $g = h^{\frac{p-1}{q}} \bmod p$, where $1 < h < p - 1$ and $g > 1$, guaranteeing that g has an *order* of $q \bmod p$. The private key x is a random integer $0 < x < q$ and the public key is (y, g, p, q) where y is computed as $y = g^x \bmod p$. In this arrangement, y is analogous to β of the *ElGamal Digital Signature* scheme.

Once the *DSA* parameters, i.e. the private and public keys, have been established, signing of the message M is performed as follows:

1. Choose $0 < k < q$.

2. Compute $r = (g^k \bmod p) \bmod q$.

3. Compute $s = (h(M) + x \cdot r) \cdot k^{-1} \bmod q$.

where $h(M)$ is the output of the *Hash Function SHA-1* which is then converted to an integer prior to use in computing s. Thus the *Digital Signature* is the pair $sig_{K_{PR}}(M, k) = (r, s)$.

Verification of the *Digital Signature* is achieved via the following process:

1. Compute $w = s^{-1} \bmod q$.

2. Compute $u_1 = h(M) \cdot w \bmod q$, where $h(M)$ is the output of the *Hash Function SHA-1* which is then converted to an integer prior to use.

3. Compute $u_2 = r \cdot w \bmod q$.

4. Compute $v = (g^{u_1} \cdot y^{u_2} \bmod p) \bmod q$.

If $v \equiv r$, then verification is successful; otherwise, verification fails. Recall that p and q are prime such that q is a prime factor of $p - 1$. Let $0 < h < p$ and $g = h^{\frac{p-1}{q}} \bmod p$. In such case:

$$g^q \bmod p = (h^{\frac{p-1}{q}} \bmod p)^q \bmod p$$

$$g^q \bmod p = h^{p-1} \bmod p$$

$$g^q \bmod p = 1 \bmod p$$

Therefore, $g^q \bmod p \equiv 1 \bmod p$ using *Fermat's Little Theorem*. Moreover, if $m \bmod q = n + k \cdot q \equiv n \bmod q$, then:

$$g^m \bmod p = g^{n + k \cdot q} \bmod p$$

$$g^m \bmod p = g^n \bmod p \cdot (g^q \bmod p)^k \bmod p$$

However, as previously demonstrated, $g^q \bmod p \equiv 1$, and thus:

$$g^m \bmod p = g^n \bmod p \cdot (1)^k \bmod p$$

$$g^m \bmod p = g^n \bmod p$$

Based on these results, the equality $v \equiv r$ may be shown to hold true for a successful verification by substituting into the equation for v:

$$v = (g^{u_1} \cdot y^{u_2} \bmod p) \bmod q$$

$$v = (g^{h(M) \cdot w \bmod q} \cdot y^{r \cdot w \bmod q} \bmod p) \bmod q$$

The equation for v may be further reduced by substituting $y = g^x \bmod p$ into the equation for v and taking advantage of the prior conclusions:

$$v = (g^{h(M) \cdot w \bmod q} \cdot (g^x \bmod p)^{r \cdot w \bmod q} \bmod p) \bmod q$$

$$v = (g^{h(M) \cdot w \bmod q} \cdot g^{x \cdot r \cdot w \bmod q} \bmod p) \bmod q$$

$$v = (g^{h(M) \cdot w + x \cdot r \cdot w \bmod q} \bmod p) \bmod q$$

$$v = (g^{w \cdot (h(M) + x \cdot r \bmod q)} \bmod p) \bmod q$$

Recall that $s = (h(M) + x \cdot r) \cdot k^{-1} \bmod q$. Therefore, w may be computed as:

$$w = s^{-1} \bmod q$$

$$w = ((h(M) + x \cdot r) \cdot k^{-1})^{-1} \bmod q$$

$$w = (h(M) + x \cdot r)^{-1} \cdot k \bmod q$$

Substituting $w = (h(M) + x \cdot r)^{-1} \cdot k \bmod q$ into the equation for v yields:

$$v = (g^{((h(M) + x \cdot r)^{-1} \cdot k \ mod \ q) \cdot (h(M) + x \cdot r \ mod \ q)} \ mod \ p) \ mod \ q$$

$$v = (g^{((h(M) + x \cdot r)^{-1} \ mod \ q) \cdot (h(M) + x \cdot r \ mod \ q) \cdot k} \ mod \ p) \ mod \ q$$

$$v = (g^{(1 \cdot k)} \ mod \ p) \ mod \ q$$

$$v = (g^k \ mod \ p) \ mod \ q$$

Therefore, $v = (g^k \ mod \ p) \ mod \ q = r$, indicating that verification is successful [225].

10.1.3   Elliptic Curves

Elliptic Curve Digital Signature schemes are composed of two stages: set-up and signing/verification. The set-up stage generates the private and public keys as follows:

1. Choose an *Elliptic Curve* over the set Z_p, for $p > 3$, of the form $y^2 \equiv x^3 + a \cdot x + b \ mod \ p$, where a and b are contained in the set Z_p and $4 \cdot a^3 + 27 \cdot b^2 \neq 0 \ mod \ p$.

2. Choose a *primitive element* α, a point on the *Elliptic Curve*, denoted as $\alpha = (x_\alpha, y_\alpha)$.

3. Choose a secret key $k \ \epsilon \ \{2, 3, 4, \ldots \#E - 1\}$.

4. Compute $\beta = k \cdot \alpha = (x_\beta, y_\beta)$.

Upon completion of the set-up stage, the public key is denoted as $K_{PUB} = (E, \beta, \alpha, p)$ and the private key is denoted as $K_{PR} = (k)$.

Once the private and public keys have been established, signing of the message $M = (x_M, y_M)$ to form the *Elliptic Curve Digital Signature* is performed as follows:

1. Choose $m \in \{2, 3, 4, \ldots \#E - 1\}$.

2. Compute $\gamma = m \cdot \alpha = (x_\gamma, y_\gamma)$.

3. Compute $r = x_\gamma \bmod \#E$. If $r \equiv 0 \bmod \#E$ then go to Step 1.

4. Compute $s = m^{-1} \cdot (x_M + k \cdot r) \bmod \#E$. If $s \equiv 0 \bmod \#E$ then go to Step 1.

where the plaintext M is a point on the *Elliptic Curve* and the *Elliptic Curve Digital Signature* is the pair $sig_{K_{PR}}(M, k) = (r, s)$. Verification of the signature is achieved as follows:

1. Compute $c = s^{-1} \bmod \#E$.

2. Compute $u_1 = x_M \cdot c \bmod \#E$.

3. Compute $u_2 = r \cdot c \bmod \#E$.

4. Compute $\delta = u_1 \cdot \alpha + u_2 \cdot \beta = (x_\delta, y_\delta)$.

5. Compute $v = x_\delta \bmod \#E$.

Verification of the signature $ver_{K_{PUB}}(M, (r, s))$ is successful if $v = r$.

Example 10.3: Using the *Elliptic Curve Digital Signature* scheme with the *Elliptic Curve* $y^2 \equiv x^3 + x + 6 \bmod 11$ and the parameters $k = 2, m = 2, \#E = 13$, and $\alpha = (3, 5)$, sign the message $M = (4, 4)$ and then verify the signature.

Generation of the *Elliptic Curve Digital Signature* begins with the computation of β:

$$\beta = k \cdot \alpha$$
$$\beta = 2 \cdot (3, 5)$$
$$\beta = (3, 5) + (3, 5)$$

$$\lambda = \frac{3x_1^2 + a}{2y_1} \bmod p$$
$$\lambda = \frac{3 \cdot 3^2 + 1}{2 \cdot 5} \bmod 11$$
$$\lambda = \frac{3 \cdot 9 + 1}{10} \bmod 11$$
$$\lambda = \frac{28}{10} \bmod 11$$
$$\lambda = \frac{6}{10} \bmod 11$$
$$\lambda = 6 \cdot 10^{-1} \bmod 11$$
$$\lambda = 6 \cdot 10 \bmod 11$$
$$\lambda = 60 \bmod 11$$

$$\lambda \;=\; 5 \bmod 11$$

$$x_3 \;\equiv\; \lambda^2 \;-\; x_2 \;-\; x_1 \bmod p$$

$$x_3 \;\equiv\; 5^2 \;-\; 3 \;-\; 3 \bmod 11$$

$$x_3 \;\equiv\; 25 \;-\; 3 \;-\; 3 \bmod 11$$

$$x_3 \;\equiv\; 19 \bmod 11$$

$$x_3 \;\equiv\; 8 \bmod 11$$

$$y_3 \;\equiv\; \lambda \cdot (x_1 \;-\; x_3) \;-\; y_1 \bmod p$$

$$y_3 \;\equiv\; 5 \cdot (3 \;-\; 8) \;-\; 5 \bmod 11$$

$$y_3 \;\equiv\; 5 \cdot -5 \;-\; 5 \bmod 11$$

$$y_3 \;\equiv\; -25 \;-\; 5 \bmod 11$$

$$y_3 \;\equiv\; -30 \bmod 11$$

$$y_3 \;\equiv\; 3 \bmod 11$$

$$\beta \;=\; (8, \; 3)$$

Signing is then performed by computing γ:

$$\gamma \;=\; m \cdot \alpha$$

$$\gamma \;=\; 2 \cdot (3, \; 5)$$

$$\lambda \;=\; \frac{3x_1^2 \;+\; a}{2y_1} \bmod p$$

$$\lambda \;=\; \frac{3 \cdot 3^2 \;+\; 1}{2 \cdot 5} \bmod 11$$

$$\lambda \;=\; \frac{3 \cdot 9 \;+\; 1}{10} \bmod 11$$

$$\lambda \;=\; \frac{28}{10} \bmod 11$$

$$\lambda = \frac{6}{10} \ mod \ 11$$

$$\lambda = 6 \cdot 10^{-1} \ mod \ 11$$

$$\lambda = 6 \cdot 10 \ mod \ 11$$

$$\lambda = 60 \ mod \ 11$$

$$\lambda = 5 \ mod \ 11$$

$$x_3 \equiv \lambda^2 - x_2 - x_1 \ mod \ p$$

$$x_3 \equiv 5^2 - 3 - 3 \ mod \ 11$$

$$x_3 \equiv 25 - 3 - 3 \ mod \ 11$$

$$x_3 \equiv 19 \ mod \ 11$$

$$x_3 \equiv 8 \ mod \ 11$$

$$y_3 \equiv \lambda \cdot (x_1 - x_3) - y_1 \ mod \ p$$

$$y_3 \equiv 5 \cdot (3 - 8) - 5 \ mod \ 11$$

$$y_3 \equiv 5 \cdot -5 - 5 \ mod \ 11$$

$$y_3 \equiv -25 - 5 \ mod \ 11$$

$$y_3 \equiv -30 \ mod \ 11$$

$$y_3 \equiv 3 \ mod \ 11$$

$$\gamma = (8, \ 3)$$

Having computed $\gamma = (8, \ 3)$, r is computed as:

$$r = x_\gamma \ mod \ \#E$$

$$r = 8 \ mod \ 13$$

Finally, s is computed as:

$$s = m^{-1} \cdot (x_M + k \cdot r) \bmod \#E$$
$$s = 2^{-1} \cdot (4 + 2 \cdot 8) \bmod 13$$
$$s \equiv 7 \cdot (4 + 16) \bmod 13$$
$$s \equiv 7 \cdot (4 + 3) \bmod 13$$
$$s \equiv 7 \cdot 7 \bmod 13$$
$$s \equiv 49 \bmod 13$$
$$s \equiv 10 \bmod 13$$

Thus the *Elliptic Curve Digital Signature* is the pair $sig_{K_{PR}}(M, k) = (r, s) = (8, 10)$.

Verification of the signature $(r, s) = (8, 10)$ is achieved by computing:

$$c = s^{-1} \bmod \#E$$
$$c = 10^{-1} \bmod 13$$
$$c \equiv 4 \bmod 13$$

$$u_1 = x_M \cdot c \bmod \#E$$
$$u_1 = 4 \cdot 4 \bmod 13$$
$$u_1 = 16 \bmod 13$$
$$u_1 \equiv 3 \bmod 13$$

$$u_2 \;=\; r \cdot c \; mod \; \#E$$

$$u_2 \;=\; 8 \cdot 4 \; mod \; 13$$

$$u_2 \;=\; 32 \; mod \; 13$$

$$u_2 \;\equiv\; 6 \; mod \; 13$$

$$\delta \;=\; u_1 \cdot \alpha + u_2 \cdot \beta$$

$$\delta \;=\; 3 \cdot (3,\,5) + 6 \cdot (8,\,3)$$

Therefore, computing δ requires the computation of $3 \cdot (3,\,5)$:

$$2 \cdot (3,\,5) \;=\; (3,\,5) + (3,\,5)$$

$$\lambda \;=\; \frac{3x_1^2 + a}{2y_1} \; mod \; p$$

$$\lambda \;=\; \frac{3 \cdot 3^2 + 1}{2 \cdot 5} \; mod \; 11$$

$$\lambda \;=\; \frac{3 \cdot 9 + 1}{10} \; mod \; 11$$

$$\lambda \;=\; \frac{28}{10} \; mod \; 11$$

$$\lambda \;\equiv\; \frac{6}{10} \; mod \; 11$$

$$\lambda \;\equiv\; 6 \cdot 10^{-1} \; mod \; 11$$

$$\lambda \;\equiv\; 6 \cdot 10 \; mod \; 11$$

$$\lambda \;\equiv\; 60 \; mod \; 11$$

$$\lambda \;\equiv\; 5 \; mod \; 11$$

$$x_3 \;\equiv\; \lambda^2 - x_2 - x_1 \; mod \; p$$

$$x_3 \equiv 5^2 - 3 - 3 \bmod 11$$

$$x_3 \equiv 25 - 3 - 3 \bmod 11$$

$$x_3 \equiv 19 \bmod 11$$

$$x_3 \equiv 8 \bmod 11$$

$$y_3 \equiv \lambda \cdot (x_1 - x_3) - y_1 \bmod p$$

$$y_3 \equiv 5 \cdot (3 - 8) - 5 \bmod 11$$

$$y_3 \equiv 5 \cdot -5 - 5 \bmod 11$$

$$y_3 \equiv -25 - 5 \bmod 11$$

$$y_3 \equiv -30 \bmod 11$$

$$y_3 \equiv 3 \bmod 11$$

$$2 \cdot (3, \ 5) = (8, \ 3)$$

$$3 \cdot (3, \ 5) = (8, \ 3) + (3, \ 5)$$

$$\lambda = \frac{y_2 - y_1}{x_2 - x_1} \bmod p$$

$$\lambda = \frac{5 - 3}{3 - 8} \bmod 11$$

$$\lambda = \frac{2}{-5} \bmod 11$$

$$\lambda \equiv \frac{2}{6} \bmod 11$$

$$\lambda \equiv 2 \cdot 6^{-1} \bmod 11$$

$$\lambda \equiv 2 \cdot 2 \bmod 11$$

$$\lambda \equiv 4 \bmod 11$$

$$x_3 \equiv \lambda^2 - x_2 - x_1 \bmod p$$

$$x_3 \equiv 4^2 - 3 - 8 \bmod 11$$

$$x_3 \equiv 16 - 3 - 8 \; mod \; 11$$

$$x_3 \equiv 5 \; mod \; 11$$

$$y_3 \equiv \lambda \cdot (x_1 - x_3) - y_1 \; mod \; p$$

$$y_3 \equiv 4 \cdot (8 - 5) - 3 \; mod \; 11$$

$$y_3 \equiv 4 \cdot 3 - 3 \; mod \; 11$$

$$y_3 \equiv 12 - 3 \; mod \; 11$$

$$y_3 \equiv 9 \; mod \; 11$$

$$3 \cdot (3, \; 5) = (5, \; 9)$$

Similarly, computing δ requires the computation of $6 \cdot (8, \; 3)$:

$$2 \cdot (8, \; 3) = (8, \; 3) + (8, \; 3)$$

$$\lambda = \frac{3x_1^2 + a}{2y_1} \; mod \; p$$

$$\lambda = \frac{3 \cdot 8^2 + 1}{2 \cdot 3} \; mod \; 11$$

$$\lambda = \frac{3 \cdot 64 + 1}{6} \; mod \; 11$$

$$\lambda = \frac{193}{6} \; mod \; 11$$

$$\lambda \equiv \frac{6}{6} \; mod \; 11$$

$$\lambda \equiv 6 \cdot 6^{-1} \; mod \; 11$$

$$\lambda \equiv 6 \cdot 2 \; mod \; 11$$

$$\lambda \equiv 12 \; mod \; 11$$

$$\lambda \equiv 1 \; mod \; 11$$

$$x_3 \equiv \lambda^2 - x_2 - x_1 \; mod \; p$$

$$x_3 \equiv 1^2 - 8 - 8 \bmod 11$$

$$x_3 \equiv 1 - 8 - 8 \bmod 11$$

$$x_3 \equiv -15 \bmod 11$$

$$x_3 \equiv 7 \bmod 11$$

$$y_3 \equiv \lambda \cdot (x_1 - x_3) - y_1 \bmod p$$

$$y_3 \equiv 1 \cdot (8 - 7) - 3 \bmod 11$$

$$y_3 \equiv 1 \cdot 1 - 3 \bmod 11$$

$$y_3 \equiv 1 - 3 \bmod 11$$

$$y_3 \equiv -2 \bmod 11$$

$$y_3 \equiv 9 \bmod 11$$

$$2 \cdot (8, \; 3) = (7, \; 9)$$

Note that $6 \cdot (8, \; 3) \equiv 3 \cdot (7, \; 9)$. However, it is known that $3 \cdot (7, \; 9) \equiv (3, \; 6)$ from **Example 9.1**. Therefore:

$$\delta = 3 \cdot (3, \; 5) + 6 \cdot (8, \; 3)$$

$$\delta = (5, \; 9) + (3, \; 6)$$

$$\lambda = \frac{y_2 - y_1}{x_2 - x_1} \bmod p$$

$$\lambda = \frac{6 - 9}{3 - 5} \bmod 11$$

$$\lambda = \frac{-3}{-2} \bmod 11$$

$$\lambda \equiv \frac{8}{9} \bmod 11$$

$$\lambda \equiv 8 \cdot 9^{-1} \bmod 11$$

$$\lambda \equiv 8 \cdot 5 \bmod 11$$

$$\lambda \equiv 40 \bmod 11$$

$$\lambda \equiv 7 \bmod 11$$

$$x_3 \equiv \lambda^2 - x_2 - x_1 \bmod p$$

$$x_3 \equiv 7^2 - 3 - 5 \bmod 11$$

$$x_3 \equiv 49 - 3 - 5 \bmod 11$$

$$x_3 \equiv 41 \bmod 11$$

$$x_3 \equiv 8 \bmod 11$$

$$y_3 \equiv \lambda \cdot (x_1 - x_3) - y_1 \bmod p$$

$$y_3 \equiv 7 \cdot (5 - 8) - 9 \bmod 11$$

$$y_3 \equiv 7 \cdot -3 - 9 \bmod 11$$

$$y_3 \equiv -21 - 9 \bmod 11$$

$$y_3 \equiv -30 \bmod 11$$

$$y_3 \equiv 3 \bmod 11$$

$$\delta = (8,\ 3)$$

Finally, v is computed as:

$$v = x_\delta \bmod \#E$$

$$v = 8 \bmod 13$$

Because $v = r = 8$, verification is successful.

The security of an *Elliptic Curve Digital Signature* scheme relies on the security of *Elliptic Curve* cryptosystems, and the best known attack against *Elliptic Curve* cryptosystems combines the *Pohlig-Hellman Algorithm* with either *Shank's Algorithm* or *Pollard's Rho Method*. As discussed in Section 8.6, the complexity of the *Pohlig-Hellman Algorithm* is $e_t \cdot \sqrt{p_t}$, where p_t is the largest prime factor of $\#E$. Therefore, p_t must be chosen for long-term security such that $p_t \geq 2^{256}$ to ensure a complexity of $\approx 2^{128}$, i.e. equivalent security to a 128-bit block cipher, so that an attack using the *Pohlig-Hellman Algorithm* is not computationally feasible in practice.

FIPS Standard 186-2, the *Digital Signature Standard* (DSS), specifies algorithms for use in generating *Digital Signatures*, including the *Elliptic Curve Digital Signature* scheme [225], though the scheme itself is described in ANSI standard X9.62 [16]. Note that the *Elliptic Curve Digital Signature* scheme described above follows the format of the scheme described in ANSI standard X9.62 as used by the *DSS*, with the only difference being that the use of the x coordinate x_M of the message M during signing/verification is replaced by $h(M)$, where $h(M)$ is the output of the *Hash Function SHA-1* [16]. In terms of security, ANSI standard X9.62 specifies that $p_t \geq 2^{160}$, where p_t is the largest prime factor of $\#E$ to guard against an attack using the *Pohlig-Hellman Algorithm*. ANSI standard X9.62 also describes particular conditions resulting in weak *Elliptic Curves* that are vulnerable to reduction attacks [200] or are anomalous [270, 294]. However, the *DSS* specifies the recommended *Elliptic Curves* for use by United States federal government agencies, thus ensuring that weak *Elliptic Curves* are not selected. Note that the *DSS* allows for the use of both *Prime Fields* and *Binary Fields*. In the case of *Binary Fields*, there are 2^m elements for a *Field* of degree m and each element is represented as an m-bit quantity where *Field* arithmetic is performed on the m-bit quantities [225].

10.1.4 Efficient Implementation

Efficient implementation of the *RSA*, *ElGamal*, and *Elliptic Curve Digital Signature* schemes relies upon the efficient implementation of the underlying public-key cryptosystems. These topics have been discussed in detail in Section 7.2 for the *RSA* cryptosystem, Section 8.4 for cryptosystems based on the *Discrete Logarithm* problem, and Section 9.3 for *Elliptic Curve* cryptosystems.

10.1.5 Homework Problems

Homework Problem 10.1.5.1: Given an *RSA Digital Signature* scheme with the public key $(n = 9,797, b = 131)$. Which of the following *Digital Signatures* are valid?

a) $(x = 123, sig(x) = 6,292)$

b) $(x = 4,333, sig(x) = 4,768)$

c) $(x = 4,333, sig(x) = 1,424)$

Homework Problem 10.1.5.2: If the *RSA* algorithm is used as a *Digital Signature* scheme:

a) How many multiplications are required on average to sign a message? How many multiplications are required on average to verify a *Digital Signature*? Assume all variables have as many bits as p, i.e. $l = \lceil log_2 p \rceil$ bits, and that the *Square-and-Multiply Algorithm* is used for both signing and verification. Derive general expressions using l as a variable.

b) What process takes longer, signing or verification?

c) Assume a computer operating with 32-bit data structures. Each variable, e.g. p or a, is represented by an array with $n = \lceil \frac{l}{32} \rceil$ elements. Assume that one multiplication of two of these variables modulo p requires n^2 clock cycles. How long does it take to compute a *Digital Signature* if the clock frequency of the computer is 10 MHz (100 ns clock period) and p has 512 bits? How long does it take to perform a verification operation? How long will both the signing and verification operations take if p has 1,024 bits? Switching to a faster computer with a clock frequency of 100 MHz (10 ns clock period), how long will the signing and verification operations take for both cases of p?

d) Philips and Siemens produce smart cards with an 8051 microprocessor kernel. The 8051 is an 8-bit microprocessor. What clock rate is required in order to perform one *Digital Signature* generation in 50 ms if p has 512 bits? What clock rate is required in order to perform one *Digital Signature* generation in 50 *ms* if p has 1,024 bits? Are these clock frequencies feasible?

Homework Problem 10.1.5.3: Let $p = 467$ and $\alpha = 2$. Using the *ElGamal Digital Signature* scheme, write a C program to sign the messages:

    a) $K_{PR} = 127,\ k = 213,\ x = 33$

    b) $K_{PR} = 127,\ k = 123,\ x = 33$

    c) $K_{PR} = 300,\ k = 45,\ x = 248$

    d) $K_{PR} = 300,\ k = 47,\ x = 248$

For each message, determine if k is a valid choice, compute $(\gamma,\ \delta)$, and verify each *Digital Signature*. This will require writing functions to compute $a^b \bmod m$ and $a^{-1} \bmod m$.

Homework Problem 10.1.5.4: Upon examination of the four messages of **Homework Problem 10.1.5.3**, it is evident that the *ElGamal Digital Signature* scheme is non-determinist — a given message x has many valid *Digital Signatures* because both $x = 33$ and $x = 248$ are shown to have two valid *Digital Signatures*.

    a) Why is the *ElGamal Digital Signature* scheme non-deterministic?

    b) Develop a general expression for the number of valid *Digital Signatures* for each message x.

c) How many valid *Digital Signatures* are there for the cryptosystem in **Homework Problem 10.1.5.3**?

Homework Problem 10.1.5.5: Consider the performance of an *ElGamal Digital Signature* scheme with $\lceil log_2 p \rceil = 768$. Assume a timing model such that multiplication or squaring modulo p of an n-bit number takes $(\lceil \frac{n}{32} \rceil)^2$ clock cycles. What is the required clock frequency to be able to perform one *Digital Signature* verification in not more than 10 *ms* on average?

Homework Problem 10.1.5.6: Consider an attack against the *RSA Digital Signature* scheme. The parameters of *Alice's Digital Signature* are $n = 10{,}403$ and the verification key $K_{PUB} = 129$. Construct a message/*Digital Signature* pair which can be verified as correct. Any *Digital Signature* y other than $y = 1$ is acceptable.

Homework Problem 10.1.5.7: Consider an *ElGamal Digital Signature* scheme used with $p = 31$, $\alpha = 3$, and $\beta = 6$. The message $x = 10$ is received twice with the *Digital Signatures* $(\gamma, \delta) = (17, 5)$ and $(\gamma, \delta) = (13, 15)$.

a) Are both *Digital Signatures* valid?

b) How many valid *Digital Signatures* are there for each message x using the parameters chosen for this *Digital Signature* scheme?

Homework Problem 10.1.5.8: Consider an *RSA Digital Signature* scheme used with parameters $p = 31$, $q = 19$. Assume

$b_B = 17$ is *Bob's* public key and $b_A = 11$ is *Alice's* public key. *Alice* receives the message $(y, \ sig(x)) = (281, \ 504)$.

a) Is the *Digital Signature* valid?

b) How many valid *Digital Signatures* are there for each message x using the parameters chosen for this *Digital Signature* scheme?

Homework Problem 10.1.5.9: Consider the performance of an *Elliptic Curve Digital Signature* scheme that employs a curve where the number of points on the curve $\#E \approx 2^{256}$. Assume that point addition and point doubling each require $(\frac{log_2 \#E}{4})^2$ clock cycles. What is the required clock frequency for calculating a *Digital Signature* in no more than 100 *ms* on average?

Homework Problem 10.1.5.10: Consider the performance of an *RSA* cryptosystem with a prime modulus $n \approx 2^{2048}$, two large prime numbers $p \approx q \approx 2^{1024}$, and $\phi(n)$ is known. The cryptosystem is used to generate *RSA Digital Signatures*. Assume that the time required to perform a multiplication is 1 *ms* and that this is twice the time required to perform a squaring. What is the average time required to compute the *Digital Signature*? What is the average time to verify the *Digital Signature*?

Homework Problem 10.1.5.11: An *RSA Digital Signature* scheme has the set-up parameters $p = 31$ and $q = 37$. The public key is $b = 17$.

a) Find the private key and sign the message $x = 2$ using the *Chinese Remainder Theorem*.

b) Verify your *Digital Signature* without using the *Chinese Remainder Theorem*.

Homework Problem 10.1.5.12: Why is it that the *Chinese Remainder Theorem* cannot be applied for verification of *RSA Digital Signatures*?

Homework Problem 10.1.5.13: Sign the message $x = 3$ using *RSA Digital Signatures* and the *Chinese Remainder Theorem*. The parameters are $p = 29$, $q = 31$, and $a = 37$. Note that $31^{-1} \equiv 15 \bmod 29$ and $29^{-1} \equiv 15 \bmod 31$.

Homework Problem 10.1.5.14: Assume an *RSA* cryptosystem implementation where the exponents are restricted to a length of $t + 1 = 60$ bits. One modular multiplication (or modular squaring) takes 105 processor clock cycles. What clock frequency, in Hz, is required if an *RSA Digital Signature* verification should not take longer than 10 *ms* on average:

a) using the *Square-and-Multiply Algorithm*?

b) using the *k-ary Method* with $k = 3$?

c) using the *Improved k-ary Method* with $k = 3$?

Homework Problem 10.1.5.15: Assume a 1024-bit *RSA* cryptosystem implementation. *Oscar* chooses a *Digital Signature y* and computes the associated message $x = y^b \bmod n$, where $K_{PUB} = (n,\ b)$ is *Alice's* public key. A format requirement on the message x is imposed by the *Digital Signature* scheme such that the 50 most significant bits must be all ones and the 100 least significant bits must be all zeros.

a) What is the probability that the message x computed by *Oscar* meets the message format requirements of the *Digital Signature* scheme?

b) What is the effective message space of the *Digital Signature* scheme?

Homework Problem 10.1.5.16: Assume that the message format requirements of **Homework Problem 10.1.5.15** are changed such that the 150 most significant bits must be all ones and the 200 least significant bits must be all zeros.

a) What is the probability that the message x computed by *Oscar* meets the message format requirements of the *Digital Signature* scheme?

b) What is the effective message space of the *Digital Signature* scheme?

10.2   Hash Functions

As discussed in Section 10.1, a significant drawback to *Digital Signature* schemes is that large messages must be broken into blocks and each block must be digitally signed prior to transmission. To address this problem, *Hash Functions* are used to reduce messages of arbitrary length to a message digest, and it is this digest that is digitally signed, resulting in the generation of a single *Digital Signature*, as shown in Figure 10.1.

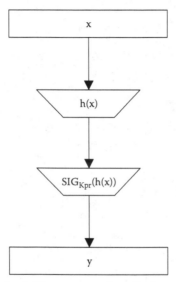

Figure 10.1: Digital Signature Applied to Message Digest

The *Hash Function* $h(x)$ is publicly known and has no key. The input message x is of arbitrary length while the output of the *Hash Function* $h(x)$ is of fixed length. To generate the output, the *Hash Function* $h(x)$ must often be applied in an iterative manner, as shown in Figure 10.2.

Therefore, for a given message x, the new protocol for transmitting a message between two communicating parties, *Alice* and *Bob*, using *Hash Functions* and *Digital Signatures*, is as follows:

1. *Alice* and *Bob* agree on a *Hash Function* and a *Digital Sig-*

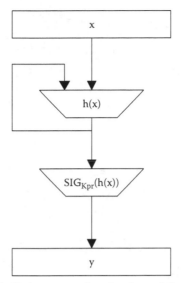

Figure 10.2: Digital Signature Applied to Message Digest Generated Iteratively

nature scheme.

2. *Bob* transmits his public key, denoted as K_{PUB_B}, to *Alice*.

3. *Bob* uses the *Hash Function* to generate the message digest $z = h(x)$.

4. *Bob* uses his private key and the *Digital Signature* signing function to sign the message digest z, yielding the *Digital Signature* $y = sig_{K_{PR_B}}(z)$.

5. *Bob* transmits the message x and the *Digital Signature* y to *Alice*.

6. *Alice* uses the *Hash Function* to generate the message digest $z = h(x)$.

7. *Alice* verifies the *Digital Signature* y for the message digest z via the *Digital Signature* verification function $ver_{K_{PUB}}(x, y)$,

yielding a value of *true* (indicating successful verification) or *false* (indicating failed verification).

Should *Oscar* attempt to substitute a message value of x' for the message x being transmitted from *Bob* to *Alice*, the new output of the *Hash Function* $z' = h(x')$ will not match the original output of the *Hash Function* $z = h(x)$, and thus when *Alice* runs the *Digital Signature* verification function, $ver_{K_{PUB}}(x', y)$, it will output a value of *false*, indicating a failed verification. If *Oscar* injects message/signature pairs of the form (x'', y'') into the data stream being sent to *Bob*, the new output of the *Hash Function*, $z'' = h(x'')$, will not generate the *Digital Signature* y'' provided by *Oscar*. This is because *Oscar* does not have *Bob's* private key, K_{PR_B}, necessary for generating the *Digital Signature* y''. However, if *Oscar* can find two messages x and x' such that $h(x) = h(x')$, i.e. *Oscar* finds a *collision*, then the *Digital Signature* verification function will output a value of *true* for both messages, indicating a successful verification. In such case, *Oscar* may substitute x' for x and *Alice* will believe that the message x' was sent by *Bob* due to the successful verification of the *Digital Signature*. Moreover, *Oscar* may save legitimate message/signature pairs of the form (x, y) by snooping the open communication channel. Later, *Oscar* may inject message pairs of the form (x', y) and *Alice* will believe that the message x' was sent by *Bob* due to the successful verification of the *Digital Signature*. Based on these possible attacks, the following requirements for a cryptographically secure *Hash Function*, denoted as $h(x)$, may be defined:

1. $h(x)$ must accept inputs of arbitrary size.

2. $h(x)$ must generate an output of fixed size.

3. $h(x)$ must be relatively easy to compute.

4. $h(x)$ must be a *One-Way* function as defined in Section 6.3.

5. $h(x)$ must be *weak collision resistant* such that *Oscar* cannot find a message x' such that $h(x') = h(x)$ given a message x and its hashed value $h(x)$.

6. $h(x)$ must be *strong collision resistant* such that *Oscar* cannot find any two message pairs (x', x) that result in $h(x') = h(x)$.

The fourth requirement, that $h(x)$ is a *One-Way* function, is critical in cases where the message x is encrypted but the hashed value produced by $h(x)$ is not encrypted prior to transmission. In this case, if the *Hash Function* $h(x)$ is not a *One-Way* function, *Oscar* can easily recover the message x. The fifth requirement, *weak collision resistance*, is necessary to thwart *Oscar's* attempt to substitute his message x' for the original message x. The sixth requirement, *strong collision resistance*, is essential to thwart *Oscar's* attempt to manipulate *white space* to find a *collision* of the form $h(x) = h(x')$. In this case, *Oscar* selects two messages, one that is legitimate, denoted as x_L, and one that is fraudulent, denoted as x_F. *Oscar's* goal is to alter both messages at non-visible locations by manipulating *white space* — tabs, spaces, and carriage returns — to create two modified messages, denoted as x_L^M

and x_F^M. These messages appear visibly identical to x_F and x_M but have the additional property that $h(x_L^M) = h(x_F^M)$, i.e. the two messages result in a *Hash Function collision*. Once *Oscar* finds the *collision*, he allows *Bob* to sign the legitimate message, resulting in $y = sig_{K_{PR_B}}(h(x_L^M))$. *Bob* transmits the message/signature pair (x_L^M, y) to *Alice*, but *Oscar* intercepts the transmission and replaces x_L^M with x_F^M. *Alice* receives the message/signature pair (x_F^M, y), and the verification function $ver_{K_{PUB_B}}(x_F^M, y)$ yields a value of *true* because $h(x_L^M) = h(x_F^M)$.

10.2.1   The Birthday Paradox

Hash Functions have *collisions* as a result of the first and second *Hash Function* requirements specified in Section 10.2. The first requirement specifies that $h(x)$ must accept inputs of arbitrary size. The second requirement specifies that $h(x)$ must generate an output of fixed size. Therefore, the size of the input message space is significantly larger than the size of the output hashed value space. As a result, there must exist multiple messages that map to the same hashed value.

The nature of *collisions* is illustrated through a phenomenon known as the *Birthday Paradox*. Consider the question of how many people must be present so that there is a 50 % probability that at least two of the people have the same birth date. If leap years are ignored such that February 29th is not a viable birth date, then there are 365 possible birth dates. Therefore, the probability that a person has a given birth date is $\frac{1}{365}$. Thus the probability that two people do not have the same birth date, i.e. that there is no *collision*, is $1 - \frac{1}{365}$. In the case where there are three people, the probability that no two people have the same birth date is:

$$P(no\ collision) = (1 - \frac{1}{365}) \cdot (1 - \frac{2}{365})$$

Similarly, when there are four people, the probability that no two people have the same birth date is:

$$P(no\ collision) = (1 - \frac{1}{365}) \cdot (1 - \frac{2}{365}) \cdot (1 - \frac{3}{365})$$

Finally, if there are p people, the probability that no two people have the same birth date is:

$$P(no\ collision) = (1 - \frac{1}{365}) \cdot (1 - \frac{2}{365})$$
$$\cdot (1 - \frac{3}{365}) \cdot \ldots \cdot (1 - \frac{p-1}{365})$$
$$P(no\ collision) = \prod_{i=1}^{p-1} (1 - \frac{i}{365})$$

Generalizing this equation for n possible random values instead of the 365 possible birth dates, the probability that no *collision* occurs if there are p random elements is $\prod_{i=1}^{p-1} 1 - \frac{i}{n}$. This equation may be further reduced by considering the Taylor Series:

$$e^{-x} \; = \; 1 \; - \; x \; + \; \frac{x^2}{2!} \; - \; \frac{x^3}{3!} \; + \; \frac{x^4}{4!} \; - \; \ldots$$

If $x \ll 1$, then $e^{-x} \approx 1 - x$. Therefore, the probability that no *collision* occurs if there are p random elements may be rewritten as:

$$P(no\ collision) \; \approx \; \prod_{i=1}^{p-1} e^{\frac{-i}{n}}$$

$$P(no\ collision) \; \approx \; e^{\frac{-1}{n}} \cdot e^{\frac{-2}{n}} \cdot e^{\frac{-3}{n}} \cdot \ldots \cdot e^{\frac{-(p-1)}{n}}$$

$$P(no\ collision) \; \approx \; e^{\frac{-(1 + 2 + 3 + \ldots + p - 1)}{n}}$$

Note, however, that:

$$1 + 2 + 3 + \ldots + p - 1 \; = \; \frac{p \cdot (p - 1)}{2}$$

Therefore, the probability that no *collision* occurs if there are p random elements may be rewritten as:

$$P(no\ collision) \; \approx \; e^{-p \cdot \frac{p-1}{2n}}$$

Having determined the probability that no *collision* occurs if there are p random elements, the probability that at least one *collision* occurs may be determined as:

$$P(\textit{at least one collision}) \approx 1 - P(\textit{no collision})$$
$$P(\textit{at least one collision}) \approx 1 - e^{-p \cdot \frac{p-1}{2n}}$$

If ε is used to denote the probability that at least one *collision* occurs, then:

$$\varepsilon \approx 1 - e^{-p \cdot \frac{p-1}{2n}}$$
$$e^{-p \cdot \frac{p-1}{2n}} \approx 1 - \varepsilon$$
$$\frac{-p \cdot (p-1)}{2n} \approx \ln(1 - \varepsilon)$$
$$p \cdot (p-1) \approx -2n \cdot \ln(1 - \varepsilon)$$
$$p^2 - p \approx 2n \cdot \ln(\frac{1}{1 - \varepsilon})$$

For large values of p, i.e. a large number of random elements to be tested to find a *collision*, p^2 is significantly larger than p. Therefore:

$$p^2 \approx 2n \cdot \ln(\frac{1}{1 - \varepsilon})$$
$$p \approx \sqrt{2n \cdot \ln(\frac{1}{1 - \varepsilon})}$$

Therefore, the probability that at least one *collision* occurs is $\sqrt{2n \cdot \ln(\frac{1}{1 - \varepsilon})}$. It is now possible to answer the question posed by the *Birthday Paradox*.

Example 10.4: How many people must be present so that there is a 50 % probability that at least two of the people have the same birth date if leap years are ignored such that February 29th is not a viable birth date, i.e. that $n = 365$?

A 50 % probability that at least two of the people have the same birth date results in $\varepsilon = 0.50$, i.e. that the probability that at least one *collision* occurs is 50 %. Therefore, the number of people that must be present so that there is a 50 % probability that at least two of the people have the same birth date is:

$$p \approx \sqrt{2n \cdot ln(\frac{1}{1 - \varepsilon})}$$

$$p \approx \sqrt{2 \cdot 365 \cdot ln(\frac{1}{1 - 0.50})}$$

$$p \approx \sqrt{730 \cdot ln(\frac{1}{0.50})}$$

$$p \approx \sqrt{730 \cdot ln(2)}$$

$$p \approx \sqrt{730 \cdot 0.693}$$

$$p \approx \sqrt{505.89}$$

$$p \approx 22.5$$

Therefore, if there are approximately twenty-three people present, there is a 50 % probability that at least two of the people have the same birth date.

The *Birthday Paradox* may now be extended to *Hash Functions* to determine how many random outputs must be generated such that the probability of a *collision* occurring is a specified percentage.

Example 10.5: How many random outputs are required so that there is a 50 % probability of a *collision* occurring if an 80-bit *Hash Function* is used?

A 50 % probability of a *collision* occurring results in $\varepsilon = 0.50$. Therefore, the number of random outputs that are required is:

$$p \approx \sqrt{2n \cdot ln(\frac{1}{1 - \varepsilon})}$$

$$p \approx \sqrt{2 \cdot 2^{80} \cdot ln(\frac{1}{1 - 0.50})}$$

$$p \approx \sqrt{2 \cdot 2^{80} \cdot ln(\frac{1}{0.50})}$$

$$p \approx \sqrt{2 \cdot 2^{80} \cdot ln(2)}$$

$$p \approx \sqrt{2 \cdot 2^{80} \cdot 0.693}$$

$$p \approx \sqrt{2^{80} \cdot 1.386}$$

$$p \approx \sqrt{2^{80}} \cdot \sqrt{1.386}$$

$$p \approx 2^{40} \cdot 1.177$$

Therefore, there is a 50 % probability of a *collision* occurring if there are approximately 2^{40} random *Hash Function* outputs for the given 80-bit *Hash Function*.

As a result of the *Birthday Paradox*, current *Hash Functions* have at least 256 output bits, resulting in the need for $p \approx 1.177 \cdot 2^{128}$ random outputs for there to be a 50 % probability of a *collision* occurring, i.e. equivalent security to a 128-bit block cipher.

10.2.2   Algorithms

Hash Functions may be classified as one of three types of algorithms — block cipher based, customized, and modular arithmetic based. Modular arithmetic based *Hash Functions* are extremely rare and frequently are not secure. As a result, this Section will focus on block cipher based and customized *Hash Functions*. Block cipher based *Hash Functions* construct *Hash Functions* using an existing block cipher as a core element. Customized *Hash Functions* are algorithms specifically designed for use as *Hash Functions*. Although many customized *Hash Functions* exist, focus will be placed on the set of related algorithms based on the *MD4 Hash Function* given their wide deployment, standardization, and progression through various levels of security.

10.2.2.1 Block Cipher Based Algorithms

Hash Functions based on block ciphers use the block cipher's encryption function in an iterative manner similar to *CBC* mode, as described in Section 5.1.3.2. The final output of the function is the hashed output for the entire message. Figure 10.3 shows an example of a *Hash Function* constructed from a block cipher.

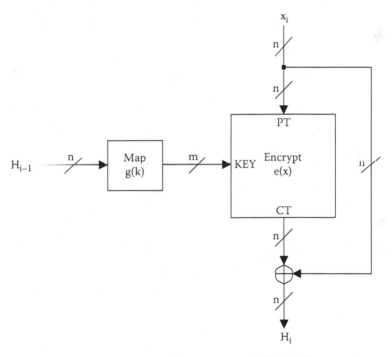

Figure 10.3: Block Cipher Based Hash Function

As shown in Figure 10.3, the plaintext x is encrypted using the encryption function, e, and the encrypted result is combined with the plaintext via the XOR operation to form the output of the *Hash Function* H_i. The previous *Hash Function* output, H_{i-1}, is used to generate the key for the block cipher. H_{i-1} is passed through a mapping function, g, to generate an appropriately sized key for the block cipher encryption function e. If the bit length of H_{i-1} matches the bit length of the key for the block cipher encryption function e, then g may be eliminated. The output of the *Hash Function* is the output produced after processing the final plaintext block.

The choice of block cipher used to create the *Hash Function* is critical towards ensuring the security of the *Hash Function*. *Hash Functions* based on block ciphers should only be constructed using block ciphers with block sizes greater than 128 bits. Ideally, the block cipher should have a block size of at least 256 bits, resulting in the need for $p \approx 1.177 \cdot 2^{128}$ random outputs for there to be a 50 % probability of a *collision* occurring, as detailed in Section 10.2.1.

The *Hash Function* constructed in Figure 10.3 is known to be secure and is represented by the equation $H_i = e_{g(H_{i-1})}(x_i) \oplus x_i$. It is desirable that the block cipher key changes during each iteration of the *Hash Functions* and the construct of Figure 10.3 achieves this goal. Other known secure constructs include $H_i = H_{i-1} \oplus e_{x_i}(H_{i-1})$, where the plaintext x_i is used as the key to the block cipher encryption function e, and $H_i = H_{i-1} \oplus e_{g(H_{i-1})}(x_i) \oplus x_i$, which is equivalent to the construct shown in Figure 10.3, with the value of the previous *Hash Function* output, H_{i-1}, also included in the combination of terms via the XOR operation to form the output of the *Hash Function* H_i.

10.2.2.2 MD4

An example of customized *Hash Functions* is the set of related algorithms based on the *Message Digest-4* (MD4) *Hash Function*. *MD4*, a 128-bit 3-round *Hash Function*, was originally developed by Ron Rivest in 1990 and operates on 512-bit input blocks [252].

MD4 begins by defining a number of constants [202]:

Initial Chaining Values

$$h_1 = 67452301_{16}$$
$$h_2 = EFCDAB89_{16}$$
$$h_3 = 98BADCFE_{16}$$
$$h_4 = 10325476_{16}$$

Additive Constants

$$y_j = \begin{cases} 00000000_{16} & 0 \le j \le 15 \\ 5A827999_{16} & 16 \le j \le 31 \\ 6ED9EBA1_{16} & 32 \le j \le 47 \end{cases}$$

Order for Accessing Source Words

$$z_0 \ldots z_{15} \;=\; 0, 1, 2, 3, 4, 5, 6, 7, 8, 9, 10, 11, 12, 13, 14, 15$$
$$z_{16} \ldots z_{31} \;=\; 0, 4, 8, 12, 1, 5, 9, 13, 2, 6, 10, 14, 3, 7, 11, 15$$
$$z_{32} \ldots z_{47} \;=\; 0, 8, 4, 12, 2, 10, 6, 14, 1, 9, 5, 13, 3, 11, 7, 15$$

Left Rotate Bit Positions

$$s_0 \ldots s_{15} \;=\; 3, 7, 11, 19, 3, 7, 11, 19, 3, 7, 11, 19, 3, 7, 11, 19$$
$$s_{16} \ldots s_{31} \;=\; 3, 5, 9, 13, 3, 5, 9, 13, 3, 5, 9, 13, 3, 5, 9, 13$$
$$s_{32} \ldots s_{47} \;=\; 3, 9, 11, 15, 3, 9, 11, 15, 3, 9, 11, 15, 3, 9, 11, 15$$

Prior to passing the input x to *MD4*, it must be padded such that the total bit length is a multiple of 512. If the bit length of the input x is $b \;=\; \lceil log_2 x \rceil$, then padding is achieved via the following steps [202]:

1. Append a single bit, whose value is set to 1, to the input x.

2. Compute the smallest r such that $b + r \bmod 512 \;=\; 448$. Append $r - 1$ bits, whose values are set to 0, to the result of Step 1.

3. Compute the 64-bit value $b \bmod 2^{64}$ and append this value to the result of Step 2 using little-endian notation, i.e. the lower 32-bit word followed by the upper 32-bit word.

This process yields a string of length $b + r + 64$ which must be a multiple m of 512 bits and thus may be represented as $(16 \cdot m)$ 32-bit blocks. Therefore, the input to *MD4* may be represented as $x'_0, x'_1, x'_2, \ldots x'_{16m - 1}$, where each x'_i is a 32-bit block. Once the input x has been padded to form x', *MD4* completes its set-up phase by establishing the initial values for working variables [202]:

1. $H_1 \ = \ h_1, \ H_2 \ = \ h_2, \ H_3 \ = \ h_3, \ H_4 \ = \ h_4$

2. For $i \ = \ 0 \, To \, m \, - \, 1$

   (a) For $j \ = \ 0 \, To \, 15$

      i. $Temp[j] \ = \ x'_{16i \, + \, j}$

3. $A \ = \ H_1, \ B \ = \ H_2, \ C \ = \ H_3, \ D \ = \ H_4$

MD4 processes the input data via three rounds that are each executed sixteen times. Each round employs a different function, and these functions are defined as [202]:

$$f(u, \ v, \ w) \ = \ (u \cdot v) \ + \ (\overline{u} \cdot w)$$
$$g(u, \ v, \ w) \ = \ (u \cdot v) \ + \ (u \cdot w) \ + \ (v \cdot w)$$
$$h(u, \ v, \ w) \ = \ u \oplus v \oplus w$$

where $\cdot$ represents a bit-wise AND, $+$ represents a bit-wise OR, $\oplus$ represents bit-wise XOR, and $\overline{u}$ represents the logical complement of u. Based on these functions and the initialized working variables, *MD4* computes the hashed value of x' via the following pseudo-code [202]:

Round 1

1. For $j = 0$ *To* 15

    (a) $t = A + f(B, C, D) + Temp[z_j] + y_j$

    (b) $A = D, B = t \ll s_j, C = B, D = C$

Round 2

1. For $j = 16$ *To* 31

    (a) $t = A + g(B, C, D) + Temp[z_j] + y_j$

    (b) $A = D, B = t \ll s_j, C = B, D = C$

Round 3

1. For $j = 32$ *To* 47

    (a) $t = A + h(B, C, D) + Temp[z_j] + y_j$

    (b) $A = D, B = t \ll s_j, C = B, D = C$

where $\ll q$ represents a circular left rotation by q bit positions and $+$ represents 32-bit addition. Following the completion of the third round, a final update occurs [202]:

$$H_1 = H_1 + A$$
$$H_2 = H_2 + B$$

$$H_3 = H_3 + C$$

$$H_4 = H_4 + D$$

After this update, the hashed value of x' is denoted as $H_1 \parallel H_2 \parallel H_3 \parallel H_4$, where $\parallel$ represents concatenation and each H_i is represented in little-endian notation.

Because *MD4* employs 32-bit Boolean and arithmetic operations, high speed implementations of the *Hash Function* are easily achieved in both software and hardware. Moreover, the use of little-endian notation results in *MD4* mapping extremely well to Intel microprocessors, which typically employ little-endian memory models for data storage [275]. In terms of security, collisions have been found after 2^{20} computations during the compression portion of *MD4*, i.e. the round functions, and thus *MD4* is no longer considered to be *collision resistant* [202].

10.2.2.3   MD5

In response to proposed attacks against *MD4* [29, 64], *MD4* was strengthened by Ron Rivest to remove symmetry and increase the *avalanche effect* inherent in the *Hash Function* [275], resulting in the *MD5* algorithm. *MD5* is a 128-bit 4-round *Hash Function* that processes 512-bit input blocks [253].

MD5 follows the same model of *MD4*. However, *MD5* processes the input data via four rounds as opposed to the three rounds used by *MD4*. *MD5* begins by defining a number of constants. Although the *Initial Chaining Values* remain the same as those of *MD4*, the *Additive Constants, Order for Accessing Source Words*, and *Left Rotate Bit Positions* have all been strengthened in *MD5* [202]:

Initial Chaining Values

$$h_1 = 67452301_{16}$$
$$h_2 = EFCDAB89_{16}$$
$$h_3 = 98BADCFE_{16}$$
$$h_4 = 10325476_{16}$$

Additive Constants

$$y_j = |\, sin(j + 1)\, |\; ;\; 0 \leq j \leq 63$$

where $|\, q\, |$ denotes the absolute value of q and j is an angle in radians. Note that the number of *Additive Constants* has been expanded from 48 to 64 to account for the additional round present in *MD5*.

Order for Accessing Source Words

$$
\begin{array}{rcl}
z_0 \ldots z_{15} & = & 0,\ 1,\ 2,\ 3,\ 4,\ 5,\ 6,\ 7,\ 8,\ 9,\ 10,\ 11,\ 12,\ 13,\ 14,\ 15 \\
z_{16} \ldots z_{31} & = & 1,\ 6,\ 11,\ 0,\ 5,\ 10,\ 15,\ 4,\ 9,\ 14,\ 3,\ 8,\ 13,\ 2,\ 7,\ 12 \\
z_{32} \ldots z_{47} & = & 5,\ 8,\ 11,\ 14,\ 1,\ 4,\ 7,\ 10,\ 13,\ 0,\ 3,\ 6,\ 9,\ 12,\ 15,\ 2 \\
z_{48} \ldots z_{63} & = & 0,\ 7,\ 14,\ 5,\ 12,\ 3,\ 10,\ 1,\ 8,\ 15,\ 6,\ 13,\ 4,\ 11,\ 2,\ 9
\end{array}
$$

Note that the *Order for Accessing Source Words* for the second and third rounds in *MD5* have changed versus the *Order for Accessing Words* in *MD4*. Also note that the number of *Word Access Orders* has been expanded from 48 to 64 to account for the additional round present in *MD5*.

Left Rotate Bit Positions

$$
\begin{array}{rcl}
s_0 \ldots s_{15} & = & 7,\ 12,\ 17,\ 22,\ 7,\ 12,\ 17,\ 22,\ 7,\ 12,\ 17,\ 22,\ 7,\ 12,\ 17,\ 22 \\
s_{16} \ldots s_{31} & = & 5,\ 9,\ 14,\ 20,\ 5,\ 9,\ 14,\ 20,\ 5,\ 9,\ 14,\ 20,\ 5,\ 9,\ 14,\ 20 \\
s_{32} \ldots s_{47} & = & 4,\ 11,\ 16,\ 23,\ 4,\ 11,\ 16,\ 23,\ 4,\ 11,\ 16,\ 23,\ 4,\ 11,\ 16,\ 23 \\
s_{48} \ldots s_{63} & = & 6,\ 10,\ 15,\ 21,\ 6,\ 10,\ 15,\ 21,\ 6,\ 10,\ 15,\ 21,\ 6,\ 10,\ 15,\ 21
\end{array}
$$

Note that the *Left Rotate Bit Positions* for all rounds in *MD5* have changed versus the *Left Rotate Bit Positions* for all rounds in *MD4*. Also note that the number of *Left Rotate Bit Positions* has been expanded from 48 to 64 to account for the additional round present in *MD5*.

Prior to passing the input x to *MD5*, it must be padded such that the total bit length is a multiple of 512. If the bit length of the input x is $b = \lceil log_2 x \rceil$, then padding is achieved via the following steps [202]:

1. Append a single bit, whose value is set to 1, to the input x.

2. Compute the smallest r such that $b + r \bmod 512 = 448$. Append $r - 1$ bits, whose values are set to 0, to the result of Step 1.

3. Compute the 64-bit value $b \bmod 2^{64}$ and append this value to the result of Step 2 using little-endian notation, i.e. the lower 32-bit word followed by the upper 32-bit word.

This process yields a string of length $b + r + 64$ which must be a multiple m of 512 bits and thus may be represented as $16 \cdot m$ 32-bit blocks. Therefore, the input to *MD5* may be represented as x'_0, x'_1, x'_2, ... x'_{16m-1}, where each x'_i is a 32-bit block. Once the input x has been padded to form x', *MD5* completes its set-up phase by establishing the initial values for working variables [202]:

1. $H_1 = h_1$, $H_2 = h_2$, $H_3 = h_3$, $H_4 = h_4$

2. For $i = 0 \, To \, m - 1$

   (a) For $j = 0 \, To \, 15$

      i. $Temp[j] = x'_{16i + j}$

3. $A = H_1$, $B = H_2$, $C = H_3$, $D = H_4$

MD5 processes the input data via four rounds that are each executed sixteen times. Note that *MD5* uses an additional fourth round as opposed to the three rounds used by *MD4*. Each of the *MD5* rounds employs a different function, and these functions are defined as [202]:

$$f(u,\ v,\ w)\ =\ (u\ \cdot\ v)\ +\ (\overline{u}\ \cdot\ w)$$

$$g(u,\ v,\ w)\ =\ (u\ \cdot\ w)\ +\ (v\ \cdot\ \overline{w})$$

$$h(u,\ v,\ w)\ =\ u\ \oplus\ v\ \oplus\ w$$

$$k(u,\ v,\ w)\ =\ v\ \oplus\ (u\ +\ \overline{w})$$

where $\cdot$ represents a bit-wise AND, $+$ represents a bit-wise OR, $\oplus$ represents bit-wise XOR, and $\overline{u}$ represents the logical complement of u. Note that the function $g(u,\ v,\ w)$ used in the second round of $MD5$ has been changed versus its original definition in $MD4$. Also note that the new function $k(u,\ v,\ w)$ has been defined for use in the fourth round of $MD5$. Based on these functions and the initialized working variables, $MD5$ computes the hashed value of x' via the following pseudo-code [202]:

Round 1

1. For $j\ =\ 0\ To\ 15$

    (a) $t\ =\ A\ +\ f(B,\ C,\ D)\ +\ Temp[z_j]\ +\ y_j$

    (b) $A\ =\ D,\ B\ =\ B\ +\ (t\ \ll\ s_j),\ C\ =\ B,\ D\ =\ C$

Note that the update of the working variable B now includes the addition of the output from the previous iteration. This change is present in each of the $MD5$ rounds.

Round 2

1. For $j = 16$ *To* 31

   (a) $t = A + g(B, C, D) + Temp[z_j] + y_j$

   (b) $A = D, B = B + (t \ll s_j), C = B, D = C$

Round 3

1. For $j = 32$ *To* 47

   (a) $t = A + h(B, C, D) + Temp[z_j] + y_j$

   (b) $A = D, B = B + (t \ll s_j), C = B, D = C$

Round 4

1. For $j = 48$ *To* 63

   (a) $t = A + k(B, C, D) + Temp[z_j] + y_j$

   (b) $A = D, B = B + (t \ll s_j), C = B, D = C$

where $\ll q$ represents a circular left rotation by q bit positions and $+$ represents 32-bit addition. Following the completion of the fourth round, a final update occurs [202]:

$$H_1 = H_1 + A$$
$$H_2 = H_2 + B$$

$$H_3 = H_3 + C$$

$$H_4 = H_4 + D$$

After this update, the hashed value of x' is denoted as $H_1 \parallel H_2 \parallel H_3 \parallel H_4$, where $\parallel$ represents concatenation and each H_i is represented in little-endian notation.

As was the case with *MD4*, because *MD5* employs 32-bit Boolean and arithmetic operations, high speed implementations of the *Hash Function* are easily achieved in both software and hardware. Although the computation of $y_j = | sin(j + 1) |$ is complex, this operation is only performed once to yield a set of constants and does not contribute to the operating speed of the compression portion of *MD5*. The use of little-endian notation results in *MD5* mapping extremely well to Intel microprocessors, as was the case for *MD4*. In terms of security, collisions have been found during the compression portion of *MD5* [65, 255, 256], i.e. the round functions, and thus *MD5* is no longer considered to be *collision resistant* [202, 275].

10.2.2.4   Secure Hash Algorithm

The *Secure Hash Algorithm* (SHA-1) is a 160-bit *Hash Function* that processes 512-bit input blocks. As first discussed in Section 10.1.1, the *DSS* specifies the use of the *SHA-1 Hash Function*, which in turn is specified in the *Secure Hash Standard* (SHS). The *SHS* was developed by NIST and is specified in FIPS Standard

180-2 [224]. *SHA-1* is used to generate a message digest for use in computing and verifying *Digital Signatures*.

SHA-1 follows the same model of *MD4*. However, *SHA-1* processes the input data via four rounds as opposed to the three rounds used by *MD4*. *SHA-1* begins by defining a number of constants. To match the bit width of *SHA-1*, a fifth constant is added to the *Initial Chaining Values* and new *Additive Constants* are defined. Also, unlike *MD4*, *SHA-1* does not require constants for the *Order for Accessing Source Words* and the *Left Rotate Bit Positions* [202]:

Initial Chaining Values

$$h_1 = 67452301_{16}$$
$$h_2 = EFCDAB89_{16}$$
$$h_3 = 98BADCFE_{16}$$
$$h_4 = 10325476_{16}$$
$$h_5 = C3D2E1F0_{16}$$

Additive Constants

$$y_1 = 5A827999_{16}$$
$$y_2 = 6ED9EBA1_{16}$$
$$y_3 = 8F1BBCDC_{16}$$
$$y_4 = CA62C1D6_{16}$$

Note that the number of *Additive Constants* has been reduced to four, one for each round of *SHA-1*.

Prior to passing the input x to *SHA-1*, it must be padded such that the total bit length is a multiple of 512. If the bit length of the input x is $b = \lceil log_2 x \rceil$, then padding is achieved via the following steps [202]:

1. Append a single bit, whose value is set to 1, to the input x.

2. Compute the smallest r such that $b + r \bmod 512 = 448$. Append $r - 1$ bits, whose values are set to 0, to the result of Step 1.

3. Compute the 64-bit value $b \bmod 2^{64}$ and append this value to the result of Step 2 using big-endian notation, i.e. the upper 32 bit word followed by the lower 32-bit word.

This process yields a string of length $b + r + 64$ which must be a multiple m of 512 bits and thus may be represented as $16 \cdot m$ 32-bit blocks. Therefore, the input to *SHA-1* may be represented as $x'_0,\ x'_1,\ x'_2,\ \ldots\ x'_{16m - 1}$, where each x'_i is a 32-bit block. Note that the byte ordering for the parameter b in Step 3 is reversed versus the byte ordering of the parameter b in *MD4*. Once the input x has been padded to form x', *SHA-1* completes its set-up phase by establishing the initial values for working variables [202]:

1. $H_1 = h_1,\ H_2 = h_2,\ H_3 = h_3,\ H_4 = h_4,\ H_5 = h_5$

2. For $i = 0\ To\ m - 1$

(a) For $j = 0$ To 15

   i. $Temp[j] = x'_{16i + j}$

3. $A = H_1, B = H_2, C = H_3, D = H_4, E = H_5$

4. For $j = 16$ To 79

   (a) $Temp[j] = (Temp[j - 3] \oplus Temp[j - 8] \oplus Temp[j - 14] \oplus Temp[j - 16]) \ll 1$

SHA-1 processes the input data via four rounds that are each executed sixteen times. Note that *SHA-1* uses an additional fourth round as opposed to the three rounds used by *MD4*. Each of the *SHA-1* rounds employs one of three functions, and these functions are the same functions used in *MD4*:

$$f(u,\ v,\ w) = (u \cdot v) \oplus (\overline{u} \cdot w)$$
$$g(u,\ v,\ w) = (u \cdot v) \oplus (u \cdot w) \oplus (v \cdot w)$$
$$h(u,\ v,\ w) = u \oplus v \oplus w$$

where $\cdot$ represents a bit-wise AND, $\oplus$ represents bit-wise XOR, and $\overline{u}$ represents the logical complement of u. Based on these functions and the initialized working variables, *SHA-1* computes the hashed value of x' via the following pseudo-code [202]:

Round 1

1. For $j = 0$ *To* 19

    (a) $t = (A \ll 5) + f(B, C, D) + Temp[z_j] + y_1 + E$

    (b) $A = t, B = A, C = B \ll 30, D = C, E = D$

Round 2

1. For $j = 20$ *To* 39

    (a) $t = (A \ll 5) + h(B, C, D) + Temp[z_j] + y_2 + E$

    (b) $A = t, B = A, C = B \ll 30, D = C, E = D$

Round 3

1. For $j = 40$ *To* 59

    (a) $t = (A \ll 5) + g(B, C, D) + Temp[z_j] + y_3 + E$

    (b) $A = t, B = A, C = B \ll 30, D = C, E = D$

Round 4

1. For $j = 60$ *To* 79

    (a) $t = (A \ll 5) + h(B, C, D) + Temp[z_j] + y_4 + E$

    (b) $A = t, B = A, C = B \ll 30, D = C, E = D$

where $\ll q$ represents a circular left rotation by q bit positions and $+$ represents 32-bit addition. Following the completion of the fourth round, a final update occurs [202]:

$$H_1 = H_1 + A$$
$$H_2 = H_2 + B$$
$$H_3 = H_3 + C$$
$$H_4 = H_4 + D$$
$$H_5 = H_5 + E$$

After this update, the hashed value of x' is denoted as $H_1 \parallel H_2 \parallel H_3 \parallel H_4 \parallel H_5$, where $\parallel$ represents concatenation and each H_i is represented in big-endian notation, i.e. the upper byte followed by the lower byte.

As was the case with *MD4*, because *SHA-1* employs 32-bit Boolean and arithmetic operations, high speed implementations of the *Hash Function* are easily achieved in both software and hardware. In terms of security, *SHA-1*, like *MD5*, removes symmetry by changing the access order for the second and third rounds. *SHA-1* also increases the *avalanche effect* inherent in the *Hash Function* through the addition of the output from the previous iteration that is reflected in the update of the A working variable for each round. Moreover, because the *SHA-1* rounds add in the fifth working variable E instead of any of the working variables B, C, or

D (used in the functions $f(u,\ v,\ w)$, $g(u,\ v,\ w)$, and $h(u,\ v,\ w)$), the attack against *MD4* proposed in [64] cannot be applied to *SHA-1*. Finally, because of the increased bit length of *SHA-1* versus the bit lengths of *MD4* and *MD5* (160 bits versus 128 bits), *SHA-1* is more resistant to exhaustive *collision* searches that attempt to take advantage of the *Birthday Paradox* [275]. However, in 2005, collisions were found in *SHA-1* after 2^{69} computations and thus *SHA-1* is no longer considered to be *collision resistant* [324]. As a result, other options were made available via the August 2002 change notice to the *SHS*. As part of FIPS Standard 180-2 [224], *SHA-256,*, *SHA-384*, and *SHA-512* are specified in addition to *SHA-1*. The different properties associated with each of these *Hash Functions* are detailed in Table 10.1 from [224].

Hash Algorithm	Message Size	Block Size	Word Size	Digest Size	Security Size
SHA-1	$< 2^{64}$	512	32	160	80
SHA-256	$< 2^{64}$	512	32	256	128
SHA-384	$< 2^{128}$	1,024	64	384	192
SHA-512	$< 2^{128}$	1,024	64	512	256

Table 10.1: Secure Hash Algorithm Properties [224]

Note that all sizes are in bits and the *Security Size* is based on taking advantage of the *Birthday Paradox*, resulting in the complexity of a *collision* search being approximately equivalent to the square root of the *Digest Size* in bits. However, FIPS Standard 180-2 [224] was published prior to the attack published in 2005 [324] that reduces the *Security Size* of *SHA-1* to 2^{69} computations.

SHA-256 is a 256-bit *Hash Function* that processes 512-bit input blocks and is specified in FIPS Standard 180-2 [224]. *SHA-256* follows the same model of *SHA-1* and begins by defining a number of constants. To match the bit width of *SHA-256*, eight 32-bit constants are used as *Initial Chaining Values* and new 32-bit *Additive Constants* are defined [224]:

Initial Chaining Values

$$h_0 = 6A09E667_{16}$$

$$h_1 = BB67AE85_{16}$$

$$h_2 = 3C6EF372_{16}$$

$$h_3 = A54FF53A_{16}$$

$$h_4 = 510E527F_{16}$$

$$h_5 = 9B05688C_{16}$$

$$h_6 = 1F83D9AB_{16}$$

$$h_7 = 5BE0CD19_{16}$$

Additive	Constants
$y_0 = 428A2F98_{16}$	$y_1 = 71374491_{16}$
$y_2 = B5C0FBCF_{16}$	$y_3 = E9B5DBA5_{16}$
$y_4 = 3956C25B_{16}$	$y_5 = 59F111F1_{16}$
$y_6 = 923F82A4_{16}$	$y_7 = AB1C5ED5_{16}$
$y_8 = D807AA98_{16}$	$y_9 = 12835B01_{16}$
$y_{10} = 243185BE_{16}$	$y_{11} = 550C7DC3_{16}$
$y_{12} = 72BE5D74_{16}$	$y_{13} = 80DEB1FE_{16}$
$y_{14} = 9BDC06A7_{16}$	$y_{15} = C19BF174_{16}$
$y_{16} = E49B69C1_{16}$	$y_{17} = EFBE4786_{16}$
$y_{18} = 0FC19DC6_{16}$	$y_{19} = 240CA1CC_{16}$
$y_{20} = 2DE92C6F_{16}$	$y_{21} = 4A7484AA_{16}$
$y_{22} = 5CB0A9DC_{16}$	$y_{23} = 76F988DA_{16}$
$y_{24} = 983E5152_{16}$	$y_{25} = A831C66D_{16}$
$y_{26} = B00327C8_{16}$	$y_{27} = BF597FC7_{16}$
$y_{28} = C6E00BF3_{16}$	$y_{29} = D5A79147_{16}$
$y_{30} = 06CA6351_{16}$	$y_{31} = 14292967_{16}$
$y_{32} = 27B70A85_{16}$	$y_{33} = 2E1B2138_{16}$
$y_{34} = 4D2C6DFC_{16}$	$y_{35} = 53380D13_{16}$
$y_{36} = 650A7354_{16}$	$y_{37} = 766A0ABB_{16}$
$y_{38} = 81C2C92E_{16}$	$y_{39} = 92722C85_{16}$
$y_{40} = A2BFE8A1_{16}$	$y_{41} = A81A664B_{16}$
$y_{42} = C24B8B70_{16}$	$y_{43} = C76C51A3_{16}$
$y_{44} = D192E819_{16}$	$y_{45} = D6990624_{16}$
$y_{46} = F40E3585_{16}$	$y_{47} = 106AA070_{16}$
$y_{48} = 19A4C116_{16}$	$y_{49} = 1E376C08_{16}$
$y_{50} = 2748774C_{16}$	$y_{51} = 34B0BCB5_{16}$
$y_{52} = 391C0CB3_{16}$	$y_{53} = 4ED8AA4A_{16}$
$y_{54} = 5B9CCA4F_{16}$	$y_{55} = 682E6FF3_{16}$
$y_{56} = 748F82EE_{16}$	$y_{57} = 78A5636F_{16}$
$y_{58} = 84C87814_{16}$	$y_{59} = 8CC70208_{16}$
$y_{60} = 90BEFFFA_{16}$	$y_{61} = A4506CEB_{16}$
$y_{62} = BEF9A3F7_{16}$	$y_{63} = C67178F2_{16}$

Prior to passing the input x to *SHA-256*, it must be padded such that the total bit length is a multiple of 512. If the bit length of the input x is $b = \lceil log_2 x \rceil$, then padding is achieved via the following steps [224]:

1. Append a single bit, whose value is set to 1, to the input x.

2. Compute the smallest r such that $b + r \bmod 512 = 448$. Append $r - 1$ bits, whose values are set to 0, to the result of Step 1.

3. Compute the 64-bit value $b \bmod 2^{64}$ and append this value to the result of Step 2 using big-endian notation, i.e. the upper 32-bit word followed by the lower 32-bit word.

This process yields a string of length $b + r + 64$ which must be a multiple m of 512 bits and thus may be represented as $16 \cdot m$ 32-bit blocks. Therefore, the input to $SHA\text{-}256$ may be represented as $x'_0, x'_1, x'_2, \ldots x'_{16m-1}$, where each x'_i is a 32-bit block. Note that the byte ordering for the parameter b in Step 3 is reversed versus the byte ordering of the parameter b in $MD4$. Once the input x has been padded to form x', $SHA\text{-}256$ completes its set-up phase by establishing the initial values for working variables [224]:

1. $H_0 = h_0$, $H_1 = h_1$, $H_2 = h_2$, $H_3 = h_3$, $H_4 = h_4$, $H_5 = h_5$, $H_6 = h_6$, $H_7 = h_7$

2. For $i = 0\ To\ m - 1$

   (a) For $j = 0\ To\ 15$

      i. $Temp[j] = x'_{16i + j}$

3. $A = H_0$, $B = H_1$, $C = H_2$, $D = H_3$, $E = H_4$, $F = H_5$, $G = H_6$, $H = H_7$

4. For $j = 16 \; To \; 63$

(a) $Temp[j] = \sigma_1(Temp[j - 2]) + (Temp[j - 7]) + \sigma_0(Temp[j - 15]) + (Temp[j - 16)])$

where the functions $\sigma_0(q)$ and $\sigma_1(q)$ are defined as:

$$\sigma_0(u) = (u \gg 7) \oplus (u \gg 18) \oplus (u \ggg 3)$$
$$\sigma_1(u) = (u \gg 17) \oplus (u \gg 19) \oplus (u \ggg 10)$$

where $\oplus$ represents bit-wise XOR, $\gg q$ represents a circular right rotation by q bit positions, and $\ggg q$ represents a right shift by q bit positions. As opposed to *SHA-1* and *MD4*, which employ three functions to process the input data, *SHA-256* processes the input data via 64 iterations that employ four functions:

$$\Sigma_0(u) = (u \gg 2) \oplus (u \gg 13) \oplus (u \gg 22)$$
$$\Sigma_1(u) = (u \gg 6) \oplus (u \gg 11) \oplus (u \gg 25)$$
$$f(u, v, w) = (u \cdot v) \oplus (\overline{u} \cdot w)$$
$$g(u, v, w) = (u \cdot v) \oplus (u \cdot w) \oplus (v \cdot w)$$

where $\cdot$ represents a bit-wise AND, $\oplus$ represents bit-wise XOR, $\gg q$ represents a circular right rotation by q bit positions, and $\overline{u}$ represents the logical complement of u. Based on these functions and the initialized working variables, *SHA-256* computes the hashed value of x' via the following pseudo-code [224]:

1. For $j = 0$ *To* 63

   (a) $t_1 = H + \Sigma_1(E) + f(E, F, G) + y_j + Temp[j]$

   (b) $t_2 = \Sigma_0(A) + g(A, B, C)$

   (c) $A = t_1 + t_2, B = A, C = B, D = C, E = D + t_1,$
   $F = E, G = F, H = G$

Following the completion of the 64 iterations, a final update occurs [224]:

$$
\begin{aligned}
H_0 &= H_0 + A \\
H_1 &= H_1 + B \\
H_2 &= H_2 + C \\
H_3 &= H_3 + D \\
H_4 &= H_4 + E \\
H_5 &= H_5 + F \\
H_6 &= H_6 + G \\
H_7 &= H_7 + H
\end{aligned}
$$

After this update, the hashed value of x' is denoted as:

$$
h(x) = H_0 \parallel H_1 \parallel H_2 \parallel H_3 \parallel H_4 \parallel H_5 \parallel H_6 \parallel H_7
$$

where $\parallel$ represents concatenation and each H_i is represented in big-endian notation, i.e. the upper byte followed by the lower byte.

As was the case with *SHA-1*, because *SHA-256* employs 32-bit Boolean and arithmetic operations, high speed implementations of the *Hash Function* are easily achieved in both software and hardware. In terms of security, *SHA-256* increases the *avalanche effect* inherent in the *Hash Function* through the addition of the output from the previous iteration that is reflected in the update of the A and E working variables. Moreover, because *SHA-256* adds in the working variable D instead of any of the working variables used in the functions $f(u,\ v,\ w)$ and $g(u,\ v,\ w)$, when updating the working variable E, the attack against *MD4* proposed in [64] cannot be applied to *SHA-256*. Finally, because of the increased bit length of *SHA-256* versus the bit length of *SHA-1* (256 bits versus 160 bits), *SHA-256* is more resistant to exhaustive *collision* searches that attempt to take advantage of the *Birthday Paradox* [275].

SHA-512 is a 512-bit *Hash Function* that processes 1024-bit input blocks and is specified in FIPS Standard 180-2 [224]. *SHA-512* follows the same model of *SHA-256* and begins by defining a number of constants. To match the bit width of *SHA-512*, eight 64-bit constants are used as *Initial Chaining Values* and new 64-bit *Additive Constants* are defined [224]:

Initial Chaining Values

$$h_0 = 6A09E667F3BCC908_{16}$$

$$h_1 = BB67AE8584CAA73B_{16}$$

$$h_2 = 3C6EF372FE94F82B_{16}$$

$$h_3 = A54FF53A5F1D36F1_{16}$$

$$h_4 = 510E527FADE682D1_{16}$$

$$h_5 = 9B05688C2B3E6C1F_{16}$$

$$h_6 = 1F83D9ABFB41BD6B_{16}$$

$$h_7 = 5BE0CD19137E2179_{16}$$

Additive	Constants
$y_0 = 428A2F98D728AE22_{16}$	$y_1 = 7137449123EF65CD_{16}$
$y_2 = B5C0FBCFEC4D3B2F_{16}$	$y_3 = E9B5DBA58189DBBC_{16}$
$y_4 = 3956C25BF348B538_{16}$	$y_5 = 59F111F1B605D019_{16}$
$y_6 = 923F82A4AF194F9B_{16}$	$y_7 = AB1C5ED5DA6D8118_{16}$
$y_8 = D807AA98A3030242_{16}$	$y_9 = 12835B0145706FBE_{16}$
$y_{10} = 243185BE4EE4B28C_{16}$	$y_{11} = 550C7DC3D5FFB4E2_{16}$
$y_{12} = 72BE5D74F27B896F_{16}$	$y_{13} = 80DEB1FE3B1696B1_{16}$
$y_{14} = 9BDC06A725C71235_{16}$	$y_{15} = C19BF174CF692694_{16}$
$y_{16} = E49B69C19EF14AD2_{16}$	$y_{17} = EFBE4786384F25E3_{16}$
$y_{18} = 0FC19DC68B8CD5B5_{16}$	$y_{19} = 240CA1CC77AC9C65_{16}$
$y_{20} = 2DE92C6F592B0275_{16}$	$y_{21} = 4A7484AA6EA6E483_{16}$
$y_{22} = 5CB0A9DCBD41FBD4_{16}$	$y_{23} = 76F988DA831153B5_{16}$
$y_{24} = 983E5152EE66DFAB_{16}$	$y_{25} = A831C66D2DB43210_{16}$
$y_{26} = B00327C898FB213F_{16}$	$y_{27} = BF597FC7BEEF0EE4_{16}$
$y_{28} = C6E00BF33DA88FC2_{16}$	$y_{29} = D5A79147930AA725_{16}$
$y_{30} = 06CA6351E003826F_{16}$	$y_{31} = 142929670A0E6E70_{16}$
$y_{32} = 27B70A8546D22FFC_{16}$	$y_{33} = 2E1B21385C26C926_{16}$
$y_{34} = 4D2C6DFC5AC42AED_{16}$	$y_{35} = 53380D139D95B3DF_{16}$
$y_{36} = 650A73548BAF63DE_{16}$	$y_{37} = 766A0ABB3C77B2A8_{16}$
$y_{38} = 81C2C92E47EDAEE6_{16}$	$y_{39} = 92722C851482353B_{16}$
$y_{40} = A2BFE8A14CF10364_{16}$	$y_{41} = A81A664BBC423001_{16}$
$y_{42} = C24B8B70D0F89791_{16}$	$y_{43} = C76C51A30654BE30_{16}$
$y_{44} = D192E819D6EF5218_{16}$	$y_{45} = D69906245565A910_{16}$
$y_{46} = F40E35855771202A_{16}$	$y_{47} = 106AA07032BBD1B8_{16}$
$y_{48} = 19A4C116B8D2D0C8_{16}$	$y_{49} = 1E376C085141AB53_{16}$
$y_{50} = 2748774CDF8EEB99_{16}$	$y_{51} = 34B0BCB5E19B48A8_{16}$
$y_{52} = 391C0CB3C5C95A63_{16}$	$y_{53} = 4ED8AA4AE3418ACB_{16}$
$y_{54} = 5B9CCA4F7763E373_{16}$	$y_{55} = 682E6FF3D6B2B8A3_{16}$
$y_{56} = 748F82EE5DEFB2FC_{16}$	$y_{57} = 78A5636F43172F60_{16}$
$y_{58} = 84C87814A1F0AB72_{16}$	$y_{59} = 8CC702081A6439EC_{16}$
$y_{60} = 90BEFFFA23631E28_{16}$	$y_{61} = A4506CEBDE82BDE9_{16}$
$y_{62} = BEF9A3F7B2C67915_{16}$	$y_{63} = C67178F2E372532B_{16}$
$y_{64} = CA273ECEEA26619C_{16}$	$y_{65} = D186B8C721C0C207_{16}$
$y_{66} = EADA7DD6CDE0EB1E_{16}$	$y_{67} = F57D4F7FEE6ED178_{16}$
$y_{68} = 06F067AA72176FBA_{16}$	$y_{69} = 0A637DC5A2C898A6_{16}$
$y_{70} = 113F9804BEF90DAE_{16}$	$y_{71} = 1B710B35131C471B_{16}$
$y_{72} = 28DB77F523047D84_{16}$	$y_{73} = 32CAAB7B40C72493_{16}$
$y_{74} = 3C9EBE0A15C9BEBC_{16}$	$y_{75} = 431D67C49C100D4C_{16}$
$y_{76} = 4CC5D4BECB3E42B6_{16}$	$y_{77} = 597F299CFC657E2A_{16}$
$y_{78} = 5FCB6FAB3AD6FAEC_{16}$	$y_{79} = 6C44198C4A475817_{16}$

Prior to passing the input x to *SHA-512*, it must be padded such that the total bit length is a multiple of 1,024. If the bit length of the input x is $b = \lceil log_2 x \rceil$, then padding is achieved via the following steps [224]:

1. Append a single bit, whose value is set to 1, to the input x.

2. Compute the smallest r such that $b + r \bmod 1,024 = 896$. Append $r - 1$ bits, whose values are set to 0, to the result of Step 1.

3. Compute the 128-bit value $b \bmod 2^{128}$ and append this value to the result of Step 2 using big-endian notation, i.e. the upper 64-bit word followed by the lower 64-bit word.

This process yields a string of length $b + r + 128$ which must be a multiple m of 1,024 bits and thus may be represented as $16 \cdot m$ 64-bit blocks. Therefore, the input to *SHA-512* may be represented as x'_0, x'_1, x'_2, ... x'_{16m-1}, where each x'_i is a 64-bit block. Note that the byte ordering for the parameter b in Step 3 is reversed versus the byte ordering of the parameter b in *MD4*. Once the input x has been padded to form x', *SHA-512* completes its set-up phase by establishing the initial values for working variables [224]:

1. $H_0 = h_0, H_1 = h_1, H_2 = h_2, H_3 = h_3, H_4 = h_4,$ $H_5 = h_5, H_6 = h_6, H_7 = h_7$

2. For $i = 0\, To\, m - 1$

   (a) For $j = 0\, To\, 15$

i. $Temp[j] = x'_{16i + j}$

3. $A = H_0, B = H_1, C = H_2, D = H_3, E = H_4, F = H_5,$ $G = H_6, H = H_7$

4. For $j = 16\ To\ 79$

(a) $Temp[j] = \sigma_1(Temp[j - 2]) + (Temp[j - 7]) + \sigma_0(Temp[j - 15]) + (Temp[j - 16)])$

where the functions $\sigma_0(q)$ and $\sigma_1(q)$ are defined as:

$$\sigma_0(u) = (u \gg 1) \oplus (u \gg 8) \oplus (u >>> 7)$$
$$\sigma_1(u) = (u \gg 19) \oplus (u \gg 61) \oplus (u >>> 6)$$

where $\oplus$ represents bit-wise XOR, $\gg q$ represents a circular right rotation by q bit positions, and $>>> q$ represents a right shift by q bit positions. As opposed to SHA-256, which processes the input data via 64 iterations, SHA-512 processes the input data via 80 iterations that employ four functions:

$$\Sigma_0(u) = (u \gg 28) \oplus (u \gg 34) \oplus (u \gg 39)$$
$$\Sigma_1(u) = (u \gg 14) \oplus (u \gg 18) \oplus (u \gg 41)$$
$$f(u, v, w) = (u \cdot v) \oplus (\bar{u} \cdot w)$$
$$g(u, v, w) = (u \cdot v) \oplus (u \cdot w) \oplus (v \cdot w)$$

where $\cdot$ represents a bit-wise AND, $\oplus$ represents bit-wise XOR, $\gg q$ represents a circular right rotation by q bit positions, and $\bar{u}$ represents the logical complement of u. Based on these functions and the initialized working variables, *SHA-512* computes the hashed value of x' via the following pseudo-code [224]:

1. For $j = 0 \, To \, 79$

    (a) $t_1 = H + \Sigma_1(E) + f(E, F, G) + y_j + Temp[j]$

    (b) $t_2 = \Sigma_0(A) + g(A, B, C)$

    (c) $A = t_1 + t_2, B = A, C = B, D = C, E = D + t_1,$
    $F = E, G = F, H = G$

Following the completion of the 80 iterations, a final update occurs [224]:

$$H_0 = H_0 + A$$
$$H_1 = H_1 + B$$
$$H_2 = H_2 + C$$
$$H_3 = H_3 + D$$
$$H_4 = H_4 + E$$
$$H_5 = H_5 + F$$
$$H_6 = H_6 + G$$
$$H_7 = H_7 + H$$

After this update, the hashed value of x' is denoted as:

$$h(x) \quad = \quad H_0 \parallel H_1 \parallel H_2 \parallel H_3 \parallel H_4 \parallel H_5 \parallel H_6 \parallel H_7$$

where $\parallel$ represents concatenation and each H_i is represented in big-endian notation, i.e. the upper byte followed by the lower byte.

As was the case with *SHA-256*, because *SHA-512* employs 64-bit Boolean and arithmetic operations, high speed implementations of the *Hash Function* are easily achieved in both software and hardware. In terms of security, *SHA-512* increases the *avalanche effect* inherent in the *Hash Function* through the addition of the output from the previous iteration that is reflected in the update of the A and E working variables. Moreover, because *SHA-512* adds in the working variable D instead of any of the working variables used in the functions $f(u, v, w)$ and $g(u, v, w)$, when updating the working variable E, the attack against *MD4* proposed in [64] cannot be applied to *SHA-512*. Finally, because of the increased bit length of *SHA-512* versus the bit length of *SHA-256* (512 bits versus 256 bits), *SHA-512* is more resistant to exhaustive *collision* searches that attempt to take advantage of the *Birthday Paradox* [275].

SHA-384 is a 384-bit *Hash Function* that processes 1024-bit input blocks and is specified in FIPS Standard 180-2 [224]. *SHA-384* follows the same model of *SHA-512* with two differences. The first difference is that *SHA-384* defines different *Initial Chaining Values* versus those of *SHA-512* [224]:

Initial Chaining Values

$$h_0 = CBBB9D5DC1059ED8_{16}$$

$$h_1 = 629A292A367CD507_{16}$$

$$h_2 = 9159015A3070DD17_{16}$$

$$h_3 = 152FECD8F70E5939_{16}$$

$$h_4 = 67332667FFC00B31_{16}$$

$$h_5 = 8EB44A8768581511_{16}$$

$$h_6 = DB0C2E0D64F98FA7_{16}$$

$$h_7 = 47B5481DBEFA4FA4_{16}$$

The second difference is that at the completion of processing the input data, the 384-bit hashed value of x' is denoted as $H_0 \parallel H_1 \parallel H_2 \parallel H_3 \parallel H_4 \parallel H_5$, where $\parallel$ represents concatenation and each H_i is represented in big-endian notation, i.e. the upper byte followed by the lower byte.

As was the case with *SHA-512*, because *SHA-384* employs 64-bit Boolean and arithmetic operations, high speed implementations of the *Hash Function* are easily achieved in both software and hardware. In terms of security, *SHA-384* increases the *avalanche effect* inherent in the *Hash Function* through the addition of the output from the previous iteration that is reflected in the update of the A and E working variables. Moreover, because *SHA-384* adds in the working variable D instead of any of the working variables used in the functions $f(u, v, w)$ and $g(u, v, w)$, when updating the working variable E, the attack against *MD4* proposed in [64] cannot be applied to *SHA-384*. Finally, because the internal bit length of *SHA-384* is the same as the bit length of *SHA-512* (512 bits), *SHA-384* exhibits the same resistance as *SHA-512* to exhaustive *collision* searches that attempt to take advantage of the *Birthday Paradox* [275]. However, because of the decreased bit length of the message digest output of *SHA-384* versus the message digest output of *SHA-512*, *SHA-384* is more susceptible to *Guessing* attacks.

10.2.2.5 RIPEMD-160

The *RIPEMD-160 Algorithm* was developed by Hans Dobbertin, Antoon Bosselaers, and Bart Preneel in 1996 [72]. *RIPEMD-160* is a 160-bit *Hash Function* that processes 512-bit input blocks. *RIPEMD-160* follows the same model of *MD4*. However, *RIPEMD-160* processes the input data via five rounds as opposed to the three rounds used by *MD4*. Moreover, *RIPEMD-160* maintains two compression functions, denoted as the *left line* and the *right line*, and processes each input block simultaneously through both compression functions before combining the outputs to form the final hashed output.

RIPEMD-160 begins by defining a number of constants. To match the bit width of *RIPEMD-160*, a fifth constant is added to the *Initial Chaining Values* of *MD4*. The three *MD4 Additive Constants* are used for the *left line* and two new constants are also defined for the *left line* along with five new constants for the *right line*. New constants are also defined for the *Order for Accessing Source Words* and the *Left Rotate Bit Positions* for both the *left line* and the *right line* [202]:

Initial Chaining Values

$$h_1 = 67452301_{16}$$
$$h_2 = EFCDAB89_{16}$$
$$h_3 = 98BADCFE_{16}$$
$$h_4 = 10325476_{16}$$
$$h_5 = C3D2E1F0_{16}$$

Additive Constants

$$y_{L_j} = \begin{cases} 00000000_{16} & 0 \le j \le 15 \\ 5A827999_{16} & 16 \le j \le 31 \\ 6ED9EBA1_{16} & 32 \le j \le 47 \\ 8F1BBCDC_{16} & 48 \le j \le 63 \\ A953FD4E_{16} & 64 \le j \le 79 \end{cases}$$

$$
y_{R_j} = \begin{cases} 50A28BE6_{16} & 0 \le j \le 15 \\ 5C4DD124_{16} & 16 \le j \le 31 \\ 6D703EF3_{16} & 32 \le j \le 47 \\ 7A6D76E9_{16} & 48 \le j \le 63 \\ 00000000_{16} & 64 \le j \le 79 \end{cases}
$$

Order for Accessing Source Words

$$
\begin{aligned}
z_{L_0} \cdots z_{L_{15}} &= 0,\ 1,\ 2,\ 3,\ 4,\ 5,\ 6,\ 7,\ 8,\ 9,\ 10,\ 11,\ 12,\ 13,\ 14,\ 15 \\
z_{L_{16}} \cdots z_{L_{31}} &= 7,\ 4,\ 13,\ 1,\ 10,\ 6,\ 15,\ 3,\ 12,\ 0,\ 9,\ 5,\ 2,\ 13,\ 11,\ 8 \\
z_{L_{32}} \cdots z_{L_{47}} &= 3,\ 10,\ 14,\ 4,\ 9,\ 15,\ 8,\ 1,\ 2,\ 7,\ 0,\ 6,\ 13,\ 11,\ 5,\ 12 \\
z_{L_{48}} \cdots z_{L_{63}} &= 1,\ 9,\ 11,\ 10,\ 0,\ 8,\ 12,\ 4,\ 13,\ 3,\ 7,\ 15,\ 14,\ 5,\ 6,\ 2 \\
z_{L_{64}} \cdots z_{L_{79}} &= 4,\ 0,\ 5,\ 9,\ 7,\ 12,\ 2,\ 10,\ 14,\ 1,\ 3,\ 8,\ 11,\ 6,\ 15,\ 13 \\
\\
z_{R_0} \cdots z_{R_{15}} &= 5\ 14,\ 7,\ 0,\ 9,\ 2,\ 11,\ 4,\ 13,\ 6,\ 15,\ 8,\ 1,\ 10,\ 3,\ 12 \\
z_{R_{16}} \cdots z_{R_{31}} &= 6,\ 11,\ 3,\ 7,\ 0,\ 13,\ 5,\ 10,\ 14,\ 15,\ 8,\ 12,\ 4,\ 9,\ 1,\ 2 \\
z_{R_{32}} \cdots z_{R_{47}} &= 15,\ 5,\ 1,\ 3,\ 7,\ 14,\ 6,\ 9,\ 11,\ 8,\ 12,\ 2,\ 10,\ 0,\ 4,\ 13 \\
z_{R_{48}} \cdots z_{R_{63}} &= 8,\ 6,\ 4,\ 1,\ 3,\ 11,\ 15,\ 0,\ 5,\ 12,\ 2,\ 13,\ 9,\ 7,\ 10,\ 14 \\
z_{R_{64}} \cdots z_{R_{79}} &= 12,\ 15,\ 10,\ 4,\ 1,\ 5,\ 8,\ 7,\ 6,\ 2,\ 13,\ 14,\ 0,\ 3,\ 9,\ 11
\end{aligned}
$$

Left Rotate Bit Positions

$$
\begin{aligned}
s_{L_0} \cdots s_{L_{15}} &= 11,\ 14,\ 15,\ 12,\ 5,\ 8,\ 7,\ 9,\ 11,\ 13,\ 14,\ 15,\ 6,\ 7,\ 9,\ 8 \\
s_{L_{16}} \cdots s_{L_{31}} &= 7,\ 6,\ 8,\ 13,\ 11,\ 9,\ 7,\ 15,\ 7,\ 12,\ 15,\ 9,\ 11,\ 7,\ 13,\ 12 \\
s_{L_{32}} \cdots s_{L_{47}} &= 11,\ 13,\ 6,\ 7,\ 14,\ 9,\ 13,\ 15,\ 14,\ 8,\ 13,\ 6,\ 5,\ 12,\ 7,\ 5 \\
s_{L_{48}} \cdots s_{L_{63}} &= 11,\ 12,\ 14,\ 15,\ 14,\ 15,\ 9,\ 8,\ 9,\ 14,\ 5,\ 6,\ 8,\ 6,\ 5,\ 12 \\
s_{L_{64}} \cdots s_{L_{79}} &= 9,\ 15,\ 5,\ 11,\ 6,\ 8,\ 13,\ 12,\ 5,\ 12,\ 13,\ 14,\ 11,\ 8,\ 5,\ 6 \\
\\
s_{R_0} \cdots s_{R_{15}} &= 8,\ 9,\ 9,\ 11,\ 13,\ 15,\ 15,\ 5,\ 7,\ 7,\ 8,\ 11,\ 14,\ 14,\ 12,\ 6 \\
s_{R_{16}} \cdots s_{R_{31}} &= 9,\ 13,\ 15,\ 7,\ 12,\ 8,\ 9,\ 11,\ 7,\ 7,\ 12,\ 7,\ 6,\ 15,\ 13,\ 11 \\
s_{R_{32}} \cdots s_{R_{47}} &= 9,\ 7,\ 15,\ 11,\ 8,\ 6,\ 6,\ 14,\ 12,\ 13,\ 5,\ 14,\ 13,\ 13,\ 7,\ 5 \\
s_{R_{48}} \cdots s_{R_{63}} &= 15,\ 5,\ 8,\ 11,\ 14,\ 14,\ 6,\ 14,\ 6,\ 9,\ 12,\ 9,\ 12,\ 5,\ 15,\ 8 \\
s_{R_{64}} \cdots s_{R_{79}} &= 8,\ 5,\ 12,\ 9,\ 12,\ 5,\ 14,\ 6,\ 8,\ 13,\ 6,\ 5,\ 15,\ 13,\ 11,\ 11
\end{aligned}
$$

Note that all constants have been expanded to support both the *left line* and the *right line* of *RIPEMD-160* as well as the expanded bit width of *RIPEMD-160* versus *MD4* (160 bits versus 128 bits).

Prior to passing the input x to *RIPEMD-160*, it must be padded such that the total bit length is a multiple of 512. If the bit length of the input x is $b = \lceil log_2 x \rceil$, then padding is achieved via the following steps [202]:

1. Append a single bit, whose value is set to 1, to the input x.

2. Compute the smallest r such that $b + r \ mod \ 512 = 448$. Append $r - 1$ bits, whose values are set to 0, to the result of Step 1.

3. Compute the 64-bit value $b \ mod \ 2^{64}$ and append this value to the result of Step 2 using little-endian notation, i.e. the lower 32-bit word followed by the upper 32-bit word.

This process yields a string of length $b + r + 64$ which must be a multiple m of 512 bits and thus may be represented as $16 \cdot m$ 32-bit blocks. Therefore, the input to *RIPEMD-160* may be represented as x'_0, x'_1, x'_2, ... $x'_{16m - 1}$, where each x'_i is a 32-bit block. Once the input x has been padded to form x', *RIPEMD-160* completes its set-up phase by establishing the initial values for working variables [202]:

1. $H_1 = h_1, H_2 = h_2, H_3 = h_3, H_4 = h_4, H_5 = h_5$

2. For $i = 0 \ To \ m - 1$

    (a) For $j = 0 \ To \ 15$

        i. $Temp[j] = x'_{16i + j}$

3. $A_L = H_1,\ B_L = H_2,\ C_L = H_3,\ D_L = H_4,\ E_L = H_5$

4. $A_R = H_1,\ B_R = H_2,\ C_R = H_3,\ D_R = H_4,\ E_R = H_5$

Both the *RIPEMD-160 left line* and *right line* process the input data via five rounds that are each executed sixteen times. Each round employs a different function, and these functions are defined as [202]:

$$f(u,\ v,\ w) = u \oplus v \oplus w$$
$$g(u,\ v,\ w) = (u \cdot v) + (\overline{u} \cdot w)$$
$$h(u,\ v,\ w) = (u + \overline{v}) \oplus w$$
$$k(u,\ v,\ w) = (u \cdot w) + (v \cdot \overline{w})$$
$$l(u,\ v,\ w) - u \oplus (v \mid \overline{w})$$

where $\cdot$ represents a bit-wise AND, $+$ represents a bit-wise OR, $\oplus$ represents bit-wise XOR, and $\overline{u}$ represents the logical complement of u. Based on these functions and the initialized working variables, *RIPEMD-160* computes the hashed value of x' via the following pseudo-code [202]:

<u>Left Line Round 1</u>

1. For $j = 0\ To\ 15$

    (a) $t = A_L + f(B_L,\ C_L,\ D_L) + Temp[z_{L_j}] + y_{L_j}$

    (b) $A_L = E_L,\ B_L = E_L + (t \ll s_{L_j}),\ C_L = B_L,$
       $D_L = C_L \ll 10,\ E_L = D_L$

Left Line Round 2

1. For $j = 16$ To 31

  (a) $t = A_L + g(B_L, C_L, D_L) + Temp[z_{L_j}] + y_{L_j}$

  (b) $A_L = E_L, B_L = E_L + (t \ll s_{L_j}), C_L = B_L,$
      $D_L = C_L \ll 10, E_L = D_L$

Left Line Round 3

1. For $j = 32$ To 47

  (a) $t = A_L + h(B_L, C_L, D_L) + Temp[z_{L_j}] + y_{L_j}$

  (b) $A_L = E_L, B_L = E_L + (t \ll s_{L_j}), C_L = B_L,$
      $D_L = C_L \ll 10, E_L = D_L$

Left Line Round 4

1. For $j = 48$ To 63

  (a) $t = A_L + k(B_L, C_L, D_L) + Temp[z_{L_j}] + y_{L_j}$

  (b) $A_L = E_L, B_L = E_L + (t \ll s_{L_j}), C_L = B_L,$
      $D_L = C_L \ll 10, E_L = D_L$

Left Line Round 5

1. For $j = 64$ To 79

  (a) $t = A_L + l(B_L, C_L, D_L) + Temp[z_{L_j}] + y_{L_j}$

(b) $A_L = E_L, B_L = E_L + (t \ll s_{L_j}), C_L = B_L,$
$D_L = C_L \ll 10, E_L = D_L$

where $\ll q$ represents a circular left rotation by q bit positions and $+$ represents 32-bit addition. The *RIPEMD-160 right line* is executed in parallel with the *RIPEMD-160 left line* via the following pseudo-code [202]:

Right Line Round 1

1. For $j = 0 \ To \ 15$

   (a) $t = A_R + l(B_R, C_R, D_R) + Temp[z_{R_j}] + y_{R_j}$

   (b) $A_R = E_R, B_R = E_R + (t \ll s_{R_j}), C_R = B_R,$
   $D_R = C_R \ll 10, E_R = D_R$

Right Line Round 2

1. For $j = 16 \ To \ 31$

   (a) $t = A_R + k(B_R, C_R, D_R) + Temp[z_{R_j}] + y_{R_j}$

   (b) $A_R = E_R, B_R = E_R + (t \ll s_{R_j}), C_R = B_R,$
   $D_R = C_R \ll 10, E_R = D_R$

Right Line Round 3

1. For $j = 32 \ To \ 47$

   (a) $t = A_R + h(B_R, C_R, D_R) + Temp[z_{R_j}] + y_{R_j}$

(b) $A_R = E_R$, $B_R = E_R + (t \lll s_{R_j})$, $C_R = B_R$,
$D_R = C_R \lll 10$, $E_R = D_R$

Right Line Round 4

1. For $j = 48$ To 63

   (a) $t = A_R + g(B_R, C_R, D_R) + Temp[z_{R_j}] + y_{R_j}$

   (b) $A_R = E_R$, $B_R = E_R + (t \lll s_{R_j})$, $C_R = B_R$,
   $D_R = C_R \lll 10$, $E_R = D_R$

Right Line Round 5

1. For $j = 64$ To 79

   (a) $t = A_R + f(B_R, C_R, D_R) + Temp[z_{R_j}] + y_{R_j}$

   (b) $A_R = E_R$, $B_R = E_R + (t \lll s_{R_j})$, $C_R = B_R$,
   $D_R = C_R \lll 10$, $E_R = D_R$

Following the completion of the fifth round of both the *left line* and the *right line*, a final update occurs [202]:

$$t = H_1$$
$$H_1 = H_2 + C_L + D_R$$
$$H_2 = H_3 + D_L + E_R$$
$$H_3 = H_4 + E_L + A_R$$
$$H_4 = H_5 + A_L + B_R$$
$$H_5 = t + B_L + C_R$$

After this update, the hashed value of x' is denoted as $H_1 \parallel H_2 \parallel H_3 \parallel H_4 \parallel H_5$, where $\parallel$ represents concatenation and each H_i is represented in little-endian notation.

Because *RIPEMD-160* employs 32-bit Boolean and arithmetic operations, high speed implementations of the *Hash Function* are easily achieved in both software and hardware. Moreover, the use of little-endian notation results in *RIPEMD-160* mapping extremely well to Intel microprocessors, which typically employ little-endian memory models for data storage [275]. In terms of security, *RIPEMD-160*, like *MD5*, removes symmetry by changing the access order for all but the first round of the *left line* and all of the rounds of the *right line*. *RIPEMD-160*, like *SHA-1*, also increases the *avalanche effect* inherent in the *Hash Function* through the addition of the output from the previous iteration that is reflected in the update of the B_L and B_R working variables for each round. As in the case of *SHA-1*, because the *RIPEMD-160* rounds add in the fifth working variables (E_L and E_R) instead of any of the working variables B_L, B_R, C_L, C_R, D_L, or D_R (used in the functions $f(u, v, w)$, $g(u, v, w)$, $h(u, v, w)$, $k(u, v, w)$, and $l(u, v, w)$), the attack against *MD4* proposed in [64] cannot be applied to *RIPEMD-160*. Finally, because of the increased bit length of *RIPEMD-160* versus the bit lengths of *MD4* and *MD5* (160 bits versus 128 bits), *RIPEMD-160* is more resistant to exhaustive *collision* searches that attempt to take advantage of the *Birthday Paradox* [275].

10.2.3   Efficient Implementation

When considering *Hash Function* implementations, numerous ASIC implementations have been published [53, 54, 73, 105, 122, 268, 310, 322]. The best reported throughputs for *Hash Functions* from the *MD4* family are detailed in Table 10.2:

Hash Algorithm	Technology	Size (Gates)	Throughput (Mbps)
MD5 [268]	0.13 μm	17,764	2,091
SHA-1 [268]	0.13 μm	9,859	2,006
SHA-224/SHA-256 [268]	0.18 μm	15,329	2,370
SHA-384/SHA-512 [268]	0.13 μm	27,297	2,909
RIPEMD-160 [268]	0.13 μm	24,775	1,442

Table 10.2: Hash Algorithm Best Implementation Performance in ASIC

The high throughputs evidenced in [268] were achieved by avoiding logic resource sharing and using high-fanout gates, thus reducing the number of stages within the implementations.

Similarly, a wide variety of FPGA implementations of *Hash Functions* of the *MD4* family exist in the literature [4, 5, 6, 7, 8, 63, 73, 104, 105, 106, 112, 122, 128, 149, 151, 158, 162, 181, 68, 194, 198, 206, 217, 219, 280, 287, 288, 289, 290, 291, 292, 293, 308, 321, 322, 336, 339]. The best reported throughputs for *Hash Functions* from the *MD4* family are detailed in Table 10.3:

Loop unrolling and partial pipelining both provided significant contributions to the high throughputs evidenced in [198, 206, 336].

Hash Algorithm	Xilinx Technology	Size	Throughput (Mbps)
MD5 [122]	Virtex II -6	613 CLB slices + 2 BRAM	744
SHA-1 [206]	Virtex XCV150BG352	1,054 CLB slices	2,816
SHA-256 [336]	Virtex II XC2V2000	1,938 CLB slices	1,296
SHA-384 [198]	Virtex-E XCV600E-8	2,914 CLB slices + 2 BRAM	479 479
SHA-512 [336]	Virtex II XC2V2000	1,938 CLB slices	2,074
RIPEMD-160 [293]	Virtex II XC2V250FG456	2,171 CLB slices	2,017

Table 10.3: Hash Algorithm Best Implementation Performance in FPGA

Software implementations of *Hash Functions* of the *MD4* family are available targeting processors such as the Intel Pentium, DEC Alpha, and the Sun SPARC [72, 218, 224, 249, 258, 281, 302, 310]. These implementations have yielded throughputs for *Hash Functions* from the *MD4* family, as detailed in Table 10.4:

Hash Algorithm	Processor	Throughput (Mbps)
MD4 [72]	90 MHz Pentium (Assembly)	165.7
MD5 [72]	90 MHz Pentium (Assembly)	113.5
SHA-1 [249]	133 MHz DEC Alpha	41.5
SHA-256 [281]	3 GHz Pentium 4	59.8
SHA-384 [302]	800 MHz Athlon	95.0
SHA-512 [302]	800 MHz Athlon	91.5
RIPEMD-160 [249]	133 MHz DEC Alpha	48.0

Table 10.4: Hash Algorithm Best Implementation Performance in Software

10.2.4   Homework Problems

Homework Problem 10.2.4.1: Consider three different *Hash Functions* that produce outputs of length 64, 128, and 160 bits, respectively. After how many random inputs is the probability of

$\varepsilon = 0.5$ for a *collision*? After how many random inputs is the probability of $\varepsilon = 0.1$ for a *collision*?

Homework Problem 10.2.4.2: Describe exactly how you would perform a search to find a pair (x_1, x_2) such that $h(x_1) = h(x_2)$ for a given *Hash Function h*. What are the memory requirements for this type of search if the *Hash Function* has an output length of n bits?

Homework Problem 10.2.4.3: Draw a block diagram for the following *Hash Functions* built from block ciphers:

a) $H_i = H_{i-1} \oplus e_{x_i}(H_{i-1})$

b) $H_i = H_{i-1} \oplus x_i \oplus e_{g(H_{i-1})}(x_i)$

c) Describe why there is no mapping function $g(x_i)$ needed for feeding x_i into the key input of the block cipher $e()$ in part (a).

Homework Problem 10.2.4.4: Consider a protocol in which messages are not encrypted. However, the messages are hashed and then digitally signed. The *Digital Signature y* is sent with each message x over an open channel. Assume that *Oscar* is able to find a *collision* in the *Hash Functions*, i.e. that *Oscar* can find x' such that $h(x) = h(x')$. Also assume that *Oscar* can (within limits) control the contents of x'. Describe how *Oscar* can now alter *Bob's* messages such that *Alice* will still consider them to be valid messages from *Bob*.

Homework Problem 10.2.4.5: Consider a protocol in which messages are encrypted, hashed, and then digitally signed. The *Digital Signature* $sig_{K_{PR}}(h(y))$ is sent with each encrypted message y over an open channel. Assume that *Oscar* is able to find a *collision* in the *Hash Functions*, i.e. that *Oscar* can find y' such that $h(y) = h(y')$. Also assume that *Oscar* can (within limits) control the contents of y'. Can *Oscar* now alter *Bob's* messages such that *Alice* will still consider them to be valid messages from *Bob*? Why is this not a useful attack from *Oscar's* perspective?

Homework Problem 10.2.4.6: How many people must be in a room such that there is a 90 % probability of two or more people having the same birth date?

Homework Problem 10.2.4.7: A block cipher is to be used to create a *Hash Function*.

a) Explain why *DES* is a poor choice for the block cipher core of the *Hash Function*.

b) Describe how *AES* should be configured for use as the block cipher core of the *Hash Function*. Be sure to specify the values for *Nb*, *Nk*, and *Nr*.

Homework Problem 10.2.4.8: Write a C program to implement the *MD5 Hash Function*. Write a user interface that queries the user for an input file that contains the message to be hashed. The program must output the resultant hashed value to the screen in hexadecimal notation and include code that measures the time required to hash the message, outputting this information to the screen. Specify the computer model used and the amount of available RAM.

Homework Problem 10.2.4.9: Implement the *MD5 Hash Function* on a 32-bit and 64-bit computer using the C program from **Homework Problem 10.2.4.8**, being sure that the amount of available RAM on each computer is the same. Use the messages contained in the file *HW10-2-4Plaintext.txt* available on the CD included with this book. Note that messages always end with the string **END OF MESSAGE**. Compare the performance of the *MD5 Hash Function* on each computer for the messages in the file *HW10-2-4Plaintext.txt*. How does the processor word size impact the performance of the *MD5 Hash Function*?

10.3   Message Authentication Codes

Much like *Digital Signatures*, *Message Authentication Codes* (MACs) are used to validate both the integrity and the authenticity of a message. However, unlike *Digital Signatures*, which are based on public-key cryptosystems, *MACs* are based on either symmetric-key cryptosystems or *Hash Functions*. *MACs* are used to validate the authenticity of a message transmitted between two parties that share a secret key. This message authentication holds true if the only people capable of generating a valid *MAC* are the two parties that share the secret key. *MACs* must also change with each new message. Therefore, to meet both of these requirements, *MACs* must be a function of both the shared secret key and the message being sent. Such a structure allows two communicating parties, *Alice* and *Bob*, to prove that one of the parties generated a given message because only these parties have access to their shared secret key. For a given message x, the protocol for transmitting a message between two communicating parties, *Alice* and *Bob*, using *MACs* is as follows:

1. *Alice* and *Bob* agree on a *MAC* scheme.

2. *Alice* and *Bob* share a secret key, denoted as k.

3. *Bob* uses the secret key and the *MAC* function, sometimes referred to as a *cryptographic checksum*, to generate the *MAC* $y = MAC_k(x)$ for the message x.

4. *Bob* transmits the message x and the *MAC* y to *Alice*.

5. *Alice* computes the *MAC* for the received message x using the same *MAC* function, yielding the *MAC* $y' = MAC_k(x)$. *Alice* verifies the *MAC* for the message x by checking if $y = y'$, yielding a value of *true* (indicating successful verification) or *false* (indicating failed verification).

MACs exhibit the following properties:

- *MACs* generate a fixed length signature for a message x of arbitrary length.

- *MACs* based on symmetric-key cryptosystems require that the communicating parties share a secret key.

- *MACs* based on symmetric-key cryptosystems are significantly faster than *Digital Signatures* based on public-key cryptosystems.

- Limited message authentication is provided because the recipient is sure that the sender generated the message.

- Data integrity is guaranteed because an alteration of either the message x or the *MAC* y will cause the *MAC* verification process to yield a value of *false*, indicating that verification has failed.

- Both the sender and the recipient of a message can generate the *MAC* for the message. Therefore, non-repudiation is not provided because the sender can deny sending the message x by claiming that the recipient is also the sender of the message.

10.3.1   Algorithms

MACs are typically constructed using one of two types of algorithms — block ciphers and *Hash Functions*. Block cipher based *MACs* construct *MACs* using an existing block cipher as a core element, whereas *Hash Function* based *MACs* construct *MACs* using an existing *Hash Functions* as a core element.

10.3.1.1   Block Cipher Based Algorithms

MACs based on block ciphers use the block cipher's encryption function in an iterative manner similar to *CBC* mode, as described in Section 5.1.3.2. The final output of the function is the hashed output for the entire message. Figure 10.4 shows an example of a *MAC* constructed from the *DES* block cipher.

Based on Figure 10.4, the *MAC* for the message $X = x_0$, x_1, x_2, ... x_n is generated as follows:

$$y_0 = e_k(x_0 \oplus IV)$$
$$y_i = e_k(x_i \oplus y_{i-1})$$

The final y_i computed as a function of *CBC* mode, y_n, is used as the *MAC* for the message X, i.e. $MAC_k(X) = y_n$. Verification of the *MAC* is achieved by the recipient of the *MAC* regenerating the *MAC* based on the received message and comparing the result to the received *MAC*. If the two *MACs* are the same, then verification is successful; otherwise, *MAC* verification fails.

The use of *DES* in the configuration shown in Figure 10.4 is described in ANSI standard X9.17 [10]. However, ANSI standard X9.17 was withdrawn once *DES* was considered to be no longer secure as a result of *DES* Challenge II-2 being successfully completed, as discussed in Section 5.1.6.2.

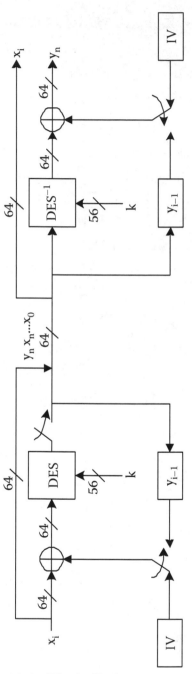

Figure 10.4: Block Cipher Based MAC

10.3.1.2 Hash Function Based Algorithms

MACs based on *Hash Functions*, also known as *Keyed Hash Functions* or *HMACs*, use the *Hash Function* to hash a key and a message and use the resultant output to authenticate the message. *HMACs* were first proposed by Mihir Bellare, Ran Canetti, and Hugo Krawczyk in 1996 [26] and were later standardized in FIPS Standard 198 [228]. Any *Hash Function* may be used to generate an *HMAC*, and *HMACs* that use the *SHA-1* and *MD5 Hash Functions* are used by the *Internet Protocol Security* (IPsec), *Secure Sockets Layer* (SSL), and *Transport Layer Security* (TLS) protocols.

The *HMAC* is defined as [26, 228]:

$$HMAC_k(x) \; = \; h([k' \oplus opad] \; || \; h([k' \oplus ipad] \; || \; x))$$

where $\oplus$ represents bit-wise XOR and $||$ represents concatenation. Note that k' is the key k with zeros appended to the most significant bits. k' must match the block size b of the *Hash Function* in length, and thus k is padded with enough zeros such that the bit length of k' is b. Also note that *ipad* is the constant 00110110_2 repeated $\frac{b}{8}$ times and *opad* is the constant 01011010_2 repeated $\frac{b}{8}$ times.

10.3.2 Efficient Implementation

Efficient implementation of *MACs* relies on the efficient implementation of the underlying block cipher or *Hash Function*. These topics have been discussed in detail in Sections 5.1.5 and 5.2.4 for block ciphers and in Section 10.2.3 for *Hash Functions*.

10.3.3 Homework Problems

Homework Problem 10.3.2.1: It is crucial for a *Hash Function* to have a sufficiently large number of output bits, e.g. 256 bits, to thwart attacks based on the *Birthday Paradox*. Why are shorter output lengths, e.g. 64 bits, sufficient for *MACs*? For your answer, assume a message x that is sent over the channel in the clear together with its *MAC* and is of the form $(x, MAC_k(x))$. Specify exactly what *Oscar* must do to attack this cryptosystem.

Homework Problem 10.3.2.2:

a) Assume the ciphertext y is computed as $y = e_k(x||h(x))$, where *h(x)* is a *Hash Function*. This technique is not suited for encryption with stream ciphers if the attacker knows the entire plaintext x. Explain exactly how an active attacker can replace x with an arbitrary x' of their choosing and compute y' such that the message recipient will verify the message correctly. Assume that x and x' are of equal length. Will this attack work if the encryption is performed using a *One-Time Pad*?

b) Is the attack described in part (a) still applicable if the checksum is computed using a keyed hash function such as a MAC? Assume y is of the form $y = e_{k_1}(x \| MAC_{k_2}(x))$ and that $e()$ is a stream cipher as in part (a). Justify your answer.

Homework Problem 10.3.2.3: Consider a protocol in which messages are not encrypted. However, a MAC is included for each message and the MAC is sent with each message x over an open channel. If *Oscar* alters the contents of the message x, describe how *Alice* will detect the alteration of the message sent by *Bob*.

Homework Problem 10.3.2.4: A block cipher is to be used to create a MAC. Describe why AES is a good choice for the block cipher core of the MAC.

Homework Problem 10.3.2.5: Consider a protocol in which messages are encrypted using AES operating in CBC mode. AES is also to be used in CBC mode to create a MAC for each message. Describe why MAC generation is redundant in this protocol.

Chapter 11

Cryptographic Protocols

A *Cryptographic Protocol* is a sequence of steps that must be performed in a specified order to achieve a particular task. Examples of such tasks include key agreement, as in the *Diffie-Hellman Key Agreement Protocol*, or privacy for wireless networks, as in the Wireless Equivalent Privacy (WEP) protocol. Increasingly, *Cryptographic Protocols* are defined to be algorithm independent, only specifying the methodology for achieving the task in question, not the underlying algorithms to be used. *Cryptographic Protocols* are designed to provide a network with a set of security services. It is this combination of services that will determine the network's security against attacks, either accidental or malicious.

11.1   Security Services

Networks may be subject to a wide variety of attacks, including but not limited to:

- Interruption of data transmission from source to destination.

- Snooping of transmitted data between source and destination.

- Interception of data transmitted by a source followed by modification and forwarding of the modified data to a destination.

- Fabrication and transmission of data to a destination by a false source.

A snooping attack is classified as a *passive attack* because it requires only that the attacker listen to the network traffic to perform the attack. All of the other attacks are classified as *active attacks* because they require an attacker to actively interrupt, modify, or generate new network traffic. In order to implement a comprehensive security plan for a given network to guarantee the security of a connection, the following services must be provided [202, 275, 298]:

- *Confidentiality*

- *Data Integrity*

- *Message Authentication*

- *Non-repudiation*

Confidentiality guarantees that information cannot be observed by an unauthorized party. This is accomplished via either public-key or symmetric-key encryption algorithms. Consider a protocol

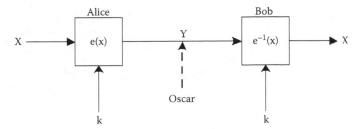

Figure 11.1: Confidentiality Through Symmetric-Key Encryption

that employs a symmetric-key encryption algorithm, as shown in Figure 11.1:

The use of a symmetric-key encryption algorithm guarantees that the information transmitted between *Alice* and *Bob*, i.e. the message X, cannot be observed by *Oscar*, assuming the symmetric-key encryption algorithm is secure. Note that this protocol also provides other security services in addition to confidentiality. If the recipient *Bob* is capable of distinguishing between valid and invalid messages, then the protocol provides weak message authentication and weak data integrity. However, these services exist only if there are a total of two communicating parties. If a third communicating party, *Charlie*, is added to the network, *Bob* is unable to determine either the validity or the integrity of a message sent by *Alice* because the message may be intercepted, decrypted, modified, re-encrypted, and then forwarded by *Charlie* to *Bob*. *Bob* is unable to detect the attack initiated by *Charlie* because all communicating parties on the network share the same key, k, for use with the symmetric-key encryption algorithm. Moreover, the use of a symmetric-key encryption algorithm does not provide any type of non-repudiation because *Bob* cannot prove that *Alice* sent a given message because *Alice* may claim that *Bob* fabricated the message and sent it to himself. *Alice* may make this claim because she and *Bob* share the same key, k, for use with the symmetric-key encryption algorithm.

An alternative protocol for providing confidentiality employs a public-key encryption algorithm, as shown in Figure 11.2:

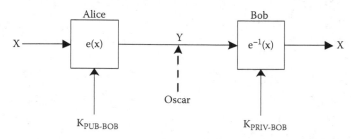

Figure 11.2: Confidentiality Through Public-Key Encryption

The use of a public-key encryption algorithm guarantees that the information transmitted between *Alice* and *Bob*, i.e. the message X, cannot be observed by *Oscar*, assuming the public-key encryption algorithm is secure. Note that this protocol also provides other security services in addition to confidentiality. If the recipient *Bob* is capable of distinguishing between valid and invalid messages, then the protocol provides weak data integrity. However, the use of a public-key encryption algorithm does not provide message authentication because *Bob* is unable to validate the authenticity of a message; anyone may send a message to *Bob* using his public key. Similarly, the protocol does not provide any type of non-repudiation for the same reason, i.e. because anyone may send a message to *Bob* using his public key.

Data integrity guarantees that transmitted data within a given communication session cannot be altered in transit due to error or an unauthorized party. This is accomplished via the use of *Hash Functions* and *Message Authentication Codes* (MACs). Consider a protocol that employs a *Hash Functions*, as shown in Figure 11.3, where || represents concatenation and + represents comparison:

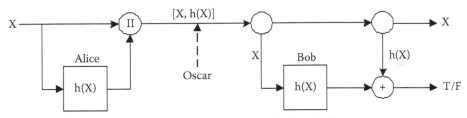

Figure 11.3: Integrity Through Hash Functions

The use of a *Hash Function* guarantees the integrity of the information transmitted between *Alice* and *Bob* assuming that the *Hash Function* is secure, i.e. that *Oscar* cannot find a *collision*. Should *Oscar* modify the message X or the hashed value $h(X)$, *Bob* will detect the modification when comparing the computed hashed value and the received hashed value. However, the use of a *Hash Function* provides no guarantee of confidentiality, i.e. that the information transmitted between *Alice* and *Bob* (the message X) cannot be observed by *Oscar*, because no encryption is performed. This protocol also does not provide either message authentication or non-repudiation because *Bob* is unable to validate either the authenticity or the source of a given message; anyone with knowledge of the *Hash Function* being used as part of the protocol may send a message to *Bob* that will pass the verification process, assuming the hashed value $h(X)$ has been properly computed.

An alternative protocol for providing data integrity employs a *MAC*, as shown in Figure 11.4, where || represents concatenation and + represents comparison:

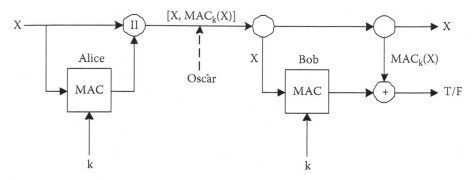

Figure 11.4: Integrity Through MACs

The use of a *MAC* provides weak data integrity for the information transmitted between *Alice* and *Bob*, assuming that the *MAC* is secure. Should *Oscar* modify the message X or the *MAC* $MAC_k(X)$, *Bob* will detect the modification when comparing the computed *MAC* value and the received *MAC* value. However, this service exists only if there are a total of two communicating parties. If a third communicating party, *Charlie*, is added to the network, *Bob* is unable to determine the integrity of the message sent by *Alice* because the message may be intercepted, modified, a new *MAC* generated, and then forwarded by *Charlie* to *Bob*. *Bob* is unable to detect the attack initiated by *Charlie* because all communicating parties on the network share the same key, k, for use with the *MAC*. Note that this protocol also provides other security services in addition to data integrity. If the recipient *Bob* is capable of distinguishing between valid and invalid messages, then the protocol provides weak message authentication for the same reason that the protocol provides weak data integrity. However, the use of a *MAC* does not provide any type of non-repudiation because *Bob* cannot prove that *Alice* sent a given message as *Alice* may claim that *Bob* fabricated the message and sent it to himself. *Alice* may make this claim because she and *Bob* share the same key, k, for use with the *MAC*. Finally, the use of a *MAC* provides no guarantee of confidentiality because no encryption is performed.

Parties within a given communication session must provide certifiable proof validating the authenticity of a message. Message authentication guarantees that this is accomplished via the use of *Digital Signatures* as shown in Figure 11.5, where $\parallel$ represents concatenation:

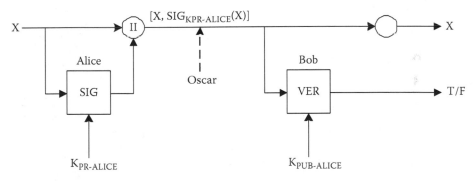

Figure 11.5: Message Authentication Through Digital Signatures

The use of a *Digital Signature* validates the authenticity of the information transmitted between *Alice* and *Bob* because only *Alice* can sign her message using her private key while anyone can verify *Alice's Digital Signature* using her public key. Note that this protocol also provides other security services in addition to message authentication. Data integrity is provided in the same manner that message authentication is provided, i.e. as a result of the use of a *Digital Signature*. Should *Oscar* modify the message X or the *Digital Signature* $sig_{K_{PR_A}}(X)$, *Bob* will detect the modification when attempting to verify the *Digital Signature*. Non-repudiation requires that neither the sender nor the receiver of a message may deny transmission. This is accomplished using *Digital Signatures* and third party notary services. Therefore, the protocol provides non-repudiation because only *Alice* can sign her message using her private key. However, the use of a *Digital Signature* provides no guarantee of confidentiality because no encryption is performed.

To develop a protocol that encompasses all of the desired security services requires a combination of cryptographic components. Consider a protocol that combines *Hash Function* with a *Digital Signature*, as shown in Figure 11.6, where || represents concatenation:

This protocol provides the same security services — data integrity, message authentication, and non-repudiation — as the protocol that employs a *Digital Signature* without the use of a *Hash Function* as shown in Figure 11.5. However, the protocol in Figure 11.6 is more realistic because it addresses the issue raised in Section 10.1.1 where large messages must be broken into blocks and each block must be digitally signed prior to transmission. To address this problem, *Hash Functions* are used to generate a message digest and it is this message digest that is digitally signed, resulting in the generation of a single *Digital Signature* for a message regardless of the size of the message.

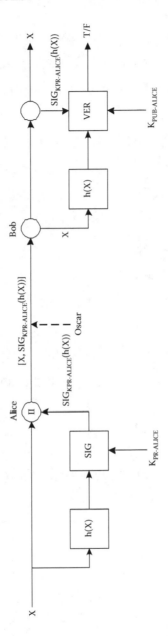

Figure 11.6: Protocol Using Hash Functions and Digital Signatures

To add confidentiality to the protocol described in Figure 11.6 requires that the information transmitted between *Alice* and *Bob* be encrypted. Modern protocols tend to be hybrid systems that utilize public-key and symmetric-key algorithms. Public-key algorithms are used for the exchange of a session key, such as through the *Diffie-Hellman Key Agreement Protocol*, and to provide data integrity, message authentication, and non-repudiation through the use of *Digital Signatures*. The session key is then used in conjunction with a symmetric-key algorithm to perform bulk data encryption of the transmitted information. This is because even the best implementations of public-key algorithms are between one and two orders of magnitude slower than equivalent implementations of symmetric-key algorithms. Figure 11.7 details such a hybrid system, where || represents concatenation:

The hybrid system shown in Figure 11.7 provides confidentiality, data integrity, message authentication, and non-repudiation. Alternatively, the *Hash Function* and *Digital Signature* in the hybrid system shown in Figure 11.7 may be replaced by a *MAC*, yielding the hybrid system shown in Figure 11.8, where || represents concatenation:

The hybrid system of Figure 11.8 provides confidentiality through the use of a symmetric-key encryption algorithm. The use of a *MAC* would normally provide weak data integrity and weak message authentication, as in the protocol shown in Figure 11.4. However, by encrypting the *MAC* output via a second shared secret key, the hybrid system of Figure 11.8 provides strong data integrity

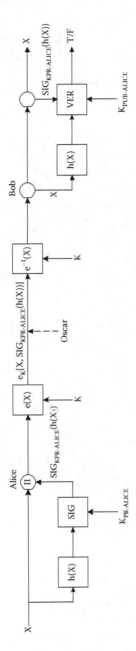

Figure 11.7: Protocol Using Hash Functions, Digital Signatures, and Symmetric-Key Encryption

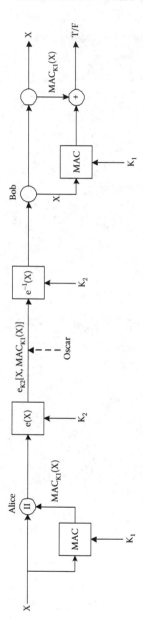

Figure 11.8: Protocol Using MACs and Symmetric-Key Encryption

and strong message authentication if there are a total of two communicating parties. Should *Oscar* modify the encrypted message $e_{k_2}[X, \ MAC_{k_1}(X)]$, *Bob* will detect the modification when comparing the decrypted received *MAC* value to the computed *MAC* value. Moreover, this protocol eliminates the need for public-key algorithms, which have already been shown to be between one and two orders of magnitude slower than equivalent implementations of symmetric-key algorithms. However, the use of a *MAC* in place of the combination of a *Hash Function* and *Digital Signature* does not provide any type of non-repudiation because *Bob* cannot prove that *Alice* sent a given message because *Alice* may claim that *Bob* fabricated the message and sent it to himself. *Alice* may make this claim because she and *Bob* share the same *MAC* and symmetric-key encryption keys, K_1 and K_2, respectively.

In addition to the security services of confidentiality, data integrity, message authentication, and non-repudiation, two additional security services are necessary when considering the secure use of a network [202, 275, 298]:

- *Entity Authentication*

- *Access Control*

The goal of entity authentication is to establish the identity of an entity, such as a person or device, whereas access control implies that appropriate controls are in place to limit access to data and resources and access is determined based on the privilege assigned to the data and resources as well as the privilege of the entity attempting to access the data and resources. Note that entity authentication differs from message authentication in that entity authentication is a run-time operation which does not require a real message.

Many forms of entity authentication exist, including user defined passwords and access codes, possession of an object such as a smart card, and *biometrics*, i.e. the use of proven unique human characteristics, such as fingerprints. Because the focus of this textbook is electronic security methods, the use of *biometrics* as a means of entity authentication will not be discussed. Clearly, user defined passwords and access codes are weak methods of entity authentication and stronger, cryptographically based methods must be considered to guarantee that users can prove their identity to another party with whom they wish to communicate without revealing their identification information to a snooping attacker. Moreover, user identification information must not be revealed to the other party with whom they wish to communicate to prevent potential identity theft. Therefore, users must provably demonstrate knowledge of some secret to authenticate their identity without revealing their identification information. This result is typically achieved through the use of a *Challenge-Response Protocol*.

Challenge-Response Protocols may be based on either symmetric-key or public-key algorithms. Should *Alice* wish to authenticate her identity to *Bob*, *Bob* must send a *challenge* to *Alice*. *Alice* must then perform some function on the *challenge* that is based on knowledge that only she possesses, generating a *response* which is sent to *Bob*. *Bob* then performs a verification function on the *response* to authenticate *Alice's* identity.

Example 11.1: Develop a *Challenge-Response Protocol* to be used by *Alice* and *Bob*, assuming the use of *AES* as the underlying protocol function and a shared key K_{AES}. If *Alice* wants to establish her identity to *Bob*, show the sequence of events that must occur if *Bob* uses the *challenge* $x_{B_{AES}}$.

If *AES* is used as the *Challenge-Response Protocol* function, then encryption (or decryption) may be used to authenticate *Alice's* identity:

1. *Bob* sends the *challenge* $x_{B_{AES}}$ to *Alice*.

2. *Alice* computes $A' = AES_{K_{AES}}(x_{B_{AES}})$.

3. *Alice* sends A' to *Bob*.

4. *Bob* computes $A = AES_{K_{AES}}(x_{B_{AES}})$.

5. *Bob* verifies that $A = A'$.

If *Oscar* modifies $x_{B_{AES}}$ in Step 1, then *Bob's* verification of *Alice's* identity will fail in Step 5. If *Oscar* modifies A' in Step 3, then *Bob's* verification of *Alice's* identity will once again fail in Step 5. If *Oscar* attempts to masquerade as *Alice*, he cannot generate a valid A' because he has no knowledge of the secret key, K_{AES}. This same protocol may be used in conjunction with a MAC as the underlying protocol function.

Example 11.2: Develop a *Challenge-Response Protocol* to be used by *Alice* and *Bob*, assuming the use of the *RSA* cryptosystem as the underlying protocol function with *Alice's* public key denoted as K_{PUB_A} and private key denoted as K_{PR_A}. If *Alice* wants to establish her identity to *Bob*, show the sequence of events that must occur if *Bob* uses the *challenge* $x_{B_{RSA}}$.

If the *RSA* cryptosystem is used as the *Challenge-Response Protocol* function, then the *RSA Digital Signature* scheme may be used to authenticate *Alice's* identity:

1. *Bob* sends the *challenge* $x_{B_{RSA}}$ to *Alice*.

2. *Alice* computes $A = sig_{K_{PR_A}}(x_{B_{RSA}}) = x_{B_{RSA}}^{K_{PR_A}} \bmod p$.

3. *Alice* sends A to *Bob*.

4. *Bob* computes $ver_{K_{PUB_A}}(A) = A^{K_{PUB_A}} \bmod p$.

5. *Bob* verifies that $ver_{K_{PUB_A}}(A) = x_{B_{RSA}}$.

If *Oscar* modifies $x_{B_{RSA}}$ in Step 1, then *Bob's* verification of *Alice's* identity will fail in Step 5. If *Oscar* modifies A in Step 3, then *Bob's* verification of *Alice's* identity will once again fail in Step 5. If *Oscar* attempts to masquerade as *Alice*, he cannot generate a valid *RSA Digital Signature A* because he has no knowledge of *Alice's* private key, K_{PR_A}.

Challenge-Response Protocols may be modified to include additional information such as serial numbers or time stamps to both protect against *Replay* attacks and to guarantee that a *response* is received within a predetermined period of time and thus thwart attacks on the underlying protocol function. Of course, the selection of operand bit lengths and the protocol function itself must be made so as to guarantee that attacks on the underlying protocol function are not feasible in practice. Note that *Challenge-Response Protocols* have been standardized in *ISO/IEC 9798*, most recently revised in 2005 [134].

11.2 Key Establishment

The goal of key establishment is the sharing of a secret key between two (or more) parties desiring to communicate in a secure manner. Key establishment is typically achieved via one of two methods:

- Key distribution — the secret key is generated and distributed by one party.

- Key agreement — the secret key is generated jointly by the parties desiring to communicate in a secure manner.

11.2.1   Key Distribution

One method of sharing a secret key is through the use of a *Trusted Authority*. A *Trusted Authority* is trusted by the parties that seek to communicate securely, and the *Trusted Authority* is capable of communicating securely with all of these parties. In this case, the *Trusted Authority* must generate a secret key for every pair of parties that seek to communicate securely, as shown in Figure 11.9:

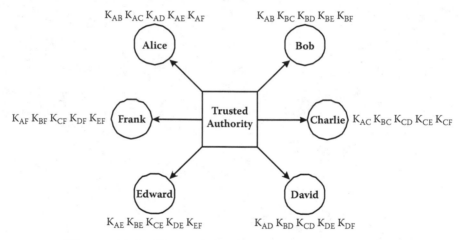

Figure 11.9: Trusted Authority Key Distribution

As shown in Figure 11.9, the use of a *Trusted Authority* requires that a secure channel exist between the *Trusted Authority* and each of the communicating parties. Moreover, for a network with n parties, the *Trusted Authority* must generate $\approx n^2$ keys, resulting in the n^2 *Key Distribution* problem. More specifically, for a network with n parties, the *Trusted Authority* must transmit $n - 1$ keys to each party and each party must store $n - 1$ keys to be able to communicate securely with every other party on the network. Therefore, the *Trusted Authority* must generate

$\frac{n \cdot (n-1)}{2} = \frac{n^2 - n}{2} \approx \frac{n^2}{2}$ keys. Moreover, the *Trusted Authority* must transmit $n \cdot (n-1) = n^2 - n \approx n^2$ keys so that all of the parties may communicate securely with each other. Finally, such an architecture scales poorly because the addition of a communicating party to the network requires that every other communicating party receive a new key to allow secure communication with the newly added party.

In an attempt to resolve the n^2 *Key Distribution* problem, an alternative model for sharing a secret key between communicating parties requires that the *Trusted Authority* act as a *Key Distribution Center*. In this model, the *Key Distribution Center* is used to generate a session key for two parties that seek to communicate securely. The session key is securely transmitted to both communicating parties by the *Key Distribution Center* because the *Key Distribution Center* shares a secret key with all communicating parties on the network. The secret keys that the *Key Distribution Center* shares with all communicating parties on the network are referred to as *key encryption keys*. The protocol for transmitting a session key from the *Key Distribution Center* to the two parties seeking to communicate securely is as follows:

1. The *Key Distribution Center* generates the session key, denoted as K_S.

2. The *Key Distribution Center* encrypts the session key, K_S, using an agreed upon symmetric-key cryptosystem and the secret keys $K_{A,KDC}$ and $K_{B,KDC}$, shared with *Alice* and *Bob*,

respectively, resulting in $y_A = e_{K_{A,KDC}}(K_S)$ and $y_B = e_{K_{B,KDC}}(K_S)$.

3. The *Key Distribution Center* transmits y_A, the encrypted session key, to *Alice* and y_B, the encrypted session key, to *Bob*.

4. *Alice* and *Bob* decrypt the session key, K_S, using the agreed upon symmetric-key cryptosystem.

Alice and *Bob* are now able to communicate securely using the session key, K_S, and an agreed upon symmetric-key cryptosystem. Note that this symmetric-key cryptosystem is not necessarily the same symmetric-key cryptosystem used to transmit the session key from the *Key Distribution Center* to *Alice* and *Bob*. In this model, the *Key Distribution Center* stores a total of n secret keys, allowing the *Key Distribution Center* to communicate with each party on the network. If a communicating party is added to the network, only one new key must be generated so that this new communicating party can communicate securely with the *Key Distribution Center*. Moreover, each party on the network must store only one key, the secret key that allows the party to communicate securely with the *Key Distribution Center*.

A modification to the protocol centered around the *Key Distribution Center* model for two parties seeking to communicate securely is as follows:

1. The *Key Distribution Center* generates the session key, denoted as K_S.

2. The *Key Distribution Center* encrypts the session key, K_S, using an agreed upon symmetric-key cryptosystem and the secret keys $K_{A,KDC}$ and $K_{B,KDC}$, shared with *Alice* and *Bob*, respectively, resulting in $y_A = e_{K_{A,KDC}}$ and $y_B = e_{K_{B,KDC}}$.

3. The *Key Distribution Center* transmits y_A and y_B to *Alice*.

4. *Alice* decrypts the session key, K_S using the agreed upon symmetric-key cryptosystem.

5. *Alice* encrypts a message x using the session key, K_S, resulting in $y = e_{K_S}(x)$, and transmits (y_B, y) to *Bob*.

6. *Bob* decrypts the session key K_S using the secret key he shares with the *Key Distribution Center* and then decrypts the message x using the session key K_S.

Once again, the symmetric-key cryptosystem used by the *Key Distribution Center* to transmit the session key K_S is not necessarily the same symmetric-key cryptosystem used to transmit information between *Alice* and *Bob*. The *Kerberos* protocol is based on this modified protocol and will be discussed in Section 11.3.1.

11.2.2 Key Agreement

An alternative method to the use of a *Trusted Authority* for sharing a secret key is the process of key agreement, where the secret key is generated jointly by the parties desiring to communicate in a secure manner. Therefore, it is of value to reexamine the *Diffie-Hellman Key Agreement Protocol* because this protocol would appear to be the most straightforward method for establishing a session key via key agreement. For the *Cyclic Group* formed by Z_p^* and the multiplication operation, the set-up stage of the *Diffie-Hellman Key Agreement Protocol* proceeds as follows:

1. Choose a large prime number, denoted as p. This process is typically implemented via a *Monte Carlo* algorithm such as the *Miller-Rabin Algorithm*, as discussed in Section 7.2.1.

2. Choose a *primitive element* α in Z_p^*.

where α and p are made publicly known.

The key establishment stage, shown in Figure 8.1, is used to establish a shared secret between two parties, *Alice* and *Bob*, who wish to communicate. As discussed in Section 8.3, solving the *Discrete Logarithm* problem is believed to be the only means of solving the *Diffie-Hellman* problem. Therefore, the *Discrete Logarithm* problem parameters used in the *Diffie-Hellman* problem are chosen to be 1024-bit values to ensure that the *Index Calculus Method* is not computationally feasible in practice. However, this assumes that only passive attacks are performed.

11.2.3 The Man-In-The-Middle Attack

Consider an active attack against the *Diffie-Hellman Key Agreement Protocol* during the key establishment stage, as shown in Figure 11.10:

Step	Alice	Oscar	Bob
1	Choose a random integer $K_{PR_A} = a_A$ where $a_A \in$ $\{2, 3, 4, \ldots p - 1\}$	Choose a random integer $K_{PR_A} = a_O$ where $a_O \in$ $\{2, 3, 4, \ldots p - 1\}$	Choose a random integer $K_{PR_B} = a_B$ where $a_B \in$ $\{2, 3, 4, \ldots p - 1\}$
2	Compute $K_{PUB_A} = b_A$ $= \alpha^{a_A} \bmod p$	Compute $K_{PUB_O} = b_O$ $= \alpha^{a_O} \bmod p$	Compute $K_{PUB_B} = b_B$ $= \alpha^{a_B} \bmod p$
3	Send b_A to *Bob* $\longrightarrow$ where b_A is really sent to *Oscar*	$\longleftarrow$ Send b_O to $\longrightarrow$ *Alice* and *Bob*	$\longleftarrow$ Send b_B to *Alice* where b_B is really sent to *Oscar*
4	Compute $K_{AO} = b_O^{a_A} \bmod p$ $= (\alpha^{a_O})^{a_A} \bmod p$ $= \alpha^{a_A a_O} \bmod p$	Compute $K_{AO} = b_A^{a_O} \bmod p$ $= (\alpha^{a_A})^{a_O} \bmod p$ $= \alpha^{a_A a_O} \bmod p$ and compute $K_{OB} = b_B^{a_O} \bmod p$ $= (\alpha^{u_B})^{a_O} \bmod p$ $= \alpha^{a_O a_B} \bmod p$	Compute $K_{OB} = b_O^{a_B} \bmod p$ $= (\alpha^{a_O})^{a_B} \bmod p$ $= \alpha^{a_O a_B} \bmod p$

Figure 11.10: Diffie-Hellman Key Agreement Protocol — Man-In-The-Middle Attack

At the completion of the *Diffie-Hellman Key Agreement Protocol* key establishment stage, *Oscar* has performed a *Man-In-The-Middle* attack. As a result of the *Man-In-The-Middle* attack, both *Alice* and *Bob* believe that they have established a secure communication session with each other although in actuality they have each established a secure communication session with *Oscar*. *Oscar* may now read, modify, and forward any message sent by one party to the other without the possibility of detection by *Alice* or *Bob*. The *Man-In-The-Middle* attack is successful because the public keys of *Alice* and *Bob* are believed to be authentic, but in fact it is *Oscar's* public key that is in use. Moreover, the *Man-In-The-Middle* attack may be applied to all public-key cryptosystems — as long as the public keys of the communicating parties are not authenticated, *Oscar* can insert himself "in the middle" during the key establishment stage of any key agreement protocol.

11.2.4   Certificates

The goal of certificates is to address the problem of public key authentication. Certificates bind identity information — user name, IP address, social security number, etc. — to a public key via the use of *Digital Signatures*. Each party that desires to communicate in a secure manner must have user identification information, denoted as *ID(U)*, where U is the user, a private key, denoted as K_{PR_U}, and a public key, denoted as K_{PUB_U}. To establish their identity, each communicating party must communicate with a *Certifying Authority*, and it is the *Certifying Authority* that issues certificates.

The *Certifying Authority* generates certificates that are of the form:

$$C(U) \;\; = \;\; [ID(U),\; K_{PUB_U}, sig_{CA}(ID(U),\; K_{PUB_U})]$$

where $sig_{CA}(ID(U), K_{PUB_U})$ is the *Digital Signature* generated by the *Certifying Authority* using its secret *Digital Signature* algorithm. When the certificate is received by the user, U, the *Digital Signature* is verified by the user via the *Certifying Authority's* verification algorithm, denoted as $ver_{CA}[C(U)]$. Note that certificate formats have been standardized in the *X.509 Public-Key and Attribute Certificate Frameworks Standard*, most recently revised in 2005 [135].

When *Alice* requests a certificate from the *Certifying Authority*, she sends her identification information and public key, denoted as $[ID(A), K_{PUB_A}]$, to the *Certifying Authority*. The *Certifying Authority* signs this information using its secret *Digital Signature* algorithm to generate $sig_{CA}(ID(U), K_{PUB_U})$ which is then sent to *Alice*. *Alice* verifies the *Digital Signature* using the *Certifying Authority's* verification algorithm $ver_{CA}[C(U)]$.

For the *Cyclic Group* formed by Z_p^* and the multiplication operation, the *Diffie-Hellman Key Agreement Protocol* key establishment stage may be modified to include the use of certificates, as shown in Figure 11.11, to establish a shared secret between two parties, *Alice* and *Bob*, who wish to communicate.

This modified version of the *Diffie-Hellman Key Agreement Protocol* prevents *Oscar* from performing a *Man-In-The-Middle* attack. Should *Oscar* intercept and replace either *Alice's* or *Bob's* public key, the corresponding *Digital Signature* of the associated certificate will fail to verify.

Step	Alice	Bob
1	Choose a random integer $K_{PR_A} = a_A$ where $a_A \in \{2, 3, 4, \ldots p - 1\}$	Choose a random integer $K_{PR_B} = a_B$ where $a_B \in \{2, 3, 4, \ldots p - 1\}$
2	Compute $K_{PUB_A} = b_A$ $= \alpha^{a_A} \bmod p$	Compute $K_{PUB_B} = b_B$ $= \alpha^{a_B} \bmod p$
3	Send $\longrightarrow$ $C(A) =$ $[ID(A),\, b_A,\, sig_{CA}(ID(A),\, b_A)]$ to *Bob*	$\longleftarrow$ Send $C(B) =$ $[ID(B),\, b_B,\, sig_{CA}(ID(B),\, b_B)]$ to *Alice*
4	Verify *Bob's* Certificate via $ver_{CA}[C(B)]$	Verify *Alice's* Certificate via $ver_{CA}[C(A)]$
5	Compute $K_{AB} = b_B^{a_A} \bmod p$ $= (\alpha^{a_B})^{a_A} \bmod p$ $= \alpha^{a_A a_B} \bmod p$	Compute $K_{AB} = b_A^{a_B} \bmod p$ $= (\alpha^{a_A})^{a_B} \bmod p$ $= \alpha^{a_A a_B} \bmod p$

Figure 11.11: Diffie-Hellman Key Agreement Protocol Key Establishment Stage Using Certificates

Unfortunately, *Oscar* may still attack the modified version of the *Diffie-Hellman Key Agreement Protocol* even when certificates are employed. If *Oscar* can convince the *Certifying Authority* that he is actually *Bob*, a legitimate user, then he may obtain a valid certificate from the *Certifying Authority* that contains his public key and *Bob's* identity information. In this case, *Oscar* has successfully masqueraded as *Bob* because the protocol has no mechanism to verify the identity of its users. However, it is still possible to use certificates in conjunction with *Digital Signatures* and the *Diffie-Hellman Key Agreement Protocol* to establish a session key in an authenticated manner. This modified protocol, shown in Figure 11.12, follows the set-up stage of the *Diffie-Hellman Key Agreement Protocol* for the *Cyclic Group* formed by Z_p^* and the multiplication operation. The protocol assumes that the *Certifying Authority's* verification algorithm, $ver_{CA}[C(U)]$, has been successfully distributed to authorized users and that *Alice* and *Bob* have received their certificates:

$$C(A) = [ID(A),\ ver_A,\ sig_{CA}(ID(A),\ ver_A)]$$
$$C(B) = [ID(B),\ ver_B,\ sig_{CA}(ID(B),\ ver_B)]$$

from the *Certifying Authority*. Note that the certificates contain *Digital Signature* verification functions for *Alice* and *Bob* as opposed to public keys, as in previous examples.

This protocol results in a shared session key, K_{AB}, that has been generated in an authenticated manner. If *Oscar* replaces b_A with his public key b_O in Step 3, then *Alice* will detect this modification in Step 10. If *Oscar* replaces b_B with his public key b_O in Step 8, then *Alice* will detect this modification in Step 10 as well. Finally, should *Oscar* attempt to modify either *Alice's* or *Bob's* certificates, then the *Digital Signatures* will fail the *Certifying Authority's* verification algorithm applied in Steps 9 and 14. This protocol is known as the *Station-to-Station Protocol* (STS) [69, 71, 134, 202].

Step	Alice	Bob
1	Choose a random integer $K_{PR_A} = a_A$ where $a_A \in \{2, 3, 4, \ldots p - 1\}$	
2	Compute $K_{PUB_A} = b_A$ $= \alpha^{a_A} \bmod p$	
3	Send b_A to $Bob \longrightarrow$	
4		Choose a random integer $K_{PR_B} = a_B$ where $a_B \in \{2, 3, 4, \ldots p - 1\}$
5		Compute $K_{PUB_B} = b_B = \alpha^{a_B} \bmod p$
6		Compute $K_{AB} = b_A^{a_B}$ $= \alpha^{a_A \cdot a_B} \bmod p$
7		Compute $sig_B(b_A, b_B)$
8		$\longleftarrow$ Send $[C(B),\ b_B,\ sig_B(b_A,\ b_B)]$ to $Alice$
9	Verify $Bob's$ Certificate via $ver_{CA}[C(B)]$	
10	Verify $Bob's$ Public Key via $ver_B[sig_B(b_A,\ b_B)]$ where $ver_B[]$ is contained in C(B)	
11	Compute $K_{AB} = b_B^{a_A}$ $= \alpha^{a_A \cdot a_B} \bmod p$	
12	Compute $sig_A(b_A, b_B)$	
13	Send $\longrightarrow$ $[C(A),\ sig_A(b_A,\ b_B)]$ to Bob	
14		Verify $Alice's$ Certificate via $ver_{CA}[C(A)]$
15		Verify $Alice's$ Public Key via $ver_A[sig_A(b_A,\ b_B)]$ where $ver_A[]$ is contained in C(A)

Figure 11.12: Authenticated Diffie-Hellman Key Agreement Protocol Key Establishment Stage Using Certificates

Another critical aspect of the use of certificates is that the *Certifying Authority's* verification algorithm, $ver_{CA}[C(U)]$, must be distributed to authorized users in an authenticated manner. If *Oscar* injects himself between the *Certifying Authority* and an authorized user (as in the *Man-In-The-Middle* attack), he can intercept and replace the *Certifying Authority's* verification algorithm, $ver_{CA}[C(U)]$, with his own verification function, $ver_O[C(U)]$, substituting his public key for the *Certifying Authority's* public key. *Oscar* then masquerades as the *Certifying Authority*, and all communications from *Oscar* to authorized users will appear to be from the *Certifying Authority* because all *Digital Signatures* from *Oscar* will verify successfully using *Oscar's* public key. Although this attack may appear to be extremely powerful, it is important to note that the distribution of the *Certifying Authority's* verification function is performed only once for each authorized user. Therefore, distribution of the *Certifying Authority's* verification function may be performed via an authenticated channel to thwart this attack given the infrequent need for performing such a communication.

Finally, when using certificates, it is possible that a user's certificate becomes compromised and thus the *Certifying Authority* must revoke the certificate. Moreover, it is often the case that a user only wants a certificate to be valid for a certain period of time. Therefore, it is essential that *Certifying Authorities* maintain certificate revocation lists, i.e. lists of certificates that are no longer valid. When an authorized user receives a certificate,

the user must check the associated *Certifying Authority's* certificate revocation list to determine if the certificate is still valid in
addition to verifying the certificate's *Digital Signature* using the
Certifying Authority's verification function.

11.3   Applications

The following sections provide a brief discussion of a number of
useful cryptographic protocols that are widely deployed and have
practical application when constructing secure systems.   These
discussions are provided as an overview for each of the protocols
— refer to the appropriate protocol specifications for complete
protocol details prior to implementation.

11.3.1   Kerberos

The *Kerberos* protocol [168, 169, 170, 208] is an authentication
protocol that was developed at MIT in 1989 for use in TCP/IP
networks. The *Kerberos* protocol assumes two parties, *Alice* and
Bob, who wish to communicate. *Alice* and *Bob* each share a secret
key with a *Trusted Authority* but they do not share a secret key
with each other. The goal of the *Kerberos* protocol is to authenticate *Alice's* identity to *Bob*. It is critical that *Alice's* identity be
authenticated to ensure that an unauthorized user masquerading
as *Alice* does not gain access to data or network services adminis-
tered by *Bob* that would otherwise be denied to the unauthorized
user [202, 275, 298].

The *Kerberos* protocol defines two types of network entities, clients and servers, and maintains a database of secret keys for each client. This database enables the *Kerberos* authentication server to perform two specific functions:

1. Provide proof of a client's identity to a server.

2. Generate and distribute session keys for encrypting data between a client and a server.

The *Kerberos* authentication server employs two types of credentials: tickets and authenticators. A ticket is issued by a *Ticket Granting Service* (TGS) and is used to pass the client's identity information to a server in a secure manner. An authenticator is used to prove to a server that the client knows the session key and to provide a time stamp to protect against a *Replay* attack.

The *Kerberos* authentication protocol proceeds as follows:

Stage 1

1. A client submits a request to the *Kerberos* authentication server for a *Ticket Granting Ticket*.

2. The *Kerberos* authentication server verifies that the client has an entry in its database of secret keys.

3. The *Kerberos* authentication server generates a *Ticket Granting Ticket*. This *Ticket Granting Ticket* is a session key for

use by the client and the *TGS* that the *Kerberos* authentication server encrypts with the client's secret key.

4. The *Kerberos* authentication server generates another *Ticket Granting Ticket*. This *Ticket Granting Ticket* contains an authenticator that authenticates the client to the *TGS* and the session key. Note that the authenticator is encrypted using the session key. This *Ticket Granting Ticket* is then encrypted by the *Kerberos* authentication server using the *TGS's* secret key.

5. The *Kerberos* authentication server sends both *Ticket Granting Tickets* to the client.

6. The client decrypts the first *Ticket Granting Ticket* using the client's secret key, extracting the session key.

Stage 2

1. The client sends the *Ticket Granting Ticket* containing its authenticator encrypted with the *TGS's* secret key to the *TGS* to obtain a ticket for every service that the client wants to access on a specified server.

2. The *TGS* decrypts the client's *Ticket Granting Ticket* using the *TGS's* secret key.

3. The *TGS* decrypts the client's authenticator using the session key extracted from the client's *Ticket Granting Ticket*.

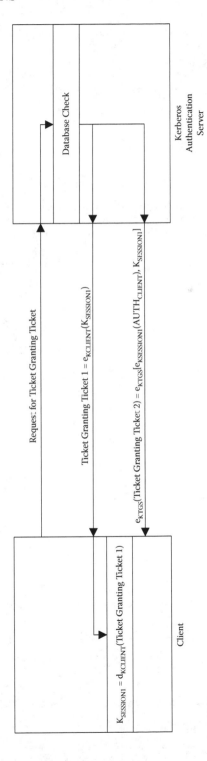

Figure 11.13: Kerberos Authentication Protocol — Stage 1

4. If the contents of the client's *Ticket Granting Ticket* match the information in the client's authenticator, the *TGS* generates a new session key for use by the client and the specified server and encrypts this session key using the session key shared by the *TGS* and the client.

5. The *TGS* generates a *Server Ticket* that contains an authenticator that authenticates the client to the specified server and the session key for use by the client and the specified server. The *Server Ticket* is encrypted using the specified server's secret key.

6. The *TGS* sends the encrypted *Server Ticket* and the encrypted session key for use by the client and the specified server to the client.

7. Using the session key shared by the client and the *TGS*, the client decrypts the session key for use by the client and the specified server.

Stage 3

1. The client creates an authenticator that is encrypted using the session key shared by the client and the specified server.

2. The client sends the encrypted *Server Ticket* and the encrypted authenticator to the specified server.

3. The specified server decrypts the client's *Server Ticket* using the specified server's secret key.

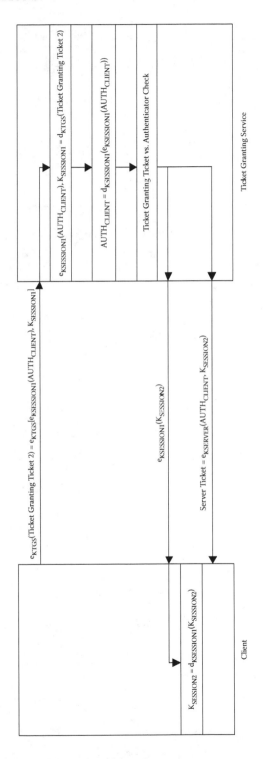

Figure 11.14: Kerberos Authentication Protocol — Stage 2

4. The specified server decrypts the client's authenticator using the session key extracted from the client's *Server Ticket*.

5. If the contents of the client's *Server Ticket* match the information in the client's authenticator, the client's identity has been authenticated to the specified server.

The *Kerberos* protocol uses *DES* for encryption and, as of Version 5, *DES* is used in *CBC* mode. With *DES* considered to be no longer secure as a result of *DES* Challenge II-2 being successfully completed, as discussed in Section 5.1.6.2, efforts are under way to integrate *AES* into Version 5 of the *Kerberos* protocol.

In terms of weaknesses, the *Kerberos* protocol is susceptible to *Replay* attacks on valid tickets with long lifetimes. Moreover, if an attacker is able to alter a server's system clock, an old authenticator may be used in a *Replay* attack. The *Kerberos* protocol is also vulnerable to password guessing dictionary attacks — when a client is a person (versus a software application), their secret key is an encrypted password and most people do not select passwords that are secure. Finally, should an attacker be able to replace the *Kerberos* protocol client software with malicious software, all passwords may be recorded for later fraudulent use [275].

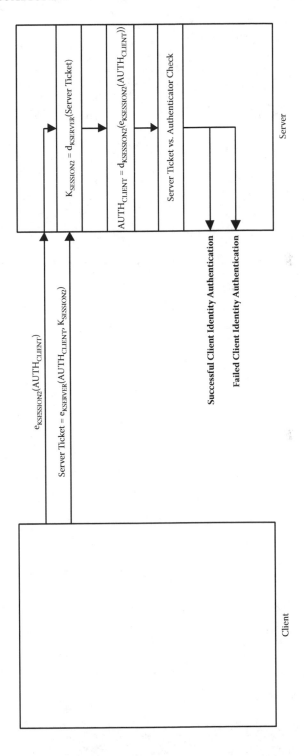

Figure 11.15: Kerberos Authentication Protocol — Stage 3

11.3.2   Pretty Good Privacy

Pretty Good Privacy (PGP) [108, 274, 297, 340, 341] is a security program developed by Phil Zimmermann in 1995 for electronic mail. *PGP* employs four cryptographic components:

1. The *IDEA*, *CAST-128*, and *Triple-DES* block ciphers for bulk data encryption.

2. *RSA* and *ElGamal* encryption for key establishment.

3. *RSA* and *DSA* for the generation of *Digital Signatures*.

4. The *SHA-1 Hash Function*.

To achieve both confidentiality and message authentication, the *PGP* email transmission process begins with the sender's sequence of operations:

Sender Sequence of Operations

1. The electronic mail message to be sent is passed through the *SHA-1 Hash Function* to generate a 160-bit hashed value.

2. The 160-bit hashed value is signed via one of the approved *Digital Signature* algorithms using the sender's private key.

3. The signed hashed value is concatenated with the electronic mail message.

4. The sender generates a session key.

5. The signed hashed value concatenated with the electronic mail message is encrypted via one of the approved block ciphers using the session key.

6. The session key is encrypted via one of the approved public-key encryption algorithms using the recipient's public key.

7. The encrypted signed hashed value concatenated with the electronic mail message is concatenated with the encrypted session key and then sent to the recipient.

Recipient Sequence of Operations

1. The encrypted signed hashed value concatenated with the electronic mail message is separated from the encrypted session key.

2. The session key is decrypted via one of the approved public-key encryption algorithms using the recipient's private key.

3. The signed hashed value concatenated with the electronic mail message is decrypted via one of the approved block ciphers using the session key.

4. The signed hashed value is separated from the electronic mail message.

5. The electronic mail message is passed through the *SHA-1 Hash Function* to generate a 160-bit hashed value.

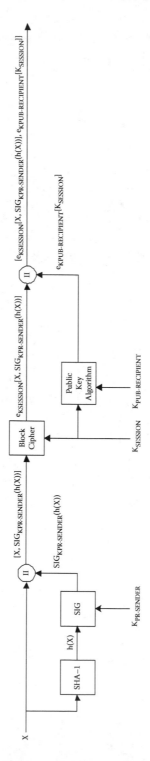

Figure 11.16: PGP Email Transmission — Sender Operations

6. The signed 160-bit hashed value is is verified via one of the approved *Digital Signature* algorithms using the sender's public key and the 160-bit hashed value generated by the recipient.

PGP email transmission allows for the use of either confidentiality or message authentication services individually, with corresponding adjustments to Figures 11.16 and 11.17 based on the implemented security service.

Management of public keys is achieved through a trust model. Every user maintains a library of collected public keys that are associated with other users. Each of these public keys is assigned a *key legitimacy* value, indicating *PGP's* trust in the validity of the public key belonging to the associated user. *PGP* also collects *Digital Signatures* that certify the validity of a public key. Each of these *Digital Signatures* has a *signature trust* value, indicating *PGP's* trust in the associated signer's ability to certify the validity of a public key. Finally, an *owner trust* value is also maintained, indicating *PGP's* trust in a user to certify other users' public keys as valid. Through the use of this trust model, a *PGP* user may make informed decisions as to their level of trust in the validity of the binding of a given user to their associated public key. This trust model is an alternative method for addressing the problem of public key authentication, eliminating the need for certificates and the requisite communication with a *Certifying Authority* [298].

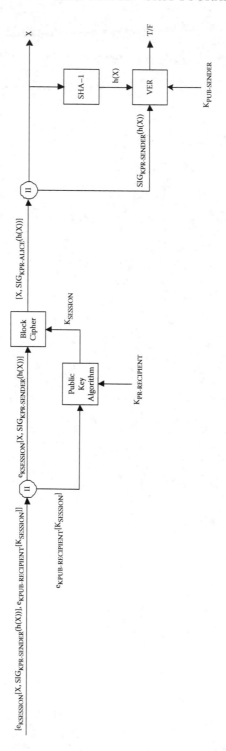

Figure 11.17: PGP Email Transmission — Recipient Operations

11.3.3 Secure Sockets Layer

Secure Sockets Layer (SSL) was originally developed by Netscape®
(now owned by AOL LLC) and the design of *SSL* Version 3 was
open to public scrutiny. The goal of *SSL* is to provide end-to-
end security over TCP via two protocol layers that form the *SSL
Protocol Stack*. The *SSL Record Protocol* resides above the TCP
layer on the *SSL Protocol Stack* and provides security services to
upper layer protocols, including the *Hypertext Transfer Protocol*
(HTTP). *SSL* also defines three upper layer protocols that reside
above the TCP layer on the *SSL Protocol Stack* — the *SSL Handshake Protocol*, the *SSL Change Cipher Spec Protocol*, and the
SSL Alert Protocol [298].

SSL initiates an association between a client and a server that
is termed a *Session*. The establishment of a *Session* defines the
cryptographic parameters to be used by the communicating parties. A *Session* is established via the *SSL Handshake Protocol*. An
SSL Connection is a peer-to-peer transport that is associated with
a *Session*. Typically there are multiple *SSL Connections* during
a given *Session*.

The *SSL Record Protocol* provides two security services — confidentiality and data integrity. The *SSL Record Protocol* encrypts
data using a shared secret key and generates a *MAC* using another
shared secret key, both of which are obtained through the use of
the *SSL Handshake Protocol*. The *SSL Record Protocol* performs
the following process before transmitting data over the TCP layer:

1. The message is *fragmented* into blocks whose maximum size is 16 Kbytes.

2. An optional *compression* algorithm is applied to each block. Note that *SSL* Version 3 specifies no compression algorithm.

3. A *MAC* is computed for each block. The *MAC* is appended to the end of the block.

4. Each block is encrypted using a symmetric-key algorithm. If a block cipher is used for encryption as opposed to a stream cipher, the *MAC* may be padded to ensure that the length of the block with the appended *MAC* is a multiple of the block size of the block cipher.

5. An *SSL Record Header* is prepended to the beginning of each block.

Note that the *MAC* employs either the *MD5* or the *SHA-1 Hash Function* and a shared secret key. Also note that *SSL* encryption supports the use of the block ciphers *AES*, *IDEA*, *RC2-40*, *DES-40*, *DES*, *Triple-DES*, and *Fortezza* in addition to the stream ciphers *RC4-40* and *RC4-128*. Clearly, many of these encryption algorithms are no longer considered to be secure. However, *SSL* allows communicating parties to negotiate the encryption algorithm on a per-session basis. Therefore, algorithms no longer considered secure must be given the lowest priority for selection whereas secure algorithms must be given the highest priority for selection to guarantee the security of the connection.

The *SSL Change Cipher Spec Protocol* uses the *SSL Record Protocol* to transmit a message that causes the update of the current state and thus updates the *Connection's* list of supported cryptographic algorithms, termed the *Cipher Suite*. The *Cipher Suite* lists algorithms in order of preference with the most preferred algorithm listed first. Each list element also defines a key exchange method and the *Cipher Spec*, which specifies the encryption algorithm and the *Hash Function* used for *MAC* generation.

The *SSL Alert Protocol* uses the *SSL Record Protocol* to transmit alert messages to the *Connection's* other peer. *Fatal* alert messages result in the immediate termination of the *Connection*. *Warning* messages do not cause the termination of the *Connection* but are still indications of serious error conditions.

The *SSL Handshake Protocol* allows for mutual authentication of the client and server and the negotiation of the encryption algorithm, the *MAC* algorithm, and the keys. The *SSL Handshake Protocol* must be executed to establish a *Connection* before data transmission may take place. The *SSL Handshake Protocol* proceeds according to the following process:

Establishing Client/Server Capabilities

1. The client sends a *hello* message to the server. The *hello* message contains:

   (a) The highest version of *SSL* supported by the client.

   (b) The client's *Cipher Suite*.

(c) A list of *compression* algorithms supported by the client.

(d) Nonces to prevent *Replay* attacks during the key exchange process.

(e) A *Session* identifier.

2. The server sends a *hello* message to the client with entries for the associated parameters:

(a) The version that is the lesser of the highest version of *SSL* supported by the client and the highest version of *SSL* supported by the server.

(b) The *Cipher Suite* chosen by the server from the client's list.

(c) The *compression* algorithm chosen by the server from the client's list.

(d) Nonces to prevent *Replay* attacks during the key exchange process.

(e) Either the client's *Session* identifier if the identifier was non-zero or a new *Session* identifier.

The *Cipher Suite* specifies multiple parameters, including the key exchange method, the encryption algorithm, and the *MAC* algorithm. The *SSL Handshake Protocol* supports key exchange methods based on the *RSA* algorithm, the *Diffie-Hellman Key Agreement Protocol*, and *Fortezza*. Three key exchange methods based on the *Diffie-Hellman Key Agreement Protocol* are available:

1. The Fixed *Diffie-Hellman Key Agreement Protocol*, which generates an authenticated fixed shared secret key between the client and the server.

2. The Ephemeral *Diffie-Hellman Key Agreement Protocol*, which generates an authenticated temporary shared secret key between the client and the server.

3. The Anonymous *Diffie-Hellman Key Agreement Protocol*, which generates a shared secret key between the client and the server without authentication.

Server Authentication and Key Exchange

1. The server sends its certificate to the client so that the client can authenticate the server's identity. Note that this step does not occur if the Anonymous *Diffie-Hellman Key Agreement Protocol* was selected as the key exchange method.

2. The server sends a key exchange message to the client containing algorithm parameters. Note that this step does not occur if the Fixed *Diffie-Hellman Key Agreement Protocol* was selected as the key exchange method.

3. The server sends a certificate request to the client. Note that this step does not occur if the Anonymous *Diffie-Hellman Key Agreement Protocol* was selected as the key exchange method.

4. The server sends a *done* message to the client to indicate the completion of the server *hello* message.

Client Authentication and Key Exchange

1. The client verifies the server's certificate if the server has sent its certificate to the client.

2. The client sends its certificate to the server if the server has requested the client's certificate.

3. The client sends a key exchange message to the server containing algorithm parameters.

4. The client sends a *certificate verify* message to the server for cases where the client has the ability to generate a *Digital Signature*. This message proves that the client owns the private key for their certificate.

Protocol Completion

1. The client sends a *change Cipher Spec* message to the server and updates the client's current *Cipher Spec*.

2. The client sends a *finished* message to the server using the new *change Cipher Spec*.

3. The server sends a *change Cipher Spec* message to the client and updates the server's current *Cipher Spec*.

4. The server sends a *finished* message to the client using the new *change Cipher Spec*.

SSL was originally developed by Netscape®. Today, Internet browsers, such as Netscape®/AOL LLC's Mozilla Firefox and Navigator and Microsoft® Corporation's Internet Explorer®, are delivered with *SSL* built into the application. Note that *Transport Layer Security* (TLS) is a standardized version of *SSL* [67] that is based on *SSL* Version 3 [298].

11.3.4 Internet Protocol Security

The *Internet Protocol Security* (IPsec) architecture is comprised of a suite of protocols [153, 154, 155] developed to ensure the security services of data integrity, confidentiality, and authentication of data communications over an IP network [116, 243]. *IPsec* is capable of both encrypting and authenticating all network traffic at the IP level and thus is highly flexible, able to be integrated into a wide range of applications [298] . Although the flexibility of the *IPsec* standard has drawn the interest of the commercial sector, this same flexibility has resulted in several problems being identified with the protocols because of their complexity [96]. *IPsec* may be used in three different security domains — Virtual Private Networks (VPNs), application level security, and routing security. When used in application level security or routing security, *IPsec* is not a complete solution and must be coupled with other security measures in order to be effective, hindering its deployment in these domains [36].

IPsec has two modes of operation — *Transport Mode* and *Tunnel Mode*. When operating in *Transport Mode*, the source and

destination hosts must directly perform all cryptographic operations. Encrypted data is sent through a single tunnel that is created with *Layer 2 Tunneling Protocol* (L2TP). Data is encrypted
by the source host and retrieved by the destination host. This
mode of operation establishes end-to-end security. When operating in *Tunnel Mode*, special gateways also perform cryptographic
processing in addition to the source and destination hosts. Here,
many tunnels are created in series between gateways, establishing gateway-to-gateway security [285]. When using either of these
modes, it is important to provide all gateways with the ability to
verify that a packet is real and to authenticate the packet at both
ends, dropping any invalid packets [330].

Two types of *Data Packet Encodings* (DPEs) are required in
IPsec. These are the *Authentication Header* (AH) and the *Encapsulating Security Payload* (ESP) *DPEs*. These encodings offer
network level security for the data [36]. The *AH* provides authenticity and integrity for the packet. The authentication is made
available through *Keyed Hash Functions* or *HMACs*. This header
also prohibits illegal modification and has the option of providing
anti-replay security. The *AH* can establish security between multiple hosts, multiple gateways, or multiple hosts and gateways, all
implementing the *AH* [153]. The *ESP* header provides encryption, data encapsulation, and confidentiality. Confidentiality is
made available through symmetric-key encryption [243].

When passing through the various tunnels and gateways, additional headers are added to a packet. On each pass through a

gateway, a datagram is wrapped in a new header. Included in this header is the *Security Protection Index* (SPI). The *SPI* specifies the algorithms and keys that were used by the last system to view the packet. The payload is also protected in this system because any change or error in the data will be detected and will cause the receiving party to drop the packet. The headers are applied at the beginning of each tunnel and are verified and removed at the end of each tunnel. This method prevents the build-up of unnecessary overhead [116].

An important part of *IPsec* is the *Security Association* (SA). The *SA* uses the *SPI* number that is carried in the *AH* and the *ESP* to indicate which *SA* was used for the packet. An IP destination address is also included to indicate the endpoint — this may be a firewall, router, or end user. An *SA Database* (SAdb) is used to store all *SAs* that are used. A *Security Policy* (SP) is used by the *SAdb* to indicate what the router should do with the packet, such as dropping the packet altogether, dropping only the *SA*, or substituting a different *SA*. All of the *SPs* in use are stored in an *SP Database* (SPdb) [330].

Most *IPsec* implementations are composed of the *SAdb* and its management routines, the *IPsec* protocol engine, and the cryptographic transforms and algorithms [232]. The *SAdb* management routines are used to enforce specific system policies, including the type of information that the system is willing to send or receive in any direction. The *IPsec* protocol engine usually consists of two separate elements — one for outgoing data and one for incoming data. These elements control the application of the input and output cryptographic algorithms to the data, perform verification of authentication data, and modify the IP headers if necessary [232].

Software implementation of *IPsec* occurs predominately at the Operating System (OS) level. An OS level implementation has many advantages. This type of implementation enables developers to write applications that take advantage of *IPsec*. Because developers do not have to develop their own *IPsec* module for their applications, implementation errors are less likely to occur. Security issues also play a significant role in choosing to implement *IPsec* at the OS level. If applications are required to access *IPsec* through the OS, it is less likely that malicious applications will be able to take advantage of any unforeseen ambiguities in the *IPsec* protocol, and in such cases, a single update to the OS is preferable to multiple patches to individual applications. However, systems exist that require the implementation of all or part(s) of *IPsec* at the application level (or in hardware) when developing custom applications. Examples include software applications for embedded systems that either do not use an OS or target an OS that does not incorporate *IPsec*. However, *IPsec* is considered to be a significant improvement versus previously available security protocols. As an example, consider *SSL*, which is widely deployed in various applications. *SSL* is inherently limited in that it is used on the transport/application layer, requiring modifications to any application that wants to include the ability to use *SSL* whereas *IPsec* does not impose this requirement by allowing implementation of the protocol at the OS level.

The continuing upgrade from IPv4 networks to IPv6 networks has affected many protocols, including *IPsec*. One of the main reasons contributing to the need for IPv6 networks is the limited 32-bit address field available in IPv4 networks. Further exacerbating this limitation is the fact that the address field is not used to its full efficiency. IPv6 networks provide a 128-bit address space and manage these addresses more efficiently than IPv4 networks. As an example, IPv4 networks must manually renumber to connect to the Internet, whereas IPv6 networks perform this function automatically [311]. Another issue with IPv4 networks is the need for Network Address Translation (NAT) for internal devices on a network (for example, a home network) [43]. IPv6 networks specify mandatory support of *IPsec*. This enables IPv6 networks to provide all of the features that come with *IPsec*, including strong integrity and authentication of IP packets through the *AH* header and strong integrity and confidentiality of IP packets through the *ESP* header [311].

11.4   Homework Problems

Homework Problem 11.4.1: Why does message authentication imply data integrity? Is the opposite true, i.e. does data integrity imply message authentication? Justify your answers.

Homework Problem 11.4.2: Assume a cryptosystem where the message x is hashed and the hashed result, y, is then concatenated with x and encrypted with a block cipher such that $e_K(x, y)$ is sent over the open channel. Discuss which security services this cryptosystem provides. What services are not provided?

Homework Problem 11.4.3: Assume a cryptosystem where the message x is hashed and the hashed result is digitally signed, resulting in $y = sig_{K_{PR}}(h(x))$. The value y is then concatenated with x such that (x, y) is sent over the open channel. Discuss which security services this cryptosystem provides. What services are not provided?

Homework Problem 11.4.4: Consider **Homework Problem 8.7.6** part (a) which dealt with the *Diffie-Hellman Key Agreement Protocol*. Assume that *Oscar* runs an active *Man-In-The-Middle* attack against the key exchange. *Oscar* uses the value $o = 16$. Compute the key pairs K_{AO} and K_{BO} the way that *Oscar* computes them and the way that *Alice* and *Bob* compute them.

Homework Problem 11.4.5: Assume that *Oscar* attempts to use an active substitution attack against the *Diffie-Hellman Key Agreement Protocol* with certificates as follows:

a) *Alice* wants to communicate with *Bob*. When *Alice* obtains *C(B)* from *Bob*, *Oscar* replaces it with a valid *C(O)*. How will this forgery be detected?

b) Assume the same scenario as part (a) but *Oscar* tries to replace only *Bob's* public key b_B with his own public key b_O. How will this forgery be detected?

Homework Problem 11.4.6: Describe in detail how *Oscar* can create conflict if he manages to trick a *Certifying Authority* into believing that he is *Alice*. What kind of information will the certificate now contain? Show how an authenticated *Diffie-Hellman Key Agreement Protocol* between *Bob* and *Oscar* would look.

Homework Problem 11.4.7: It would seem that *Oscar* could easily run a *Man-In-The-Middle* attack if a party requests a certificate. Assume a certificate is requested by *Alice* by sending the ID and the public key to the *Certifying Authority*. Who will easily detect if *Oscar* replaces *Alice's* public key in the certificate request with his own public kcy?

Homework Problem 11.4.8: Assume *Oscar* has full control over all of *Bob's* communications, i.e. *Oscar* can alter all messages to and from *Bob*. *Oscar* replaces the *Certifying Authority's* public key with his own. Note that *Bob* has no means to authenticate the key that he receives, so he believes that he received the *Certifying Authority's* public key.

a) *Bob* requests a certificate by sending a request containing his ID, *ID(B)*, and his public key, b_B, from the *Certifying Authority*. Describe exactly what *Oscar* must do so that *Bob* does not find out that he has the wrong public *Certifying Authority* key.

b) Describe what *Oscar* must do to establish a session key with *Bob* using the authenticated *Diffie-Hellman Key Agreement Protocol* such that *Bob* thinks he is executing the protocol with *Alice*.

Homework Problem 11.4.9: *Oscar* manages to bribe the *Trusted Authority* in the *Diffie-Hellman Key Agreement Protocol* predistribution scheme. The *Trusted Authority* replaces *Bob's* public key b_B in *Bob's* certificate with b_O, which is known by *Oscar*, and the *Trusted Authority* signs the public key correctly.

a) Is *Oscar* now able to perform a generalized *Man-In-The-Middle* attack, i.e. undetected reading and altering of encrypted messages from *Alice* and *Bob*?

b) What kind of undetected attack can *Oscar* perform? Describe the specific limitations of this attack.

Homework Problem 11.4.10:

a) Describe an attack against which time stamps protect.

b) Draw a simple protocol for a time stamp service involving *Alice* and a *Trusted Authority*. Assume a message x (to be time stamped), a public *Hash Function* $h(x)$, the *Digital Signature* algorithm sig_{TA} of the *Trusted Authority*, and a time stamp TS.

Homework Problem 11.4.11: Consider an authenticated *RSA* encryption cryptosystem where the key information is obtained via a *Trusted Authority*. Assume that in the set-up phase of the cryptosystem, *Oscar* was capable of performing a successful *Man-*

In-The-Middle attack. Show where *Oscar* must inject himself into the process to guarantee that he can read (and alter) encrypted messages from *Alice* to *Bob* and from *Bob* to *Alice* without *Alice* or *Bob* noticing.

Homework Problem 11.4.12: Consider an authenticated *RSA* encryption cryptosystem.

a) Show how an authenticated *RSA* encryption cryptosystem works if *Alice* has the correct *Certifying Authority* verification key. Assume *Alice* sends a message to *Bob*. Do not assume an attacker for this part of the problem. Use the variables (b_B, n_B) for *Bob's* public key and a_B for *Bob's* private key.

b) Assume now that in the set-up phase of the cryptosystem *Oscar* was capable of performing a successful *Man-In-The-Middle* attack such that *Alice* received *Oscar's* public verification key ver_O rather than the one of the *Certifying Authority*. *Alice* again wants to encrypt a message and send it to *Bob*. Show all steps of a protocol in which *Oscar* runs a *Man-In-The-Middle* attack such that he can read (and alter) encrypted messages from *Alice* to *Bob* without *Alice* or *Bob* noticing. Start with *Alice's* attempt to get *Bob's* public key.

Homework Problem 11.4.13: The *Diffie-Hellman Key Agreement Protocol* is as secure as the *Diffie-Hellman* problem which is probably as hard as the *Discrete Logarithm* problem in the *Cyclic Group* Z_p^*. However, this only holds for passive attacks, i.e. if *Os-*

car is only capable of eavesdropping. If *Oscar* can manipulate the messages between *Alice* and *Bob*, the key agreement protocol can be easily broken. Develop an attack against the *Diffie-Hellman Key Agreement Protocol* with *Oscar* in the middle being able to alter messages.

Homework Problem 11.4.14: Compute the two public keys and the common key for the *Diffie-Hellman Key Agreement Protocol* with the parameters $p = 467$, $\alpha = 2$, $a_A = 3$, and $a_B = 5$. Assume that *Oscar* runs an active *Man-In-The-Middle* attack against the key exchange. *Oscar* uses the value $a_O = 16$. Compute the key pairs K_{AO} and K_{BO} the way that *Oscar* computes them and the way that *Alice* and *Bob* compute them.

Homework Problem 11.4.15: Explain why *DES* would be a poor choice as the underlying function for a *Challenge-Response Protocol*.

References

[1] A. Z. Alkar and R. Sönmez. A Hardware Version of the RSA Using the Montgomery's Algorithm with Systolic Arrays. *Integration, the VLSI Journal*, 38(2):299–307, December 2004.

[2] N. Abu-Khader and P. Siy. Systolic Galois Field Exponentiation in a Multiple-Valued Logic Technique. *Integration, the VLSI Journal*, 39(3):229–251, June 2006.

[3] C. Adams. The CAST-256 Encryption Algorithm. In *First Advanced Encryption Standard (AES) Conference*, Ventura, California, USA, 1998.

[4] I. Ahmad and A. Shoba Das. Hardware Implementation Analysis of SHA-256 and SHA-512 Algorithms on FPGAs. *Computers and Electrical Engineering*, 31(6):345–360, September 2005.

[5] F. Aisopos, K. Aisopos, D. Schinianakis, H. Michail, and A. P. Kakarountas. A Novel High-Throughput Implementation of a Partially Unrolled SHA-512. In *Proceedings of the Thirteenth IEEE Mediterranean Electrotechnical Conference — MELECON 2006*, pages 61–65, Malaga, Spain, May 16–19 2006.

[6] K. Aisopos, A. P. Kakarountas, H. Michail, and C. E. Goutis. High Throughput Implementation of the New Secure Hash Algorithm Through Partial Unrolling. In *Proceedings of the 2005 IEEE International Workshop on Signal Processing Systems — SIPS '05*, pages 99–103, Athens, Greece, November 2–4 2005.

[7] ALMA Technologies. ALMA Technologies Products. http://www.alma-tech.com.

[8] Amphion. Amphion Products. http://www.amphion.com/index.html.

[9] B. Ansari and M. Anwar Hasan. High Performance Architecture of Elliptic Curve Scalar Multiplication. Technical

Report CACR 2006-01, University of Waterloo, Waterloo, Ontario, Canada, 2006.

[10] ANSI X9.17-1995. *Financial Institution Key Management (Wholesale)*. American National Standards Institute, Washington, DC, USA, 1995.

[11] ANSI X9.30-1. *Public Key Cryptography Using Irreversible Algorithms — Part 1: The Digital Signature Algorithm (DSA)*. American National Standards Institute, Washington, DC, USA, 1997.

[12] ANSI X9.30-2. *Public Key Cryptography Using Irreversible Algorithms — Part 2: The Secure Hash Algorithm (SHA-1)*. American National Standards Institute, Washington, DC, USA, 1997.

[13] ANSI X9.31. *Digital Signatures Using Reversible Public Key Cryptography for the Financial Services Industry (rDSA)*. American National Standards Institute, Washington, DC, USA, 1998.

[14] ANSI X9.32. *Data Compression in Financial Telecommunications*. American National Standards Institute, Washington, DC, USA, 2006.

[15] ANSI X9.42. *Public Key Cryptography for the Financial Services Industry: Agreement of Symmetric Keys Using Discrete Logarithm Cryptography*. American National Standards Institute, Washington, DC, USA, 2003.

[16] ANSI X9.62. *Public Key Cryptography for the Financial Services Industry, The Elliptic Curve Digital Signature Algorithm (ECDSA)*. American National Standards Institute, Washington, DC, USA, 2005.

[17] ANSI X9.63. *Public Key Cryptography for the Financial Services Industry, Key Agreement and Key Transport Using Elliptic Curve Cryptography*. American National Standards Institute, Washington, DC, USA, 2003.

[18] S. Bajracharya, C. Shu, K. Gaj, and T. El-Ghazawi. Implementation of Elliptic Curve Cryptosystems Over $GF(2^n)$ in Optimal Normal Basis on a Reconfigurable Computer. In J. Becker, M. Platzner, and S. Vernalde, editors, *Proceedings of the International Conference on Field Programmable Logic and Applications — FPL '04*, volume LNCS 3203, pages 1001–1005, Leuven, Belgium, August 30–September 1 2004. Springer-Verlag.

[19] P. S. L. M. Barreto. Optimized Rijndael C Code v3.0. http://homes.esat.kuleuven.be/~rijmen/rijndael-fst-3.0.zip.

[20] P. D. Barrett. Implementing the Rivest Shamir and Adleman Public Key Encryption Algorithm on a Standard Digital Signal Processor. In A. M. Odlyzko, editor, *Advances in*

Cryptology – CRYPTO '86, volume LNCS 263, pages 311–323, Santa Barbara, California, USA, August 11–15 1986. Springer-Verlag.

[21] S. Bartolini, I. Branovic, R. Giorgi, and E. Martinelli. A Performance Evaluation of ARM ISA Extension for Elliptic Curve Cryptography Over Binary Finite Fields. In *Proceedings of the Sixteenth Symposium on Computer Architecture and High Performance Computing — SBC-PAD 2004*, pages 238–245, Foz do Iguaçu, Brazil, October 27–29 2004.

[22] L. Batina, G. Bruin-Muurling, and S. B. Örs. Flexible Hardware Design for RSA and Elliptic Curve Cryptosytems. In *Proceedings of the Cryptographer's Track at the RSA Conference — CT-RSA*, volume LNCS 2964, pages 250–263, San Francisco, California, USA, February 23–27 2004. Springer-Verlag.

[23] L. Batina, S. B. Örs, B. Preneel, and J. Vandewalle. Hardware Architectures for Public Key Cryptography. *Integration, the VLSI Journal*, 34(1-2):1–64, May 2003.

[24] M. Bednara, M. Daldrup, J. Teich, J. von zur Gathen, and J. Shokrollahi. Tradeoff Analysis of FPGA Based Elliptic Curve Cryptography. In *Proceedings of the 2002 International Symposium on Circuits and Systems — ISCAS 2002*, volume 5, pages 797–800, Scottsdale, Arizona, USA, May 26–29 2002.

[25] M. Bednara, M. Daldrup, J. von zur Gathen, J. Shokrollahi, and J. Teich. Reconfigurable Implementation of Elliptic Curve Crypto Algorithms. In *Proceedings of the Sixteenth International Parallel and Distributed Processing Symposium, Reconfigurable Architectures Workshop — IPDPS 2002, RAW 2002*, Fort Lauderdale, Florida, USA, April 15 2002.

[26] M. Bellare, R. Canetti, and H. Krawczyk. Keying Hash Functions for Message Authentication. In N. Koblitz, editor, *Advances in Cryptology — CRYPTO '96*, volume LNCS 1109, pages 1–15, Santa Barbara, California, USA, August 18–22 1996. Springer-Verlag.

[27] G. Bertoni, L. Breveglieri, P. Fragneto, M. Macchetti, and S. Marchesin. Efficient Software Implementation of AES on 32-Bit Platforms. In B. S. Kaliski Jr., Ç. K. Koç, and C. Paar, editors, *Workshop on Cryptographic Hardware and Embedded Systems — CHES 2002*, volume LNCS 2523, pages 159–171, Redwood Shores, California, USA, August 13–15 2002. Springer-Verlag.

[28] T. Beth and D. Gollmann. Algorithm Engineering for Public

Key Algorithms. *IEEE Journal on Selected Areas in Communications*, 7(4):458–466, May 1989.

[29] E. Biham. On the Applicability of Differential Cryptanalysis to Hash Functions. In *EIES Workshop on Cryptographic Hash Functions*, Santa Barbara, California, USA, March 1992. Workshop Lecture.

[30] E. Biham. New Types of Cryptanalytic Attacks Using Related Keys. In T. Helleseth, editor, *Advances in Cryptology – EUROCRYPT '93*, volume LNCS 765, pages 398–409, Lofthus, Norway, May 23–27 1993. Springer-Verlag.

[31] E. Biham. A Fast New DES Implementation in Software. In E. Biham, editor, *Fourth International Workshop on Fast Software Encryption*, volume LNCS 1267, pages 260–272, Haifa, Israel, January 20–22 1997. Springer-Verlag.

[32] E. Biham and A. Shamir. Differential Cryptanalysis of DES-like Cryptosystems. In A. J. Menezes and S. A. Vanstone, editors, *Advances in Cryptology — CRYPTO '90*, volume LNCS 537, pages 2–21, Santa Barbara, California, USA, August 11–15 1990. Springer-Verlag.

[33] I. Blake, G. Seroussi, and N. Smart. *Elliptic Curves in Cryptography*. Cambridge University Press, London Mathematical Society Lecture Notes Series 265, 1999.

[34] T. Blum and C. Paar. Montgomery Modular Multiplication on Reconfigurable Hardware. In *14th IEEE Symposium on Computer Arithmetic (ARITH-14)*, Adelaide, Australia, April 14–16 1999.

[35] T. Blum and C. Paar. High Radix Montgomery Modular Exponentiation on Reconfigurable Hardware. *IEEE Transactions on Computers*, 50(7):759–764, November 2001.

[36] T. C. Bressoud. IP Security Paper Summary. Technical report, Mathematics and Computer Science Department, Denison University, Granville, Ohio, USA, September 2003.

[37] E. F. Brickell. A Fast Modular Multiplication Algorithm with Application to Two Key Cryptography. In D. Chaum, R. L. Rivest, and A. T. Sherman, editors, *Advances in Cryptology — CRYPTO '82*, pages 51–60, Santa Barbara, California, USA, 1982.

[38] E. F. Brickell, D. M. Gordon, K. S. McCurley, and D. B. Wilson. Fast Exponentiation with Precomputation. In R. A. Rueppel, editor, *Advances in Cryptology – EUROCRYPT '92*, volume LNCS 658, pages 200–207, Balatonfüred, Hungary, May 1992. Springer-Verlag.

[39] J. Burke, J. McDonald, and T. M. Austin. Architectural Support for Fast Symmetric-Key Cryptography. In *Proceedings of the Ninth International Conference on Archi-*

tectural Support for Programming Languages and Operating Systems — AS-PLOS 2000, pages 178–189, Cambridge, Massachusetts, USA, November 12–15 2000.

[40] K.-Y. Chang, D. Hong, and H.-S. Cho. Low Complexity Bit-Parallel Multiplier for $GF(2^m)$ Defined by All-One Polynomials Using Redundant Representation. *IEEE Transactions on Computers*, 54(12):1628–1630, December 2005.

[41] P.-S. Chen, S.-A. Hwang, and C.-W. Wu. A Systolic RSA Public Key Cryptosystem. In *Proceedings of the 1996 International Symposium on Circuits and Systems — ISCAS 1996*, volume 4, pages 408–411, Atlanta, Georgia, USA, May 12–15 1996. IEEE, Inc.

[42] K. S. Cho, J. H. Ruy, and J. D. Cho. High-Speed Modular Multiplication Algorithm for RSA Cryptosystem. In *Proceedings of the 27th Annual Conference of the IEEE Industrial Electronics Society — IECON 2001*, volume 1, pages 479–483, Denver, Colorado, USA, November 29–December 2 2001. IEEE Inc.

[43] T. Chown. IPv6 in the Home Makes Sense. Technical report, EU IPv6 Task Force, University of Southampton, September 2002.

[44] J. W. Chung, S. G. Sim, and P. J. Lee. Fast Implementation of Elliptic Curve Defined over $GF(p^m)$ on CalmRISC with MAC2424 Coprocessor. In Ç. K. Koç and C. Paar, editors, *Workshop on Cryptographic Hardware and Embedded Systems — CHES 2000*, volume LNCS 1965, pages 57–70, Worcester, Massachusetts, USA, August 2000. Springer-Verlag.

[45] A. Cilardo, L. Coppolino, N. Mazzocca, and L. Romano. Elliptic Curve Cryptography Engineering. *Proceedings of the IEEE*, 94(2):395–406, February 2006.

[46] A. Cilardo, A. Mazzeo, L. Romano, and G. Saggese. Exploring the Design-Space for FPGA-Based Implementation of RSA. *Microprocessors and Microsystems*, 28(4):183–191, May 2004.

[47] A. Cilardo, A. Mazzeo, L. Romano, and G. P. Saggese. Carry-Save Montgomery Modular Exponentiation on Reconfigurable Hardware. In *Proceedings of the 2004 Conference on Design, Automation and Test in Europe Conference and Exhibition — DATE 2004*, volume 3, pages 206–211, Paris, France, February 16–20 2004.

[48] H. Cohen, A. Miyaji, and T. Ono. Efficient Elliptic Curve Exponentiation Using Mixed Coordinates. In K. Ohta and D. Pci, editors, *Advances in Cryptology — ASIACRYPT'98*, volume LNCS 1514, pages 51–65. Springer-Verlag, 1998.

[49] D. Coppersmith. The Data Encryption Standard (DES) and Its Strength Against Attacks. *IBM Journal of Research and Development*, 38(3):243, May 1994.

[50] D. Coppersmith, H. Krawczyk, and Y. Mansour. The Shrinking Generator. In D. R. Stinson, editor, *Proceedings of the 13th Annual International Cryptology Conference on Advances in Cryptology*, volume LNCS 773, pages 22–39, Santa Barbara, California, USA, August 22–26 1993. Springer-Verlag.

[51] D. Coppersmith, A. Odlyzko, and R. Schroeppel. Discrete Logarithms in GF(p). *Algorithmica*, 1(1):1–15, 1986.

[52] M. Curtin. *Brute Force: Cracking the Data Encryption Standard.* Springer, 2005.

[53] L. Dadda, M. Macchetti, and J. Owen. An ASIC Design for a High Speed Implementation of the Hash Function SHA-256 (384, 512). In D. Garrett, J. Lach, and C. A. Zukowski, editors, *Proceedings of the Fourteenth ACM Great Lakes Symposium on VLSI*, pages 421–425, Boston, Massachusetts, USA, April 26–28 2004.

[54] L. Dadda, M. Macchetti, and J. Owen. The Design of a High Speed ASIC Unit for the Hash Function SHA-256 (384, 512). In *Proceedings of the 2004 Conference on Design, Automation and Test in Europe Conference and Exhibition — DATE 2004*, volume 3, pages 70–75, Paris, France, February 16–20 2004.

[55] J. Daemen. *Cipher and Hash Function Design Strategies Based on Linear and Differential Cryptanalysis.* PhD thesis, Katholieke Universiteit Leuven, The Netherlands, March 1995.

[56] J. Daemen, L. Knudsen, and V. Rijmen. The Block Cipher SQUARE. In E. Biham, editor, *Fourth International Workshop on Fast Software Encryption*, volume LNCS 1267, pages 149–165, Haifa, Israel, January 20–22 1997. Springer-Verlag.

[57] J. Daemen and V. Rijmen. AES Proposal: Rijndael. In *First Advanced Encryption Standard (AES) Conference*, Ventura, California, USA, 1998.

[58] J. Daemen and V. Rijmen. *The Design of Rijndael.* Springer, New York, New York, USA, 2002.

[59] A. Daly and W. Marnane. Efficient Architectures for Implementing Montgomery Modular Multiplication and RSA Modular Exponentiation on Reconfigurable Logic. In *ACM/SIGDA International Symposium on Field Programmable Gate Arrays 2002 — FPGA '02*, pages 40–49, Monterey, California, USA, February 24–26 2002. ACM

Press.

[60] A. Daly, W. Marnane, T. Kerins, and E. Popovici. An FPGA Implementation of a GF(p) ALU for Encryption Processors. *Microprocessors and Microsystems*, 28(5-6):253–260, August 2004.

[61] A. K. Daneshbeh and M. A. Hasan. Area Efficient High Speed Elliptic Curve Cryptoprocessor for Random Curves. In *Proceedings of the Symposium on Information Technology: Coding and Computing — ITCC 2004*, volume 2, pages 588–592, Las Vegas, Nevada, USA, April 5–7 2004.

[62] G. M. de Dormale and J.-J. Quisquater. High-Speed Hardware Implementations of Elliptic Curve Cryptography: A Survey. *Journal of Systems Architecture*, 53(2-3):72–84, February 2007.

[63] J. Deepakumara, H. M. Heys, and R. Venkatesan. FPGA Implementation of MD5 Hash Algorithm. In *Proceedings of the Canadian Conference on Electrical and Computer Engineering — CCECE 2001*, volume 2, pages 919–924, Toronto, Ontario, Canada, May 13–16 2001.

[64] B. den Boer and A. Bosselaers. An Attack on the Last Two Rounds of MD4. In J. Feigenbaum, editor, *Advances in Cryptology — CRYPTO '91*, volume LNCS 576, pages 194–203, Santa Barbara, California, USA, August 11–15 1991. Springer-Verlag.

[65] B. den Boer and A. Bosselaers. Collisions for the Compression Function of MD5. In T. Helleseth, editor, *Advances in Cryptology — EUROCRYPT '93*, volume LNCS 765, pages 293–304, Lofthus, Norway, May 23–27 1993. Springer-Verlag.

[66] C. D'Halluin, G. Bijnens, V. Rijmen, and B. Preneel. Attack on Six Rounds of Crypton. In L. R. Knudson, editor, *Sixth International Workshop on Fast Software Encryption*, volume LNCS 1636, pages 46–59, Rome, Italy, March 24–26 1999. Springer-Verlag.

[67] T. Dierks and C. Allen. *RFC 2246: The TLS Protocol Version 1.0*. Corporation for National Research Initiatives, Internet Engineering Task Force, Network Working Group, Reston, Virginia, USA, January 1999.

[68] M. J. Diez, S. Bojanić, L. J. Stanimirović, C. Carreras, and O. Nieto-Taladriz. Hash Algorithms for Cryptographic Protocols: FPGA Implementations. In *Proceedings of the Telecommunications Forum — TELFOR 2002*, pages 26–28, Belgrade, Yugoslavia, November 26–28 2002.

[69] W. Diffie. The First Ten Years of Public-Key Cryptography. *Proceedings of the IEEE*, 76(5):560–577, May 1988.

[70] W. Diffie and M. E. Hellman. New Directions in Cryptogra-

phy. *IEEE Transactions on Information Theory*, IT-22:644–654, 1976.

[71] W. Diffie, P. C. Van Oorschot, and M. J. Weiner. Authentication and Authenticated Key Exchanges. *Designs, Codes and Cryptography*, 2(2):107–125, June 1992.

[72] H. Dobbertin, A. Bosselaers, and B. Preneel. RIPEMD-160, A Strengthened Version of RIPEMD. In D. Gollmann, editor, *Third International Workshop on Fast Software Encryption*, volume LNCS 1039, pages 71–82, Cambridge, United Kingdom, February 21-23 1996. Springer-Verlag.

[73] S. Dominikus. A Hardware Implementation of MD4-Family Hash Algorithms. In *Proceedings of the Ninth International Conference on Electronics, Circuits and Systems — ICECS '02*, volume 3, pages 1143–1146, Dubrovnik, Croatia, September 15–18 2002.

[74] P. W. Dowd and J. T. McHenry. Network Security: It's Time to Take It Seriously. *IEEE Computer*, 31(9):24–28, September 1998.

[75] M. Dworkin. *NIST Special Publication SP800-38A*. National Institute of Standards and Technology, Gaithersburg, Maryland, USA, December 2001.

[76] M. Dworkin. *NIST Special Publication SP800-38C*. National Institute of Standards and Technology, Gaithersburg, Maryland, USA, May 2004.

[77] M. Dworkin. *NIST Special Publication SP800-38B*. National Institute of Standards and Technology, Gaithersburg, Maryland, USA, May 2005.

[78] Z. Dyka and P. Langendoerfer. Area Efficient Hardware Implementation of Elliptic Curve Cryptography by Iteratively Applying Karatsuba's Method. In *Proceedings of the 2005 Design, Automation, and Test in Europe Conference and Exhibition — DATE 2005*, volume 3, pages 70–75, Munich, Germany, March 7–11 2005.

[79] H. Eberle, N. Gura, and S. Chang-Shantz. A Cryptographic Processor for Arbitrary Elliptic Curves Over $GF(2^m)$. In *Proceedings of the Fourteenth IEEE International Conference on Application-Specific Systems, Architectures and Processors — ASAP 2003*, pages 455–468, The Hague, The Netherlands, June 24–26 2003.

[80] H. Eberle, N. Gura, S. Chang-Shantz, V. Gupta, L. Rarick, and S. Sundaram. A Public-Key Cryptographic Processor for RSA and ECC. In *Proceedings of the Fifteenth IEEE International Conference on Application-Specific Systems, Architectures and Processors — ASAP 2004*, pages 98–110, Galveston, Texas, USA, September 27–29 2004.

[81] H. Eberle, S. Shantz, V. Gupta, N. Gura, L. Rarick, and L. Spracklen. Accelerating Next-Generation Public-Key Cryptosystems on General-Purpose CPUs. *IEEE Micro*, 25(2):52–59, March-April 2005.

[82] A. J. Elbirt. *Reconfigurable Computing for Symmetric-Key Algorithms*. PhD thesis, Worcester Polytechnic Institute, Worcester, Massachusetts, USA, April 2002.

[83] A. J. Elbirt. Efficient Implementation of Galois Field Fixed Field Constant Multiplication. In *Proceedings of the International Conference on Information Technology: New Generation — ITNG '06*, pages 172–177, Las Vegas, Nevada, USA, April 10–12 2006.

[84] A. J. Elbirt. Fast and Efficient Implementation of AES Via Instruction Set Extensions. In *Proceedings of the Third IEEE International Symposium on Security in Networks and Distributed Systems*, pages 396–403, Niagara Falls, Canada, May 21–23 2007.

[85] A. J. Elbirt, W. Yip, B. Chetwynd, and C. Paar. An FPGA Implementation and Performance Evaluation of the AES Block Cipher Candidate Algorithm Finalists. In *The Third Advanced Encryption Standard Candidate Conference*, pages 13–27, New York, New York, USA, April 13–14 2000. National Institute of Standards and Technology.

[86] A. J. Elbirt, W. Yip, B. Chetwynd, and C. Paar. An FPGA-Based Performance Evaluation of the AES Block Cipher Candidate Algorithm Finalists. *IEEE Transactions on Very Large Scale Integration (VLSI) Systems*, 9(4):545–557, August 2001.

[87] S. E. Eldridge and C. D. Walter. Hardware Implementation of Montgomery's Modular Multiplication Algorithm. *IEEE Transactions on Computers*, 42(6):693–699, July 1993.

[88] Wikipedia: The Free Encyclopedia. Cryptography/History of Cryptography. http://en.wikipedia.org/wiki/History_of_cryptography, November 1 2006.

[89] Wikipedia: The Free Encyclopedia. Cryptography. http://en.wikipedia.org/wiki/Cryptography, February 20 2007.

[90] Wikipedia: The Free Encyclopedia. Gilbert Vernam. http://en.wikipedia.org/wiki/Gilbert_Vernam, February 11 2007.

[91] Wikipedia: The Free Encyclopedia. Lorenz Cipher. http://en.wikipedia.org/wiki/Lorenz_cipher, January 18 2007.

[92] M. Ernst, M. Jung, F. Madlener, S. Huss, and R. Blümel.

A Reconfigurable System on Chip Implementation for Elliptic Curve Cryptography Over $GF(2^m)$. In B. S. Kaliski Jr., Ç. K. Koç, and C. Paar, editors, *Workshop on Cryptographic Hardware and Embedded Systems — CHES 2002*, volume LNCS 2523, pages 381–399, Redwood Shores, California, USA, August 13–15 2002. Springer-Verlag.

[93] M. Ernst, S. Klupsh, O. Hauck, and S. A. Huss. Rapid Prototyping for Hardware Accelerated Elliptic Curve Public-Key Cryptosystems. In *Proceedings of the Twelfth International Workshop on Rapid System Prototyping — RSP 2001*, pages 24–29, Monterey, California, USA, June 25–27 2001.

[94] H. Feistel. Cryptography and Computer Privacy. *Scientific American*, 228(5):15–23, May 1973.

[95] N. Ferguson, J. Kelsey, S. Lucks, B. Schneier, M. Stay, D. Wagner, and D. Whiting. Improved Cryptanalysis of Rijndael. In *Seventh International Workshop on Fast Software Encryption*, volume LNCS 1978, pages 213–230, New York, New York, USA, April 10–12 2000. Springer-Verlag.

[96] N. Ferguson and B. Schneier. A Cryptographic Evaluation of IPsec. Technical report, Counterpane Internet Security, Inc., Mountain View, California, USA, 1999.

[97] A. P. Fournaris and O. Koufopavlou. A New RSA Encryption Architecture and Hardware Implementation Based on Optimized Montgomery Multiplication. In *Proceedings of the 2005 IEEE International Symposium on Circuits and Systems — ISCAS 2005*, volume 5, pages 4645–4648, Kobe, Japan, May 23–26 2005. IEEE, Inc.

[98] Free Software Foundation, Inc. Documentation for the GNU MP Long Number Library Functions. http://www.gnu.org/software/gmp/manual/, June 19 2002.

[99] W. F. Friedman and L. D. Callimahos. *Military Cryptanalytics Part I — Volume 2*. Aegean Park Press, Laguna Hills, California, USA, 1985.

[100] W. Gai and H. Chen. A Systolic Linear Array for Modular Multiplication. In *Proceedings of the Second IEEE International Conference on ASIC*, pages 171–174, Shanghai, China, October 21–24 1996.

[101] H. F. Gaines. *Cryptanalysis*. Dover Publications, Inc., New York, New York, USA, 1956.

[102] K. Gaj and P. Chodowiec. Comparison of the Hardware Performance of the AES Candidates Using Reconfigurable Hardware. In *The Third Advanced Encryption Standard Candidate Conference*, pages 40–54, New York, New York, USA, April 13–14 2000. National Institute of Standards and

Technology.

[103] T. El Gamal. A Public-Key Cryptosystem and a Signature Scheme Based on Discrete Logarithms. *IEEE Transactions on Information Theory*, 31(4):469–472, 1985.

[104] T. S. Ganesh, M. T. Frederick, T. S. B. Sudarshan, and A. K. Somani. Hashchip: A Shared-Resource Multi-Hash Function Processor Architecture on FPGA. *Integration, the VLSI Journal*, 40(1):11–19, January 2007.

[105] T. S. Ganesh and T. S. B. Sudarshan. ASIC Implementation of a Unified Hardware Architecture for Non-Key Based Cryptographic Hash Primitives. In *Proceedings of the International Conference on Information Technology: Coding and Computing — ITCC '05*, volume 1, pages 580–585, Las Vegas, Nevada, USA, April 4–6 2005.

[106] T. S. Ganesh, T. S. B. Sudarshan, N. K. Srinivasan, and K. Jayapal. Pre-Silicon Prototyping of a Unified Hardware Architecture for Cryptographic Manipulation Detection Codes. In *Proceedings of the Third IEEE International Conference on Field Programmable Technology — ICFPT 2004*, pages 323–326, Brisbane, Australia, December 6–8 2004.

[107] F. Gang. Design of Modular Multiplier Based on Improved Montgomery Algorithm and Systolic Array. In *Proceedings of the First International Multi-Symposiums on Computer and Computational Sciences — IMSCCS '06*, volume 2, pages 356–359, Hangzhou, China, April 20–24 2006.

[108] S. L. Garfinkel. *PGP: Pretty Good Privacy*. O'Reilly and Associates, Sebastopol, California, USA, 1995.

[109] W. Geiselmann and R. Steinwandt. A Redundant Representation of $GF(q^n)$ for Designing Arithmetic Circuits. *IEEE Transactions on Computers*, 52(7):848–853, July 2003.

[110] P. Gil. How Big Is the Internet? http://netforbeginners.about.com/cs/technoglossary/ f/FAQ3.htm, 2005.

[111] C. Grabbe, M. Bednara, J. von zur Gathen, J. Shokrollahi, and J. Teich. A High Performance VLIW Processor for Finite Field Arithmetic. In *Proceedings of the Seventeenth International Parallel and Distributed Processing Symposium, Reconfigurable Architectures Workshop — IPDPS 2003, RAW 2003*, Nice, France, April 22 2003.

[112] T. Grembowski, R. Lien, K. Gaj, N. Nguyen, P. Bellows, J. Flidr, T. Lehman, and B. Schott. Comparative Analysis of the Hardware Implementations of Hash Functions SHA-1 and SHA-512. In A. H. Chan and V. Gligor, editors, *Proceedings of the Fifth International Information Security*

Conference — ISC 2002, volume LNCS 2433, pages 75–89, Sao Paulo, Brazil, September 30–October 2 2002. Springer-Verlag.

[113] J. H. Guo and C. L. Wang. A Novel Digit-Serial Systolic Array for Modular Multiplication. In *Proceedings of the 1998 International Symposium on Circuits and Systems — ISCAS 1998*, volume 2, pages 177–180, Monterey, California, USA, May 31–June 3 1998. IEEE, Inc.

[114] J.-H. Guo, C.-L. Wang, and H.-C. Hu. Design and Implementation of an RSA Public-Key Cryptosystem. In *Proceedings of the 1999 International Symposium on Circuits and Systems — ISCAS 1999*, pages 504–507, Orlando, Florida, USA, May 30–June 2 1999.

[115] N. Gura, S. Chang-Shantz, H. Eberle, D. Finchelstein, S. Gupta, V. Gupta, and D. Stebila. An End-to-End Systems Approach to Elliptic Curve Cryptography. In B. S. Kaliski Jr., Ç. K. Koç, and C. Paar, editors, *Workshop on Cryptographic Hardware and Embedded Systems — CHES 2002*, volume LNCS 2523, pages 349–365, Redwood Shores, California, USA, August 13–15 2002. Springer-Verlag.

[116] J. D. Guttman, A. L. Herzog, and F. J. Thayer. Authentication and Confidentiality via IPsec. In F. Cuppens, Y. Deswarte, D. Gollmann, and M. Waidner, editors, *Proceedings of the Sixth European Symposium on Research in Computer Security — ESORICS 2000*, volume LNCS 1895, pages 255–272, Toulouse, France, October 4–6 2000.

[117] M. K. Hani, T. S. Lin, and N. Shaikh-Husin. FPGA Implementation of RSA Public-Key Cryptographic Coprocessor. In *Proceedings — TENCON 2000*, volume 3, pages 6–11, Kuala Lampur, Malaysia, September 24–27 2000.

[118] F. A. Harris. *Solving Simple Substitution Ciphers*. USA American Cryptograph Association, 1959.

[119] M. A. Hasan and M. Ebtedaei. Efficient Architectures for Computations Over Variable Dimensional Galois Fields. *IEEE Transactions on Circuits and Systems I*, 45(11):1205–1211, November 1998.

[120] O. Hauck, A. Katock, and S. A. Huss. VLSI System Design Using Asynchronous Wave Pipelines: A 0.35 μm CMOS 1.5 GHz Elliptic Curve Public Key Cryptosystem Chip. In *Proceedings of the Sixth International Symposium on Asynchronous Circuits and Systems — ASYNC 2000*, pages 188–197, Eilat, Israel, April 2–6 2000.

[121] The Government Communications Headquarters. Public-Key Encryption — How GCHW Got There First! http://www.gchq.gov.uk/about/pke.html.

[122] Helion Technology. Helion IP Core Products. http://www.heliontech.com/core.htm/.

[123] T. Hisakadot, N. Kobayashi, S. Goto, T. Ikenagat, K. Higashi, I. Kitao, and Y. Tsunoo. 61.5mW 2048-Bit RSA Cryptographic Co-Processor LSI Based on N Bit-Wised Modular Multiplier. In *Proceedings of the 2006 International Symposium on VLSI Design, Automation and Test*, pages 1–4, Hsinchu, Tiawan, April 26–28 2006.

[124] A. Hodjat and I. Verbauwhede. A 21.54 Gbit/s Fully Pipelined AES Processor on FPGA. In *Proceedings of the Twelfth Annual IEEE Symposium on Field-Programmable Custom Computing Machines — FCCM 2004*, pages 308–309, Napa, California, USA, April 20–23 2004. IEEE, Inc.

[125] A. Hodjat and I. Verbauwhede. Interfacing a High Speed Crypto Accelerator to an Embedded CPU. In *Proceedings of the 38th Asilomar Conference on Signals, Systems, and Computers*, volume 1, pages 488–492, Los Angeles, California, USA, November 7–10 2004.

[126] A. Hodjat and I. Verbauwhede. Minimum Area Cost for a 30 to 70 Gbits/s AES Processor. In *Proceedings of the IEEE Computer Society Annual Symposium on VLSI Emerging Trends in VLSI System Design — ISVLSI'04*, pages 83–88, Lafayette, Louisiana, USA, February 19–20 2004. IEEE, Inc.

[127] J.-H. Hong and C.-W. Wu. Radix-4 Modular Multiplication and Exponentiation Algorithms for the RSA Public-Key Cryptosystem. In *Proceedings of the 2000 Asia and South Pacific Design Automation Conference — ASP-DAC 2000*, pages 565–570, Yokohama, Japan, January 25–28 2000.

[128] L. Hong-Qiang and M. Chang-Yun. Hardware Implementation of Hash Function SHA-512. In *Proceedings of the First International Conference on Innovative Computing, Information and Control — ICICIC '06*, volume 2, pages 38–42, Beijing, China, August 30–September 1 2006.

[129] J. Hughes. Implementation of NBS/DES Encryption Algorithm in Software. In *Colloquium on Techniques and Implications of Digital Privacy and Authentication Systems*, 1981.

[130] S. A. Huss, M. Jung, and F. Madlener. High Speed Elliptic Curve Crypto Processors: Design Space Exploration by Means of Reconfigurable Hardware. In *Proceedings of the International Scientific and Applied Conference — Information Security*, July 2004.

[131] T. Ichikawa, T. Kasuya, and M. Matsui. Hardware Evaluation of the AES Finalists. In *The Third Advanced Encryption Standard Candidate Conference*, pages 279–285, New York, New York, USA, April 13–14 2000. National Institute

of Standards and Technology.

[132] IEEE P1363. *IEEE Standard Specifications for Public-Key Cryptography*. The Institute of Electrical and Electronics Engineers, Inc., New York, New York, USA, 2000.

[133] IEEE P1363a. *IEEE Standard Specifications for Public-Key Cryptography — Amendment 1: Additional Techniques*. The Institute of Electrical and Electronics Engineers, Inc., New York, New York, USA, 2004.

[134] International Organization for Standardization, Geneva, Switzerland. *ISO/IEC 9798 Information Technology — Security Techniques — Entity Authentication*, 2005.

[135] International Telecommunication Union Telecommunication Standardization Sector. *X.509: Information Technology — Open Systems Interconnection — The Directory: Public-Key and Attribute Certificate Frameworks*, Geneva, Switzerland 2005.

[136] S. Ishii, K. Ohyama, and K. Yamanaka. A Single-Chip RSA Processor Implemented in a 0.5 μm Rule Gate Array. In *Proceedings of the Seventh Annual IEEE International ASIC Conference and Exhibit*, pages 433–436, Rochester, New York, USA, September 19–23 1994.

[137] K. Itoh, M. Takenaka, N. Torii, S. Temma, and Y. Kurihara. Fast Implementation of Public-Key Cryptography on a DSP TMS320C6201. In Ç. K. Koç and C. Paar, editors, *Workshop on Cryptographic Hardware and Embedded Systems — CHES 1999*, volume LNCS 1717, pages 61–72, Worcester, Massachusetts, USA, August 12–13 1999. Springer-Verlag.

[138] K. Iwamura, T. Matsumoto, and H. Imai. Montgomery Modular-Multiplication Method and Systolic Arrays Suitable for Modular Exponentiation. *Electronics and Communications in Japan*, 77(3):40–50, January 1994.

[139] J. Großchädl. The Chinese Remainder Theorem and Its Application in a High-Speed RSA Crypto Chip. In *Proceedings of the Sixteenth Annual Conference on Computer Security Applications — ACSAC '00*, pages 384–393, New Orleans, Louisiana, USA, December 11–15 2000.

[140] J. Großchädl and E. Savas. Instruction Set Extensions for Fast Arithmetic in Finite Fields GF(p) and GF(2^m). In M. Joye and J.-J. Quisquater, editors, *Workshop on Cryptographic Hardware and Embedded Systems — CHES 2004*, volume LNCS 3156, pages 133–147, Cambridge, Massachusetts, USA, August 11–13 2004. Springer-Verlag.

[141] J. Großchädl and G.-A. Kamendje. Instruction Set Extension for Fast Elliptic Curve Cryptography Over Binary Finite Fields GF(2^m). In *Proceedings of the Fourteenth IEEE*

International Conference on Application-Specific Systems, Architectures and Processors — ASAP 2003, pages 455–468, The Hague, The Netherlands, June 24–26 2003.

[142] J. Irwin and D. Page. Using Media Processors for Low-Memory AES Implementation. In *Proceedings of the Fourteenth IEEE International Conference on Application-Specific Systems, Architectures and Processors — ASAP 2003*, pages 144–154, The Hague, The Netherlands, June 24–26 2003.

[143] T. Jakobsen and L. R. Knudsen. The Interpolation Attack on Block Ciphers. In E. Biham, editor, *Fourth International Workshop on Fast Software Encryption*, volume LNCS 1267, pages 28–40, Haifa, Israel, January 20–22 1997. Springer-Verlag.

[144] K. Järvinen, M. Tommiska, and J. Skyttä. A Fully Pipelined Memoryless 17.8 Gbps AES-128 Encryptor. In *ACM/SIGDA International Symposium on Field Programmable Gate Arrays 2003 — FPGA '03*, pages 207–215, Monterey, California, USA, February 23–25 2003. ACM Press.

[145] K. Järvinen, M. Tommiska, and J. Skyttä. A Scalable Architecture for Elliptic Curve Point Multiplication. In O. Diessel and J. Williams, editors, *Proceedings of the 2004 IEEE International Conference on Field-Programmable Technology — FPT 2004*, pages 303–306, Brisbane, Australia, December 6–8 2004.

[146] Y. Jeong and W. Burleson. VLSI Array Algorithms and Architectures for RSA Modular Multiplication. *IEEE Transactions on Very Large Scale Integration (VLSI) Systems*, 5(2):211–217, May 1997.

[147] M. Joye and S. M. Yen. The Montgomery Powering Ladder. In B. S. Kaliski Jr., Ç. K. Koç, and C. Paar, editors, *Workshop on Cryptographic Hardware and Embedded Systems — CHES 2002*, volume LNCS 2523, pages 291–302, Redwood Shores, California, USA, August 13–15 2002. Springer-Verlag.

[148] D. Kahn. *The Codebreakers. The Story of Secret Writing.* Macmillan, 1967.

[149] A. P. Kakarountas, G. Theodoridis, T. Laopoulos, and C. E. Goutis. High-Speed FPGA Implementation of the SHA-1 Hash Function. In *Proceedings of the IEEE Workshop on Intelligent Data Acquisition and Advanced Computing Systems: Technology and Applications — IDAACS 2005*, pages 211–215, Sofia, Bulgaria, September 5–7 2005.

[150] M.-S. Kang and F. J. Kurdahi. A Novel Systolic VLSI Architecture for Fast RSA Modular Multiplication. In *Proceedings*

of the Third IEEE Asia-Pacific Conference on ASIC, pages 81–84, Taipei, Taiwan, August 6–8 2002.

[151] Y. K. Kang, D. W. Kim, T. W. Kwon, and J. R. Choi. An Efficient Implementation of Hash Function Processor for IPSec. In *Proceedings of the Third IEEE Asia-Pacific Conference on ASIC*, pages 93–96, Taipei, Taiwan, August 6–8 2002.

[152] J. Kelsey, B. Schneier, and D. Wagner. Key-Schedule Cryptanalysis of IDEA, GDES, GOST, SAFER, and Triple-DES. In N. Koblitz, editor, *Advances in Cryptology — CRYPTO '96*, volume LNCS 1109, pages 237–252, Santa Barbara, California, USA, August 18–22 1996. Springer-Verlag.

[153] S. Kent and R. Atkinson. *RFC 2401: Security Architecture for the Internet Protocol.* Corporation for National Research Initiatives, Internet Engineering Task Force, Network Working Group, Reston, Virginia, USA, November 1998.

[154] S. Kent and R. Atkinson. *RFC 2402: IP Authentication Header.* Corporation for National Research Initiatives, Internet Engineering Task Force, Network Working Group, Reston, Virginia, USA, November 1998.

[155] S. Kent and R. Atkinson. *RFC 2406: IP Encapsulating Security Payload.* Corporation for National Research Initiatives, Internet Engineering Task Force, Network Working Group, Reston, Virginia, USA, November 1998.

[156] A. Kerckhoffs. La Cryptographie Militaire. *le Journal des Sciences Militaires*, 1883.

[157] T. Kerins, W. P. Marnane, and E. M. Popovici. An FPGA Implementation of a Flexible Secure Elliptic Curve Cryptography Processor. In *Proceedings of the International Workshop on Applied Reconfigurable Computing: Architectures and Applications — ARC 2005*, Algarve, Portugal, February 22–23 2005.

[158] E. Khan, M. W. El-Kharashi, F. Gebali, and M. Abd-El-Barr. An FPGA Design of a Unified Hash Engine for IPSec Authentication. In *Proceedings of the Fifth International Workshop on System-on-Chip for Real-Time Applications — IWSOC 2005*, pages 450–453, Banff, Alberta, Canada, July 20–24 2005.

[159] H.-S. Kim, S.-W. Lee, and K.-Y. Yoo. Partitioned Systolic Architecture for Modular Multiplication in $GF(2^m)$. *Information Processing Letters*, 76(3):135–139, December 2000.

[160] H. W. Kim and S. Lee. Design and Implementation of a Private and Public Key Crypto Processor and Its Application to a Security System. *IEEE Transactions on Consumer Electronics*, 50(1):214–224, February 2004.

[161] Y. S. Kim, W. S. Kang, and J. R. Choi. Asynchronous Implementation of 1024-Bit Modular Processor for RSA Cryptosystem. In *Proceedings of the Second IEEE Asia Pacific Conference on ASICs — AP-ASIC 2000*, pages 187–190, Cheju Island, Korea, August 28–30 2000.

[162] P. Kitsos, N. Sklavos, and O. Koufopavlou. An Efficient Implementation of the Digital Signature Algorithm. In *Proceedings of the Ninth IEEE International Conference on Electronics, Circuits and Systems — ICECS 2002*, volume 3, pages 1151–1154, Croatia, September 15–18 2002.

[163] P. Kitsos, G. Theodoridis, and O. Koufopavlou. An Efficient Reconfigurable Multiplier Architecture for Galois Field $GF(2^m)$. *Microelectronics Journal*, 34(10):975–980, October 2003.

[164] P. Kitsos, G. Theodoridis, and O. Koufopavlou. An Reconfigurable Multiplier in $GF(2^m)$ for Elliptic Curve Cryptosystem. In *Proceedings of the Tenth IEEE International Conference on Electronics, Circuits and Systems — ICECS 2003*, volume 2, pages 699–702, Sharjah, United Arab Emirates, December 14–17 2003.

[165] L. R. Knudson. Truncated and Higher Order Differentials. In B. Preneel, editor, *Second International Workshop on Fast Software Encryption*, volume LNCS 1008, pages 196–211, Leuven, Belgium, December 14–16 1994. Springer-Verlag.

[166] D. E. Knuth. *The Art of Computer Programming. Volume 2: Seminumerical Algorithms*. Addison-Wesley, Reading, Massachusetts, USA, 2nd edition, 1981.

[167] N. Koblitz. Elliptic Curve Cryptosystems. *Mathematics of Computation*, 48(177):203–209, 1987.

[168] J. T. Kohl and B. C. Neuman. The Kerberos Network Authentication Service. Technical Report RFC 1510, Department of Electrical Engineering and Computer Science, Massachusetts Institute of Technology, Cambridge, Massachusetts, USA, September 1993.

[169] J. T. Kohl, B. C. Neuman, and T. Ts'o. The Evolution of the Kerberos Authentication System. In *Distributed Open Systems*. IEEE Computer Society Press, Los Alamitos, California, USA, 1994.

[170] J. T. Kohl, B. C. Neuman, and T. Y. Ts'o. The Evolution of the Kerberos Authentication Service. In *Proceedings of the 1991 EurOpen Conference*, pages 295–313, Tromso, Norway, May 1991.

[171] P. Kornerup. A Systolic, Linear-Array Multiplier for a Class of Right-Shift Algorithms. *IEEE Transactions on Computers*, 43(8):892–898, August 1994.

[172] A. Krishnamurthy, Y. Tang, C. Xu, and Y. Wang. An Efficient Implementation of Multi-Prime RSA on DSP Processor. In *Proceedings of the 2003 International Conference on Multimedia and Expo — ICME '03*, volume 3, pages III–437–III–440, Baltimore, Maryland, USA, July 6–9 2003.

[173] K. Kumar, D. Mukhopadhyay, and D. R. Chowdhury. A Programmable Parallel Structure to Perform Galois Field Exponentiation. In *Proceedings of the Ninth International Conference on Information Technology — ICIT '06*, Bhubaneswar, India, December 18–21 2006.

[174] S.-Y. Kung. *VLSI Array Processing.* Prentice-Hall, 1988.

[175] H. Kuo, I. Verbauwhede, and P. Schaumont. A 2.29 Gbits/sec, 56 mW Non-Pipelned Rijndael AES Encryption IC in a 1.8V, 0.18 μm CMOS Technology. In *Proceedings of the IEEE 2002 Custom Integrated Circuits Conference*, pages 147–150, Orlando, Florida, USA, May 12–15 2002.

[176] T.-W. Kwon, C.-S. You, W.-S. Heo, Y.-K. Kang, and J.-R. Choi. Two Implementation Methods of a 1024-Bit RSA Cryptoprocessor Based on Modified Montgomery Algorithm. In *Proceedings of the 2001 International Symposium on Circuits and Systems — ISCAS 2001*, volume 4, pages 650–653, Sydney, Australia, May 6–9 2001.

[177] C.-Y. Lee. Low-Complexity Bit-Parallel Systolic Multipliers Over $GF(2^m)$. *Integration, the VLSI Journal*, To Appear.

[178] K.-J. Lee and K.-Y. Yoo. Systolic Multiplier for Montgomery's Algorithm. *Integration, the VLSI Journal*, 32(1-3):99–109, November 2002.

[179] H. Li and Z. Friggstad. An Efficient Architecture for the AES Mix Columns Operation. In *Proceedings of the 2005 IEEE International Symposium on Circuits and Systems — ISCAS 2005*, pages 4637–4640, Kobe, Japan, May 23–26 2005. IEEE, Inc.

[180] R. Lidl and H. Niederreiter. *Finite Fields*, volume 20 of *Encyclopedia of Mathematics and Its Applications*. Addison-Wesley, Reading, Massachusetts, USA, 1983.

[181] R. Lien, T. Grembowski, and K. Gaj. A 1 Gbit/s Partially Unrolled Architecture of Hash Functions SHA-1 and SHA-512. In T. Okamoto, editor, *The Cryptographers' Track at the RSA Conference — CT-RSA 2004*, volume LNCS 2964, pages 324–338, San Francisco, California, USA, February 23–27 2004. Springer-Verlag.

[182] Q. Liu and X. Cheng. Architectural Exploration of High Performance Montgomery Modular Multipliers. In *Proceedings of the 48th IEEE International Midwest Symposium on Circuits and Systems*, volume 2, pages 1314–1317, Cincinnati,

Ohio, USA, August 7–10 2005.

[183] Q. Liu, F. Ma, D. Tong, and X. Cheng. A Regular Parallel RSA Processor. In *Proceedings of the 47th IEEE International Midwest Symposium on Circuits and Systems*, volume 3, pages 467–470, Hiroshima, Japan, July 15–28 2004.

[184] Q. Liu, F. Ma, D. Tong, and X. Cheng. Efficient Implementation of the RSA Crypto Processor in Deep Submicron Technology. In *Proceedings of the ICISA Second International Conference on Applied Cryptography and Network Security — ACNS 2004*, pages 106–114, Yellow Mountain, China, June 8–11 2004.

[185] Q. Liu, D. Tong, and X. Cheng. Non-Interleaving Architecture for Hardware Implementation of Modular Multiplication. In *Proceedings of the 2005 IEEE International Symposium on Circuits and Systems — ISCAS 2005*, volume 1, pages 660–663, Kobe, Japan, May 23–26 2005. IEEE, Inc.

[186] J. Lopez and R. Dahab. Improved Algorithms for Elliptic Curve Arithmetic in GF(2^m). In S. Tavares and H. Meijer, editors, *Fifth Annual Workshop on Selected Areas in Cryptography*, volume LNCS 1556, pages 201–212, Kingston, Ontario, Canada, August 1998. Springer-Verlag.

[187] J. Lopez and R. Dahab. Fast Multiplication on Elliptic Curves Over GF(2^m). In Ç. Koç and C. Paar, editors, *Workshop on Cryptographic Hardware and Embedded Systems — CHES 1999*, volume LNCS 1717, pages 316–327, Worcester, Massachusetts, USA, August 12–13 1999. Springer-Verlag.

[188] J. Lutz and M. A. Hasan. High Performance FPGA Based Elliptic Curve Cryptographic Co-Processor. In *Proceedings of the Symposium on Information Technology: Coding and Computing — ITCC 2004*, volume 2, pages 486–492, Las Vegas, Nevada, USA, April 5–7 2004.

[189] P. Mackenzie and S. Patel. Hard Bits of the Discrete Log with Applications to Password Authentication. In A. Menezes, editor, *Topics in Cryptology — CT-RSA 2005*, volume LNCS 3376, pages 209–226, San Francisco, California, USA, February 14–18 2005.

[190] W. P. Marnane. Optimised Bit Serial Modular Multiplier for Implementation on Field Programmable Gate Arrays. *Electronic Letters*, 34(8):738–739, 1998.

[191] M. A. G. Martinez, G. M. Luna, and F. R. Henriquez. Hardware Implementation of the Binary Method for Exponentiation in $GF(2^m)$. In E. Chávez, J. Favela, M. Mejía, and A. Oliart, editors, *Proceedings of the Fourth Mexican International Conference on Computer Science*, pages 131–134,

Tlaxcala, Mexico, September 8–12 2003.

[192] M. Matsui. Linear Cryptoanalysis Method for DES Cipher. In T. Helleseth, editor, *Advances in Cryptology – EURO-CRYPT '93*, volume LNCS 765, pages 386–397, Lofthus, Norway, May 23–27 1993. Springer-Verlag.

[193] A. Mazzeo, L. Romano, G. P. Saggese, and N. Mazzocca. FPGA-Based Implementation of a Serial RSA Processor. In *Proceedings of the 2003 Design, Automation and Test in Europe Conference and Exhibition*, pages 582–587, Messe Munich, Germany, March 3–7 2003.

[194] R. P. McEvoy, F. M. Crowe, C. C. Murphy, and W. P. Marnane. Optimisation of the SHA-2 Family of Hash Functions on FPGAs. In *Proceedings of the 2006 IEEE Computer Society Annual Symposium on VLSI — ISVLSI 2006*, pages 317–322, Karlsruhe, Germany, March 2–3 2006.

[195] C. McIvor, M. McLoone, and J. McCanny. An FPGA Elliptic Curve Cryptographic Accelerator Over GF(p). In *Proceedings of the Irish Signals and Systems Conference — ISSC 2004*, pages 589–594, Belfast, Northern Ireland, June 30–July 2 2004.

[196] C. McIvor, M. McLoone, and J. V. McCanny. A High-Speed, Low Latency RSA Decryption Silicon Core. In *Proceedings of the 2003 International Symposium on Circuits and Systems — ISCAS 2003*, volume 4, pages IV133–IV136, Bangkok, Thailand, May 25–28 2003.

[197] C. McIvor, M. McLoone, and J. V. McCanny. Fast Montgomery Modular Multiplication and RSA Cryptographic Processor Architectures. In *Proceedings of the 37th Asilomar Conference on Signals, Systems, and Computers*, volume 1, pages 379–384, November 9–12 2003.

[198] M. McLoone and J. V. McCanny. Efficient Single-Chip Implementation of SHA-384 & SHA-512. In *Proceedings of the 2002 IEEE International Conference on Field-Programmable Technology — FPT 2002*, pages 457–459, Hong Kong, Hong Kong, December 16–18 2002.

[199] M. McLoone and J. V. McCanny. Rijndael FPGA Implementations Utilising Look-Up Tables. *Journal of VLSI Signal Processing Systems for Signal, Image, and Video Technology*, 34(3):261–275, July 2003.

[200] A. Menezes, T. Okamoto, and S. Vanstone. Reducing Elliptic Curve Logarithms to Logarithms in a Finite Field. *IEEE Transactions on Information Theory*, 39(5):1639–1646, September 1993.

[201] A. Menezes and S. Vanstone. Elliptic Curve Cryptosystems and Their Implementation. *Journal of Cryptology*, 6(4):209–

224, 1993.

[202] A. J. Menezes, P. C. van Oorschot, and S. A. Vanstone. *Handbook of Applied Cryptography*. CRC Press, Boca Raton, Florida, USA, 1997.

[203] Q. Meng, Y.-F. Liu, and Z.-B. Dai. FPGA Implementation of Expandable RSA Public-Key Cryptographic Coprocessor. In *Proceedings of the 2006 First International Symposium on Pervasive Computing and Applications*, pages 552–555, Urumqi, China, August 3–5 2006.

[204] N. Mentens, S. B. Örs, and B. Preneel. An FPGA Implementation of an Elliptic Curve Processor $GF(2^m)$. In *Proceedings of the ACM Great Lakes Symposium on VLSI*, pages 454–457, Boston, Massachusetts, USA, April 26–28 2004.

[205] N. Mentens, K. Sakiyama, L. Batina, I. Verbauwhede, and B. Preneel. FPGA-Oriented Secure Data Path Design: Implementation of a Public Key Coprocessor. In *Proceedings of the International Conference on Field Programmable Logic and Applications — FPL '06*, pages 1–6, Madrid, Spain, August 28–30 2006.

[206] H. Michail, A. P. Kakarountas, O. Koufopavlou, and C. E. Goutis. A Low-Power and High-Throughput Implementation of the SHA-1 Hash Function. In *Proceedings of the 2005 IEEE International Symposium on Circuits and Systems — ISCAS 2005*, volume 4, pages 4086–4089, Kobe, Japan, May 23–26 2005. IEEE, Inc.

[207] E. A. Michalski and D. A. Buell. A Scalable Architecture for RSA Cryptography on Large FPGAs. In *Proceedings of the International Conference on Field Programmable Logic and Applications — FPL '06*, pages 1–8, Madrid, Spain, August 28–30 2006.

[208] S. P. Miller, B. C. Neuman, J. I. Schiller, and J. H. Saltzer. Kerberos Authentication and Authorization System. Technical Report Section E.2.1: Project Athena Technical Plan, Department of Electrical Engineering and Computer Science, Massachusetts Institute of Technology, Cambridge, Massachusetts, USA, October 27 1987.

[209] V. Miller. Uses of Elliptic Curves in Cryptography. In H. C. Williams, editor, *Advances in Cryptology — CRYPTO '85*, volume LNCS 218, pages 417–426, Santa Barbara, California, USA, August 18–22 1985. Springer-Verlag.

[210] P. L. Montgomery. Modular Multiplication without Trial Division. *Mathematics of Computation*, 44(170):519–521, April 1985.

[211] N. Nedjah and L. de Macedo Mourelle. Three Hardware Ar-

chitectures for the Binary Modular Exponentiation: Sequential, Parallel, and Systolic. *IEEE Transactions on Circuits and Systems I*, 53(3):627–633, March 2006.

[212] K. Nadehara, M. Ikekawa, and I. Kuroda. Extended Instructions for the AES Cryptography and Their Efficient Implementation. In *Proceedings of the Eighteenth IEEE Workshop on Signal Processing Systems — SIPS 2004*, pages 152–157, Austin, Texas, USA, October 13–15 2004.

[213] E. Nahum, S. O'Malley, H. Orman, and R. Schroeppel. Towards High Performance Cryptographic Software. Technical report, The University of Arizona Tucson Department of Computer Science, Tucson, Arizona, USA, 1995. TR-95-04.

[214] National Institute of Standards and Technology. Modes of Operation for Symmetric Key Block Ciphers. http://csrc.nist.gov/CryptoToolkit/modes/, April 28 2005.

[215] J. Nechvatal, E. Barker, D. Dodson, M. Dworkin, J. Foti, and E. Roback. Status Report on the First Round of the Development of The Advanced Encryption Standard. http://csrc.nist.gov/encryption/aes/round1/r1report.pdf, August 9 1999.

[216] N. Nedjah and L. de Macedo Mourelle. Fast Reconfigurable Systolic Hardware for Modular Multiplication and Exponentiation. *Journal of Systems Architecture*, 49(7–9):387–396, October 2003.

[217] N. Nedjah and L. de Macedo Mourelle, editors. *Unified Hardware Architecture for the Secure Hash Standard*. Nova Science Publishers, 2004. Chapter author: A. Satoh.

[218] W. Nevelsteen and B. Preneel. Software Performance of Universal Hash Functions. In J. Stern, editor, *Advances in Cryptology – EUROCRYPT '99*, volume LNCS 1592, pages 24–41, Prague, Czech Republic, 1999. Springer-Verlag.

[219] C.-W. Ng, T.-S. Ng, and K.-W. Yip. A Unified Architecture of MD5 and RIPEMD-160 Hash Algorithms. In *Proceedings of the 2004 International Symposium on Circuits and Systems — ISCAS 2004*, volume 2, pages 889–892, Vancouver, Canada, May 23–26 2004.

[220] N. Nguyen, K. Gaj, D. Caliga, and T. El-Ghazawi. Implementation of Elliptic Curve Cryptosystems on a Reconfigurable Computer. In *Proceedings of the 2003 IEEE International Conference on Field-Programmable Technology — FPT 2003*, pages 60–67, Tokyo, Japan, December 15–17 2003.

[221] O. Nibouche, A. Belatreche, and M. Nibouche. Speed and Area Trade-Offs for FPGA-Based Implementation of RSA

Architectures. In *Proceedings of the Second Annual IEEE Northeast Workshop on Circuits and Systems — NEWCAS 2004*, pages 217–220, Montreal, Canada, June 20–23 2004.

[222] O. Nibouche, M. Nibouche, and A. Bouridane. High Speed FPGA Implementation of RSA Encryption Algorithm. In *Proceedings of the 2003 Tenth IEEE International Conference on Electronics, Circuits and Systems — ICECS 2003*, volume 1, pages 204–207, Sharjah, United Arab Emirates, December 14–17 2003.

[223] O. Nibouche, M. Nibouche, A. Bouridane, and A. Belatreche. Fast Architectures for FPGA-Based Implementation of RSA Encryption Algorithm. In O. Diessel and J. Williams, editors, *Proceedings of the 2004 IEEE International Conference on Field-Programmable Technology — FPT 2004*, pages 271–278, Brisbane, Australia, December 6–8 2004.

[224] NIST FIPS PUB 180-2. *Secure Hash Standard (SHS)*. National Institute of Standards and Technology, Gaithersburg, Maryland, USA, February 2004.

[225] NIST FIPS PUB 186-2. *Digital Signature Standard (DSS)*. National Institute of Standards and Technology, Gaithersburg, Maryland, USA, October 5 2001.

[226] NIST FIPS PUB 196. *Entity Authentication Using Public Key Cryptography*. National Institute of Standards and Technology, Gaithersburg, Maryland, USA, February 1997.

[227] NIST FIPS PUB 197. *Specification for the Advanced Encryption Standard (AES)*. Federal Information Processing Standards, National Bureau of Standards, U.S. Department of Commerce, November 26 2001.

[228] NIST FIPS PUB 198. *Specification for the Advanced Encryption Standard (AES)*. Federal Information Processing Standards, National Bureau of Standards, U.S. Department of Commerce, March 6 2002.

[229] NIST FIPS PUB 46-3. *Data Encryption Standard*. Federal Information Processing Standards, National Bureau of Standards, U.S. Department of Commerce, 1977.

[230] NIST FIPS PUB 74. *Guidelines for Implementing and Using the NBS Data Encryption Standard*. Federal Information Processing Standards, National Bureau of Standards, U.S. Department of Commerce, April 1 1981.

[231] W. Nuan, D. Z. Bin, and Z. Y. Fu. FPGA Implementation of Alterable Parameters RSA Public-Key Cryptographic Coprocessor. In *Proceedings of the Sixth International Conference on ASIC — ASICON 2005*, volume 2, pages 769–773, Shanghai, China, October 24–27 2005.

[232] National Institute of Standards and Technology. NIST

Cerberus, An IPsec Reference Implementation for Linux. http://w3.antd.nist.gov/tools/cerberus/index.html, 2000.

[233] S. Okada, N. Torii, K. Itoh, and M. Takenaka. Implementation of Elliptic Curve Cryptographic Coprocessor Over $GF(2^m)$ on an FPGA. In Ç. K. Koç and C. Paar, editors, *Workshop on Cryptographic Hardware and Embedded Systems — CHES 2000*, volume LNCS 1965, pages 25–40, Worcester, Massachusetts, USA, August 2000. Springer-Verlag.

[234] D. Oliva, R. Buchty, and N. Heintze. AES and the Cryptonite Crypto Processor. In J. H. Moreno, P. K. Murthy, T. M. Conte, and P. Faraboschi, editors, *Proceedings of the 2003 International Conference on Compilers, Architecture and Synthesis for Embedded Systems — CASES 2003*, pages 198–209, San Jose, California, USA, October 30–November 1 2003. ACM Press.

[235] G. Orlando and C. Paar. A High-Performance Reconfigurable Elliptic Curve Processor for $GF(2^m)$. In Ç. K. Koç and C. Paar, editors, *Workshop on Cryptographic Hardware and Embedded Systems — CHES 2000*, volume LNCS 1965, pages 41–56, Worcester, Massachusetts, USA, August 2000. Springer-Verlag.

[236] G. Orlando and C. Paar. A Scalable GF(p) Elliptic Curve Processor Architecture for Programmable Hardware. In Ç. K. Koç, D. Naccache, and C. Paar, editors, *Workshop on Cryptographic Hardware and Embedded Systems — CHES 2001*, volume LNCS 2162, pages 356–371, Paris, France, May 14–16 2001. Springer-Verlag.

[237] S. B. Örs, L. Batina, B. Preneel, and J. Vandewalle. Hardware Implementation of a Montgomery Modular Multiplier in a Systolic Array. In *Proceedings of the Seventeenth International Parallel and Distributed Processing Symposium — IPDPS 2003*, Nice, France, April 22–26 2003. IEEE, Inc.

[238] S. B. Örs, L. Batina, B. Preneel, and J. Vandewalle. Hardware Implementation of an Elliptic Curve Processor Over GF(p). In *Proceedings of the Fourteenth IEEE International Conference on Application-Specific Systems, Architectures and Processors — ASAP 2003*, pages 433–443, The Hague, The Netherlands, June 24–26 2003.

[239] H. Orup. A 100 Kbits/s Single Chip Modular Exponentiation Processor. In *HOT Chips VI, Symposium Record*, pages 53–59, Stanford, California, USA, August 14–16 1994.

[240] C. Paar. Optimized Arithmetic for Reed-Solomon Encoders. In *1997 IEEE International Symposium on Infor-*

mation Theory, page 250, Ulm, Germany, June 29–July 4 1997.

[241] D. Page and N. P. Smart. Parallel Cryptographic Arithmetic Using a Redundant Montgomery Representation. *IEEE Transactions on Computers*, 53(11):1474–1482, November 2004.

[242] B. Penner. What Is Gate Count? What Are Gate Count Metrics for Virtex/Spartan-II/4K Devices? Electronic Mail Personal Correspondence, January 2003. Xilinx Inc.

[243] R. Perlman and C. Kaufman. Analysis of the IPSec Key Exchange Standard. In *Proceedings of the Tenth IEEE International Workshop on Enabling Technologies: Infrastructure for Collaborative Enterprises — WET ICE 2001*, pages 150–156, Cambridge, Massachusetts, USA, June 20–22 2001.

[244] A. Pfitzmann and R. Assman. More Efficient Software Implementations of (Generalized) DES. *Computers & Security*, 12(5):477–500, 1993.

[245] T. Pionteck, T. Staake, T. Stiefmeier, L. D. Kabulepa, and M. Geisner. Design of a Reconfigurable AES Encryption/Decryption Engine for Mobile Terminals. In *Proceedings of the 2004 International Symposium on Circuits and Systems — ISCAS 2004*, volume 2, pages 545–548, Vancouver, Canada, May 23–26 2004.

[246] S. C. Pohlig and M. E. Hellman. An Improved Algorithm for Computing Logarithms Over $GF(p)$ and its Cryptographic Significance. *IEEE Transactions on Information Theory*, 24(1):106–110, January 1978.

[247] J. M. Pollard. Monte Carlo Methods for Index Computation (mod p). *Mathematics of Computation*, 32(143):918–924, July 1978.

[248] E. M. Popovici and P. Fitzpatrick. Algorithm and Architecture for a Galois Field Multiplicative Arithmetic Processor. *IEEE Transactions on Information Theory*, 49(12):3303–3307, December 2003.

[249] B. Preneel. Software Performance of Encryption Algorithms and Hash Functions. In *Proceedings of the Second Annual Workshop on Selected Areas in Cryptography — SAC 1995*, pages 89–98, Ottawa, Canada, May 18–19 1995. Springer-Verlag.

[250] S. Ravi, A. Raghunathan, N. Potlapally, and M. Sankaradass. System Design Methodologies for a Wireless Security Processing Platform. In *Proceedings of the 2002 Design Automation Conference — DAC 2002*, pages 777–782, New Orleans, Louisiana, USA, June 10–14 2002.

[251] V. Rijmen. Rijndael Reference Code in ANSI C v2.2. http://homes.esat.kuleuven.be/~rijmen/rijndaelref.zip.

[252] R. Rivest. The MD4 Message Digest Algorithm. In A. J. Menezes and S. A. Vanstone, editors, *Advances in Cryptology — CRYPTO '90*, volume LNCS 537, pages 303–311, Santa Barbara, California, USA, August 11–15 1990. Springer-Verlag.

[253] R. Rivest. The MD5 Message-Digest Algorithm. Internet Request for Comments, April 1992. Presented at Rump Session of Advances in Cryptology — CRYPTO '91.

[254] R. Rivest, A. Shamir, and L. M. Adleman. Cryptographic Communications System and Method. United States Patent, Patent Number 4405829, September 20 1983.

[255] M. J. B. Robshaw. Implementations of the Search for Pseudo-Collisions in MD5. Technical Report TR-103 Version 2.0, RSA Laboratories, November 1993.

[256] M. J. B. Robshaw. On Pseudo-Collisions in MD5. Technical Report TR-102 Version 1.1, RSA Laboratories, July 1994.

[257] F. Rodríguez-Henríquez and Ç. Koç. On Fully Parallel Karatsuba Multipliers for $GF(2^m)$. In S. Sahni, editor, *Proceedings of Computer Science and Technology — CST 2003*, pages 405–410, Cancun, Mexico, May 19–21 2003.

[258] M. Roe. Performance of Block Ciphers and Hash Functions — One Year Later. In B. Preneel, editor, *Second International Workshop on Fast Software Encryption*, volume LNCS 1008, pages 359–362, Leuven, Belgium, December 14–16 1994. Springer-Verlag.

[259] P. Rogaway and D. Wagner. A Critique of CCM. http://eprint.iacr.org/2003/070/, April 2003. Cryptology ePrint Archive: Report 2003/070.

[260] A. Royo, J. Morán, and J. C. López. Design and Implementation of a Coprocessor for Cryptography Applications. In *Proceedings of the 1997 European Design and Test Conference*, pages 213–217, March 17–20 1997.

[261] RSA Laboratories. The RSA Factoring Challenge FAQ. http://www.rsa.com/rsalabs/node.asp?id=2094, 2007.

[262] S. Tillich and J. Großchädl. A Simple Architectural Enhancement for Fast and Flexible Elliptic Curve Cryptography Over Binary Finite Fields $GF(2^m)$. In *Proceedings of the Ninth Asia-Pacific Conference on Advances in Computer Systems Architecture — ACSAC 2004*, volume LNCS 3189, pages 282–295, Beijing, China, September 7–9 2004. Springer-Verlag.

[263] S. Tillich and J. Großchädl. Instruction Set Extensions

for Efficient AES Implementation on 32-bit Processors. In L. Goubin and M. Matsui, editors, *Workshop on Cryptographic Hardware and Embedded Systems — CHES 2006*, volume LNCS 4249, pages 270–284, Yokohama, Japan, October 10–13 2006. Springer-Verlag.

[264] G. P. Saggese, L. Romano, N. Mazzocca, and A. Mazzeo. A Tamper Resistant Hardware Accelerator for RSA Cryptographic Applications. *Journal of Systems Architecture*, 50(12):711–727, December 2004.

[265] N. A. Saqib, F. Rodriguez-Henriquez, and A. Diaz-Pérez. AES Algorithm Implementation — An Efficient Approach for Sequential and Pipeline Architectures. In *Proceedings of the Fourth Mexican International Conference on Computer Science — ECC'03*, pages 126–130, Apizaco, Mexico, September 8–12 2003. IEEE, Inc.

[266] N. A. Saqib, F. Rodríguez-Henríquez, and A. Díaz-Pérez. A Parallel Architecture for Computing Scalar Multiplication on Hessian Elliptic Curves. In *Proceedings of the Symposium on Information Technology: Coding and Computing — ITCC 2004*, volume 2, pages 493–497, Las Vegas, Nevada, USA, April 5–7 2004.

[267] N. A. Saqib, F. Rodríguez-Henríquez, and A. Díaz-Pérez. A Parallel Architecture for Fast Computation of Elliptic Curve Scalar Multiplication Over $GF(2^m)$. In *Proceedings of the Eighteenth International Parallel and Distributed Processing Symposium — IPDPS 2004*, Santa Fe, New Mexico, USA, April 26–30 2004.

[268] A. Satoh and T. Inoue. ASIC-Hardware-Focused Comparison for Hash Functions MD5, RIPEMD0160, and SHS. In *Proceedings of the International Conference on Information Technology: Coding and Computing — ITCC '05*, volume 1, pages 532–537, Las Vegas, Nevada, USA, April 4–6 2005.

[269] A. Satoh and K. Takano. A Scalable Dual-Field Elliptic Curve Cryptographic Processor. *IEEE Transactions on Computers*, 52(4):449–460, July 2003.

[270] T. Satoh and K. Araki. Fermat Quotients and the Polynomial Time Discrete Log Algorithm for Anomalous Elliptic Curves. *Commentarii Mathematici Universitatis Sancti Pauli*, 1998(47):81–92, 1998.

[271] P. Schaumont, K. Sakiyama, A. Hodjat, and I. Verbauwhede. Embedded Software Integration for Coarse-Grain Reconfigurable Systems. In *Proceedings of the Eighteenth International Parallel and Distributed Processing Symposium — IPDPS 2004*, pages 137–142, Santa Fe, New Mexico, USA,

April 26–30 2004.

[272] M. Schimmler, B. Schmidt, H.-W. Lang, and S. Heithecker. An Area-Efficient Bit-Serial Integer and $GF(2^n)$ Multiplier. *Microelectronic Engineering*, 84(2):253–259, February 2007.

[273] O. Schirokauer. Discrete Logarithms and Local Units. *Philosophical Transactions: Physical Sciences and Engineering*, 345(1676):409–423, November 1993.

[274] B. Schneier. *E-Mail Security (with PGP and PEM)*. John Wiley & Sons Inc., New York, New York, USA, 1995.

[275] B. Schneier. *Applied Cryptography*. John Wiley & Sons Inc., New York, New York, USA, second edition, 1996.

[276] B. Schneier. Cryptographic Design Vulnerabilities. *IEEE Computer*, 31(9):29–33, September 1998.

[277] B. Schneier and J. Kelsey. Unbalanced Feistel Networks and Block Cipher Design. In D. Gollmann, editor, *Third International Workshop on Fast Software Encryption*, volume LNCS 1039, pages 121–144, Cambridge, United Kingdom, February 21–23 1996. Springer-Verlag.

[278] Security Group. *ATM Security Specification Version 1.0*. ATM Forum.

[279] A. Selby and C. Mitchell. Algorithms for Software Implementations of RSA. *IEE Proceedings on Computers and Digital Techniques*, 136(3):166–170, May 1989.

[280] G. Selimis, N. Sklavos, and O. Koufopavlou. VLSI Implementation of the Keyed-Hash Message Authentication Code for the Wireless Application Protocol. In *Proceedings of the Tenth IEEE International Conference on Electronics, Circuits and Systems — ICECS 2003*, volume 2, pages 24–27, Sharjah, United Arab Emirates, December 14–17 2003.

[281] Shamus Software Ltd. Multiprecision Integer and Rational Arithmetic C/C++ Library (MIRACL). http://www.shamus.ie/.

[282] M. Shand and J. Vuillemin. Fast Implementations of RSA Cryptography. In E. E. Swartzlander, M. S. Irwin, and J. Jullien, editors, *Proceedings of the Eleventh IEEE Symposium on Computer Arithmetic*, pages 252–259, Windsor, Ontario, Canada, June 29–July 2 1993.

[283] C. E. Shannon. Communication Theory of Secrecy Systems. *Bell System Technical Journal*, 27(4):656–715, 1949.

[284] J.-B. Shin, J. Kim, and H. Lee-Kwang. Optimisation of Montgomery Modular Multiplication Algorithm for Systolic Arrays. *Electronic Letters*, 34(19):1830–1831, September 17 1998.

[285] D. Shinder. Securing Data in Transit with IPSec. *WindowSecurity.com*, February 17 2003.

[286] C. Shu, K. Gaj, and T. El-Ghazawi. Low Latency Elliptic Curve Cryptography Accelerators for NIST Curves on Binary Fields. In *Proceedings of the 2005 IEEE International Conference on Field-Programmable Technology — FPT 2005*, pages 309–310, Singapore, December 11–13 2005.

[287] N. Sklavos, E. Alexopoulos, and O. Koufopavlou. Networking Data Integrity: High Speed Architectures and Hardware Implementations. *The International Arab Journal of Information Technology*, 1(0):54–59, July 2003.

[288] N. Sklavos, G. Dimitroulakos, and O. Koufopavlou. An Ultra High Speed Architecture for VLSI Implementation of Hash Functions. In *Proceedings of the 2003 Tenth IEEE International Conference on Electronics, Circuits and Systems — ICECS 2003*, volume 3, pages 990–993, Sharjah, United Arab Emirates, December 14–17 2003.

[289] N. Sklavos, P. Kitsos, E. Alexopoulos, and O. Koufopavlou. Open Mobile Alliance (OMA) Security Layer: Architecture, Implementation and Performance Evaluation of the Integrity Unit. *New Generation Computing: Computing Paradigms and Computational Intelligence*, 23(1):77–100, 2005.

[290] N. Sklavos, P. Kitsos, K. Papadomanolakis, and O. Koufopavlou. Random Number Generator Architecture and VLSI Implementation. In *Proceedings of the IEEE International Symposium on Circuits and Systems - ISCAS 2002*, volume 4, pages 854–857, Scottsdale, Arizona, USA, May 26–29 2002.

[291] N. Sklavos and O. Koufopavlou. On the Hardware Implementations of the SHA-2 (256, 384, 512) Hash Functions. In *Proceedings of the IEEE International Symposium on Circuits and Systems — ISCAS 2003*, volume 5, pages 153–156, Bangkok, Thailand, May 25–28 2003.

[292] N. Sklavos and O. Koufopavlou. Implementation of the SHA-2 Hash Family Standard Using FPGAs. *Journal of Supercomputing*, 31(3):227–248, 2005.

[293] N. Sklavos and O. Koufopavlou. On the Hardware Implementation of RIPEMD Processor: Networking High Speed Hashing, Up to 2 Gbps. *Computers and Electrical Engineering*, 31(6):361–379, September 2005.

[294] N. Smart. The Discrete Logarithm Problem on Elliptic Curves of Trace One. *Journal of Cryptology*, 12(3):193–196, 1999.

[295] F. Sozzani, G. Bertoni, S. Turcato, and L. Breveglieri. A Parallelized Design for an Elliptic Curve Cryptosystem Coprocessor. In *Proceedings of the Symposium on Information Technology: Coding and Computing — ITCC 2005*, vol-

ume 1, pages 626–630, Las Vegas, Nevada, USA, April 4–6 2005.

[296] W. Stallings. *Network and Internetwork Security – Principles and Practice.* Prentice Hall, Englewood Cliffs, New Jersey, USA, 1995.

[297] W. Stallings. *Protect Your Privacy: A Guide for PGP Users.* Prentice Hall, Englewood Cliffs, New Jersey, USA, 1995.

[298] W. Stallings. *Cryptography and Network Security.* Prentice Hall, Upper Saddle River, New Jersey, USA, second edition, 1999.

[299] F. X. Standaert, G. Rouvroy, J. J. Quisquater, and J. D. Legat. Efficient Implementation of Rijndael Encryption in Reconfigurable Hardware: Improvements and Design Trade-offs. In *Workshop on Cryptographic Hardware and Embedded Systems — CHES 2003*, volume LNCS 2778, pages 334–350, Cologne, Germany, September 7–10 2003. Springer-Verlag.

[300] K. Stevens and O. A. Mohamed. Single-Chip FPGA Implementation of a Pipelined, Memory-Based AES Rijndael Encryption Design. In *Proceedings of the Eighteenth Annual Canadian Conference on Electrical and Computer Engineering — CCECE'05*, pages 1296–1299, Saskatoon, Saskatchewan, Canada, May 1–4 2005. IEEE, Inc.

[301] D. R. Stinson. *Cryptography, Theory and Practice.* CRC Press, Boca Raton, Florida, USA, 1995.

[302] StreamSec. StrSec Performance. http://www.streamsec.com/prod_strsec2_perf.asp, 2002.

[303] C. Studholme. *The Discrete Log Problem.* PhD thesis, University of Toronto, Toronto, Canada, June 2002. Research Key Milestone Paper.

[304] C.-Y. Su, S.-A. Hwang, P.-S. Chen, and C.-W. Wu. An Improved Montgomery Algorithm for High-Speed RSA Public-Key Cryptosystem. *IEEE Transactions on Very Large Scale Integration (VLSI) Systems*, 7(2):280–284, June 1999.

[305] Suetonius. *De Vita Caesarum: Julius*, volume I. Harvard University Press, Cambridge, Massachusetts, USA, 1920. Translated by J. C. Rolfe.

[306] N. Takagi. A Radix-4 Modular Multiplication Hardware Algorithm Efficient for Iterative Modular Multiplications. In P. Kornerup and D. W. Matula, editors, *Proceedings of the Tenth IEEE Symposium on Computer Arithmetic — ARITH-10*, pages 35–42, Grenoble, France, June 26–28 1991.

[307] S. Tillich, J. Großchädl, and A. Szekely. An Instruction Set Extension for Fast and Memory-Efficient AES Implementation. In J. Dittmann, S. Katzenbeisser, and A. Uhl, editors,

Proceedings of the Ninth International Conference on Communications and Multimedia Security — CMS 2005, volume LNCS 3677, pages 11–21, Salzburg, Austria, September 19–21 2005. Springer-Verlag.

[308] K. K. Ting, S. C. L. Yuen, K. H. Lee, and P. H. W. Leong. An FPGA Based SHA-256 Processor. In *Proceedings of the Twelfth International Conference on Field-Programmable Logic and Applications — FPL 2002*, volume LNCS 2438, pages 577–585, Montpellier, France, September 2–4 2002. Springer-Verlag.

[309] A. A. Tiountchik. Systolic Modular Exponentiation via Montgomery Algorithm. *IEE Electronics Letters*, 34(9):874–875, April 1998.

[310] J. Touch. Performance Analysis of MD5. In *Proceedings of the ACM SIGCOMM '95 Conference*, pages 77–86, Cambridge, Massachusetts, USA, August 28–September 1 1995.

[311] A. Trachtenberg. Internet Protocol Version 6: IPv4 vs. IPv6. Technical report, Electrical and Computer Engineering Department, Boston University, Boston, Massachusetts, USA.

[312] S. Trimberger, R. Pang, and A. Singh. A 12 Gbps DES Encryptor/Decryptor Core in an FPGA. In Ç. K. Koç and C. Paar, editors, *Workshop on Cryptographic Hardware and Embedded Systems — CHES 2000*, volume LNCS 1965, pages 156–163, Worcester, Massachusetts, USA, August 17–18 2000. Springer-Verlag.

[313] W.-C. Tsai, C. B. Shung, and S.-J. Wang. Two Systolic Architectures for Modular Multiplication. *IEEE Transactions on Very Large Scale Integration (VLSI) Systems*, 8(1):103–107, February 2000.

[314] A. Tyagi. A Reduced-Area Scheme for Carry-Select Adders. *IEEE Transactions on Computers*, 42(10):1163–1170, October 1993.

[315] J. von zur Gathen and J. Shokrollahi. Efficient FPGA-Based Karatsuba Multipliers for Polynomials Over F_2. In *Twelfth Annual Workshop on Selected Areas in Cryptography*, volume LNCS 1556, pages 359–369, Kingston, Ontario, Canada, August 11–12 2005. Springer-Verlag.

[316] J. E. Vuillemin, P. Bertin, D. Roncin, M. Shand, H. H. Touati, and P. Boucard. Programmable Active Memories: Reconfigurable Systems Come of Age. *IEEE Transactions on Very Large Scale Integration (VLSI) Systems*, 4(1):56–69, March 1996.

[317] C. Walter. Fast Modular Multiplication Using Power-2 Radix. *International Journal of Computer Mathematics*, 39(1–2):21–28, 1991.

[318] C. D. Walter. Systolic Modular Multiplication. *IEEE Transactions on Computers*, 42(3):376–378, March 1993.

[319] C. D. Walter. Improved Linear Systolic Array for Fast Modular Exponentiation. *IEE Computers and Digital Techniques*, 147(5):323–328, September 2000.

[320] C.-L. Wang. Bit-Level Systolic Array for Fast Exponentiation in $GF(2^m)$. *IEEE Transactions on Computers*, 43(7):838–841, July 1994.

[321] G. Wang. An Efficient Implementation of SHA-1 Hash Function. In *Proceedings of the 2006 IEEE International Conference on Electro/information Technology*, pages 575–579, East Lansing, Michigan, USA, May 7–10 2006.

[322] M.-Y. Wang, C.-P. Su, C.-T. Huang, and C.-W. Wu. An HMAC Processor with Integrated SHA-1 and MD5 Algorithms. In M. Imai, editor, *Proceedings of the 2004 Conference on Asia South Pacific Design Automation: Electronic Design and Solution Fair*, pages 456–458, Yokohama, Japan, January 27–30 2004.

[323] P. A. Wang, W.-C. Tsai, and C. B. Shung. New VLSI Architectures of RSA Public-Key Cryptosystem. In *Proceedings of the 1997 International Symposium on Circuits and Systems — ISCAS 1997*, volume 3, pages 2040–2043, Hong Kong, Hong Kong, June 9–12 1997. IEEE, Inc.

[324] X. Wang, Y. L. Yin, and H. Yu. Finding Collisions in the Full SHA-1. In V. Shoup, editor, *Advances in Cryptology — CRYPTO 2005*, volume LNCS 3621, pages 17–36, Santa Barbara, California, USA, August 14–18 2000. Springer-Verlag.

[325] N. Weaver and J. Wawrzynek. A Comparison of the AES Candidates Amenability to FPGA Implementation. In *The Third Advanced Encryption Standard Candidate Conference*, pages 28–39, New York, New York, USA, April 13–14 2000. National Institute of Standards and Technology.

[326] B. Weeks, M. Bean, T. Rozylowicz, and C. Ficke. Hardware Performance Simulations of Round 2 Advanced Encryption Standard Algorithms. In *The Third Advanced Encryption Standard Candidate Conference*, pages 286–304, New York, New York, USA, April 13–14 2000. National Institute of Standards and Technology.

[327] D. C. Wilcox, L. Pierson, P. Robertson, E. Witzke, and K. Gass. A DES ASIC Suitable for Network Encryption at 10 Gbps and Beyond. In Ç. Koç and C. Paar, editors, *Workshop on Cryptographic Hardware and Embedded Systems — CHES 1999*, volume LNCS 1717, pages 37–48, Worcester, Massachusetts, USA, August 12–13 1999. Springer-Verlag.

[328] T. Wollinger, J. Guajardo, and C. Paar. Security on FP-GAs: State-of-the-Art Implementations and Attacks. *ACM Transactions on Embedded Computing Systems*, 3(3):534–574, August 2004.

[329] C.-H. Wu, J.-H. Hong, and C.-W. Wu. RSA Cryptosystem Design Based on the Chinese Remainder Theorem. In *Proceedings of the 2001 Asia and South Pacific Design Automation Conference — ASP-DAC 2001*, pages 391–395, Yokohama, Japan, January 30–February 2 2001.

[330] C.-L. Wu, S. F. Wu, and R. Narayan. IPSec/PHIL (Packet Header Information List): Design, Implementation, and Evaluation. In *Proceedings of the Tenth International Conference on Computer Communications and Networks*, pages 206–211, Scottsdale, Arizona, USA, October 15–17 2001.

[331] L. Wu, C. Weaver, and T. Austin. CryptoManiac: A Fast Flexible Architecture for Secure Communication. In B. Werner, editor, *Proceedings of the 28th Annual International Symposium on Computer Architecture — ISCA-2001*, pages 110–119, Goteborg, Sweden, June 30–July 4 2001.

[332] C.-C. Yang, T.-S. Chang, and C.-W. Jen. A New RSA Cryptosystem Hardware Design Based on Montgomery's Algorithm. *IEEE Transactions on Circuits and Systems*, 45(7):908–913, July 1998.

[333] S. Yeşil, A. N. İsmailoğlu, Y. C. Tekmen, and M. Aşkar. A Simple Architectural Enhancement for Fast and Flexible Elliptic Curve Cryptography Over Binary Finite Fields $GF(2^m)$. In *Proceedings of the 2004 International Symposium on Circuits and Systems — ISCAS 2004*, volume 2, pages II–557–II–560, Vancouver, Canada, May 23–26 2004.

[334] S.-M. Yoo, D. Kotturi, D. W. Pan, and J. Blizzard. An AES Crypto Chip Using a High-Speed Parallel Pipelined Architecture. *Microprocessors and Microsystems*, 29(7):317–326, September 2005.

[335] D. Yuliang, M. Zhigang, Y. Yizheng, and W. Tao. Implementation of RSA Cryptoprocessor Based on Montgomery Algorithm. In *Proceedings of the 1998 Fifth International Conference on Solid-State and Integrated Circuit Technology*, pages 524–526, Beijing, China, October 21–23 1998.

[336] M. Zeghid, B. Bouallegue, A. Baganne, M. Machhout, and R. Tourki. A Reconfigurable Implementation of the New Secure Hash Algorithm. In *Proceedings of the Second International Conference on Availability, Reliability, and Security — ARES '07*, pages 281–285, Barcelona, Spain, April 10–13 2007.

[337] D. Zhang, M. Gao, L. Li, Z. Cheng, and X. Wang. An Implementation Method of a RSA Crypto Processor Based on Modified Montgomery Algorithm. In *Proceedings of the Fifth International Conference on ASIC — ASICON 2003*, volume 2, pages 1332–1336, Beijing, China, October 21–24 2003.

[338] X. Zhang and K. K. Parhi. Implementation Approaches for the Advanced Encryption Standard Algorithm. *IEEE Circuits and Systems Magazine*, 2(4):25–46, 2002.

[339] D. Zibin and Z. Ning. FPGA Implementation of SHA-1 Algorithm. In *Proceedings of the Fifth International Conference on ASIC — ASICON 2003*, volume 2, pages 1321–1324, Beijing, China, October 21–24 2003.

[340] P. Zimmermann. *PGP Source Code and Internals*. MIT Press, Cambridge, Massachusetts, USA, 1995.

[341] P. Zimmermann. *The Official PGP User's Guide*. MIT Press, Cambridge, Massachusetts, USA, 1995. Second Printing.

Index